weather

architecture

Weather Architecture further extends Jonathan Hill's investigation of authorship by recognising the creativity of the weather. At a time when environmental awareness is of growing relevance, the overriding aim is to understand a history of architecture as a history of weather and thus to consider the weather as an architectural author that affects design, construction and use in a creative dialogue with other authors such as the architect and user.

Grounding environmental awareness in historical understanding, *Weather Architecture* emphasises that a critical investigation of the past can be a catalyst to creativity, and recognises the emergence of a hybridised weather that is industrial and electromagnetic as well as natural. The evolving relations between architecture and weather are a means to encourage buildings that co-exist with their immediate and wider environments and acknowledge time, decay and change.

Environmental discussions in contemporary architecture tend to focus on the practical or the poetic but here they are considered together. The analysis of weather's effects on the design and experience of specific buildings and gardens is interwoven with a historical survey of changing attitudes to the weather and climate in the arts, sciences and society, which integrates architecture's relations to the weather into a wider discussion of cultural and social influences on architecture and leads to a critical re-evaluation of contemporary responses to climate change.

An architect and architectural historian, **Jonathan Hill** is Professor of Architecture and Visual Theory at the Bartlett School of Architecture, UCL, where he directs the MPhil/PhD Architectural Design programme. Jonathan is the author of *The Illegal Architect* (1998), *Actions of Architecture* (2003) and *Immaterial Architecture* (2006), editor of *Occupying Architecture* (1998) and *Architecture—the Subject is Matter* (2001), and co-editor of *Critical Architecture* (2007).

WEATHER ARCHITECTURE

Jonathan Hill

Routledge
Taylor & Francis Group
LONDON AND NEW YORK

First published 2012
by Routledge
2 Park Square, Milton Park, Abingdon, Oxon OX14 4RN

Simultaneously published in the USA and Canada
by Routledge
711 Third Avenue, New York, NY 10017

Routledge is an imprint of the Taylor & Francis Group, an informa business

British Library Cataloguing in Publication Data
A catalogue record for this book is available from the British Library

Library of Congress Cataloging in Publication Data
Hill, Jonathan, 1958–
Weather architecture / Jonathan Hill.
p. cm.
Includes bibliographical references and index.
1. Architecture and climate. 2. Architecture and society.
3. Weather–Social aspects. I. Title.
NA2541.H55 2011
720'.4–dc23 2011024761

ISBN: 978-0-415-66860-6 (hbk)
ISBN: 978-0-415-66861-3 (pbk)

Typeset in News Gothic
by Keystroke, Station Road, Codsall, Wolverhampton

FSC www.fsc.org MIX Paper from responsible sources FSC® C004839

Printed and bound in Great Britain by
TJ International Ltd, Padstow, Cornwall

CONTENTS

FIGURES

COVER

1 THINGS OF A NATURAL KIND

2 THE SEASONS OF A LIFE

3 A LIFE IN RUINS

4 THE GARDEN OF ARCHITECTURE

5 PIGMENTS AND POLLUTION

6 THE WEATHER OF OUR HOUSES

7 SUBMITTING TO THE SEASONS

8 FOG, GLARE AND GLOOM

9 SWEET GARDEN OF VANISHED PLEASURES

ACKNOWLEDGEMENTS

Weather Architecture developed from my teaching and research at the Bartlett School of Architecture, University College London. I particularly wish to thank Matthew Butcher and Elizabeth Dow, my teaching partners in MArch Unit 12, whose ideas and advice have been stimulating and generous. My colleagues in the MPhil/PhD Architectural Design programme offered invaluable criticism and encouragement, especially Dr Marjan Colletti, Dr Marcos Cruz, Dr Penelope Haralambidou, Dr Yeoryia Manolopoulou, Professor Jane Rendell and Professor Phil Tabor. Also at the Bartlett, I wish to thank Abi Abdolwahabi, Professor Iain Borden, Dr Ben Campkin, Max Dewdney, Professor Adrian Forty, Professor Murray Fraser, Professor Christine Hawley, Dr Jan Kattein, Chee-Kit Lai, Professor CJ Lim, Dr Barbara Penner, Dr Peg Rawes, Bob Sheil and Professor Phil Steadman. Dialogue with an exceptional group of MArch and PhD students has influenced the character of this book, notably Anton Ambrose, John Ashton, Emma Cheatle, James Church, Charlie de Bono, Alex Hill, Rosalie Kim, Taeyoung Kim, Kwang Guan Lee, Tom Noonan, David Potts, Tom Reynolds, Ruth Silver and Alan Worn. Supported by the Bartlett Architectural Research Fund, the image permissions were very ably arranged by Catalina Mejia Moreno and Anna Solarska.

I very much appreciate the suggestions and support of many friends and colleagues. Dr Sophia Psarra, Bartlett School of Graduate Studies, read the final manuscript and offered invaluable and inspiring advice. I am also indebted to Dr Ana Araujo, Chelsea College of Art and Design; Morag Bain; Carolyn Butterworth, University of Sheffield; Barbara-Ann Campbell-Lange, Architectural Association School of Architecture; Professor Nat Chard, University of Manitoba; Dr Willem de Bruijn; Chris Davy; Dr Davide Deriu, University of Westminster; Professor Mark Dorrian, University of Newcastle; Professor Anthony Dunne and Fiona Raby, Royal College of Art; Paul Fineberg; William Firebrace, University of Westminster; Alex Gino and Jason Griffiths, Arizona State University; Professor Katja Grillner, Royal Institute of Technology, Stockholm; Dr Christos Hadjichristos, University of Cyprus; Catherine Harrington; Paul Hodgson; Professor Rolf Hughes, Konstfack, Stockholm; Udi Kassif; Bekir Kaya; Dr Amy Kulper and Perry Kulper, University of Michigan; Constance Lau, University of Westminster; Justin Lyons, Farnsworth House and the National Trust for Historic Preservation; Dr Lesley Lokko; Mark Lumley; Igor Marjanovic, Washington University, St Louis; Ganit Mayslits; Ben Nicholson, Art Institute of Chicago; Jean Oh; Ulrike Passe, Iowa State University; Rahesh Ram; Neil Rawson; Ro Spankie, University of Westminster; Dr Bradley Starkey, University for the Creative Arts; Kay Ngee Tan; Professor Jeremy Till,

University of Westminster; Dr Victoria Watson, University of Westminster; and Alex Zambelli. Sharing a fascination for gardens, Emma Jones encouraged my investigation of the eighteenth century. Generous assistance and advice was offered by individuals at institutions where I conducted research, notably Stephen Astley and Susan Palmer, respectively the Curator of Drawings and Archivist at Sir John Soane's Museum, London; Colin Harris, Superintendent of the Special Collections Reading Rooms at the Bodleian Library, Oxford; and Christine Hiskey and Dr Suzanne Reynolds, respectively the Archivist and Manuscript Curator at Holkham Hall, Norfolk. *Weather Architecture* is my sixth book to be published by Routledge, and I am especially grateful to Fran Ford, Kyle Duggan, Georgina Johnson and Laura Williamson for their continuing support.

ILLUSTRATIONS

Considerable effort has been made to trace copyright holders of images. The author and publishers apologise for any errors and omissions, and, if notified, will endeavour to correct these at the earliest available opportunity.

introduction

WEATHER AND CLIMATE

This book has been in my thoughts for many years. Growing up in the south-west of England, contemporary mythologies presented the landscape as largely docile, bucolic and benign. Writing at the cusp of the twentieth century, Thomas Hardy's fictional Wessex offered an alternative and more convincing rural tradition in which the weather was a complex protagonist in events. But Hardy's novels differ from *Weather Architecture* in that they fatalistically focus on weather's influence on people, while this book is concerned with the interdependence of nature and culture and considers urban as well as rural life.[1] To oil the wheel of polite conversation, the English mention the weather incessantly. But here, as in many countries and continents, the weather, as a phenomenon and a metaphor, is also a means to explore and engage the relations between nature and culture, time and space, and life and death.

The name given to atmospheric conditions closer to the earth's surface, the weather results from differences in air pressure and temperature, which the atmosphere attempts to redress.[2] This book considers climate as well as weather but its principal focus is everyday experience so that environmental awareness is informed by context and history. Weather and climate differ in duration and scale. Unlike the weather, which we can see and feel at a specific time and place, we cannot directly perceive climate because it is an idea aggregated over many years and across a region.

1 For example, Hardy, *The Woodlanders*, pp. 367–385, when stormy weather divides the principal characters, Grace Melbury and Giles Winterborne, who dies as a consequence.

2 The atmosphere's five layers are the outer exosphere, thermosphere, mesosphere, stratosphere and inner troposphere.

WEATHER, ARCHITECTURE AND AUTHORSHIP

Its supposed opposition to weather, which represents a physical and psychological threat, has often been used to define architecture. Banister Fletcher writes that 'Architecture . . . must have had a simple origin in the primitive efforts of mankind to provide protection against inclement weather, wild beasts and human enemies.'[3] As I question its opposition to architecture, the weather is a means to reconsider architectural authorship, which is the underlying theme of all my research. In *The Illegal Architect*, 1998, and *Actions of Architecture*, 2003, I state that architecture is an experience as well as an object or space.[4] Consequently, I conclude that architecture is made by use as well as by design and state that the user can be as creative as the designer. Arguing that user creativity should be a central concern of architectural design, I also recognise that use may involve design, and vice versa. In *Immaterial Architecture*, 2006, I focus on the perceived absence of matter more

3 Fletcher, p. 1.

4 Architecture is also a subject, discipline and practice. Hill, *The Illegal Architect*, p. 34; Hill, *Actions of Architecture*, pp. 63–89.

than the actual absence of matter in order to devise further means to explore the creativity of the designer and the user, which may be complementary or conflicting. The user decides whether architecture is immaterial. But the architect, or any other designer, devises material conditions in which that decision can be made. Emphasising that architecture is not just conventional building fabric, *Immaterial Architecture* concludes with an 'Index' of thirty architectural 'materials' that can be perceived as immaterial, such as condensation, glass and rust.[5] *Weather Architecture* further extends my investigation of authorship by identifying the weather as a creative architectural force alongside the designer and user. Although I acknowledge the influence of the client, contractor and engineer, the relations between the designer, user and weather are the focus of this book.

5 Hill, *Immaterial Architecture*, pp. 79–200.

THE PICTURESQUE AND ROMANTICISM

Grounding environmental awareness in historical understanding, *Weather Architecture* begins in the Enlightenment, recognising its influence on subsequent and present-day attitudes to the weather and climate. Empiricism was the principal British contribution to Enlightenment theory. The concern for experience gave new attention to subjectivity and the natural world, so that one became a means to discover the other. Reconfiguring the relations between nature and culture stimulated an expanded understanding of architectural authorship. The aloof and individual authorship of the Italian Renaissance emphasised the artistic and intellectual creation of an architect who was in command of drawing and distant from the construction site. In the eighteenth century an alternative conception of the architect acknowledged a new type of design and a new way of designing that valued the ideas and emotions evoked through experience and recognised the creative influences of the weather as well as the user. No longer was architecture a cohesive body of knowledge based on universal ideas. Instead, ideas were provisional, changeable and dependent on experience at conception, production and reception. The changing weather became synonymous with changing perception and was considered to be as exceptional as the imagination. Consequently, the eighteenth century recognised not only the effects of nature on people, and vice versa, but also weather's role as an architectural author.

Marking a significant transformation in design practice, these principles were first combined in the early eighteenth-century picturesque garden. One of the main aims of this book is to redeem the picturesque from the unfortunate connotations of its name. Frequently dismissed as superficial and indulgent, the picturesque is assumed to be solely concerned with appearances and largely ignorant of social, cultural and political questions. The picturesque is a deceptive term because it does not readily acknowledge the importance of the senses and the seasons to experience, understanding and the imagination in the eighteenth-century garden. In a significant design innovation, the picturesque gave new emphasis to the environment, exploring human activity in dialogue with an evolving natural world. Just as the daily weather was part of a larger weather pattern, the picturesque garden was a means to engage the social as well as the subjective. History, politics, love and death were all represented and discussed among garden glades and monuments.

The attention given to subjectivity inevitably and increasingly led to questions of mortality. For the self-aware and questioning mind, the seasons drew attention to the past, present and future. In the picturesque garden, time was tangible in plants and trees and represented in monuments and buildings, which were also seen to age. Weathering and decay were acknowledged and even celebrated. Equating the seasons of a garden to the seasons of a life, references to impending winter, and death, were indicative of delights made sweeter because they were fleeting. In the picturesque, architecture became temporal. Rather than a complete and timeless object, a garden building was understood as an incident in an environment with which it conversed. Establishing a profound influence on subsequent centuries, environmental awareness became central to the architectural imagination. The dialogue between architecture and weather is a means to encourage buildings that coexist with their immediate and wider environments and acknowledge time, decay and change.

Alongside a re-evaluation of the picturesque, a reassessment of romanticism is a further aim of this book. The term 'romantic' is often applied pejoratively, suggesting disengagement and retreat from contemporary concerns. Instead, collaborations and conversations between painters, poets and scientists characterised early nineteenth-century romanticism, which accommodated intellect as well as emotion, and was not indifferent to reason. For example, rather than a retreat to nature, J.M.W. Turner's romanticism fully acknowledged the complexity of his time, its climate and weather.

PICTURESQUE AND ROMANTIC MODERNISM

Analysing attitudes to a changing environment, *Weather Architecture* identifies a picturesque and romantic thread that began in the eighteenth century and was revived in the mid-twentieth century as a means to reconsider and reconfigure modernist architecture. Modernism has often been associated with progress. But in the twentieth century as well as the eighteenth, a critical understanding of the past was a catalyst to creativity. Architects looked to the past to imagine the future, studying an earlier architecture not to replicate it but to understand and transform it, revealing its relevance to the present. Critical of modernist disregard for cultural, social and geographic differences, designers and writers drew attention to the picturesque and romanticism in order to question one modernism – international, mechanical and insensitive – in favour of another – local, emotive and environmentally aware.

Precedents for modernism's rationalising tendencies can be identified in the Enlightenment as well as the scientific management of labour on the factory floor. Although technocratic modernism has received much criticism, many of its principles remain in architectural discourse and practice, significantly because of the demands of an increasingly structured building industry and architects' need to identify specific expertise in defence of their status. The architect as problem solver is one such, largely unquestioned principle, which favours solutions that are widely applicable and reduces nature–culture relations to a merely technical concern. Architects refer to climate more often than weather because it is representative of a norm. Enforcing the assumption that architecture is opposed to weather, architects adopt climatic performance as a reassuring model for design, presenting a consistent and comfortable environment as an ideal. As early as 1915 Le Corbusier proposed a universal 'neutralising wall' to isolate inside from outside and guarantee a stable internal temperature. In architectural discourse this tradition is eloquently expressed in Reyner Banham's *The Architecture of the Well-tempered Environment*, 1984.[6] Even when the architect's design approach is more poetic, the architect as problem solver often prevails because of the need to identify precise skills that generate economic, social and cultural benefits for the client, user and architect. Architectural publications often reflect this prejudice, presenting the architect as a creative and skilful environmental manager. Questioning the narrowly technocratic notion of the architect as problem solver and moderator of climatic performance, this book offers an alternative model of architectural authorship that allows for a wider and more discursive engagement with a range of issues and values. In *Weather Architecture*, the relationship between architecture and the environment is one of mutual dependence, which requires the architect to develop a subtle and complex understanding of time and context, accept the inevitability of unexpected change and acknowledge weather's creative influence.

6 First devised for the Villa Schwob, La Chaux de Fonds, 1915. Refer to Le Corbusier, *Precisions,* pp. 65–66; Banham, *The Architecture of the Well-tempered Environment*, pp. 156–163.

A HISTORY OF WEATHER

The detailed discussion of buildings and gardens is the focus of my research method. I also consider the ideas, images and opinions of architects, artists and theorists because my concern is the design as well as the experience of architecture, in particular how an awareness of users' creativity may inform designers' creativity, and vice versa.

In giving particular emphasis to architecture as an experience and focusing on the weather's contribution to perception and understanding, the picturesque initiated an influential architectural environmentalism. The first five chapters consider the work of William Kent, John Soane and J.M.W. Turner so as to analyse and categorise picturesque and romantic attitudes to the environment at a time when science and industry were transforming society. As industries multiplied, the weather increasingly became a hybrid of the artificial and the natural, while perception was mediated through devices such as the Claude Glass. To cast this history in a more contemporary light, and discuss the appropriation and translation of picturesque and romantic principles, the following four chapters focus on Ludwig Mies van der Rohe, Alison and Peter Smithson, Sverre Fehn and Sigurd Lewerentz, and Derek Jarman. Specific influences are discussed in detail, such as Mies's debt to Karl Friedrich Schinkel. As in my previous books, I consider architects and other architectural designers, noting that the architectural profession does not have a monopoly on innovative design. Consistent with the picturesque and romanticism, each of my protagonists acknowledged the weather as a significant authorial voice that complemented his or her own, albeit to varying degrees. Each of them recognised a different atmosphere, reflecting specific aspects of an emergent hybridised weather that was becoming increasingly industrial, electromagnetic and radioactive as well as natural.

Environmental discussions in architecture tend to focus on the practical or the poetic but my aim is to consider them together. Rather than investigate architecture's relations to the weather in isolation I integrate them into a wider discussion of cultural and social influences on architecture. My analysis of weather's effects on the design and experience of specific buildings and gardens is interwoven with a historical survey of changing attitudes to the weather in the arts, sciences and society, which leads to a critical re-evaluation of contemporary responses to climate change. At a time when environmental awareness is of growing relevance, my overriding aim is to understand a history of architecture as a history of weather and thus to consider the weather as an architectural author that influences design, construction and use in a creative dialogue with other authors such as the architect and user.

1

things of a natural kind

INTRODUCTION

The new reverence given to subjectivity and nature in the eighteenth century, and the association of one with the other, encouraged a new type of design and a new way of designing, which valued the ideas and emotions evoked through experience. The early eighteenth-century picturesque is the subject of this chapter and William Kent is its central figure. The chapter is organised into three interconnecting sections, each with a specific theme, which together consider the ideas and places that informed the picturesque. The first, 'Magnificence Beyond the Formal Mockery of Princely Gardens', addresses the philosophical, cultural and political contexts to the 'natural' garden in eighteenth-century England, which gave special attention to weather as a means to discover the qualities of a person and a place. The second, 'Signor Kentino', discusses the Roman and Italian influences that Kent translated for an English climate. The third, 'More than Picturesque', analyses the origins of the term and questions its appropriateness to the early eighteenth-century English garden. Concluding my investigation of the early picturesque, Chapter 2 provides a detailed study of Kent's garden at Rousham, Oxfordshire.

MAGNIFICENCE BEYOND THE FORMAL MOCKERY OF PRINCELY GARDENS

The Natural Light of Reason

Beginning in the mid-seventeenth century and extending into most of the subsequent century, the Enlightenment – the natural light of reason – was founded on the assumption that humanity and nature are subject to the same laws of divine reason, can be understood by reason and progress by reason. The principal British contribution to Enlightenment theory was empiricism, which promoted reason but made it specific rather than generic. The term is derived from the ancient Greek term for experience: *empeiria*. Empirical investigation was applied extensively, notably to the operations of the mind. In *An Essay concerning Human Understanding*, 1690, John Locke describes diverse peoples and beliefs to support his assumption that knowledge, personality and morality are acquired not innate. He concludes that the mind begins as a 'White Paper', an empty cabinet, which experience furnishes with understanding.[1]

1 Locke, *An Essay concerning Human Understanding*, bk. 2, ch. 1, p. 104. Refer to Davies, *A History of Europe*, p. 598; Porter, *Enlightenment*, p. 9.

> *External, Material things, as the Objects of SENSATION; and the Operations of our own Minds within, as the Objects of Reflection, are, to me the only Originals, from whence all our* Ideas *take their beginnings.*[2]

Associating illumination with understanding, Locke gives special attention to vision but acknowledges the influence of all the senses.[3] He distinguishes between the simple ideas of sensations, over which the mind has no control, and complex ones, which the mind creates by selecting, rejecting and combining simple ideas. Memory and judgement allow complex ideas to develop and for one to be associated with another. Recognising that experience is iterative, Locke values the continuing return to the simple ideas of sensations as a necessary means to affirm or deny complex ones. Consequently, understanding depends on an evolving dialogue between the external world, the senses and the mind. As ideas are provisional and always subject to experience, *An Essay concerning Human Understanding* undermines the neo-Platonist and Cartesian traditions in which knowledge is acquired by the mind alone.[4]

Locke's theories were influential but not unquestioned. The assumption that there is a direct relationship between the observer and the observed generated disagreement because it ignored the observer's role in shaping that experience. Considered untenable, it was discarded by later eighteenth-century empiricist philosophers such as Archibald Alison, Thomas Reid and Dugald Stewart. *An Essay concerning Human Understanding* was also criticised as an attack on faith. Locke asserts that reason and faith are relevant to different concerns: 'Nothing that is contrary to, and inconsistent with the clear and self-evident Dictates of Reason, has a Right to be urged, or assented to, as a matter of Faith, wherein Reason has nothing to do.'[5] The resurrection, for example, is a question of faith. The consequence of this distinction was to focus attention on reasoned investigation; spiritual concerns were largely ignored. The authority of the emergent secular elite was increased and that of the Church diminished.

Dismissing the search for ultimate truth, which had received so much previous attention, Locke accepts that there are limits to what we can know: 'When we consider the vast distance of the known and visible parts of the World, and the Reasons we have to think, that what lies within our Ken is but a small part of the Universe, we shall then discover an huge Abyss of Ignorance.'[6] Consequently, he argues that conclusions must be in proportion to the evidence: 'Our business here is not to know all things, but those which concern our conduct.'[7] Locke's empiricism may seem modest and sensible but it can spawn a mode of investigation

2 Locke, *An Essay concerning Human Understanding*, bk. 2, ch. 1, p. 105.

3 Locke, *An Essay concerning Human Understanding*, bk. 2, ch. 2, pp. 119–121.

4 Descartes, *Meditations on First Philosophy*, p. 53.

5 Locke, *An Essay concerning Human Understanding*, bk, 4, ch. 18, p. 696.

6 Locke, *An Essay concerning Human Understanding*, bk. 4, ch. 3, p. 555.

7 Locke, *An Essay concerning Human Understanding*, bk, 1, ch. 1, p. 46.

that recognises only what it can define and objectify, dismissing any means to understanding that does not follow its methods.

A model of education – a person learning through experience in a measured and reasonable manner – is at the heart of *An Essay concerning Human Understanding*. The Lockean self is self-controlled, punctual, industrious and drawn to self-improvement and socially acceptable pleasures. The personal liberty and responsible behaviour that Locke conjoins in *An Essay concerning Human Understanding* mirror the political freedoms of the citizen in the civil society he describes in *Two Treatises of Government*, also published in 1690.

As morality and standards of behaviour are acquired not innate, an extensive chain of ideas can nourish a responsible mind, indicating learning and judgement. Wishing not to deny creativity but to contain it, Locke assumes that understanding grounded in experience is more likely to resist the inappropriate association of ideas, which, he concludes, result from shock more often than habit and may lead to unfortunate consequences such as unhappiness or even madness.[8] According to Ernest Tuveson:

> *Here we encounter an authentic note of 'modernism' . . . The wrong associations are a part of the history of what passes in man's mind, and we must reconstruct that history to find out the real causes of his mental malaise . . . To take this step towards psychoanalysis, however, required almost two centuries. It took a long time before an explicit theory of the unconscious emerged, even though it is implicit in Locke's discussion.*[9]

Indeed, in a famous reference to Socrates awake and asleep, Locke acknowledges that one person may have different mental states and more than one personality and opinion: 'If the same *Socrates* waking and sleeping do not partake of the same *consciousness*, *Socrates* waking and sleeping is not the same Person.'[10]

From classical antiquity to the seventeenth century, beauty was certain. But the eighteenth century opened it to subjective interpretation. In 'Of the Standard of Taste', 1757, David Hume employs empiricism to conclude: 'Beauty is no quality in things themselves: it exists merely in the mind which contemplates them; and each mind perceives a different beauty.'[11] Hume offers an equally subtle understanding of the relationship between mind and matter: 'Though it be certain that beauty and deformity but belong to the sentiment, internal or external, it must be allowed, that there are certain qualities in objects which are fitted by nature to produce those particular feelings'.[12] Hume recognises that opinions may vary from person to person but, determined to defend his class, still maintains that rules are

8 The chapter 'Of the Association of Ideas' appears in the fourth edition of 1700, although it was written somewhat earlier. Locke, *An Essay concerning Human Understanding*, bk. 2, ch. 33, pp. 394–401. Refer to Ballantyne, pp. 144–145; Forty, pp. 208–209; Hunt and Willis, 'Introduction', pp. 37–38; Taylor, *Sources of the Self*, pp. 159–176; Tuveson, p. 75.

9 Tuveson, pp. 35–36.

10 Locke, *An Essay concerning Human Understanding*, bk. 2, ch. 27, p. 342.

11 Hume, 'Of the Standard of Taste', pp. 136–137.

12 Hume, 'Of the Standard of Taste', p. 141.

not absent. Reinforcing the eighteenth-century concern for taste, which coupled cultural and social refinement, he identifies 'those models and principles which have been established by the uniform consent and experience of nations and ages'.[13] Hume concludes that access to genuine beauty is limited to the most educated: 'the general principles of taste are uniform in human nature: where men vary in their judgements, some defect or perversion in their faculties may commonly be remarked'.[14] Using mist as a metaphor for confusion, he remarks: 'A perfect serenity of mind, a recollection of thought, a due attention to the object; if any of these circumstances be wanting our experiment will be fallacious, and we shall be unable to judge of the catholic and universal beauty.'[15]

Empiricism's contribution to British life has been profound and enduring, establishing measured and modest behaviour as a model. But in drawing attention to the ambiguities of identity and limits of objectivity, empiricism's success could only be relative. Increasingly in the eighteenth century, the recognition that we make our own reality and associate seemingly unrelated ideas was exploited for its creative potential, contradicting Locke's grounded reasonableness of a mechanistic mind and Hume's defence of educated opinion. Individuality was lauded and affirmed while it was recognised to be uncertain. Undoubtedly this was part of its attraction. The elusive quarry stimulated the hunt, establishing principles that have influenced the arts ever since.

13 Hume, 'Of the Standard of Taste', p. 143.

14 Hume, 'Of the Standard of Taste', p. 149.

15 Hume, 'Of the Standard of Taste', pp. 143, 139.

Microscopes and Telescopes

In the Renaissance, nature was admired for its God-given beauty but was often treated with suspicion unless it was cultivated. Mountains and forests were not enjoyed. As Tuveson remarks, the immaterial soul, 'as a visitor in matter' could not 'be truly at home in nature'.[16] The early Enlightenment depended on Deism, according to which God created the natural world for human benefit and offered no further intervention, leaving it in trust to humanity. Now synonymous with reason, nature was eulogised from poetry to geology. In 1660 the Royal Society was founded for the advance of scientific knowledge and received a royal charter two years later, while in 1675 the Royal Observatory was established in Greenwich.[17] With the development of modern scientific instruments such as the microscope and the telescope, increasingly detailed observation focused more on the properties of natural objects and less on their immediate value to humans, although this concern was never distant. Favouring the collection, analysis and ordering of information according to a complete system, the Enlightenment also concentrated attention on

16 Tuveson, p. 11.

17 At the time, the term 'natural philosophy' was used in place of science.

the relations between natural objects, which had previously been primarily measured against a human standard. Astronomers, botanists and zoologists classified planets, plants and animals, while geologists established the earth's age. In 1683 Anton van Leeuwenhoek declared 'that there were more animals in his own mouth than there were people in the United Provinces' of the Netherlands.[18] The discovery of new plants, places and creatures, and greater understanding of those already known, further stimulated appreciation of the natural world. A concern for all the earth's creatures is a characteristic of the Judaeo-Christian tradition. But it was more often latent until the late seventeenth century when scientists concluded that any natural object, however humble, could be admired if it fulfilled a purpose. Science detached nature from culture so that it was available for investigation, encouraging an alternative concern for unfettered nature that was less evident in earlier societies.[19]

18 Thomas, referring to Dobell, pp. 174, 243.

19 Hulme, pp. 343–344.

A Philosophical Rhapsody

Believing that the mind is at first empty, Locke must have cherished his role as tutor to Anthony Ashley Cooper, the future third Earl of Shaftesbury. As physician and secretary to the first Earl, Locke even attended the birth of the child, who later described his tutor as my 'foster-father'.[20] The pupil confirmed the tutor's appreciation of liberty and reason but tempered Locke's empiricism and rejected his egalitarianism: 'Twas Mr. Locke that struck at all fundamentals, threw all order and virtue out of the world.'[21]

On the natural world their opinions diverged. In *Two Treatises of Government* Locke mentions 'the Woods and Forests, where the irrational untaught Inhabitants kept right by following Nature, are fitter to give us Rules, than Cities and Palaces, where those that call themselves Civil and Rational, go out of their way, by the Authority of Example'.[22] But in *An Essay concerning Human Understanding* he discusses the natural world only so far as it affects human knowledge and describes mental confusion as a weather condition: mist before the eyes.[23]

Published as a three-volume collection in 1711, *Characteristicks of Men, Manners, Opinions, Times* established Shaftesbury as a persuasive influence on eighteenth-century thought, notably informing Edmund Burke and Richard Boyle – third Earl of Burlington – in England, Jean-Jacques Rousseau in France, and Johann Gottfried von Goethe, Johann Gottfried Herder and Immanuel Kant in Germany.[24] The first volume promotes the political, moral and cultural authority of an educated elite and praises their moderation and polite behaviour. According to

20 Shaftesbury quoted in Ayres, p. xiv.

21 Shaftesbury, *The Life, Unpublished Letters, and Philosophical Regimen of Anthony, Earl of Shaftesbury*, p. 403.

22 Locke, *Two Treatises of Government*, p. 201, bk. I, para. 58.

23 Locke, *An Essay concerning Human Understanding*, bk. 3, ch. 10, p. 493.

24 The first two volumes had earlier been published separately but were substantially revised for the 1711 three-volume collection.

Shaftesbury, beauty follows objective, moral and universal standards that only the most cultured can appreciate.[25] Praising the moral and aesthetic virtues of a restrained classicism as well as restrained behaviour, he dismisses the buildings of Sir Christopher Wren and Sir John Vanbrugh.[26]

Shaftesbury's conception of beauty was indebted to Plato. In *Timaeus*, *c.*360 BC, Plato claims that all the things we perceive in the material world are modelled on divine, immaterial and ideal forms, which are defined by geometrical relationships.[27] Consequently, there are two distinct realms. One consists of ideal originals, which only the intellect can comprehend, the other of imperfect, natural and material copies that are subject to decay. Named in recognition of the revival and reinterpretation of classical antiquity, the Renaissance promoted a concept of beauty based on geometry's universal proportions. According to Marsilio Ficino, who founded the Platonic Academy in Florence and provided the first translation of Plato's works into Latin: 'The beauty of bodies does not consist in the shadow of materiality, but in the clarity and gracefulness of form, not in the hidden bulk, but in a kind of luminous harmony, not in an inert and stupid weight, but in a fitting number and measure.'[28] Informed by the Cambridge Platonists such as Henry More – author of *An Antidote Against Atheism*, 1652, and *The Exploration of the Grand Mystery of Godliness*, 1660 – Shaftesbury acknowledged an ideal order but, rather than debased, he conceived nature as a means to contemplate the divine.

The second volume of *Characteristicks* praises nature, incorporating ideas that Shaftesbury previously considered in *The Moralists, A Philosophical Rhapsody*, which was written in 1705 and published in 1709. Recuperation in nature was not a new theme but it found new expression in the eighteenth century, when nature and moral virtue were associated with each other for the first time. Sensitivity to one's environment became as necessary as sensitivity to others. In a eulogy to nature and the weather that has, until recently, been seen as advocating the flowing lines of the early eighteenth-century garden, Shaftesbury writes:

> *I shall no longer resist the Passion growing in me for Things of a* natural *kind; where neither* Art*, nor the* Conceit *or* Caprice *of Man has spoil'd their* genuine Order, *by breaking in upon that* primitive State. *Even the* Rocks, *the mossy* Caverns, *the irregular unwrought* Grotto's, *and broken* Falls *of Waters, with all the horrid* Graces *of the* Wilderness *it-self, as representing NATURE more, will be the more engaging, and appear with a Magnificence beyond the formal Mockery of Princely Gardens.*[29]
>
> *HOW comfortable is it to those who come out hence alive, to breathe a purer AIR! To see the rejoicing Light of* Day! *And tread the fertile Ground! How gladly they*

25 Shaftesbury, *Characteristicks*, vol. 1, pp. 77–78, 118–119.

26 'A Letter Concerning The Art, or Science of Design' was written in 1709 and widely read at that time, appearing in the fifth edition of the *Characteristicks* in 1732.

27 Plato, *Timaeus*, p. 121.

28 Ficino refers to Plato's allegory of the cave. Ficino, letter to Giovanni Cavalcanti, quoted in Hofstadter and Kuhns, p. 204; Plato, *The Republic*, pp. 203–206.

29 Shaftesbury, *Characteristicks*, vol. 2, p. 101.

contemplate the Surface of the Earth, their habitation heated and enliven'd by the Sun, *and temper'd by the fresh AIR of fanning* Breezes*! These exercise the resty Plants, and scour the unactive Globe. And when the* Sun *draws hence thick clouded Steams and Vapours, 'tis only to digest exalt the unwholesom Particles, and commit 'em to the sprightly AIR; which soon imparting its quick and vital Spirit, renders 'em again with improvement to the Earth, in gentle Breathings, or in rich Dews and fruitful Showers.*[30]

30 Shaftesbury, *Characteristicks*, vol. 2, p. 94.

Anthony Ashley Cooper, third Earl of Shaftesbury, *Characteristicks of Men, Manners, Opinions, Times*, 1711. The 1714 frontispiece to the second edition. Courtesy of the British Library.

As Roy Porter poignantly remarks, 'Shaftesbury was lastingly charmed by the flair and creativity of his own genius.'[31] In the 1714 frontispiece to the second edition he poses as a Roman senator.[32] Leaning on a book-laden pedestal, Shaftesbury stands in front of a neo-classical arch, which frames the sequential arrangement of three natures: distant wooded hills, abundant orchards and formal gardens. In *De Natura Deorum* (On the Nature of the Gods), written in the first century BC, Cicero referred to *alteram naturam*, an alternative, second nature of human fabrication: 'We sow corn, we plant trees, we fertilize the soil by irrigation, we dam the rivers and direct them where we want. In short, by means of our hands we try to create as it were a second nature within the natural world.'[33] In 1541 and 1559 respectively, Jacopo Bonfadio and Bartoleomeo Taegio described gardens as a 'third nature', a companion to the other two.[34]

Within Shaftesbury's statements on nature, Christopher Hussey recognises 'the Augustan's continual difficulty in deciding what Nature meant to them: whether the sum of visible phenomena not made by artifice; or the "ideal" form, theoretically achievable' if not practically possible.[35] Concluding that the 1714 frontispiece illustrates the formality of Shaftesbury's own garden at Wimborne St Giles in Dorset, David Leatherbarrow writes:

> *Shaftesbury's praise of uncultivated nature cannot be taken as an anticipation of the early or mid-eighteenth-century preference for uncut trees and contrived informality in gardens. His rhapsody on nature must be taken as part of a philosophy of ungraspable beauty and truth in nature.*[36]

But Shaftesbury influenced the early eighteenth-century garden whether or not he predicted it. Locke connected understanding to experience but required a degree of critical detachment from the natural world. In the second volume of *Characteristicks* nature's purpose is more profound, as Charles Taylor recognises: 'though disengaged reason is not repudiated, we participate in God's plan through a re-engagement'.[37]

The Pleasures of the Imagination

Influenced by Locke's concern for everyday experience and the association of ideas and Shaftesbury's appreciation of wild nature and classical precedent, Joseph Addison and Alexander Pope furthered the philosophical and literary gestation of the early eighteenth-century garden. In 1712 Addison published eleven essays on 'The

31 Porter, *Flesh in the Age of Reason*, p. 135.

32 Most likely conceived in consultation with Shaftesbury, Simon Gribelin's engraving was based on a John Closterman portrait of 1700–1701 and was completed in 1714, one year after Shaftesbury's death. Although the second edition is dated 1714, it actually appeared in 1715. Ayres, 'Introduction', pp. xxxi–xxxiv.

33 *De natura deorum* was translated into English as *Cicero's Three Books Touching on the Nature of the Gods*, 1683. Cicero, quoted in Hunt, *Greater Perfections*, p. 33.

34 Taegio refers to the term in his treatise, *La Villa*, 1559, while Bonfadio mentions it in correspondence with Plinio Tomacello. Refer to Hunt, *Greater Perfections*, p. 32.

35 Hussey, *English Gardens and Landscapes*, p. 29.

36 Leatherbarrow, p. 353.

37 Taylor, *Sources of the Self*, p. 265.

· Attitudes to nature: caprice of man.

Pleasures of the Imagination' in *The Spectator*, the daily journal he had founded with Richard Steele. Previously, nature was most often explored in paintings and books. But Addison concluded that this appreciation was secondary to the primary pleasures of direct experience, which could cultivate a healthy body, an alert mind and a sociable manner.[38] References to the weather's influence on conversation, behaviour and health appear throughout his articles. Addison particularly recommended that his readers maintain a diary to encourage self-awareness. Eighteenth-century empiricism placed great emphasis on activities that led to personal development. The individual drawn to socially acceptable pleasures was also useful to an expanding capitalist economy because of the resulting demand for goods associated with such pleasures, whether clothes, guidebooks or drawing instruments.

38 Addison, 'From *The Spectator* (21, 23 and 25 June 1712)', p. 235.

Following Locke, Addison identifies, first, passive appreciation and then creative proposition as essential to the imagination. He describes sight as 'the most perfect and most delightful of all our Senses . . . which furnishes the Imagination with its Ideas'. Although Addison values the other senses, their purpose is more prosaic. For example, 'The Sense of Feeling can indeed give us a Notion of Extension, Shape, and all Other Ideas that enter at the Eye, except Colours; but at the same time it is very streightned and confined in its Operations, to the number, bulk and distance of its particular Objects.'[39]

39 Addison, 'From *The Spectator* (21, 23 and 25 June 1712)', p. 234.

Citing the Pantheon in Rome, he appreciates architecture's ability to evoke a single, vast idea, notably the divine.[40] Mountains have a similar power but Addison also notes that wild nature is especially conducive to the imagination because it offers a multitude of ideas for association.

40 Addison, 'From *The Spectator* (26 June 1712)', pp. 254–255.

> *There is something more bold and masterly in the rough careless Strokes of Nature, than in the nice Touches and Embellishments of Art. The Beauties of the most stately Garden or Palace lie in a narrow Compass, the Imagination immediately runs them over, and requires something else to gratifie her; but, in the wide Fields of Nature, the Sight wanders up and down without Confinement, and is fed with an infinite variety of Images, without any Stint or Number.*[41]

41 Addison, 'From *The Spectator* (21, 23 and 25 June 1712)', p. 238.

But rather than the natural world per se, he focuses on the art of making a garden appear natural, drawing a parallel with the cultivation of natural behaviour: 'The fashionable world is grown free and easy; our manners sit more loose upon us: nothing is so modish as an agreeable negligence.'[42] Concluding that the 'artificial rudeness' of a garden modelled on nature 'gives us a nobler and more exalted kind of Pleasure', Addison even suggests that it may be more widely applied: 'why may not a whole Estate be thrown into a kind of Garden?'[43]

42 Addison, *Selections from Addison's Papers*, p. 263.

43 Addison, 'From *The Spectator* (21, 23 and 25 June 1712)', p. 238.

As Addison associates the imagination with spiritual needs, Tuveson describes 'The Pleasures of the Imagination' as 'the first work ever written on aesthetics as a wholly autonomous subject' and recognises a precursor to romanticism: 'The possibility that imagination, far from being an ideal ally of reason, is its inveterate rival and antagonist, now emerges into the open.'[44] But the degree to which imagination and reason were compatible, or not, was a concern throughout the century, which neither the picturesque nor romanticism answered categorically. Equally, the mimetic purpose of the arts was questioned by the increasing emphasis on the imagination but there was no resolution to the debate, as John Dixon Hunt remarks:

44 Tuveson, pp. 92, 97, 117 and 131.

> *Garden aesthetics in the eighteenth century increasingly fell into the gap between the traditional notion of imitation (where representation of nature and human nature in history are stressed) and a rival view which proposed the affective power of art (and therefore gave prominence to the interior and autonomous imagination).*[45]

45 Hunt, *Garden and Grove*, p. 97.

The Famous Grotto

Echoing Shaftesbury, Pope praised 'the amiable simplicity of unadorned nature' and sought justification in divine order and classical precedent: 'this was the taste of the ancients in their gardens'.[46] His concern for classical antiquity led him to translate Homer – to make him 'speak good *English*' – and adopt Horace as a literary model.[47] Rather than a direct and literal translation, his references to classical antiquity were intended to cultivate principles suited to England.

46 Pope, 1713, quoted in Hussey, 'Introduction', p. 21. Refer to Jackson, p. 4.

47 Sir William Trumball, in Pope, vol. 1, pp. 45–46.

Pope influenced early eighteenth-century gardens as a designer as well as a poet. At Twickenham, adjacent to the River Thames, his house was on one side of the road and his garden was on the other. To connect the two he created a tunnel, which became the famous grotto, begun around 1719. The first grottoes were caves where shrines to the water spirits were constructed in ancient Greece. Built on the site of a natural spring, Pope's grotto included a sequence of rooms, varied watery environments, verdant mosses and encrusted surfaces that glistened with shells, flints, crystals, corals and fossils from many countries, either found by Pope or donated by his friends. The lamp hanging at its centre caused light to flicker across its surfaces, distorting the scale of the grotto as the flame swayed and varied in the breeze. Popular in ancient Rome and Renaissance Italy, grottoes were not new to England. But Pope's fame drew attention to his grotto, inspiring other grottoes in picturesque gardens and offering a poetic model for garden buildings that allowed weather into their interiors.

Beyond the grotto, Pope's garden included numerous means to entice the visitor and punctuate journeys: a grove of lime trees, circular lawn, viewing mound, shell temple, vineyard, orangery, obelisk, urns and statues. Pope created alternative routes, some formal, others meandering, and varied views, either within the garden or to the Thames beyond. Designed to appear bigger than its five acres, Pope's garden was as complex and intense as the grotto's surfaces.

The Temple of British Worthies

The early eighteenth-century garden was richly resonant of its time because its purpose was political as well as literary, philosophical and artistic. In 1688 a confrontation between the absolutist Catholic king, James II, and the dominant Protestant parliamentary grouping, the Whigs, led to James's daughter, Mary, and son-in-law, William of Orange, becoming constitutional monarchs with the overriding power of parliament affirmed. In 1714 the ascent of the first Hanoverian monarch, George I, continued these principles seven years after the union of England and Scotland. Arguments for a limited monarchy and strong parliament found a model in 'the Roman pattern of consuls (=Monarch), patricians (=Lords), and *comitiae* (=Commons)'.[48] Ancient Rome offered Georgian London a semblance of authority and a model to emulate and surpass. According to John Brewer:

48 Hunt, *William Kent*, p. 57.

> *Foreign visitors and commentators emphasized England's liberty and modernity. Its vigorous political culture, epitomized by the most fully developed European newspaper press, the absence of prior censorship (the Licensing Act had lapsed in 1695), the existence of religious toleration and of freedom to worship, the concern for subjects' rights and the openness of society all impressed foreigners because they were conspicuous by their absence elsewhere.*[49]

49 Brewer, pp. xxiv–xxviii.

A coalition of factions rather than a coherent organisation, the Whigs dominated all areas of society and included Locke, who only returned to England in 1688. *Characteristicks* has often been linked to the Whig ascendancy but Shaftesbury was loyal to his principles rather than those of a particular party. The transformations in English society were not exclusively due to Whig influence. For example, Pope was a Tory and Addison claimed to be neutral.[50]

50 Li, pp. 157–158; Voitle, p. 70.

Just as political power was increasingly concentrated in parliament, cultural influence moved away from the royal court to assembly rooms, learned societies, literary journals and country estates. The focus of political, economic and cultural power in London ensured that garden developments were English first and British second. Before the eighteenth century, English gardens were ordered into a series of room-like spaces. The newly 'natural' picturesque garden was just as contrived but the choices it offered were associated with the choices available to the prosperous members of English society, where empiricism thrived alongside a liberal democracy and constitutional monarchy. Advocates of the picturesque noted that the axial geometry of the French garden expanded outwards from the château and its occupant, while the early eighteenth-century English house was not at the garden's centre and was but one element among others. The readily apparent order of the French garden provided a setting for ceremonial gatherings and was associated with an absolutist monarchy. In *Elements of Criticism*, 1762, Henry Home, Lord Kames, disparagingly concludes: 'The gardens of Versailles, executed with infinite expense by men at that time of high repute, are a lasting monument of a taste the most vicious and depraved.'[51]

51 Kames, vol. 2, p. 331.

A member of a leading aristocratic Whig family and once a general in the Duke of Marlborough's army, Richard Temple, first Viscount Cobham, conceived Stowe – the grandest eighteenth-century English garden – as a political and cultural statement. In the 1730s he commissioned the Elysian Fields, named after the paradise dedicated to the heroes of classical antiquity. But villains were also featured. As a counterpoint to the pristine Temple of Ancient Virtue, the Temple of Modern Virtue was built as a ruin and housed a headless sculpture dedicated to Sir Robert Walpole, the first British Prime Minister. Although both were Whigs, Cobham opposed Walpole, advocating a more expansionist foreign policy and questioning the 1733 Excise Duty, a widespread tax on goods. Also in the Elysian Fields, the Temple of British Worthies is reminiscent of a semi-circular Roman shrine. Each of its twelve niches contains a bust and is surmounted by an inscription, commemorating Whig heroes as varied as the Black Prince, King Alfred, Francis Bacon, John Milton, Alexander Pope and Walter Raleigh. One bust depicts Locke, who through Addison inspired Stowe's Elysian Fields.[52] His inscription reads:

Who best of all Philosophers,
understood the powers of the human mind:
the nature, end, and bounds of civil government;
and with equal courage and sagacity, refused
the slavish systems of usurped authority
over the rights, the consciences, or the reason of mankind.

52 John Dixon Hunt and Peter Willis write that one of Addison's 'essays in *The Tatler* (No. 123) even seems to have provided the programme of images and their associated ideas for Stowe's Elysian Fields'. Hunt and Willis, 'Introduction', p. 37.

For all the grandeur of Cobham's political proclamation, the Temple of British Worthies is modest not bombastic. A nationalistic desire to express British ascendance was tempered by Lockean empiricism, which acknowledged the limits of understanding.

William Kent, Elysian Fields, Stowe, c.1735. The bust of John Locke in the Temple of British Worthies. Photograph, Jonathan Hill.

53 *The History of the Modern Taste in Gardening* was written in the late 1760s and printed in 1771 but not published until 1780 as part of Walpole's *Anecdotes of Painting in England*. In 1785 it was published on its own. Walpole, *The History of the Modern Taste in Gardening*, p. 43.

SIGNOR KENTINO

Multiple Perspectives

Addison imagined an estate as a garden. But in *The History of the Modern Taste in Gardening*, 1771, Sir Robert's youngest son, Horace Walpole, remarks that it was William Kent – the designer of the Elysian Fields and the Temple of British Worthies – who first 'leaped the fence, and saw that all nature was a garden'.[53]

For eighteenth-century architects, painters and patrons, the Grand Tour was invaluable. Born in Yorkshire in 1685, the son of a joiner, Kent had little formal education but his drawing skill was recognised. Supported by various patrons, in 1709 he left London to study art, architecture and gardens in Italy, remaining there for ten years. Kent acted as a guide and adviser to prosperous English visitors, establishing connections that would be important throughout his career. In 1712 he briefly encountered Shaftesbury. Two years later he met Burlington, to whom he remained close throughout his life. The 'Will of William Kent' begins with his request to be buried in the Burlington family vault at Chiswick parish church.[54] Also in 1714, Kent met Thomas Coke, for whom he designed buildings and gardens at Holkham, Norfolk, between the 1720s and 1740s. A neighbour, distant relative and political protégé of Sir Robert Walpole, Coke became the first Earl of Leicester in 1744.[55] For patrons old and new, Kent maintained a steady supply of antiquities, paintings and sculptures, both originals and copies. The *Holkham Household Accounts* for 1717 show four payments to Kent of 100, 300, 500 and 300 Roman crowns.[56] For Burrell Massingberd, an early patron, he even acquired 'Naples soap, fans and dictionaries.'[57]

At first, painting was assumed to be Kent's principal talent. Massingberd even encouraged him to be *'Raphael secundus',* a second Raphael.[58] Kent travelled widely in Italy but spent most of his time in Rome, where he studied under the painter Giuseppe Chiari,[59] who he referred to as 'my master'.[60] Chiari was a pupil of Carlo Maratti and both were indebted to the mature Raphael.[61] But Kent proved to be a mediocre painter; his principal commission was to complete the ceiling of San Giuliano del Fiamminghi in 1717, a Baroque church built in 1681 to the design of Antonio Maria Borioni, one of Gian Lorenzo Bernini's assistants.

In 1714 Kent began a diary, which records his journeys around Italy.[62] Given the liveliness of his drawings and his friends' frequent references to his hedonism, Kent's diary is at first a surprisingly sober account of buildings, paintings and gardens. Sometimes written in English, at other times in Italian, it includes small

54 Kent, 'Will of William Kent', in Jourdain, p. 89.

55 Coke's grandmother married Sir Robert's uncle. In 1733 he became Postmaster General, remaining in office until his death in 1759. Schmidt, Keller and Feversham, *Holkham*, pp. 34–36.

56 Jourdain, p. 51.

57 Hunt, *William Kent*, p. 12.

58 Massingberd, draft letter to Kent, 5 July 1714, quoted in Mowl, *William Kent*, p. 46.

59 Cereghini and Jourdain mention that Kent studied under Benedetto Luti, while Harris, Hunt, Mowl and Sicca cite Chiari and Wilson mentions both painters. Cereghini, p. 320; Harris, *William Kent,* p. 4; Hunt, *William Kent*, p. 11; Jourdain, p. 30; Mowl, *William Kent*, pp. 29–30; Sicca, p. 136; Wilson, *William Kent*, p. 12, p. 252.

60 Kent, letter to Massingberd, 24 November 1714, quoted in Wilson, *William Kent*, p. 252.

61 Sicca, p. 136.

62 The diary continues into 1715 and briefly mentions 1717. Kent, 'Italian diary of 1714–1715', ff. 1–36.

drawings and diagrams in the margins and text. The opening pages refer to his travels with Coke in 1714.[63] Arriving in Venice on 22 July Kent first visits Andrea Palladio's San Giorgio Maggiore, 1780. Leaving the city on 18 August he separates from Coke's party at Padua and proceeds to Vicenza, where he stays just one day. There, Kent admires Palladio's Teatro Olimpico, 1580, which he illustrates with a tiny plan that identifies the elliptical seating, empty stage and perspectival street scenes. Elsewhere in Vicenza he refers merely to 'several other palaces', offering no mention of Palladio's Villa Rotonda, 1569.[64] Kent's garden accounts are more evocative. In addition to valued patrons, Italy introduced him to visual languages and mythological narratives that informed his later designs. At the Medici villa at Pratolino, north of Florence, he notes 'a very fine Situation & very fine Grotos adorn'd with Shells & pietrified stone work with pretty water works a Galatea coming out of her Grotto drawn by Delfini'.[65] At Guilio Romano's Palazzo del Tè in Mantua, *c.*1530, he notices 'in grotta at end of ye garden are very fine grottesque'.[66] Kent is also known to have admired the Renaissance gardens at the Villa Aldobrandini at Frascati and must have been a frequent visitor to the gardens of the Villa Borghese in Rome and the Villa d'Este in Tivoli.[67] Later in the diary, Kent turns his attention to artistic techniques: 'to paint a tempera one egg with white & yolk to-gether & tow eggs of water, after put stalk of fig leaves, or lemon pel'.[68] But the most impressive section is the final one, which contains beautiful and delicate illustrations of perspective techniques in line and wash.[69]

63 Listing all his master's expenses, including over seventy while they were in Venice, Edward Jarrett, Coke's treasurer and valet, provided an alternative account of their journey with a slightly different chronology. Jarrett, 'Account of Thomas Coke's Grand Tour'.

64 Kent, 'Italian Diary', f. 13.

65 Kent, 'Italian Diary', f. 3.

66 Kent, 'Italian Diary', f. 14.

67 Hunt, *William Kent*, p. 26; Sicca, p. 140.

68 Kent, 'Italian Diary', f. 24.

69 Kent, 'Italian Diary', ff. 25–36.

Andrea Palladio, Villa Rotonda, Vicenza, 1570. Photograph, Jonathan Hill.

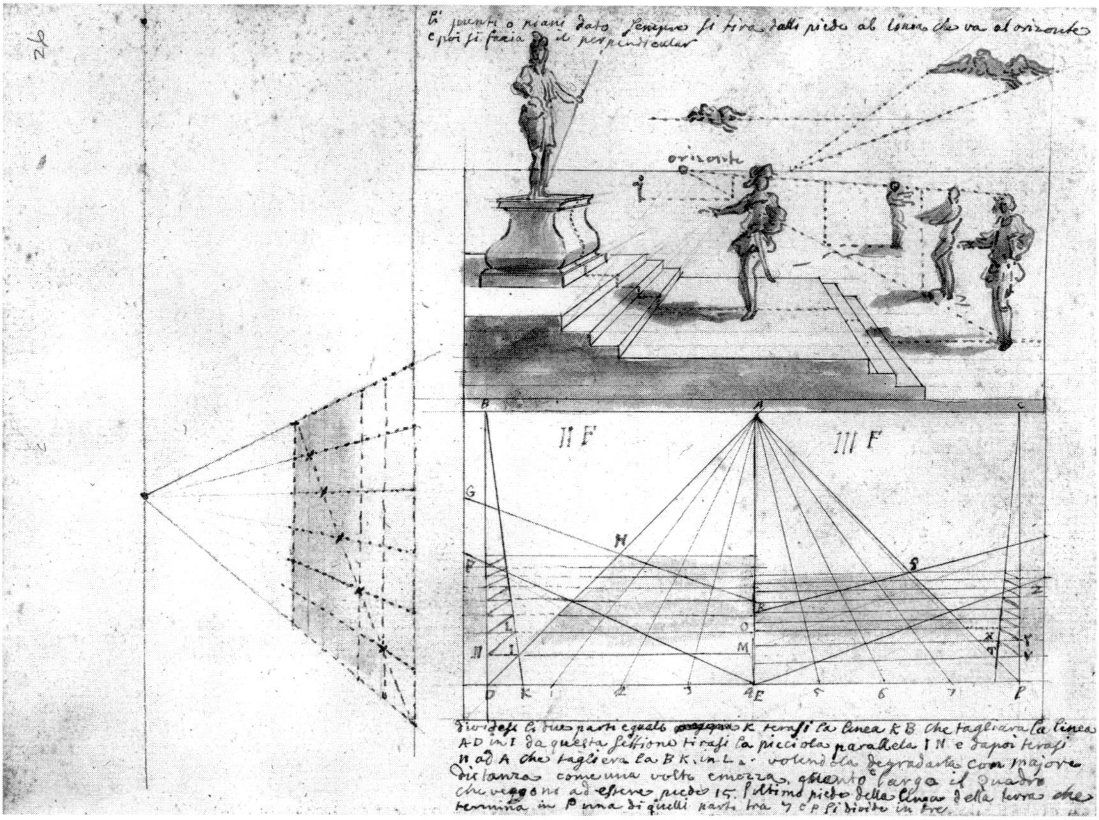

William Kent, Italian Diary, 1714–1715, fol. 26r. Courtesy of the Bodleian Library, Oxford.

Hunt argues that Kent's garden designs were equally influenced by two painting traditions that he appreciated in Italy. Raphael, the acknowledged master of history painting, exemplified one attitude, while Titian represented the other, which placed greater emphasis on formal play.[70] Elisabetta Cereghini notes another debt, to the *quadratura* painters who developed 'geometric devices and perspectives to represent the spatial effects of architecture on a flat surface'.[71] Kent met the noted *quadratura* painter, Giovanni Paolo Panini, while working in the studio of Benedetto Luti, who, like Chiari, was taught by Maratti.[72] In Renaissance art, ruins were familiarly depicted in the background but Panini placed them in the foreground, making ruins the subject of his paintings more than any other painter before him. Panini was a pupil of the architect and theatre designer Ferdinando Galli Bibiena, who described the technique of multiple perspectives in *L'Architettura Civile*, 1711.[73] Cereghini concludes that Kent applied his knowledge of the *quadraturisti* to garden drawings and garden designs:

multiple perspective.

70 Hunt, *William Kent*, p. 35.

71 *Quadratura* means 'squaring' in English. Cereghini, p. 320.

72 Panini is sometimes referred to as Pannini.

73 Rykwert, *The First Moderns*, p. 110.

> *Instead of devising a space based on a single perspective line, along which the eye of the spectator travelled from a fixed viewpoint in a formally organized sequence (as in the Baroque garden), Kent adopted a technique based on the use of oblique perspectives comprised of two or more axial lines converging from points outside the 'scene', which no longer corresponded with the line of vision of the spectator. This prompted the spectator to seek out viewpoints independently rather than be confined to any single perspective prescribed by the architect.*[74]

74 Cereghini, p. 320.

Kent's earliest surviving design for a garden building appears in a 1715 letter to Massingberd. Remarking that his design should be 'agreeable to our climate',[75] Kent was already considering how he could translate to a different culture and climate what he had experienced In Italy. Kent left Italy in 1719 and in January 1720, barely a month after returning to England, he complained that his 'Italian constitution' could not endure the winter weather of 'this Gothick country'.[76] Given Kent's extensive use of 'Gothick' designs, his remark was at least partly in jest. But his affection for Italy was deep and sincere. Recognising the value of his Italian experience to his English reputation, Kent scattered Italian phrases and terms throughout his letters and was happily known as 'Signor', 'Giuglielmo', 'Kentino'.

75 Kent, letter to Massingberd, 12 October 1715, quoted in Hunt, *William Kent*, p. 140.

76 Kent, letter, 30 January 1720, quoted in Hunt, *William Kent*, p. 51.

The Villas of the Ancients

Eulogising ancient and Renaissance Rome, an 'Italian constitution' was common among Kent's contemporaries. Renaissance allusions to classical antiquity relied on garden descriptions rather than the gardens themselves, of which there was little evidence. Mentioning frescoes, fountains, fruit trees, terraces and rural views, Pliny the Younger's first century AD description of his Tuscan villa in the Apennines and Laurentian villa on the coast near Rome was particularly influential. The term 'villa' derives from the Latin for farm but Pliny's account was an urbanite's impression of the countryside, like many others after him. Evoking a relaxed and abundant rural life Pliny notes the interdependence of house, gardens and fields, which English travellers on the Grand Tour later recognised in the luxuriant Italian countryside. As early as 1610 a visitor described the journey from Sienna to Pisa as 'a most pleasant and delightful garden',[77] preceding Addison by a hundred years and Walpole's praise for Kent by fifty further years.[78] But Addison and Walpole meant something more because, following Shaftesbury, they associated nature with moral virtue.

In the third volume of *Vitruvius Britannicus* Campbell describes Burlington as 'not only a great Patron of all Arts, but the first Architect', an opinion confirmed by

77 Quoted in Hunt, *Garden and Grove*, p. 37.

78 Addison, 'From *The Spectator* (21, 23 and 25 June 1712)', p. 238; Walpole, *The History of the Modern Taste in Gardening*, p. 43.

the subject of Campbell's sycophancy, who signed himself 'Burlington architectus'.[79] Burlington's influence and patronage included funding the publication of *The Villas of the Ancients Illustrated*, 1728, in which Robert Castell provided an English translation alongside Pliny's original Latin account of his two villas. Castell's engraved plan of the Apennine garden gave greater emphasis to 'wild' nature than was familiar in the Renaissance, when, for all the manipulation of views, levels and wooded walks, a geometrical organisation closer to the house was the principal

79 Campbell, vol. 3, p. 1.

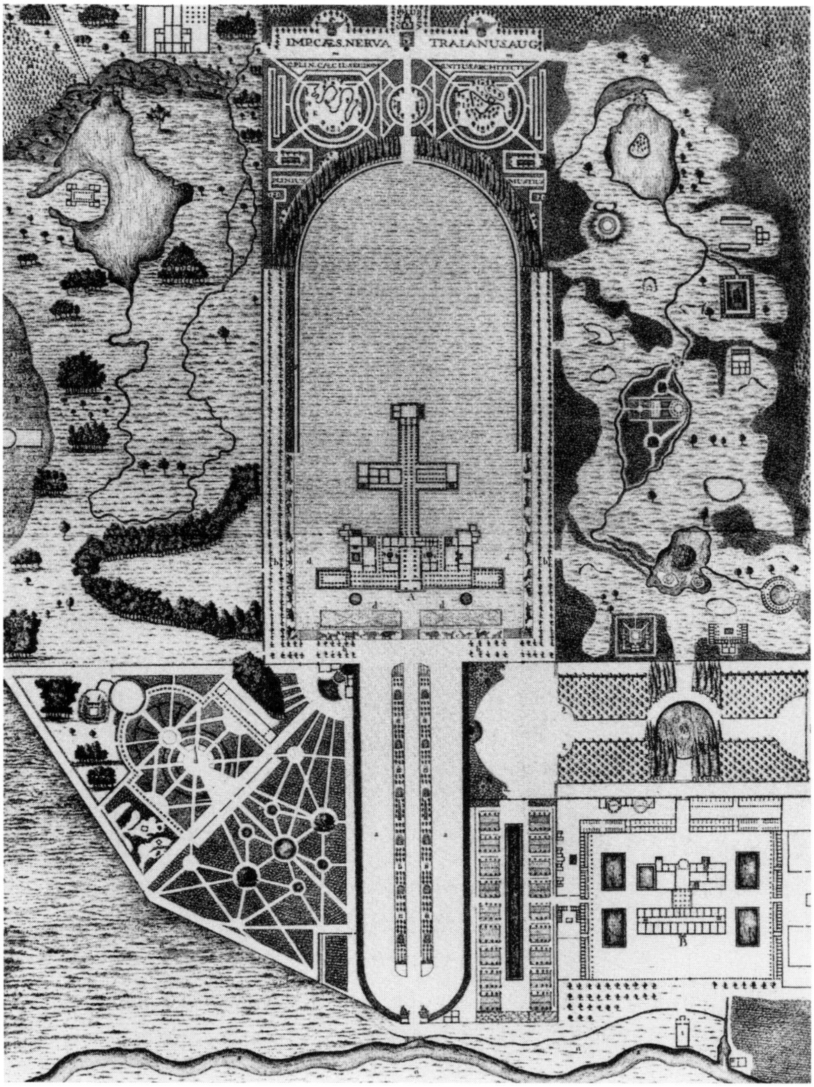

Robert Castell, *The Villas of the Ancients Illustrated*, 1728. Reconstructed plan of the gardens and buildings at Pliny the Younger's Tuscan villa. Courtesy of the British Library.

focus.[80] It is likely that Burlington did not welcome Castell's conclusions, expecting ancient Roman gardens to be as rigid as the one that Kent and he created in the 1720s and 1730s at Chiswick House, which includes meandering paths but emphasises linearity.[81] But for his subscribers, and also for Kent, Castell offered a valuable historical precedent for early eighteenth-century taste for the picturesque. His commentary identifies a formal garden, a natural garden, and one that combines the two, particularly in evidence at Pliny's Tuscan villa:

80 Castell, pp. 126–127.

81 Mowl, *William Kent*, p. 144.

> *By the accounts we have . . . it seems as if from the two former Manners a third had been formed, whose Beauty consisted in a close Imitation of Nature; where, tho' the parts are disposed with the greatest Art, the Irregularity is still preserved; so that their Manner may not improperly be said to be an artful Confusion, where there is no Appearance of that Skill which is made use of, their* Rocks, Cascades, *and* Trees, *bearing their natural Forms.*[82]

82 Castell, pp. 116–117.

An English Palladio

Kent has often been cited as a principal exponent of Palladian architecture in England. Early eighteenth-century reverence for Palladio followed a previous revival by Inigo Jones, who was celebrated among Burlington's circle, included in the Temple of British Worthies, and published in William Kent's *The Designs of Inigo Jones, Consisting of Plans and Elevations for Publick and Private Buildings*, 1727.[83] Palladio's extensive influence on English architecture was principally due to *I Quattro Libri dell' Archittetura* (The Four Books on Architecture), 1570. Renaissance architects published treatises to affirm their status as exponents of intellectual and artistic labour, establishing a practice that became essential to the development and dissemination of architectural ideas. Copies of *I Quattro Libri dell' Archittetura* were soon available in England and Jones owned one. The first complete English edition did not appear until 1721 when a Venetian architect, Giacomo, or James, Leoni replaced the original woodcut illustrations with his own versions engraved in copper. Dismissive of Leoni's publication, Burlington commissioned his own translation by Isaac Ware, which was published in 1738 with more precise copper engravings of the original woodcuts.

83 *Some Designs of Mr. Inigo Jones and Mr. William Kent* appeared in 1744.

The buildings illustrated in *The Four Books on Architecture* are not the ones actually built. As Vincent Scully notes: 'the contrast between the built building and the published drawing is a perfect one in terms of the Renaissance aesthetic, since it is between the Real and the Ideal, the realities of material practice and the immaterial perfection of the Neoplatonic world view'.[84] Rather than just a distinction between the drawing and the building, the discourse of the Ideal and the Real is apparent in the villas themselves. Their inexact proportions refer to the immaterial and its uncertain presence in the built world. The Villa Rotonda is seemingly symmetrical across its axes. But a different garden design is seen from each of its four elevations and, often unnoticed, one axis is slightly wider than the other. James S. Ackerman acknowledges that 'Palladio thought of strict uniformity as literally unnatural; this his neo-Classical admirers never understood.'[85] The villas also engage and celebrate everyday life. They are mostly working farms in the tradition of the modest classical villa and country estate, evoking the pleasures of rural life and the harmony of humanity and nature. The Villa Emo, Fanzolo di Vedelago, 1565, consists of a central pedimented block flanked on each side by an arcaded farm building terminated by a dovecote. The central ramped staircase provides entry to the principal rooms and a surface for threshing grain.

84 Scully, p. 317.

85 Ackerman, p. 164. Refer to Holberton, pp. 156–163.

Andrea Palladio, Villa Emo, Fanzolo di Vedelago, 1565. Photograph, Jonathan Hill.

Palladio also conceived a villa as an aid to health. Born in the fifth century BC, Hippocrates assumed that illnesses were seasonal and varied according to the astronomical calendar and the physical environment. The Hippocratic tradition was acknowledged by Vitruvius in the first century BC and widely disseminated in the Renaissance, notably by Leon Battista Alberti.[86] The influence of climate on health, and the assumption that a good body and a good building share good proportions, was essential to the Hippocratic tradition, which particularly emphasised the benefits of air movement. The Villa Rotonda is unusual in that it is not attached to a farm. Placed on a hill, cool air circulates horizontally between the four axially located entrances and vertically between the underground chamber and a floor grating in the central hall. As the dome's oculus was originally open to the sky, vertical and horizontal ventilation extended throughout the villa.[87]

86 *Airs, Waters, Places* and *Breaths* were highly influential texts but it is uncertain whether the treatises attributed to Hippocrates were actually written by him. Refer to Alberti, pp. 9–11; Vitruvius, pp. 170–171.

87 Kenda, pp. 11–13.

As few English patrons and architects visited the villas, these subtle distinctions were mostly ignored. Palladio's most significant churches were frequently studied because they were in Venice. Scattered across the countryside, his villas were less accessible and their elegant but rustic charms were largely unappreciated. Kent spent years in Rome and weeks in Venice but only days in and around the Veneto, including just one in Vicenza. Contradicting Kent's frequently cited association with Palladio and noting his lengthy stay in Rome, Cinzia Maria Sicca argues that his principal influences were not Venetian:

> *Kent's conception of the wall as a three-dimensional and sculptural element was not a Venetian feature, indeed it had been the core of the architectural debate developing in Rome in the course of the sixteenth century from Bramante to Raphael and his pupils.*[88]

88 Sicca, p. 134.

> *The sharply chiselled* bozze *of Kent's London works and more refined country houses give way to rough, unhewn blocks in his 'natural' garden buildings and cascades. In the latter, as in the cascade of the Villa Madama, the stone blocks look as if they had been thrown together by Nature itself. Kent's architecture, unlike Burlington's, is constantly pervaded by the theme of the tension between art and nature, a theme . . . central to the post-Raphaelesque architectural and figurative culture diffused by Giulio and theorized by Serlio in the 1550s.*[89]

89 The Villa Madama, Rome, was begun in *c.*1516 by Raphael and others. Giulio is Giulio Romano, Serlio is Sebastiano Serlio. Sicca, p. 146.

Timothy Mowl argues that Burlington's visit to the Veneto was equally cursory because Palladio was a means to an end not the focus of his interest:

> *Lord Burlington was not aiming so much at the revival of Palladio's domestic architecture of the sixteenth century as at the supposed architecture of senatorial*

> *Rome, sixteen hundred years earlier. He assumed, in his ignorance, that Palladio's Orders in his* First Book, *together with his semi-scholarly reconstructions of Roman public bath houses, would provide an easy route to an authentic neo-classical revival.*[90]

90 Mowl, *William Kent*, pp. 76–77.

The designs copied by architects and patrons were the ones illustrated in *The Four Books on Architecture* not the buildings themselves. Colen Campbell lavishly praises Palladio in his influential three-volume *Vitruvius Britannicus*, which was completed in 1725, the year that he created Mereworth Castle in Kent, a copy of the Villa Rotonda. But he never visited Italy. For all the era's empiricism, the architect's traditional concern for the idea expressed in a drawing was favoured over actual experience.

The Italian House and the English Garden

Raphael, *Madonna dell'Impannata*, 1514. Courtesy of the Palazzo Pitti/Foto Scala, Florence.

Campbell's first-hand knowledge of Italy was non-existent but Kent's was extensive. Although Kent gave Palladio little attention, Italian Renaissance gardens and the *quadraturisti* were more certain influences. As a painter and an architect, Raphael's influence on Kent has also been noted. Discussing the figures in Raphael's *Madonna dell'Impannata*, 1514, Robin Evans writes: 'They look closely on one another, stare myopically into eyes and at flesh, grasp, embrace, hold and finger each other's bodies as if their recognition rested more firmly on touch than on sight.'[91] Evans then considers Raphael's villa on the slopes of the Monte Mario on the outskirts of Rome, which was begun around 1516. Only a part of the extensive design, later to be called the Villa Madama, was completed after Raphael's death with the assistance of Antonio da Sangallo the Younger, Giulio Romano and Giovanni da Udine.[92] Kent studied the Villa Madama under Chiari's direction and came to revere the building,[93] which Evans describes:

91 Evans, 'Figures, Doors and Passages', p. 59.

92 A letter from Raphael confirms his authorship. Refer to Jones and Penny, p. 247.

93 Sicca, pp. 136, 139.

> *Although most spaces within the villa were symmetrically composed, there were no duplications; every room was different. Uniformity was restricted to the parts where it could be immediately apprehended; the building as a whole was diverse. Yet, despite this striving to create a singularity of place, it is very difficult to tell from the plan which parts are enclosed, and which are open, as the relationship between all the spaces is much the same throughout. The chambers, loggias, courts and gardens all register as walled shapes – like large rooms – which add up to fill the site. The building seems to have been conceived as an accumulation of these enclosures, with the component spaces being more regular than the overall pattern.*[94]

94 Evans, 'Figures, Doors and Passages', p. 60.

Colin Rowe and Leon Satkowski associate Raphael's initial design with the *casale*, a contemporary building type in which a house and farm are grouped around an open court. Identifying an earlier model, they conclude that the Villa Madama was intended to provide a setting comparable to Pliny's villas, in which 'the pursuit of activities free of urban distractions, could be re-created through study, bathing, theatrical and musical performance, and even gastronomy'.[95] Evans, however, identifies a more widespread condition that recalls the close proximity of figures in Raphael's *Madonna dell'Impannata*:

95 Rowe and Satkowski, p. 72.

> *In the Villa Madama, as in virtually all domestic architecture prior to 1650, there is no qualitative distinction between the way through the house and the inhabited spaces within it . . . The matrix of connected rooms is appropriate to a type of society which feeds on carnality, which recognizes the body as the person, and in*

which gregariousness is habitual. The features of this kind of life can be discerned in Raphael's architecture and painting. Such was the typical arrangement of household space in Europe until challenged in the seventeenth century, and finally displaced in the nineteenth by the corridor plan, which is appropriate to a society that finds carnality distasteful, which sees the body as a vessel of mind and spirit, and in which privacy is habitual.[96]

A matrix is usually assumed to be regular, but rather than a geometric pattern, Evans's reference to the Villa Madama emphasises the degree of interconnection within an accumulation of differing rooms, some internal, others external. Kent had repeated experience of the matrix of interconnected rooms because it was prevalent in domestic architecture in the Italian Renaissance.[97] As Palladio also followed this arrangement and recalled the relaxed rural life evoked in classical antiquity, Kent's ignorance of his villas was partly addressed elsewhere.[98] In the Italian Renaissance villa, rooms are often defined not by function but by position, orientation, and the mythological and historical figures depicted on walls and ceilings. Views within a villa, and to the gardens beyond, suggest multiple trajectories and journeys. As the matrix of interconnected rooms offers alternative, and potentially private, routes

96 Evans, 'Figures, Doors and Passages', pp. 64–88.

97 I prefer the phrase 'matrix of interconnected rooms' to Evans's 'set' or 'matrix of connected rooms'.

98 Evans, 'Figures, Doors and Passages', pp. 62–63.

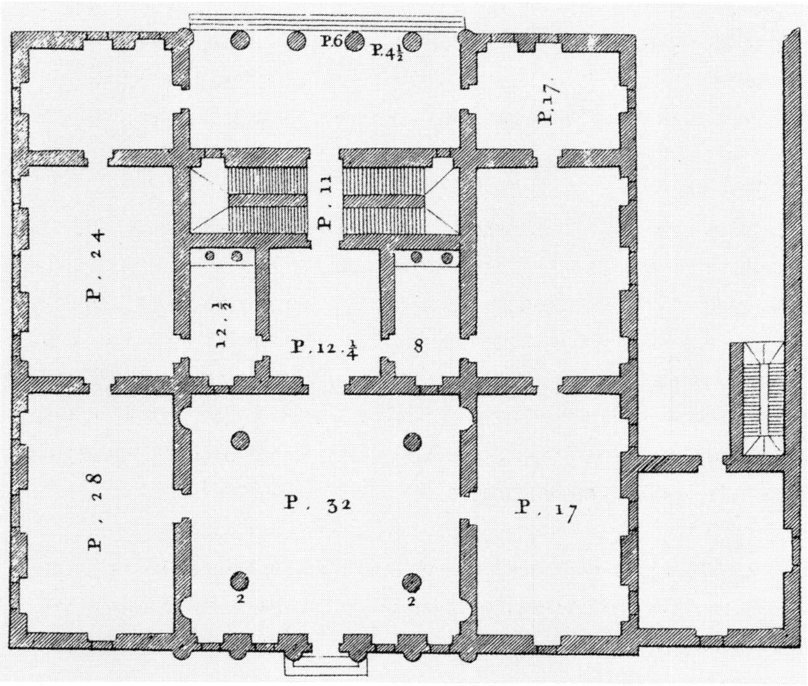

Andrea Palladio, Palazzo Antonini, Udine, 1556. Plan, from Robin Evans, *Translations from Drawing to Building and Other Essays*, 1997. Courtesy of the Architectural Association, London.

within a house, Evans may overemphasise the carnality of Renaissance society; but the potential it offers for public and private routes indicates the subtlety of its organisation.

Increasingly, the interconnected rooms common in 'hovel and mansion' were believed to have two features that 'rendered them unfit as moral dwellings', writes Evans.[99] First, they allowed people to roam from one space to another unmonitored. Second, they encouraged overcrowding and close contact between occupants. By the middle of the seventeenth century 'the subdivision of the house into day and night uses, and into formal and informal areas, had begun', states Witold Rybczynski.[100] Raffaella Sarti notes that the Netherlands 'developed architectural elements similar to "modern" corridors very early', as was the case in England where they were introduced in the seventeenth century.[101] The corridor enables a room to have a single use and a single entrance, protecting privacy and discouraging entry to anyone without a specific purpose.

99 Evans, 'Rookeries and Model Dwellings', pp. 101, 102, 104

100 Rybczynski, p. 56.

101 Evans, 'Figures, Doors and Passages', pp. 70–73; Sarti, p. 269.

The corridor plan was evident in eighteenth-century English architecture but Kent's house designs continued to favour the arrangement he had observed in Italy, which very likely influenced his garden designs as well. Defined not by function but by position, orientation and the mythological and historical figures they contain, each 'room' in a Kentian garden is particular and permeable. Hedonistic and irreverent, Kent brought to the English garden the organisation and life of the Italian Renaissance house and garden as well as the philosophies of eighteenth-century empiricism.

MORE THAN PICTURESQUE

The Pictorial and the Picturesque

Locke, Shaftesbury, Addison, Pope and Castell influenced the development of the picturesque although it was not a familiar feature of their vocabulary. In *The Picturesque: Studies on a Point of View*, 1927, Hussey recognises a changing attitude to landscape and the role of specific paintings in this transformation:

> *In the accounts of grand tours made between 1640 and 1730 a pictorial view of landscape is exceptional. In each case it can be traced fairly exactly to the actual sojourn in Rome, where the works of Claude and Salvator were to be seen. The notes upon scenery thence onward tend to become more frequent and more picturesque.*[102]

102 Hussey, *The Picturesque*, p. 84.

103 Only since the mid-nineteenth century has the term 'landscape architecture' referred to the design of landscapes rather than the depiction of buildings and landscapes in paintings. The term 'landscape architect' derives from the same period.

Claude Lorrain, *Landscape with Apollo, the Muses and a River God*, 1652. Courtesy of the National Gallery of Scotland.

Meaning 'in the manner of painters', *pittoresco* in Italian, or *pittoresque* in French, suggests a method of laying on paint in broad, bold and irregular strokes to depict not simply a detailed copy of nature but something closer to the experience of nature, including its weather. The term picturesque was applied first to paintings and only later to gardens.[103] Mid-eighteenth-century writers recognised the picturesque composition of Kent's gardens. William Shenstone mentions Kent's 'picturesque gardening' in 'Unconnected Thoughts on Gardening', 1764, while Kames, in *Elements of Criticism*, and Walpole, in *The History of the Modern Taste in Gardening*, remark that Kent's gardens are composed like paintings.[104] Kent admired the seventeenth-century painters Nicolas Poussin, Salvator Rosa and Claude Lorrain, who he imitated. Composed into fore-, middle- and background, Claude's paintings depict a pastoral Arcadia of classical temples, undulating landscapes and relaxed inhabitation, which evoke the simple, rural life praised by Virgil and Horace in classical antiquity. Rosa depicted a wilder, more dramatic landscape that fuelled the growing concern for the natural sublime.

In *The Discovery of Pictorial Composition*, 2000, Thomas Puttfarken describes Poussin's formative role in the shift from the centralised perspective of the

104 Shenstone, quoted in Hunt, *The Picturesque Garden in Europe*, p. 26; Kames, vol. 2, p. 327; Walpole, *The History of the Modern Taste in Gardening*, pp.43–44.

Salvator Rosa, *Landscape with Travellers asking the Way*, c.1641. Courtesy of the National Gallery, London.

Renaissance to the later pictorial order, which gave new emphasis to visual composition and informed the development of the picturesque.[105] Although Renaissance artists in Italy had successfully argued that the three visual arts – painting, sculpture and architecture – were liberal arts associated with intellectual labour and individual authorship rather than crafts associated with manual labour and dispersed authorship, this appreciation did not immediately extend to other countries. Painting's status in early seventeenth-century France was equivalent to that of 'the third of the five categories of the city's *arts et metiers*, along with pork butchers, millers, and clockmakers, beneath barbers, hatmakers, and dyers, and just above brewers, herring vendors, soap makers and engravers of iron and copper'.[106] Founded in 1648 to raise the status of the arts, the Académie Royale de Peinture et de la Sculpture identified Poussin as the personification of the *peintre philosophe* who created a thematic *tableau*, which Shaftesbury praised in 1713.[107]

105 Puttfarken, pp. 201–227; Macarthur, pp. 19–26.

106 Posner, p. 585.

107 Shaftesbury, *Second Characters*, pp. 30–33, referred to in Puttfarken, p. 280.

The first French reference to the picturesque appears in Roger de Piles's codification of pictorial order, *Cours de peinture par principes*, 1708, which was translated into English as *The Principles of Painting*, 1743. Depicting rugged rocks, broken branches and shaggy foliage, seventeenth-century Dutch landscape painters such as Jacob van Ruisdael were a further influence on the picturesque, especially after William of Orange's intervention in 1688 led to increased cultural trade between England and the Netherlands.

For eighteenth-century advocates of the picturesque, garden design's status as an art depended on its relations with landscape painting. But the relevance of the painting to the garden was much discussed and conclusions were inconsistent. In the opening line of *Observations on Modern Gardening, Illustrated by Descriptions*, 1770, Thomas Whately writes that 'GARDENING, in the perfection to which it has been lately brought in England, is entitled to a place of considerable rank among the liberal arts. It is as superior to landskip painting, as a reality to a representation'.[108] Later he adds that paintings 'must be only used as studies, not as models' for gardens.[109] *Observations on Modern Gardening* was an instant success.[110] In 1786 Thomas Jefferson used it as a guidebook when he visited English gardens in the company of another future American President, John Adams.[111]

108 The term landskip refers to a picture of the land not the land itself. Whately, p. 1.

109 Whately, p. 147.

110 According to de Bolla, Whately's concern for composition places him in an 'elitist cultural tradition' alongside Horace Walpole. De Bolla, pp. 110, 128.

111 Charles Miller, pp. 16, 116.

Nicolas Poussin, *Landscape with a Man Killed by a Snake*, 1648. Courtesy of the National Gallery, London.

The Painting and the Garden

In *Theory of the Avant-Garde*, 1985, Peter Bürger describes the transformation of art – painting and sculpture – from sacral, to courtly, to bourgeois. In sacral art, for example in the high Middle Ages, production was a collective craft, reception was collective and sacral, and the artwork was a religious cult object. In courtly art, for example in the reign of Louis XIV, production was individual, reception was collective and social, and the artwork was a representational object. In bourgeois art, the artwork is produced by one individual and contemplated by another because its purpose is the 'portrayal of bourgeois self-understanding'.[112] Bourgeois art was formed in the eighteenth century, fully established by the end of the century, and continues today. The transfer from one art period to another was neither smooth nor sudden, however. For example, sacral and courtly art overlapped in fifteenth-century Italy in that production was individual and reception collective, but the artwork was either a religious cult object or a representational object. The Italian Renaissance was the first stage in the development of the (relative) autonomy of art, which reached fruition in bourgeois art. The Abbé Batteux provided the first detailed categorisation of the fine arts – notably poetry, music, painting, sculpture and architecture – in *Les beaux arts reduits à un même principe*, 1746. In the eighteenth century, alongside science and morality/ethics, art emerged as one of three independent value systems within European society, each with its own specific concerns so that one did not interfere with the other. Kant provided the first detailed codification of the three systems in *Critique of Pure Reason*, *Critique of Practical Reason* and *Critique of Judgement*, published respectively in 1781, 1788 and 1790.

112 Bürger, pp. 48, 49.

In bourgeois society, the individual is usually denied in production but is necessary as a consumer. Bourgeois society cultivates the paradoxical principle that individuality is best expressed through the consumption of mass-produced goods. A self-absorbed and uncertain subject suits a mercantile economy, which creates a cycle of production and consumption that generates needs that can never be fully satisfied, ensuring that the cycle continues unbroken and ever-expanding. Art in bourgeois society may be understood as just another form of commodity production but its purpose is potentially deeper. Bürger writes: 'The citizen who, in everyday life has been reduced to a partial function (means-ends activity) can be discovered in art . . . Here one can unfold the abundance of one's talents, though with the proviso that this sphere remain strictly separate from the praxis of life.'[113] Galleries and museums were established to ensure appropriate conditions for the appreciation of art, which was isolated in its own reverential domain. Requiring

113 Bürger, pp. 48–49.

absorbed visual concentration and devaluing the other senses, contemplation established an empathetic relationship between the viewer and the viewed while the distance between them affirmed art's aura.

Art and nature were increasingly revered in the eighteenth century. Appreciating a painting was one means to explore subjectivity. Wandering in a garden was another. The picturesque developed while the codes of bourgeois art were being formulated but the garden's status was never so certain as that of a painting or sculpture. Isolating art from utility, Kant concluded that architecture's aesthetic potential was even less than that of a garden.[114]

114 Kant, *Kant's Critique of Judgement*, p. 210.

The gallery visitor moved from picture to picture and the garden visitor moved from scene to scene. But a garden scene was rarely the focus of concentrated attention and never experienced in hermetic conditions. Rather than just contemplative, garden visitors were also engaged, social and active. In the notes to his translations of Homer's *Iliad*, *c.*800 BC, Pope ascribes the picturesque to both landscape and behaviour, mirroring Addison's remarks on the natural garden and natural behaviour.[115]

115 Hunt, *The Picturesque Garden in Europe*, p. 16.

The picturesque draws attention to the pleasures and problems of seeing. It emphasises that vision is learnt, both because the eye receives inexact information and because what and how we see is cultural and historical, differing according to era and locality. Richard Gregory writes that 'visual and other perception is intelligent decision-taking from limited sensory evidence. The essential point is that sensory signals are not adequate for direct or certain perceptions, so intelligent guesswork is needed for seeing objects.'[116] Consequently, permeated by memory, 'perceptions are hypotheses . . . retinal images are open to an infinity of interpretations'.[117] With regard to the picturesque, Peter de Bolla writes: 'The point here is that "landscape" only looks the way it does on account of an interactive relation between viewer, physical land, and a cultural imaginary: we only see what we have learned to see.'[118]

116 Gregory, p. 5.

117 Gregory, p. 10.

118 De Bolla, p. 106.

The picturesque garden is experienced not in a concentrated visual moment but in motion, over time and with all the senses. What we see is affected by what we touch, feel, taste, smell and hear. In the classical tradition, the eye and the body follow the same path. But in the picturesque, the eye and the body diverge. The eye is drawn to a distant object but the path is not direct or singular. Even when the garden visitor is static, movement is implicit because any single view is understood in relation to other potential views and is but one part of a complex and changeable whole. Whether subtle or sudden, shifts in the seasons further enliven habitual experience so that the visitor is self-aware and questioning.

In a significant innovation, the picturesque gave greater emphasis to environmental concerns, thereby drawing attention to time, mood and husbandry. Rather than an independent, complete and timeless object, a garden building was understood as an incident in an environment. Consequently, the picturesque is a deceptive term because it does not readily acknowledge the importance of the senses and the seasons to perception, understanding and the imagination in the eighteenth-century garden. The association of the picturesque with painting is easily exaggerated. References to theatres and other settings for human discourse and action are as relevant.

Setting the Stage

The theatrical potential of gardens and celebrations was a theme of Kent's career. He understood the close association of gardens and theatres in Renaissance Italy, in which pastoral and mythological themes were common, and admired Jones's theatre and masque designs. Kent continued both traditions, which shared a concern for settings for human action that was also seen in contemporary history and landscape paintings.[119] The two traditions were one in that Italian Renaissance gardens informed Jones's masques.[120] They differed in that the visitors' movements were literal in the garden, while the moving scenery in Jones's masques 'allowed stationary spectators the illusion that *they* were exploring the spaces unfolded onstage'.[121] Gardens and masques also encouraged the metaphorical movement of the imagination from idea to idea and from place to place.

119 Hunt, *William Kent*, p. 32.

120 Jones visited Italy in 1600 and 1604.

121 Hunt, *William Kent*, p. 45.

Kent's concern for theatricality was widely applied. For example, he designed the set and costumes for a production at the Theatre Royal, Drury Lane, in 1724, a triumphal arch for the coronation of George II in 1727 and decorations for Princess Anne's wedding in 1734. Long and sleek, the 1732 royal barge for Prince Frederick, Prince of Wales, is his most exuberantly theatrical creation, with carved Baroque decorations throughout. Sea-lions line the prow. The royal party's cabin is at the centre. Set within a scallop shell and supported on dolphins and mermaids, the royal crest completes the stern. A barge-master directed the twenty-one oarsmen who were dressed in blue uniforms, black velvet caps and silver-gilt badges to Kent's overall design.[122]

Also shells.

122 The silversmith Paul de Lamerie created the badges. Wilson, *William Kent*, p. 132.

Whether a woodland glade or a curving hillside, many of Kent's garden drawings show nature in the form of a theatre, recalling the open-air auditorium of classical antiquity, and stimulating 'various kinds of play: social play, the play of fantasy, the play even of historical imagination'.[123] Originally painted the colour of flesh, the statues that people his gardens were not empty lead vessels but animate expressions of values and ideas, catalysts for conversation and observation.

123 Hunt, *William Kent*, p. 32.

Yes but where does this sit within conceptions of the mind. Shaftsbury / Burlington.

William Kent, *Arcadian Hermitage with Satyr and Shepherdess*, *c.* 1730. Courtesy of the Trustees of Sir John Soane's Museum, London.

Consequently, for a person or a statue, the roles of actor and spectator were interchangeable, as they were at the end of a Jones masque, when actors and spectators danced together. The early picturesque garden continued an earlier theatrical tradition that was distinct from eighteenth-century theatre, and bourgeois art in general, when the separation of actors and audiences, artworks and viewers, became increasingly common.

Concern for a primitive life in nature generated a fashion for the hermit and the hermitage, a place of play and display as much as use. In Kent's design for an Arcadian Hermitage, *c.* 1730, a grove of trees frames a rustic building, which has the inscription 'Arcadia' carved above the keystone. In the foreground, a satyr kneels before a shepherdess who may be Queen Caroline, wife of George II, who commissioned the Richmond Hermitage for which this was probably a design.[124] Completed in 1731, the rustic but classical exterior of the Richmond Hermitage contrasted with the elegance of its octagonal interior – a Greek cross in plan – which included a tented entrance, central dome and oculus, couches, bookcase and arched niches. The Richmond Hermitage received criticism, primarily because of the inappropriate busts inserted at the Queen's request.[125] In a letter to Burlington, dated 6 November 1732, Pope mentions his support for Kent:

124 Harris, *William Kent*, pp. 29–30.

125 Gordon, pp. 35–36; Mowl, *William Kent*, pp. 172–175.

> *Pray lay your Commands upon Kent, to send you the Short Dialogue I writ in his behalf between the General & myself, shewing the Cause why nobody takes notice of him when they speak of the Hermitage. He is modest, & afraid to give offence, so has kept it in his pocket, nor ever dared show it to the General, by which means my Wit is lost in obscurity.*[126]

126 Pope, vol. 3, p. 329.

As Kent refused to show Pope's helpful but teasing dialogue to General James Dormer even though they all were friends, the poet's portrayal of Kent's timidity was probably accurate and not a further tease. Given his irreverent humour, Kent's reaction may seem surprising. But irreverence and a thin skin can go together. Conscious of his image, Kent changed his surname from Cant early in his life. He may have also been concerned that poor publicity would deter further commissions. Fortunately it did not and neither did the criticism alter his designs. In 1735, again at the request of Queen Caroline, he created Merlin's Cave at Richmond. Rustic and gothic inside and out, rough columns reminiscent of tree-trunks supported a vaulted ceiling and three steeply-thatched roofs. Hunt remarks:

> *Both the materials of the Cave and the sinking of the Hermitage into the ground clearly identify the British gothick with nature rather than with art, which was classical. Contemporaries saw the Hermitage as a 'cave by nature made'. Its ruined turret announced, as do all ruins, the determining effects and contributions of nature and chance rather than art.*[127]

127 Hunt, *William Kent*, pp. 64–65.

Kent's development as a garden designer was gradual and occurred alongside his career as an architect. The intermingling of garden and building, which is evident in the Richmond Hermitage, also occurred in a much grander but equally theatrical location. In 1725 Kent was commissioned to design the principal rooms of Houghton Hall, Sir Robert Walpole's new house on his ancestral estate in Norfolk.[128] Houghton featured paintings by Chiari and Maratti, to whom a whole room, the Drawing Room, was dedicated. Walpole conceived Houghton as a fitting setting for the Prime Minister to host visiting dignitaries. Rising the full height of the house, the Great Staircase suggests the open-air courtyard of a Renaissance palazzo. Internal windows line its walls, which are decorated with mythological hunting scenes. Creating a further ambiguity between interior and exterior, the Doric temple that fills the 'courtyard' is provocatively large for the space, suggesting that it should really be in the garden to which it refers. Surmounting the temple, Hubert Le Sueur's *Gladiator* – a seventeenth-century copy of a classical original – aggressively mediates between the *trompe l'oeil* hunting scenes of the Great Staircase

128 Colen Campbell, James Gibbs, Thomas Ripley and James Ware contributed to other aspects of Houghton's design. Harris, 'The Architecture of the House', pp. 20–28.

and the muscular carving of the Stone Hall. The focus of the Stone Hall – John Michael Rysbrack's bust of Sir Robert in Roman dress – stands before a relief of *The Sacrifice of Diana*, goddess of hunting.[129] Together, the Great Staircase and Stone Hall offer a vibrant dialogue on representation and reality, the garden, the hunt and the house.

129 Cornforth, p. 32; Edwards, Moore and Archer, pp. 110–111.

A Fox and Four Chickens

A setting for discourse, celebration and adventure, the picturesque garden matched Kent's character. Recounting his love of life's varied pleasures, Kent's friends remarked on his humour, hedonism and greed. Burlington characterised him as 'the little rogue'.[130] Pope teasingly encouraged Burlington to 'eat a Mutton Stake in ye manner of that great Master Signor Kent'.[131] Elsewhere, Pope simply described his friend as 'very hot and very fat', concluding that 'he must expect not to imitate Raphael in anything but his untimely end'.[132] Indications of Kent's joyful and irreverent character appear in his garden monuments, which regularly feature satire and humour. In 1736 he designed a pyramidal monument at Stowe to celebrate a regular visitor, the dramatist William Congreve, who was known for his accounts of human folly. On an island in the lake, a monkey looks into a mirror, culminating the monument. The carved inscription attests that 'Comedy is the imitation of life

130 Burlington, quoted in Harris, *William Kent*, p. 2.

131 Pope, quoted in Harris, *William Kent*, p. 2.

132 Pope, quoted in Harris, *William Kent*, p. 2.

William Kent, *Chiswick House and Lord Burlington*. Courtesy of the Devonshire Collection, Chatsworth.

William Kent, *Chiswick Obelisk and Arch by Moonlight*. Courtesy of the Devonshire Collection, Chatsworth.

William Kent, *Four Chickens Hang a Fox in Front of the Chiswick Aviary*. Courtesy of the Devonshire Collection, Chatsworth.

William Kent, *Seat on the Mount with Irregular Basin, Holkham*, *c.*1739. Courtesy of Viscount Coke and the Trustees of the Holkham Estate.

and the mirror of society.' On the rear elevation of the Temple of British Worthies, a stone carving extols the exemplary virtues of Signor Fido. Only at the end of the inscription is it apparent that the subject of such praise is a dog.

Kent's garden drawings are equally irreverent. Beside the Chiswick House entrance portico and in front of Rysbrack's statue of Palladio, Kent gesticulates to Burlington while a dog pisses on his patron. In another drawing, the Chiswick Obelisk and western entrance Arch appear in moonlight; a figure lies on the ground and animals scamper around. In the most comical drawing of all, chickens hang a fox in front of the Chiswick Aviary. Two chickens pull on ropes looped over a branch, from which the fox dangles in a noose; two further chickens stand triumphant, one on the branch above the fox, one on the ground below. The watching crowd, including an owl, make no efforts to save the fox, except for a lady, whose pleadings are ignored. In a more genteel scene at Holkham, a gentleman drives a gig around a basin, in which a lady fishes from a rowing boat. Other drawings confirm that Kent conceived his gardens for diverse pleasures: playful abandon as well as erudite discussion.

The figures in Kent's garden drawings are active and engaged. They do not stare transfixed at a picture before them. But, according to their desires, they move from one scene to another, which offer multiple diversions and deviations. Kent's drawings affirm the garden's role in developing the alert and sociable individual. But the varied activities he depicts surpass the reasonable and measured behaviour promoted by Locke. Kent conceived the garden as a means to explore the full gamut of ideas, experiences and emotions.

2

the seasons of a life

INTRODUCTION

A companion to the first chapter, and concluding my investigation of the early picturesque, this chapter provides a detailed study of the garden that Kent designed at Rousham, Oxfordshire, between 1738 and 1741. The chapter is organised into three interconnecting sections, each with a specific theme. The first, 'The Genius of the Place', focuses on the ideas, images and emotions that Rousham evokes. Recognising two distinct attitudes to atmospheric phenomena in classical antiquity – one a theory of meteors, the other a practical guide to the weather – the second section, 'The Weather of the Place', assesses their relevance to the early eighteenth century, when rural England was yet to feel the true impact of science and industrialisation, and analyses the weather's complex contribution to Rousham's *genius loci.* The concluding section, 'Designing while Walking', recognises Rousham as an innovative reassessment of the architect's practice as it was established in the Italian Renaissance.

THE GENIUS OF THE PLACE

A Bend in the Cherwell

Philosophical and literary texts greatly informed the early eighteenth-century picturesque but its most complete works were gardens not books. Substantial garden theories appeared later in the century, including Whately's *Observations on Modern Gardening*, 1770, the first comprehensive account of the landscape garden as an artefact, practice and experience.

A graduate of Merton College, Oxford, and member of Burlington's inner circle, General Dormer served under the Duke of Marlborough, like Cobham. The General was a member of the elite Whig social club, the Kit-Cat, which was named after the mutton pie made by Christopher Cat, or Catling, a Norfolk pastry cook and the proprietor of the *Cat and Fiddle* in Gray's Inn Lane, where the Club first met. Ophelia Field remarks: 'As pies and puddings were considered the best of English cookery, the Club's favourite dish would have signified the founders' self-consciously English, as opposed to French, tastes.'[1] Active from around 1696 until 1720, the Kit-Cat's membership was mostly aristocratic but also included writers, architects and dramatists such as Addison, Steele, Vanbrugh and Congreve. Alongside the pleasures of food, wine and male company, the Kit-Cat's purpose was political influence and

1 Field, p. 35.

cultural patronage.[2] William Kent was not a member, but a number of his clients belonged to the Kit-Cat, including Burlington, Cobham, Dormer and Walpole.[3]

In 1725 General Dormer was the British envoy to the Portuguese court, where he argued with another English resident in Lisbon:

Indeed, Sir, I must own that since you went from hence I have been overrun with the spleen at finding myself so entirely neglected in England that everything made an impression to fret and vex me; so trifling a circumstance as Mr. Burnett's living in a house exactly fronting mine; where I could see what passed, has not a little contributed to exasperate me; on the feasts he has given I have the mortification to see his house all over illuminated, whilst mine has been dark; besides stories he has given out that I was to be recalled in disgrace . . .[4]

Severely agitated at being ignored, General Dormer ordered his servants to attack Burnett, who sent his servants in reply and was injured in the altercation. Having offended the King of Portugal, General Dormer was sent home, the cause of his own disgrace. In 1734 General Dormer visited his brother's estate at Rousham Park, twelve miles north of Oxford, before travelling on to Stowe. An account of the journey indicates that Pope's affectionate teasing of Kent was typical of his other friendships:

We set out yesterday, two coach-fulls of us, from Rousham. Stowe is in great beauty, the master is in excellent spirits, by which the Major General Dormer gets a new tormentor; not that his old one (Pope) was not sufficient, who has really laughed himself fat at poor Jemmy's expense, who in proportion hath fretted himself lean.[5]

In 1737, when he was nearly sixty, General Dormer inherited Rousham on the death of this brother, Colonel Robert Dormer. A garden designed by Charles Bridgeman in the 1720s was already in place, which Kent adapted and expanded. Among Kent's many drawings of different gardens, very few are plans. His drawings for Rousham are all perspectives, which depict the garden as a set of elaborately interrelated scenes. Employing the techniques of the *quadraturisti*, Kent's drawings show not a single linear perspective but multiple, oblique perspectives that suggest varied and alternative routes, as Cereghini concludes:

This spatial device involves the choice of at least three different points of view from which to frame the scene. And it now becomes clear in what way the various

2 Brewer, pp. 40–49.

3 Field, pp. 425–426.

4 General Dormer, letter to Stephen Cottrell, 30 October 1727, quoted in Cottrell Dormer, p. 53.

5 Hon. George Berkeley, letter to Countess of Suffolk, 1734, quoted in Cottrell Dormer, p. 50.

features are interrelated: a scene viewed in a direct line is comprised also of aspects of those scenes placed at the margins of the spectator's vision, in which the architectural focus is set at an oblique angle to the straight perspective. Such an arrangement creates a natural transition from one area of the garden to another, and ensures that the various features are revealed in turn, as they are in nature.[6]

The drawings' implicit recognition of subjective choices mirrored Kent's willingness to compose and adjust his design in response to the conditions found on site and the advice he received. Kent may have considered a plan of his own to be unnecessary because he accepted the general principles of Bridgeman's layout, which he softened and transformed with new avenues, buildings and statues that further exploited the site, a heavily wooded and steeply sloping bend in the River Cherwell. A witness to Colonel Dormer's will and highly trusted by both brothers, the General's steward, William White, drew the 1738 plan of Kent's design. Susan Gordon remarks that 'Other plans were also later drawn up by White and sent to Kent and Dormer. Several of White's letters to Dormer contain sketches for Kent's approval.'[7] None of Kent's garden drawings for Rousham include written instructions to workmen. His only surviving drawing with written instructions is a view from the terrace at Claremont, which he designed for Thomas Pelham, Duke of Newcastle, between 1728 and 1743. As was his usual site practice, Kent only visited Rousham once or twice a year. Sometimes he met his client in London but General Dormer, White and John Clary,[8] the head gardener, all wanted Kent to visit more often. White and Clary were responsible for the work on site, which in the spring of 1738 involved over 140 men.[9] In November 1738 White mentioned to the General that Kent 'will be most wanted, when ye Ground is brought into a rough levell, which I suppose to be about the beginning of next February, Could he then be prevaild upon to take a trip down'.[10] Later, the head gardener remarked to Sir Clement Cottrell, General Dormer's cousin and Master of Ceremonies to George III: 'if Mr. Kent don't come soon I must turn off half my men, having 44 men, which will work themselves out of work by Saturday night, without the water sinks, the weather mends or Mr Kent comes'.[11] In July 1741 General Dormer told his cousin: 'if Kent can be persuaded to come I shall take it very kindly'.[12] But Kent was busy on other projects and prepared to work collaboratively. The roads were poorly maintained and the journey from London to Rousham could take days, further limiting the time he spent on site: 'I goe to ye Generals next tuesday but shall be back ye latter end of ye week.'[13]

6 Cereghini, p. 321.

7 Gordon, p. 42. Refer to Hunt, *William Kent*, p. 80.

8 Clary is sometimes referred to as MacClary or Macclary, his original surname. He shortened his name when he realised that Clary was the surname of a seventeenth-century landowner at nearby Steeple Aston.

9 Wilson, *William Kent*, p. 215.

10 White, letter to General Dormer, 28 November 1738, quoted in Müller, p. 181.

11 Clary, letter to Sir Clement Cottrell, 15 February 1740/1741, quoted in Müller, p. 186.

12 General Dormer, letter to Sir Clement Cottrell, 21 July 1741, quoted in Müller, p. 187.

13 Kent, letter to Selina, Countess of Huntingdon, 25 September 1739, quoted in Willis, p. 164.

Making History

Embedded with meanings and conceived as a place of study in the classical tradition, which the Italian Renaissance continued, the early picturesque garden also found inspiration and affirmation in the association of ideas. According to John Dixon Hunt and Peter Willis:

> *Locke's ideas certainly sustained and even authorized the emblematic garden – its images recalled ideas that were already familiar – at the same time they also promoted an individual mind's particular reading of some scene. Such a mixed vocabulary and syntax of meanings – specific, available, public, on the one hand, vague, private, sentimental on the other . . . both precise meanings embodied or 'precoded' in a building, statue or inscription and mood and nuance.*[14]

14 Hunt and Willis, 'Introduction', p. 36.

Kent conceived Rousham according to the *genius loci* – genius of the place – a concept with classical origins that was important to the picturesque. In eighteenth-century England the genius of the place was made as much as found, the fusion of new ideas, forms and spaces with those already in place, which were often the results of earlier migrations. As much as Kent heralded a new picturesque landscape, he recalled the Italian Renaissance garden. For example, the descending pools in Rousham's Vale of Venus are reminiscent of Pratolino, while its rustic cascade refers to the upper gardens of the Villa Aldobrandini. References to English history were evident alongside English translations of classical antiquity and the Italian Renaissance:[15] According to Hunt:

15 Hunt, *Garden and Grove*, pp. 214–215.

> *Allusions to the new garden's Italian models – to the ruined Temple of Fortune at ancient Praeneste or to a sculptural group in the grounds of the Renaissance Villa de-Este – were offered along with cultural changes that the act of translation had wrought upon the classical originals. Further, throughout the relatively small garden Kent emphasized both the old and the new, classical and Gothick, often side by side; by these juxtapositions our attention is drawn to the new English location of classical ideas and forms.*[16]

16 Hunt, *Gardens and the Picturesque*, p. 11.

The house lies to the south of the garden. The view at its entrance leads through the interior to the window in the opposite façade. The landscape beyond, to the north, is carefully composed according to the three, sequential natures. Peter Scheemaker's *Lion Attacking the Horse* is in the foreground and at the centre, terminating the level lawn before it slopes down to the Cherwell. Beyond the garden,

William Kent, Rousham, 1738–1741, *The Temple of the Mill and the Triumphal Arch beyond the gardens*. Courtesy of C. Cottrell Dormer.

the Temple of the Mill is in the fields to the left and a further eye-catcher, the Triumphal Arch, is on a distant ridge to the right. Rousham's current owners, General Dormer's descendants, display Kent's drawing on a music stand, facing the viewer and repeating the actual view.[17]

The Temple of the Mill is an earlier building, which Kent's additions give the impression of a partially-ruined medieval church. Further to the left he realigned the road to reveal Heyford Bridge, which partly dates from the thirteenth century. Recalling General Dormer's military campaigns, the profile of the furthest eye-catcher is gothic, although the triumphal arch is an ancient Roman tradition. In the early eighteenth century, classical architecture was sometimes associated with republican Rome and gothic was highly regarded for its association with English history and civil liberty, a combination that the victors of 1688 understood to be their political and cultural heritage. At Stowe, the classical Temple of British Worthies celebrates King Alfred and the most significant garden building is the gothic Temple of Liberty, designed by James Gibbs and completed in 1748.

17 Except that the drawing shows the view beyond Scheemaker's *Lion Attacking the Horse*.

Working in conjunction rather than competition, the hybridisation of historical and geographical references within a building and a garden is characteristic of the picturesque. Referring to the Temple of the Mill and the Triumphal Arch beyond the garden and the Pyramid Building and the Praeneste Terrace within it, David Coffin suggests that 'The architecture of these garden buildings seems to be determined by their geographical orientation: Gothic toward the north, Egyptian at the east, and ancient Roman at the south.'[18] With regard to Townesend's Building within the garden, Coffin adds: 'One can, therefore, only conclude that Kent identified the geographical west with a classical style that was, however, less polished, perhaps even more primitive, than the mature Roman style of architecture.'[19] Coffin's interpretation is plausible. Kent's friend, Pope, who visited Rousham a number of times, developed a similar theme in his allegorical poem *The Temple of Fame*, 1715, in which he associates the orientation of façades with different geographical regions and their architectures.[20]

18 The Terrace refers to the Roman town Praeneste. Coffin, p. 419.

19 Designed by Kent and constructed by William Townesend. Coffin, p. 419.

20 Coffin, p. 420.

William Kent, Rousham, 1738–1741. View from the Praeneste Terrace towards the River Cherwell flood. Photograph, Jonathan Hill.

Garden Stories

Stourhead is the picturesque garden most obviously inspired by Claude. Begun by Henry Hoare in 1740, it references Virgil's *Aeneid*, c.29–19 BC. Hunt concludes that interpretations of Stourhead often overemphasise Virgil's text and ignore other possible meanings.[21] But it is fair to describe Stouhead as the most didactic of picturesque gardens because it directs movement in a specific pattern. The lake at its centre indicates that the principal views – across the lake and on a circuit – are those of a detached and methodical observer appropriate to Lockean empiricism.

21 Hunt, *The Afterlife of Gardens*, p. 202.

Henry Hoare, Stourhead, c.1740. View across the lake towards the Temple of Apollo. Photograph, Jonathan Hill.

The picturesque affirmed the principle of *ut pictura poesis* – as with a picture, so also with a poem – which was first established in classical antiquity. Like Stourhead, Rousham was intended for learned visitors able to uncover and understand the references encoded in its design. But its sources, meanings and routes are less certain and more varied. Upon his death, General Dormer bequeathed Rousham to Sir Clement Cottrell, who added the General's surname to his own. Also a friend of Burlington, Cottrell Dormer visited Rousham less often, maybe because he already had a country house at Twickenham, closer to London. Clary, by then Rousham's steward, wrote to the General's heirs in 1750, nine years after General Dormer's death and two years after Kent's. Enticing them to visit more often he describes the garden's pleasures such as the Grotto and Cold Bath, which he associates with Proserpina, a fertility goddess and the wife of Pluto, ruler of the Underworld.[22]

22 'Letter From John Macclary', in Batey, 'The Way to View Rousham', pp. 127–132. Refer also to Coffin, pp. 412–413.

William Kent, Rousham, 1738–1741. Watery Walk. Photograph, Nat Chard.

William Kent, Rousham, 1738–1741. Cold Bath and Watery Walk. Photograph, Nat Chard.

William Kent, Rousham, 1738–1741. Cold Bath. Photograph, Nat Chard.

Starting at the house Clary describes a clockwise route around the garden. Although he attaches a certain authority to his description, his letter does not necessarily describe Kent's intentions. 'Rowshamius Hortus', an anonymous Latin poem published in 1747, identifies a somewhat similar route and is no more reliable.[23] It portrays General Dormer as Scipio Africanus, a celebrated Roman commander who fought in Spain and retired to the country to create a compact garden featuring a cold bath. Informed by her reading of 'Rowshamius Hortus', Gordon notes similarities between Rousham and Francesco Colonna's *Hypnerotomachia Poliphili*, 1499.[24] The *Hypnerotomachia* describes the protagonist's erotic and wondrous journey through buildings and gardens in search of his beloved Polia, leading to death and rebirth after an encounter with five nymphs representing the five senses. Gordon writes:

> *The statues and ornamental features . . . which visitors meet at Rousham are also met with in the* Hypnerotomachia*: horned fauns and satyrs, Venus and Cupid, Ceres, Bacchus and Mercury, a river in a wood, streams in gravelled channels, an octagonal cold bath, fountains, temples, and a pyramidal mausoleum. That the text could have been used as a base for the entire garden seems reasonable. Many of Kent's pyramid buildings are known to have been based on woodcut illustrations from the* Hypnerotomachia*. Furthermore, Rousham's owner, James Dormer, like Kent himself, owned several copies of the text.*[25]

Kent's enthusiasm for Edmund Spenser's unfinished poem *The Faerie Queene*, 1595, was long-held and a certain influence. Michael Wilson remarks: 'That this epic work, a triumph of Elizabethan imagery masquerading as a medieval fable, could attract readers in the austere Augustan age, is proof that an undertow of romanticism was already running strongly.'[26] Kent reportedly attributed 'his taste in gardening' to 'the picturesque descriptions of Spenser'.[27] Depicting scenes from *The Faerie Queene*, Francesco Sleter's murals decorated the interiors of two of Kent's pavilions at Stowe – the Temple of Venus and the Hermitage – and late in his life Kent provided thirty-two illustrations for Thomas Birch's 1751 edition of Spenser's poem, which was published three years after Kent's death. Although many of these illustrations depict landscapes unlike Kent's gardens, and few show his garden buildings, collectively they recall his interest in sequential narrative settings and confirm his fascination for the gothic alongside the classical.[28] Hunt writes: 'And for the properly equipped and learned mind this encounter with Venus among the glades of Rousham would bring back with suitable propriety Spenser's discussions of courtesy and its connections with the countryside.'[29] This image of

23 Gordon mentions Robert Dodsley or Sir Clement Cottrell Dormer as possible authors. Gordon, pp. 69–101. Refer to Hunt, 'Verbal Versus Visual Meanings in Garden History', p. 158.

24 There is some speculation that Alberti not Colonna was the author. Vidler, 'Preface', p. 11. Refer to Colonna, *Hypnerotomachia Poliphili*; Lefaivre, *Leon Battista Alberti's Hypnerotomachia Poliphili*.

25 Gordon, pp. 71–72.

26 Wilson, *William Kent*, p. 149.

27 William Mason, *The English Garden*, 1811, quoted in Wilson, *William Kent*, p. 215.

28 The Temple of Venus and the Hermitage at Stowe appear in 'The Idle Lake' and 'Archimago's Cell'. Hunt, *Gardens and the Picturesque*, p. 248, n. 15.

29 Hunt, *Gardens and the Picturesque*, p. 86.

William Kent, Rousham, 1737–1741. *The Vale of Venus*. Courtesy of C. Cottrell Dormer.

William Kent, *Redcross Knight & Una invited by Subtle Archimago to his Cell*, illustration for Edmund Spenser's *The Faerie Queene,* 1751 edition. Kent's design for a Hermitage is seen to the left. Courtesy of the Victoria and Albert Museum, London.

educated and polite discussion is confirmed in Kent's drawing of Rousham's Vale of Venus.

Rather than definitive guides, the letter and fables indicate some of the ways in which Rousham can be understood and appreciated. As Manfredo Tafuri remarks, 'the interlocutor does not simply receive the messages, but he is asked to complete them, even to change their meaning while they are being deciphered'.[30]

30 Tafuri, *Theories and Histories of Architecture*, p. 82.

The garden has a number of entry points, including one from the house, which bifurcates, and another originally intended for public access, which leads from the road through a neo-classical gateway adjacent to the Gothic Seat, further undermining the assumption that there is a preferred route. Rousham offers no obvious hierarchy, endlessly varied routes, multiple vistas of differing dimensions and exquisite rooms that open one onto the other.[31] There is never just one way to look. It is likely that Kent did not subscribe to a specific narrative and saw no reason to do so: 'Rather it is the juxtapositions already noticed, ancient and modern, classical and gothick, natural and artificial, foreign and English, that constitute its "subject".'[32]

As the century progressed, the garden as a story was less appreciated, in part because patrons were less concerned to develop and display their learning. Subjectivity was increasingly valued, as were landscapes that most engaged feelings and emotions. In *Elements of Criticism*, Kames criticises literal devices such as the monuments that Kent designed for the Elysian Fields at Stowe, which Whately praises in *Observations on Modern Gardening* although his general argument might suggest otherwise.[33] Whately distinguishes between the emblematic, imitative and original. Criticising the emblematic because it requires careful analysis and the imitative because it depends on resemblance, he concludes that neither allows trains of thought to develop. In contrast, original character needs no mental reflection; its effects 'are obvious at a glance, and instantaneously distinguished by our feelings'.[34] Remarking that 'we soon lose sight of the means by which the character is formed', Whately concludes that original character is most conducive to the imagination because it enables an expressive mode of association that is less specific than the emblematic:[35]

> *The power of such characters is not confined to the ideas which the objects immediately suggest; for these are connected with others, which insensibly lead to subjects, far distant perhaps from the original thought, and related to it only by a similitude in the sensations they excite.*[36]

Praised by both Walpole and Whately and noted for softly rolling landscapes, Lancelot 'Capability' Brown was the pre-eminent English landscape gardener in the mid-eighteenth century.[37] Featuring a varied and intimate topography abundant in monuments and statues, Kent's gardens were there to be walked and considered. Broader and more open, with far fewer architectural and topographical incidents, Brown's gardens were less obviously intended for discourse. Stephen Bending suggests that the expressive garden had a social purpose despite its somewhat

31 Rousham's spaces and objects are specific and evocative. The Praeneste Terrace, Dying Gladiator, Octagon Pond, Upper Cascade with Venus and Cupids, Upper Ponds, Watery Walk, Cold Bath, Temple of Echo, Gothic Seat, Palladian Doorway, Statue of Antinous/Apollo, Long Walk, Lower Cascade and Pyramid, for example.

32 Hunt, *William Kent*, p. 86.

33 Kames, vol. 2, p. 353; Whately, pp. 217–221.

34 Whately, p. 153.

35 Whately, p. 155.

36 Whately, p. 154.

37 Walpole, *The History of the Modern Taste in Gardening*, p. 57; Whately, pp. 213–227.

unrelenting appearance.[38] But Hunt emphasises the subjective and emotional responses to the expressive garden and offers Stowe as an example, where Brown was head gardener between 1741 and 1750:

38 Bending, 'Horace Walpole', pp. 222–223; Bending, 'Re-reading the Eighteenth-Century Landscape Garden', pp. 391–399.

> *The Grecian Valley no longer requires the learned attention to detailed meaning; it makes no claim upon our intellect. The subtle varieties of the valley afford a landscape that seems to answer our changing moods, that allows a unique and individual response by each visitor to its unobtrusive character.*[39]

39 Hunt, *Gardens and the Picturesque*, p. 87.

But a simple opposition between emblematic and expressive gardens is untenable, and neither did one immediately replace the other. Writing 'that Pope would not have chosen to distinguish as sharply as Whately did in 1770 between the rival kinds of garden', Hunt offers Rousham as an example of an early eighteenth-century garden that is both emblematic and expressive.[40] Favouring the measured investigation and the immediate response, Rousham was intended to cultivate knowledge and debate, imagination and emotion. Just as the diverse activities depicted in Kent's garden drawings surpassed the reasonable behaviour promoted by Locke, Rousham afforded the association of ideas a freedom that Locke did not intend.

40 Hunt, *Gardens and the Picturesque*, p. 98. Refer to Harwood, p. 42; Hunt, 'Verbal Versus Visual Meanings in Garden History', p. 178.

A Beautiful Boy

In classical antiquity, the earth was feminine and the winds were masculine. Inheriting this tradition, the early eighteenth century usually categorised the natural landscape as female, which paintings and sculptures confirmed, while the person who commissioned the garden was most likely male. Differences in gender and sexuality were further acknowledged in garden statues. The rules for their selection, order and location were much discussed and a means to display learning. For example, they were extensively considered in Batty Langley's *New Principles of Gardening: Or, the Laying out and Planting Parterres, Groves, Wildernesses, Labyrinths, Avenues, Parks etc. after a more Grand and Rural Manner, than has been done before*, 1728. Kent received guidance from the 1626 Paduan edition of Vincenzo Cartari's *Imagini delli dei gl'antichi*, 1556, a popular handbook on classical mythology.[41] A particular myth or character might have had a number of variations and meanings. But as each figure or structure could represent specific ideas in relation to others in the garden its position at Rousham was carefully considered.

41 Coffin, p. 412.

William Kent, Rousham, 1738–1741. Antinous/Apollo at the end of the Long Walk. Photograph, Jonathan Hill.

The statue at the end of the Elm Walk – placed there by General Dormer – has attracted particularly intense debate among garden historians. Kenneth Woodbridge describes it as Antinous, Wilson recognises that it may be Antinous or Apollo, while Coffin proposes Antinous, Apollo or Mercury.[42] Hunt concludes that the statue is Apollo because of Rousham's 'pastoral emphasis', and Coffin agrees because the statue and garden are both associated with Arcadia.[43] Mowl, however, criticises historians who deny the garden's sensuality and the owner's sexuality:

42 Woodbridge, 'Kent's Gardening', p. 289; Wilson, *William Kent*, p. 214; Coffin, p. 418.

43 Hunt, 'Verbal Versus Visual Meanings in Garden History', p. 179; Coffin, p. 416.

> *Garden writers of a 'Georgian' complexion insist that it is a statue of Apollo, a respectable god. In fact, it is Antinous, one of three representations that the General bought and obviously relished. Antinous was the Emperor Hadrian's beautiful boy lover who came to a mysterious death in the Nile and was subsequently deified, the ultimate gay icon.*[44]

44 Mowl, *William Kent*, p. 241.

Even if Apollo was a respectable god in Georgian England the distinction between Apollo and Antinous may not to be so clear because ancient Greek gods had sexual relations with mortals, both men and women. Mowl may be correct about General Dormer's sexual preference but homoeroticism was acceptable in the early eighteenth century and not necessarily associated with homosexuality. The eighteenth-century elite was exclusively male and socialised in institutions such as the Kit-Cat. In the first volume of *Characteristicks*, Shaftesbury praises 'the Liberty of *the Club*, and of that sort of Freedom which is taken amongst *Gentlemen* and *Friends* who know one another perfectly well'.[45]

45 Shaftesbury, *Characteristicks*, vol. 1, p. 45. Refer to Cowan, p. 138.

Writing to General Dormer in November 1739, White openly reports that 'The Venus is now safe in her Nech next ye house. Antinous likewise in his place, his right Arm in two places a little bruis'd.'[46] Here, it is uncertain whether White refers to the figure at the end of the Elm Walk or another statue. His inventory – *List of the General's Bronzes, Statues, Bas Reliefs Etc. left by him at Rousham and entered of now by me in this book July ye 20th 1743* – records 'at the end of the Long Green Walk Antoinous larger than life a leaden figure'.[47] But to confuse matters, White describes himself as an unreliable witness: 'country folk can be of little acquainted with the value of Bustos, statues, or Bronzes'.[48] Associating urban with urbane, White's opinion echoed those of his employer's class on matters of culture and learning, for whom a country estate was an adjunct to London life. In an unpublished account of Rousham from 1902, Frances Elizabeth Cottrell Dormer also refers to the figure at the end of the Elm Walk as Antinous, suggesting that the family accepts this attribution.[49] But whatever Kent and Dormer's intentions, the confusion over this statue indicates that definitive interpretations of the parts as well as the whole are enjoyably contentious and elusive. Rather than be considered on its own, the meaning of any garden element depends on the complex system of relations and associations within the garden.

46 White, letter to General Dormer, 29 November 1739, quoted in Müller, p. 185.

47 White, quoted in Gordon, p. 102. Refer to Batey, 'The Way to View Rousham', p. 128.

48 White, letter to Sir Clement Cottrell, quoted in Gordon, p. 65.

49 Cottrell Dormer, p. 38.

William Kent, Rousham, 1738–1741. Detail of Antinous/Apollo at the end of the Long Walk. Photograph, Jonathan Hill.

THE WEATHER OF THE PLACE

Meteorologica

As a reality and a representation, the weather was essential to the creation of Rousham's *genius loci*, which can be seen as a response to conceptions of the atmosphere in classical antiquity and the seventeenth and eighteenth centuries. The assumption that the universe is an interconnected whole is indebted to ancient Greek philosophy, notably Plato's distinction between unchanging ideal forms and material copies that decay.[50] Influenced by Plato, many of his contemporaries associated change with imperfection, which was therefore not a subject of serious study. But in *Meteorologica*, *c.*350 BC, Aristotle provided the first comprehensive theory of meteorology, a term derived from the Greek *meteoros*, meaning 'to be raised up'. As conceived by Aristotle, meteorology considers objects and particles that are suspended in the air or fall from it. He attributed atmospheric phenomena to the actions of the sun on the earth, which result in two types of exhalation. The first is hot and dry and occurs when the sun's rays fall on dry land. The second is cool and moist and occurs when the sun's rays fall on water. The exhalations interact with each other and the elements – earth, air, fire and water – to create atmospheric movement: clouds, mists, winds, storms and other conditions. Aristotle indicated an interest in '*the totality of phenomena* produced in a specific cosmological realm, rather than a concern with weather patterns in a geographic area. Put simply, *Meteorologica* is concerned with meteors, not the weather', writes Vladimir Jankovic.[51] The acknowledged authority on the atmosphere for two thousand years, *Meteorologica*'s influence continued into the mid-eighteenth century, including the 1723 third edition of Isaac Newton's *Opticks*.[52]

50 Plato, *Timaeus*, p. 121.

51 Jankovic, p. 19.

52 At first influential but then ignored, *Meteorologica* returned to prominence in the thirteenth century due to two translations, one from Arabic and the other from Greek. Newton, *Opticks*, pp. 379–380. Refer to Boia, p. 122; Jankovic, p. 28.

The Natural History of Oxfordshire

Dependent on developments in science and philosophy, the reassessment of atmospheric phenomena occurred gradually. In the Renaissance, the invention of new scientific instruments allowed the atmosphere's properties to be categorised and measured, the first signs of a new-found confidence in humanity's place in God's natural creation. In 1450 Nicholas de Cusa invented the hygrometer to measure air moisture and in 1593 Galileo Galilei invented the thermometer to measure temperature. Another invention is usually credited to Evangelista Torricelli in 1644 but Robert Boyle was probably the first to devise the term 'barometer' and to identify its potential for measuring air pressure.

In England, Francis Bacon's publications – such as *Historia Ventorum* (History of Winds), 1622, and *Sylva Sylvarum: or A Natural History, in Ten Centuries*, 1627 – set the tone for investigations later in the seventeenth century, promoting reasoned analysis of the natural world. Emphasising that knowledge is acquired through the senses, Bacon's example was followed with varying degrees of rigour. His assumption that extraordinary weather events could be even more revealing than everyday occurrences was influential.[53] In *The Natural History of Oxfordshire, Being an Essay toward the Natural History of England*, 1677, Robert Plot consistently focuses on the exceptional. Entries include 'An *Egg* with another within it', 'An *Elm* having three trunks out of the one root', 'A great *Flood* in the River *Cherwell*', 'A *Sheep* with only one horn' and '*Stones* resembling Plants'. Plot includes human artefacts within his natural history. Delicately engraved plates include illustrations of antiquities, plants, shells, standing stones and the Woodstock Echo. The first chapter – 'Of the Heavens and Air' – places local and personal accounts of weather alongside comparable descriptions from classical antiquity:

53 Bacon, pp. 107–110, 171–175, 187. Refer to Bowen, pp. 36–57; Jankovic, pp. 44–50.

> *The second tempest of Thunder and Lightning, on the 10th of* May *1666, which though terrible enough to all parts adjacent to* Oxford, *yet was mischievous only at* Medley, *a well known House, about a mile or somwhat more distant from it; two scholars of* Wadham *College, alone in a boat, and new thrust off shore to come homewards, being struck off the head of the boat into the water, the one of them stark dead, and the other stuck fast in the mud like a post, with his feet downward, and for the present so disturbed in his senses, that he neither knew how he came out of the boat, nor could remember either Thunder or Lightning that did effect it.*[54]

54 Plot, pp. 5–6.

Furthering regional and local identities, 'Plot's work was eagerly anticipated by his aristocratic and gentlemanly subscribers'.[55] In a section on 'Garden Walks' he mentions Rousham, indicating the dramatic topography of which Kent made use:

55 Jankovic, p. 86.

> *And for a descent, there are none like the Walks at* Rousham, *in the Garden of the Worshipful* Robert Dormer *Esq; where there are no less than five one under another, leading from the* garden *above, down to the river side, having* steps *at each end, and parted with* hedges *of* Codlings *etc.*[56]

56 Plot, p. 117.

Weather Records

The work of individuals rather than institutions, weather diaries gradually became more common in the early eighteenth century and were often prepared by clerics who used their university education and parish knowledge to record exceptional local conditions, following Bacon's model. The Rev. Thomas Leigh, the vicar of Lower Heyford, close to Rousham, and a witness to Colonel Dormer's will, was one such inquisitive cleric, as Frances Elizabeth Cottrell Dormer recounts:

> *Mr. Leigh made a practice of writing down in a manuscript book any curious thing which came under his observation, this habit of storing up information made his conversation very agreeable, and the late General Dormer who was a near neighbour in the country, and had, as the world knows, an uncommonly large and curious collection of books, said that he received nothing of instruction from them in comparison to that which he enjoyed in his living library, Mr. Leigh.*[57]

57 Cottrell Dormer, p. 54.

During the first half of the eighteenth century, local weather reports were regularly published in *Philosophical Transactions,* a journal once edited by Plot and associated with the Royal Society. Alongside the clerics' local knowledge of exceptional weather, a more rigorous and consistent approach was advocated. In 'Method for Making a History of the Weather', 1667, Robert Hooke argued for regular and consistent weather records, laying the foundation of meteorological science.[58] Appointed the first keeper of the Ashmolean Museum and Professor of Chemistry at Oxford University in 1683, Plot added his encouragement. Locke also concurred, daily recording the temperature, barometric pressure and winds for many years, and editing Robert Boyle's *General History of the Air*, 1692. In *Philosophical Transactions*, Locke commented on his weather records:

58 Hooke's essay was published in Thomas Sprat's *History of the Royal Society of London, for the Improving of Natural Knowledge*. Weather data were collected in other European countries. For example, at the Accademia del Cimento in Florence in the 1650s and 1660s and the Académie des Sciences after its foundation in 1666. Refer to Gunther, vol. 4, pp. 34–35; Jankovic, p. 82.

> *I have often thought that if such a Register as this, or one that were better contriv'd, with the help of some Instruments that for exactness might be added, were kept in every County in* England, *and so constantly published many things relating to the Air, Winds, Health, Fruitfulnes, etc. might by a sagacious man be collected from them, and several Rules and Observations concerning the extent of Winds and Rains, etc, be in time establish'd, to the great advantage of Mankind.*[59]

59 Locke, 'A Register of the Weather for the Year 1692', p. 1919. Refer to Jankovic, pp. 35–36; Nebeker, p. 11.

In the early eighteenth century, even ships did not include meteorological instruments, and logbooks were compiled through observation alone. Wind force was described in terms that were widely but not consistently used such as 'fair' and 'strong' while wind direction was noted according to a 32-point compass. Mariners described the general condition of the weather as a narrative, using terms that were almost lyrical. However, the Great Storm of 1703 was the first to be measured scientifically due to barometric data prepared by William Derham of Upminster and Richard Towneley of Burnley.[60] Causing havoc on land and at sea, it remains one of the most ferocious in recorded history. The Great Storm's fame was established and maintained by Daniel Defoe's *An Historical Narrative of the Great and Tremendous Storm Which Happened on Nov. 26th, 1703*, which was published in the following year. On the morning of 26 November 1703, Defoe notes: 'About

60 Derham, pp. 1530–1534. Refer to Wheeler, pp. 419–427.

ten the barometers gave information that the night would be very tempestuous, the mercury sinking lower than had been observed before.'[61]

Weather diaries were compiled intermittently until around 1715 when they were increasingly prepared by medical doctors who were concerned to establish connections between the weather and the transmission of disease, and thus adopted a more rigorous approach than the clerics. Many of these doctors had either been educated under Herman Boerhaave at the University of Leiden or were influenced by the importance he attached to accurate records. Boerhaave's pupil, James Jurin, who was then Secretary of the Royal Society, appealed for a uniform method of observation and measurement in *Philosophical Transactions* in 1723, furthering interest in weather records. However, his advice was open to varied interpretation and did not establish a consistent system. For example, temperature readings were to be taken 'in a room facing north where a fire never burns, or as rarely as possible'.[62]

Automated means to record the weather were also proposed. In 1663 Wren presented a 'Description of a Weather Clock' to the Royal Society and in 1669 Hooke constructed the mechanical 'weather wiser', the first automated weather station that recorded air pressure, humidity and temperature, rainfall, wind direction and speed. A national network of meteorological observatories was first proposed in the 1680s but the idea did not receive widespread support until it was revived in the second half of the eighteenth century; the automated weather station only became common in the twentieth century. In the first half of the eighteenth century new scientific research still existed alongside references to classical precedent, echoing the concern for ancient models in architecture. For example, in *A Rational Account of the Weather, Showing the Signs of Its Several Changes*, 1723, John Pointer includes references to Aristotle, Pliny and Seneca.[63] Increasingly, as the century progressed, the new science emphasised detached observation and reasoned explanation, not committed engagement with nature, intuitive interpretation and classical precedent. Bacon's concern for systematic understanding was continued but investigations focused on familiar patterns, not exceptional events. Creating order as well as understanding, Latin terminology made knowledge uniform and familiar to the specialist, detaching it from local traditions and contending vernacular descriptions of plants, birds, insects and animals, which had emotional and symbolic connotations rather than scientific rigour. Between 1686 and 1704 John Ray produced his three-volume survey of plant life, *Historia Plantarum*. But Carl von Linnaeus developed the pre-eminent system of plant classification in *Critica Botanica*, 1737, *Species Plantarum*, 1753, and the tenth edition of his *Systema Naturae*, 1758. Scientific investigation was not immediately and extensively applied

61 Defoe, p. 51.

62 Jurin, 1723, quoted in Manley, p. 300.

63 A second edition appeared in 1738. Refer to Crewe, pp. 137–138; Jankovic, pp. 15, 154–156.

to the atmosphere because the weather was assumed to lack reason. But it was also recognised as an inviting challenge to rational explanation. If the weather could be categorised, then so could anything in nature. In *Discourse on Method, Optics, Geometry and Meteorology*, 1637, René Descartes expresses 'the hope that if I here express the nature of clouds in such a way that we will no longer have occasion to wonder at anything that descends from them, we will easily believe that it is similarly possible to find causes of everything that is admirable above the earth'.[64]

64 Descartes, *Discourse on Method*, p. 263.

Weather Moods

Narrating the formation of modern identity, Michel Foucault uses the phrase 'technology of the self' to describe how moral character and behaviour were constructed and maintained through a self-disciplined activity such as writing a diary.[65] The unpublished diary of an anonymous Oxford graduate details the Worcestershire weather in 1703, the year of the Great Storm. The diary refers to classical authors including Aristotle and Seneca as well as contemporary figures such as Robert Boyle, Thomas Burnet, René Descartes, Johannes Kepler and Athanasius Kircher.[66] Most contemporary weather diarists ignored clouds because they were difficult to measure but the 1703 diarist gave them special poetic attention a hundred years before they became the focus of meteorology, painting and poetry. Employing visual analogies – such as cobwebs, fleece and spun wool – he classified clouds according to eight categories.[67] The 1703 diarist was interested in the natural causes of weather but his analysis was not reasonable and moderate in the manner advocated by empirical science. While the medical practitioners wrote factually and made few personal remarks, the 1703 weather diarist profusely referred to himself and his relations with the weather, describing his diary as 'this Book of Life' and 'the grand history & picture of my own life'.[68] For the 1703 diarist, experiencing the weather and writing the weather diary were means of self-exploration and self-expression. Rather than quantify the daily weather, he describes it poetically and personally through metaphor and analogy, emphasising its effects on his thoughts and moods.[69] Depending upon the author's state of mind, differing weathers encouraged particular thoughts and perceptions, whether sublime, sexual, divine, heroic or melancholic. A lightning flash was 'so superlative & extraordinary enormous a fright I never was sensible of in all my life'.[70] Rain was 'spermatic irrigation' and 'every vegetable strutted in a vivid new-fed green and amiable freshness, swelled & distended with ye vernall succus, like a Plump vigorous face, or semole breasts full

65 Foucault, 'On the Genealogy of Ethics', p. 369.

66 Golinski suggests that the author may have been Thomas Appletree, a graduate of Balliol College, Oxford, where Robert Boyle and Robert Plot both lectured. Golinski, 'Exquisite Atmography', pp. 150, 170–171. Refer to Webster, 'Writing to Redundancy', p. 50.

67 Golinski, 'Exquisite Atmography', pp. 151, 156.

68 1703 Weather Diary, quoted in Golinski, 'Exquisite Atmography', p. 166.

69 Golinski, 'Exquisite Atmography', p. 155.

70 1703 Weather Diary, quoted in Golinski, 'Exquisite Atmography', p. 167.

of youth & blown up tight and stiff with Longing desires, & flatus of youthful lust'.[71] A heavily overcast October day was a 'temper of weather (that) exactly corresponds to my saturnine & quiet melancholy Genius'.[72] After an 'angry' storm his home 'all lookt with a decayed, antient Ruinous face, & air of desolation, as some dropping deserted work & threadbare mansion of a Lost and careless owner'.[73] Misty August drizzle 'was incomparably delicate & agreeable to my temper a distillation of divine juice, & smoothed my soul all into Raptures, melted me into a sacred & aeternall transport oh! how happy was I for ye moment, sliding into unknown joys and serenity of mind'.[74]

In comparison to the detached weather records promoted by empirical science, the 1703 diarist offered engaged appreciation of the weather and its effects on the self. Notably, he described the weather as an agent of spiritual transcendence. But the diarists effusive language was in contrast to Shaftesbury's greater restraint.[75]

71 1703 Weather Diary, quoted in Golinski, 'Exquisite Atmography', p. 168.

72 1703 Weather Diary, quoted in Golinski, 'Exquisite Atmography', p. 167.

73 1703 Weather Diary, quoted in Golinski, 'Exquisite Atmography', p. 163.

74 1703 Weather Diary, quoted in Golinski, 'Exquisite Atmography', p. 167.

75 Golinski, 'Exquisite Atmography', p. 171; Shaftesbury, *Characteristicks*, vol. 2, p. 101.

Weather Signs

In the early eighteenth century the environmental romanticism of the 1703 diarist was in its infancy, as was a purely rational approach to the weather, and an alternative was widely supported despite the influence of empiricism. In classical antiquity there were two distinct attitudes to atmospheric phenomena: one a theory of meteors, the other a practical guide to the weather. According to Jankovic:

> *The first Greek text of this nature is the* Phaenomena *by Aratus of Soli, written early in the third century* BC. *It is an astronomical poem to which a section is added on prognostic signs, entitled* Diosemiai. *This and the anonymous* De Signis Tempestates *(attributed to Theophrastus), represent two chief sources for the most influential book in the genre, the first book of Virgil's* Georgics *(37* BC*).*[76]

76 Jankovic, p. 21.

The assumption that all natural objects are part of a single interconnected world gave credence to the weather signs tradition. Verse not prose, and interpretation not explanation, the first book of the *Georgics* identifies changes in nature that foretell impending weather, such as the behaviour of insects and birds, plants and skies. The *Georgics* derives its title from *georgos*, the Greek term for farmer. Virgil equates the farmer's virtuous management of the land to the benign management of Rome and emphasises weather's influence on the arts as well as daily life. He even acknowledges inclement weather as a creative stimulus.

Virgil's *Georgics* was a model for pastoral verse in the Renaissance and afterwards. An English translation appeared in 1697, inspiring Pope's *Pastorals*, 1709.[77] The weather signs tradition continued in poems such as James Thomson's *The Seasons*, 1730, which presents human activity in dialogue with an evolving natural world to a greater extent than Pope's more restrained poetry. *The Seasons*' popularity was immediate and enduring, resulting in over three hundred editions between 1750 and 1850. Here, Thomson describes the spring:

77 The *Georgics*' translator was John Dryden. Refer to Andrews, *The Search for the Picturesque*, pp. 9–10; Hunt, *Gardens and the Picturesque*, p. 228.

Clear was the temperate air; an even calm
Perpetual reign'd, save what the zephyrs bland
Breath'd o'er the blue expanse; for then nor storms
Were taught to blow, nor hurricanes to rage;
Sound slept the Waters; no sulphureous glooms
Swell'd in the sky, and sent the lightning forth:
While sickly damps, and cold and autumnal fogs,
Sat not pernicious on the springs of life.[78]

78 Thomson, *The Seasons*, p. 20.

Alongside poems, the Georgic tradition continued in farming guides. Natural objects were trusted to offer protection against misfortune. Certain trees – 'bays, beeches and horse-leeks – were planted near the house to save it from lightning . . . Heather, swallows, owls, cattle and cats, all gave out signs of future changes in the weather . . . If the ash was out before the oak, they were bound to have a soak', writes Keith Thomas. However, it was bad luck, 'even a sign of death, to meet a hare, or to hear a howling dog, a singing swan, a chirping cricket, a croaking raven, a death-watch beetle, a bittern, or a screech-owl'. [79] Explanation was unnecessary: 'the tradition of prognostics never developed a *theoretical* account of how the rules worked. Their reliability was in their use, not in a *reasoned* defence of their validity or in a causal connection between the signs and predictions', writes Jankovic.[80] The weather signs tradition placed its trust in the intuition and experience of the farmer, not the reason and instrumentation of the scientist.

79 Thomas, pp. 75–76.

80 Jankovic, p. 130.

The clerics' weather reports focused on exceptional weather, while the weather guide – whether the *Georgics* or a later text – offered comprehensive advice. But the concern for weather anomalies and weather signs coincided when spectacular natural events were studied for their human significance. For England and the newly independent United Province of the Netherlands, founded only in 1609, the winds and tides were particularly liable to allegorical interpretation. On the eve of the Glorious Revolution in 1688, the October wind that kept William of Orange's fleet in harbour was deemed to be Papist and the strong east wind that followed in early November was praised as Protestant.

In *The Origin of Table Manners*, 1968, Claude Lévi-Strauss suggests that many everyday rules of good behaviour are intended to protect the public realm from our errant actions as much as the opposite.[81] Sensitive to people, places and situations, eighteenth-century polite behaviour avoided disruptive disagreements and oiled the flow of trade and knowledge as well as politics. Although Addison and Steele had stimulated such notions, polite society came to fruition in the second half of the eighteenth century.[82] Alongside weather signs' practical and allegorical purpose, the weather acquired an essential role in polite conversation. But Englishmen also relished their cantankerous and contrary behaviour, which they explained by reference to the fickle and variable weather.[83] The sudden variability of the British weather is due to an island location at the edge of continental Europe and the influence of the Gulf Stream, which guarantees a climate that is unusually mild for such a latitude. The weather became such a necessary catalyst to discussion – polite or otherwise – that Samuel Johnson remarked in 1758: 'It is commonly observed, that when two Englishmen meet, their first talk is of the weather; they are in haste to tell each other, what they already know, that it is hot or cold, bright or cloudy, windy or calm.'[84] Johnson attributes this national obsession to the sudden variations in the English weather but questions such fickle behaviour and dismisses trust in weather signs. He asks each Englishman to 'struggle against the tyranny of the climate, and refuse to enslave his virtue or his reason to the most variable of variations, the changes of the weather'.[85]

The application of rational order to the natural world was gradually extended to the climate and weather. Following continental Europe, in 1752 Britain and its colonies adopted the Gregorian calendar's uniform system of measurement in place of the Julian calendar, which reflected the seasonal rhythms of farming.[86] The introduction of a standard timescale allowed the climate to be more readily conceived as regular and ordered. But confidence in the weather guide persisted well into the eighteenth century. First, because it affirmed rural traditions, emphasising the social, practical and spiritual benefits that arose from the coexistence with nature, which tied many customs and celebrations to the seasonal calendar. Second, because it countered the mechanical and secular conception of time and nature, which suited the agricultural reforms of the political establishment and provided an early indication of industrialisation. However, a practical and spiritual appreciation of the weather and a mechanical and secular one were not simply opposed in class terms. The weather signs tradition was communicated to prosperous and poor alike, whether in books, artworks or oral histories. Equally, attempts to resolve the two traditions were evident. One of the best-known farming guides was written by John Claridge in 1670 and republished as *The Shepherd of*

81 Lévi-Strauss, p. 504.

82 Carter, *Men and the Emergence of Polite Society, Britain 1660–1800*, pp. 25, 27, 63.

83 Porter, *English Society in the Eighteenth Century*, p. 10.

84 Johnson, *The Idler and the Adventurer*, p. 36.

85 Johnson, *The Idler and the Adventurer*, p. 39.

86 Before 1752, New Year's Day was 25 March rather than 1 January. For example, a date that would have been classified as 3 March 1715 in 1752 would have been 3 March 1714 before then.

Banbury's Rules To Judge of the Changes of the Weather, Grounded on Forty Years Experience in 1744.[87] The subtitle of the 1744 edition describes 'A Rational Account . . . on the Principles of *Newtonian* Philosophy'. After an unexplained piece of weather advice, the author remarks:

87 Curry, p. 161; Golinski, p. 72; Jankovic, pp. 77, 153–155.

> *This must be allow'd a very extraordinary Aphorism from a Country Shepherd, but at the Same Time it is very agreeable to the Observations of Dr.* Hooke, *Dr.* Derham, *Dr.* Grew, *and other able Naturalists, who with unwearied Pains and Diligence have calculated the Quality of Rain filling in one Year and compared with what fell in another.*[88]

88 Claridge, p. 14.

Farmer George

England in Kent's lifetime was not yet subject to intensive industrialisation but the foundations of that process had begun. Jethro Tull advertised a machine-drill in *Horse-Hoeing Husbandry*, 1731, while Thomas Newcomen constructed a rudimentary steam engine in 1712, which James Watt greatly improved in 1763. Outside of the few industrial centres, England remained overwhelmingly rural and sparsely populated. Land ownership was the principal indicator of wealth, status and influence. England was reasonably prosperous but agricultural profitability was especially low in the 1720s and 1730s in spite of consistently warm summers. As the century progressed, parliamentary land enclosures transferred over six million acres from public to private use, improving the fortunes of the larger estates, benefiting landowners and tenant farmers but not the rural poor who had relied on common land for at least a part of their livelihood. Landowners' subsequent fears of social unrest were reflected in the increasing number of crimes against property that resulted in a capital offence, including servants pilfering from their masters in 1736 and sheep-stealing in 1741.[89]

89 Lamb, p. 243; Porter, *English Society*, pp. 135–137, 208–213.

The Enlightenment is familiarly, and understandably, associated with the control of nature. Between 'ancient and modern literature on the modifications of the earth by human agency' Clarence C. Glacken notes 'a sharp contrast' not only in 'the amount and rate of change' but also in 'awareness of change'.[90] Sometimes a more subtle understanding of change accompanied modification. Glacken identifies John Evelyn's *Sylva, or A Discourse of Forest-Trees, and the Propagation of Timber in His Majesties Dominions*, 1664, and the *French Forest Ordinance of 1669*, initiated by Jean-Baptiste Colbert, minister to Louis XIV, as 'the beginning of a more reserved attitude toward the modification of nature by man in the history

90 According to Glacken, the modern era began in the Renaissance. Glacken, p. 149.

of Western thought'.[91] The Royal Society's first official publication, *Sylva* reflected its Baconian empiricism and concern for managed and measured rural development. Both texts question past exploitation while Evelyn, who frequently quotes Virgil's *Georgics*, acknowledges the effects of deforestation on climate and recognises the need for forestry science, conservation and sustainable development.

Landowners did not wish to appear to be solely concerned with profit and pleasure. In *Philosophiae Naturalis Principia Mathematica* (Mathematical Principles of Natural Philosophy), 1687, Isaac Newton concludes that material objects possess mass and are dependent on forces of attraction and repulsion as in a mechanical system.[92] As nature was conceived as a machine, mankind could have been its driver and mechanic, making adjustments to improve performance. But in an era that was fortified by descriptions of rural life and yet to face the full force of industrialisation, another analogy was then more appropriate. Aware of humanity's duty to God's creation, the farmer was a model for the enlightened management of nature and society.[93] Monarch between 1760 and 1820, George III's affectionate nickname – Farmer George – confirmed him as a farmer twice over, even though by the end of his reign the agricultural metaphor was to some extent inappropriate and a means to ignore the ravages of industrialisation. Popular manuals on farm management appeared throughout the eighteenth century, including Timothy Nourse's *Compania Felix, or a Discourse on the Benefits and Improvements of Husbandry*, 1700, Arthur Young's *The Farmer's Letters to the People of England*, 1767, and Kames's *The Gentleman Farmer; Being An Attempt to Improve Agriculture by Subjecting it to the Test of Rational Principles*, 1776.

91 Glacken titles the book *Silva* rather than *Sylva*. Brown, *French Forest Ordinance of 1669*; Evelyn, *Sylva*, pp. 112–120; Glacken, p. 485.

92 Newton, *Mathematical Principles of Natural Philosophy*.

93 Barrell, pp. 8–9, 15; Porter, *Enlightenment*, pp. 303–311.

Georgic England

As land enclosures enlarged estates, gardens proliferated. Heaths and pastures were ordered into regular fields while gardens cultivated a natural image. The pleasures and liberties of the picturesque garden were as carefully monitored as those of parliamentary democracy. The creators and beneficiaries of the picturesque were wealthy, educated and most likely male; only a small proportion of the population had voting rights.

To appear natural the garden needed continuous maintenance, which was preferably unseen. Removing the villages that stood in the way of their gardens, Cobham, Coke and Walpole ensured that labour was further displaced. Ignoring the conditions of the rural poor and the inequalities of agricultural production, the pastoral Arcadia recreated in the early eighteenth-century picturesque was a means to avoid the landscape as much as it was a means to enjoy it. Consequently, according to Malcolm Andrews: 'The Picturesque eye, in other words, is anti-georgic.'[94] However, John Barrell recognises that there was a need to question as well as promote the pastoral Arcadia. It was necessary 'to admit some degree of concern for work, for the industriousness which was from now on to be regarded as chief among the virtues'.[95] Barrell cites Thomson's appreciation of the farming seasons as 'the most influential of the Georgic poems of the eighteenth century'.[96] Among painters, he identifies John Constable and Thomas Gainsborough. The English Georgic tradition accommodated the pastoral Arcadia as a complementary notion of rural life:

> *It was a mode that celebrated the comforts as well as the rigours of rural life, and one in which the harshness of actuality was carefully mitigated by ornate diction . . . It was the delicacy as well as the practicality of English Georgic that was responsible for its success, and made it well able to reflect that double image of the aristocracy, as the leisured consumers of Britain's wealth, and as the patrons of her agricultural and mercantile expansion.*[97]

Barrell concludes that the English Georgic tradition allowed 'its inhabitants a life of work and play together', and was 'concerned to soften as much as to recommend the hard moral lessons of Virgil's original *Georgics*' in which 'rewards and pleasures are always in the future'.[98] Although industriousness was a virtue for rich and poor, the prosperous were more likely to be rewarded with recreation and repose.

94 Andrews, *The Search for the Picturesque*, p. 64. Refer to Williams, p. 155.

95 Barrell, p. 15.

96 Barrell considers landscapes depicted in paintings and poems but does not extend his discussion to gardens. Barrell, p. 7.

97 Barrell, p. 12.

98 Barrell, pp. 36–37. Refer to Chambers, pp. 7–8.

Cow Castle

As in contemporary farming guides, Thomson combines a Georgic sensibility with a Newtonian conception of the universe. Thomson celebrates the variety of the weather but recognises a fundamental order in the natural sequence of the seasons, which provide a setting for the primacy of culture. In 'A Poem Sacred to the Memory of Sir Isaac Newton', which was published with *The Seasons*, nature is female, passive and subject to Newton: 'Nature herself / Stood all subdu'd by him, and open laid / Her very latent glory to his view'.[99] A drawing of Kent's pyramidal monument to Newton immediately precedes Thomson's poem to the scientist, implying that the architect and poet may have had a comparable understanding of nature. Carved in white and grey marble and installed in Westminster Abbey in

99 Thomson, 'A Poem Sacred to the Memory of Sir Isaac Newton', p. 243. Refer to Bate, 'Living with the Weather', pp. 433, 437, n. 16.

1731, Newton reclines on a sarcophagus, resting an arm on his most famous volumes.[100] Above, a figure representing astronomy surmounts a celestial globe. The Latin inscription praises 'a strength of mind almost divine, and mathematical principles peculiarly his own'. Newton also appears in Stowe's Temple of British Worthies. It is likely that, in common with his age, Kent recognised a practical and spiritual appreciation of nature and a mechanical and secular one. But rather than a discourse on Newtonian thought, his gardens and garden drawings emphasise an engaged, lyrical and hedonistic appreciation of the natural world.

100 Thomson, *The Seasons*, p. 240.

William Kent, *Spring*, illustration for James Thomson's *The Seasons*, 1730. Courtesy of the British Museum.

William Kent, *Summer*, illustration for James Thomson's *The Seasons*, 1730. Courtesy of the British Museum.

Sharing Thomson's sensitivity to the contrasting seasons, Kent provided illustrations for *Spring*, *Summer*, *Autumn* and *Winter*, no doubt recognising parallels between the relaxed and evocative flow of Thomson's poetry and his own developing gardening concerns.[101] Connecting times and places, Kent's illustrations combine classical imagery, indigenous trees and figures in modern dress. In the responses of peoples, buildings and landscapes to changing weathers they eulogise nature's drama. In *Spring* a rainbow arcs beneath a sun encircled by angels. Reclining figures rest under trees in the foreground, a mountainous landscape is

101 Andrews, *The Search for the Picturesque*, p. 10; Hunt, *William Kent*, p. 38; Hussey, *The Picturesque*, p. 54.

William Kent, *Autumn*, illustration for James Thomson's *The Seasons*, 1730. Courtesy of the British Museum.

seen in the distance and a substantial classical villa lies between them. *Summer* seems no more abundant except that attention is given to the bathing figures in the foreground; no buildings are illustrated. *Autumn* is the most populated season. Two figures converse in the foreground – one lying, the other standing – while farmers harvest and riders hunt. Further in the distance, the landscape partly obscures a classical pavilion. In *Winter* a storm rages at sea, bombarding trees on land as people and animals huddle and cower, seeking the protection of a farm building. Like the landscape, the architecture changes according to the seasons;

William Kent, *Winter*, illustration for James Thomson's *The Seasons*, 1730. Courtesy of the British Museum.

the substantial villa in *Spring* is absent in *Summer*, reappears as a pavilion in *Autumn*, and becomes a farm in *Winter*. Confirming the poem's Georgic nature, agricultural labourers appear in Kent's illustrations, while in his drawing of Rousham's Vale of Venus there is a gardener in the lower left-hand corner.

Intimacy is a defining characteristic of Rousham's *genius loci*. In contrast to the monumental grandeur of Holkham and Stowe, Rousham's scale and relationship to the land are comparable to that of a Renaissance villa, recalling the pleasures of rural life praised in classical antiquity. House, garden and farmland are adjacent and visible to each other; the farm is opposite the main entrance to the estate. In the field to the west of the house, beyond the ha-ha, General Dormer introduced long-horned cattle, partly for their aesthetic value. On the far side of the field, the original public entrance and the Gothic Seat are adjacent and set into the high wall to the road. Here agriculture and garden overlap. First, because the cattle in the west field complete the view to the garden buildings beyond. Second, because, sheltering cattle as well as people, the Gothic Seat is nicknamed the 'Cow Castle'.

William Kent, Rousham, 1738–1741. Cow Castle. Photograph, Jonathan Hill.

The *Georgics* inspired Home Park, the section of Stowe given to agriculture, but its purpose was not the efficient cultivation of crops. In contrast, the Cow Castle's purpose is agricultural, aesthetic and symbolic. The difference between Stowe and Rousham is evident in the views they create. Stowe is ordered around a central lake, which collects all the principal views and ensures that the focus is inward. At Rousham, avenues and clearings open onto rural views in all directions. Even the principal sculptures look beyond the garden.[102] Recalling the General's profession, Simon Pugh interprets the garden in terms of military surveillance:

102 Noted by Mavis Batey. Refer to Moggridge, p. 188.

> *It is no coincidence that two of the distinctive features of Rousham are the ridge (giving a 'commanding height' over the countryside) and the haha, the first derived from military tactics and the second from military architecture. It is not fortuitous either that fortifications (the castellated seat) and images of heroic militarism (the gladiator, the arch, Hercules, Marcus Aurelius and Caesar), however stylised, proliferate.*[103]

103 The ha-ha was designed by Bridgeman and retained by Kent. Pugh, pp. 57–58.

But a view can work two ways not just one. Rousham offers views in and out; the house, garden and farm are visible to each other. The interdependence of Rousham's lawns and fields, monuments and cows, aligns the picturesque with the Georgic.

Picturesque Days

As in Virgil's *Georgics*, the English Georgic tradition drew attention to the weather. But the new fascination and respect for the human subject and the natural world, and the relations between them, meant that the weather acquired further significance. Eighteenth-century authors recognised the importance of the weather to the picturesque. In 'Of the Seasons', the final chapter in *Observations on Modern Gardening*, Whately argues that the designer of gardens and garden buildings must take into account the different times of the day and the different seasons. Whately concludes that gardens must be designed for the weather's 'transitory effects' and those that are more predictable:[104]

104 Whately, p. 245.

> *To every view belongs a light which shews it to advantage; every scene and every object is in its highest beauty only at particular hours of the day; and every place is, by its situation and character, peculiarly agreeable in certain months of the year. The seasons thus become subjects of consideration in gardening . . . Different parts*

may thus be adapted to different seasons; and each in its turn will be in perfection.[105]

105 Whately, pp. 242–243.

In *The History of the Modern Taste in Gardening* Walpole only mentions the picturesque occasionally, including once when he discusses the weather. Referring to 'the few picturesque days that we enjoy' he implies that sunlight is necessary to fully appreciate a garden.[106] Kent's garden drawings also focus on fine weather but his illustrations for Thomson are suitably varied. Although he eulogised Italy, Kent understood that picturesque days are not limited to one season. Indicative of pleasurable abundance, inevitable demise and potential return, references to the seasons appear throughout his gardens, buildings, paintings and illustrations.

106 Walpole, *The History of the Modern Taste in Gardening*, p. 50.

Just as each season has its particular pleasures, so do the seasons of a life. One of Rousham's principal themes – the cycles of life and death – is tangible in plants and trees and apparent in monuments and buildings, which are also seen to decay. Kent's concern for nature as metaphor and material was long-held. He even intended to plant dead trees in the grounds of Kensington Palace as an aid to a picturesque naturalism.[107] Such rhetorical devices existed alongside his concern for the continuing effects of weather and weathering.

107 Hussey, *The Picturesque*, p. 130; Kames, vol. 2, p. 335; Price, *An Essay on the Picturesque*, pp. 186–187; Walpole, *The History of the Modern Taste in Gardening*, p. 59; Wilson, *William Kent*, p. 221.

The estate monuments and garden were Kent's principal contribution to Rousham but he also added two new wings to the house, altered its interior and façades, and designed an elegant stable block. One room in particular, the Saloon or Green Parlour – a dining room – emphasises the garden's themes. Kent's oval ceiling painting shows Ceres and Bacchus supporting Venus and Cupid, which can be interpreted as 'Food and Wine sustain Beauty and Love', a line derived from Terence: 'Sine Cerere et Baccho frigit Venus' or 'Without food and wine Love grows cold.'[108] Reminiscent of his illustrations for Thomson, Kent painted the four seasons at the corners of the ceiling: 'Spring is represented by Venus, Summer by Bacchus, Autumn by Ceres, and Winter by an old man in a hooded cloak', writes Gordon.[109] As mythological figures also appear as garden statues, they represent the seasons there as well, creating a dialogue between the actual season and the ones associated with each sculpture. Consequently, whatever the season, all the seasons are present in the garden and the house, as is an awareness of time, weather and the pleasures of food, wine, beauty and love.

108 Terence, 'Eunuch', cited in Gordon, pp. 43, 44. Refer to Cottrell Dormer, p. 37; Mowl, *William Kent*, pp. 238–239.

109 Gordon, p. 45.

Rousham refers to the Arcadian and Elysian narratives of classical antiquity and their relations with the English Georgic tradition and the newly revelatory appreciation of nature. Together, they evoke a blissful existence threatened by decay.[110] Increasingly secular, the eighteenth century emphasised the transitory pleasures of the present more often than the eternal joy of the afterlife. Whether bathed in

110 Barrell, pp. 36–37; Coffin, pp. 412–416; Hunt, 'Verbal Versus Visual Meanings in Garden History', pp. 170–171, 175.

William Kent, Rousham, 1738–1741. Mould growth on Townesend's Building. Photograph, Jonathan Hill.

light or tingling with dew, gardens are inherently sensual. As its iconography attests, erotic love is one of Rousham's principal themes. The garden's many references to impending winter, and death, are indicative of delights made sweeter because they are fleeting. At its centre, the Vale of Venus juxtaposes love and death. The statue of Venus surmounts the rustic cascade; beneath is the tomb and epitaph 'To Ringwood, the Otter-hound', celebrating its skill at the kill.[111] Close to the culmination of Clary's route, Kent's Pyramid is a building type often associated with

111 The tomb and epitaph were added after Kent's work was complete. Frances Elizabeth Cottrell Dormer states that the author was Sir Clement Cottrell Dormer. But her 1902 manuscript dates the epitaph to early in 'this century'. In pencil this is corrected to 'the last century'. Neither matches Sir Clement's era. Cottrell Dormer, 'Account of Rousham', p. 38.a

entombment. Terminating the lawn, Scheemaker's *Lion Attacking the Horse* is a copy of an early seventeenth-century sculpture at the Villa d'Este, which refers to the struggle between Rome and Tivoli – the lion and the horse – and is itself a copy of a sculpture that once stood on the Capitoline Hill in ancient Rome. Another of Scheemaker's sculptures, *Dying Gladiator*, reclines above the Praeneste Terrace. Also a copy of an ancient Roman sculpture, it most likely refers to General Dormer's declining health. Kent originally intended for the sculpture to be mounted on a sarcophagus, an even more emphatic image. As the garden work reached completion, the weather added further resonance. The bitter winter of 1739–1740 initiated the coldest year since 1659 and led to a further freezing winter in 1741.[112] Just then the General died.

112 Lamb, p. 244.

DESIGNING WHILE WALKING

Drawing Forth

The picturesque offered a significant reassessment of the architect's practice, questioning principles and techniques that were first established in the Italian Renaissance, which was indebted to classical antiquity. Plato distrusted art because it mimicked natural objects, which were assumed to already be impure copies of pure forms, merely adding one layer of misrepresentation onto another.[113] Concerned to affirm their intellectual status, Italian Renaissance artists promoted a concept of beauty based on geometric ideals but undermined Plato's argument that the artwork is always inferior to the idea it depicts. Accordingly, an idea could be formulated and drawn forth as the product of creative thought while retaining its claim to universal value. Erwin Panofsky comments that 'In the middle of the sixteenth century it even became customary to designate not only the content of artistic imagination but also the capacity for artistic imagination with the expression "idea," so that the term approximated the word *immaginazione*.'[114] However, as to be creative was to be divine, a Renaissance artist was rarely described as such and only in the eighteenth century was the term regularly applied to an artist as well as to God.[115]

Of little importance to building practice the Medieval drawing was understood as no more than a flat surface and the shapes upon it were but tokens of three-dimensional objects.[116] The Italian Renaissance introduced a fundamental change in perception, implying that the drawing truthfully depicts the three-dimensional

113 Plato distinguishes between arts that produce, and result in things, such as architecture, and arts that imitate, and result in images, such as painting, but considers the difference to be of little significance as things are but images of ideas. Refer to Tatarkiewicz, p. 45.

114 Panofsky, p. 62.

115 Kristeller, 'The Modern System of the Arts, p. 250.

116 There is some suggestion that drawing was used more frequently in the late Middle Ages.

world and is a window to that world, which places the viewer outside and in command of the view. For the first time, the drawing became essential to architectural practice. The term design comes from the Italian *disegno*, meaning drawing, suggesting both the drawing of a line on paper and the drawing forth of an idea. *Disegno* implies a direct link between an idea and a thing. As Vilém Flusser remarks: 'The word is derived from the Latin signum, meaning "sign", and shares the same ancient root.'[117] Establishing architecture, painting and sculpture as liberal arts associated with the intellect, the command of drawing, not building, unlocked the status of the architect. In the new division of labour, architecture resulted not from the accumulation of a team of anonymous craftsman working together on a construction site but the artistic creation of an individual architect in command of drawing who designed a building as a whole at a remove from construction. Joseph Rykwert notes, however, that this transition did not occur simultaneously across nations: 'The profession of architect was isolated in Italy about 1450, in France a century later, and in Britain almost a century after France. Inigo Jones was probably the first Briton to use the word in the sense in which it was coming to be used in the rest of Europe.'[118]

117 Flusser, p. 17.

118 Rykwert, *The First Moderns*, p. 121.

The sixteenth-century painter and architect Giorgio Vasari was crucial to the promotion of *disegno*: 'one may conclude that this design is nothing but a visual expression and clarification of that concept which one has in the intellect, and that which one imagines in the mind'.[119] In 1563 Vasari founded the first art academy, the *Accademia del Disegno* in Florence. A model for art and architecture schools ever since, the academy enabled painters, sculptors and architects to converse independently of the craft guilds. Replacing workshop instruction with a studio education in drawing and geometry, the academy emphasised intellectual not manual labour.

119 Vasari, p. 205.

Renaissance architects, such as Palladio, valued the pleasures of life as well as references to the ideal. But *disegno* is concerned with the immaterial idea of architecture more than the material fabric of building. Confusion arose because the architectural drawing depends on two related but distinct concepts. One claims that the drawing is the truthful representation of the building, indicating the architect's mastery of the building site. The other indicates that drawing is an intellectual, artistic activity distant from the grubby materiality of building. Education in the academy and the dissemination of architectural ideas in books led architects to ignore distinctions between the drawing and the building. As Mario Carpo remarks: 'For many Renaissance architects, the Pantheon and the Colosseum were not places in Rome. They were places in books.'[120] Whether in front of a drawing or a building, the architect could focus on the forms and proportions he had been educated to

120 Carpo, p. 46.

appreciate. But for the knowing and reflective architect, the qualities of a drawing could be a catalyst for architectural innovation, as in Kent's appreciation of the *quadraturisti*.

Design as it was first conceived has a number of failings. First, it suggests that only the architect is creative. Second, it fails to recognise the creativity of the user and others involved in the conception, production and reception of architecture. Third, it promotes the superiority of the intellect. Fourth, it denigrates the manual, material and experiential. The highly influential concept that ideas are superior to matter is nothing but a prejudice. One option is to dismiss it, concluding that its effect on architecture is only negative because it denies the materiality of architecture and encourages architects to chase after artistic status that they will never fully attain, may not need, and should question. But the original meaning of design, as the drawing of a line and the drawing forth of an idea, remains valuable to architectural practice and research as long as its limitations are acknowledged and challenged.

Imagination and Experience

The history of design from the fifteenth to the twenty-first centuries is not seamless, and an important departure occurred in the eighteenth century, when the meaning of a design and an idea changed significantly. As the fine arts were opposed to utility, the design disciplines that proliferated due to industrialisation were categorised as applied arts at best. Painters and sculptors discarded design once it became associated with collective authorship, industrial production and forms made without ideas in mind. Among the fine arts, which include the three original visual arts, only in architecture is the term regularly used today. In the discourse of architects, the older meaning of design – drawing ideas – and the newer meaning of design – drawing appliances – are both in evidence. As many people outside the architectural discipline associate design with its newer meaning, architectural design is often misunderstood.

In the Italian Renaissance an idea was understood to be intellectual, immaterial and universal. Subsequently, the Baroque drew some attention to subjective interpretation. For example, Baroque drama exploited the dialectical potential of allegory, in which meanings are not fixed but endlessly changing and open to appropriation and revision.[121] Significantly due to the influence of empiricism, the eighteenth century acknowledged that ideas are provisional and dependent on experience at conception, production and reception. The attention given to subjectivity increased

121 Benjamin, *The Origin of German Tragic Drama*, pp. 159–161.

awareness of the conditions that affect perception. Any change in the weather, the time of the day or the knowledge, position or mood of the viewer can influence understanding, so that even an object seemingly as solid as a building may not seem the same from one moment to the next. Recognition that creativity and perception are subjective and changeable transformed the visual arts, its objects, authors and viewers. Rather than being a cohesive body of knowledge dependent on universal ideas and proportions, architecture was increasingly associated with subjective imagination and experience.

As Inigo Jones was the first Briton to practise in the manner of the Italian Renaissance architect committed to *disegno*, the architect was barely established in Britain when another type of architect appeared alongside the first. The earliest example of such a design practice in the eighteenth century occurred in gardens, not buildings, because they incorporated the natural world and were more clearly subject to change. Although the pleasures of the picturesque were limited to the educated and prosperous, notable principles were established. The picturesque was the first visual language to fully recognise that beauty is subjective and dependent on experience. Valuing the individuality of the designer and the user, early eighteenth-century garden design was a significant departure in the practice of the architect. Rather than being conceived according to the rules of geometry in a distant studio, Rousham was designed the way it was experienced, by a figure moving across a landscape and imagining future movements. Rather than consider the site as a *tabula rasa*, Kent worked with an existing topography and an existing garden. Rather than follow an inflexible vision, he adjusted his design in response to the conditions found during construction and the advice of the steward and head gardener supervising the site. Rather than design with orthogonal drawings, he made no plans, sections and elevations. Instead, Kent designed through views that show not a single linear perspective but multiple perspectives and alternative routes that encourage visitors to construct personal journeys. Spaces were not intended for specific uses and Kent's garden drawings reflect the varied activities he had in mind. Rousham suggests diverse ideas and allegories. Many of the garden monuments are highly specific – a pyramid, a dying gladiator, a statue of Venus – but no overall meaning is apparent. This combination of specificity and ambiguity is essential to the garden's character.

The picturesque gave new emphasis to the environment, acknowledging the senses and the seasons and weather's contribution to perception and understanding. Exemplifying a concern for time, pleasure and decay in a garden and a life, the weather is Rousham's emblem. Daily apparent in dew and drizzle, represented in paintings and monuments, Rousham's attention to the changing seasons

suggests a garden – and a building – that is like the weather in all its subtle variety. Just as the daily weather is part of a larger weather pattern, the early eighteenth-century picturesque garden is a means to engage the subjective and the social. Set within a historical and philosophical context, Stowe is a political manifesto while Rousham's themes are life, love and death, affirming the English Georgic tradition of labour and leisure, poetry and pragmatism. But the early eighteenth-century garden also heralded an engagement with nature beyond the Georgic. Eulogising nature as the means of self-revelation, Rousham implied a burgeoning romanticism.

William Kent, Rousham, 1738–1741. Mossy cascade, Vale of Venus. Photograph, Bradley Starkey.

3

a life in ruins

INTRODUCTION

The late eighteenth- and early nineteenth-century picturesque is the focus of this chapter. Its central figure is John Soane, notably his house, office and museum at 12–14 Lincoln's Inn Fields, London, which he transformed between 1792 and 1837. Drawing parallels between Jean-Jacques Rousseau's *Confessions*, William Beckford's Fonthill Abbey and Laurence Sterne's *Tristram Shandy*, 'A Life in Ruins' discusses Soane's architectural autobiography and the themes of dynasty and decay that fuelled it. Concluding my investigation of Soane, Chapter 4 analyses his fascination for the architectural potential of gardens, climate and weather.

A HISTORY OF MY HOUSE[1]

1 In 1812 Soane wrote 'Crude Hints towards a History of My House in L(incoln's) I(nn) Fields'.

One of the residential squares that developed around the City of London, and close to the Inns of Court, Lincoln's Inn Fields was run by a trust that was founded in 1734 to maintain the square and the garden at its centre. Susan Palmer remarks:

> *All the owners of property in the square paid an annual rate to the Trust, and from this were funded the upkeep of the paving and the central garden, and the employment of a lamplighter, a gardener, a scavenger to keep the carriage and footways clean and to take away rubbish from the houses, a beadle to keep the peace and watchmen to protect the inhabitants and their houses at night.*[2]

2 Palmer, *The Soanes at Home*, p. 1.

Appointed architect to the Bank of England in 1788 and inheriting a fortune from his wife's uncle in 1790, Soane bought 12 Lincoln's Inn Fields in 1792 and soon rebuilt it, moving there in 1794. One of his earliest interventions, the Breakfast Parlour at Number 12, has a ceiling painted with a pergola and foliage, a fashion in sixteenth-century Italy that was revived in the late eighteenth century throughout Europe.[3] The house faced onto the square; to the rear was the office, entered from Whetstone Park, the lane to the north. In 1808 Soane acquired 13 Lincoln's Inn Fields, accommodating his expanded office and museum at the back of the house, which was connected to the rear of Number 12 in 1809. Beginning in 1812 Soane rebuilt the front of Number 13, including the Library–Dining Room and Breakfast Parlour. Moving there in 1813 he connected the house at the front to the office and museum at the rear of Numbers 12 and 13. Occupied by the former tenant of Number 13, the front of Number 12 was separated from the rear. In 1823 Soane bought 14 Lincoln's Inn Fields. Starting to rebuild it in 1824, he added the Picture

3 Completed in 1794, the artist was John Crace. Thornton and Dorey. p. 92.

Sir John Soane, The Breakfast Parlour, looking north, 13 Lincoln's Inn Fields. Photograph, Martin Charles. Courtesy of the Trustees of Sir John Soane's Museum, London.

Room, Monk's Parlour and Monk's Yard at the rear of Number 14 and inserted the Colonnade at the rear of Number 13.

Soane's ambition to establish an architectural dynasty was frustrated by his sons' limited ability. Instead, he established a dynasty of influence, offering his house, office and museum as a model for architects. The Soane Museum Act of Parliament, 1833, established future public access to 12–14 Lincoln's Inn Fields. The buildings' combined functions continued after Soane's death because his second floor bedroom and bathroom became the curator's apartment, a tradition that was terminated only in the mid-twentieth century.

The Renaissance revived the ancient Roman concern for collecting. Susan Feinberg Millenson writes that 'The word "museum" appeared at this time, signifying a nobleman's collection . . . The Renaissance originated two museological types: the antiquarium and the cabinet.'[4] The antiquarium is a collection of antiquities; the cabinet of curiosities is more wide-ranging, reflecting the collector's knowledge

4 Millenson, p. 129.

and personality. Soane's museum is an antiquarium and a cabinet of curiosities. It is also a public museum, a feature of the Enlightenment. Established by an Act of Parliament in 1753, the British Museum is typical of such a museum, ordering information according to a logical system in conjunction with the development of new scientific disciplines such as archaeology and ethnography. Even at the start of the twenty-first century the British Museum's director, Neil MacGregor, continued its original purpose: 'to get the whole world in one building'. [5] In the discussions that preceded the Soane Museum Act, Sir Robert Peel, in a similar spirit, proposed that Soane's collection should be absorbed within the British Museum, failing to recognise that the building is part of the collection.[6] Britain's first museum of architecture, 12–14 Lincoln's Inn Fields reflects the Enlightenment concern for categorisation by discipline; its many ancient artefacts also affirm the Enlightenment concern for origins. But Soane's museum is not ordered by subject, type or chronology. Objects and settings are composed according to mood and effect. Due to its eclectic collection, emphasis on atmosphere, poetic appreciation of history and identification with an individual, 12–14 Lincoln's Inn Fields is a museum of the romantic self as well as the rational one.[7]

FALLEN, FALLEN, FALLEN

Inserted after the 1833 Act, Sir Francis Chantrey's white marble bust of Soane is the focus of the Dome Area at the museum's centre.[8] At his request, the Act required that the house, office and museum should remain 'as nearly as possible in the state in which Sir John Soane shall leave it'.[9] Wanting to preserve 12–14 Lincoln's Inn Fields as his monument, Soane protected it from ruination but the ruin is a recurring theme of his architecture,[10] indebted to Giovanni Battista Piranesi and the picturesque in particular.[11] Late in his life Soane exclaimed: 'O Architecture! thou Queen of the Fine Arts, – my first love, – my friend through life, and the prop of my declining years, how art thou fallen, fallen, fallen.'[12]

As a metaphor for time, the fascination for ruins was known in ancient Rome and the Middle Ages and furthered in the Renaissance. While ruins were contemplated rather than constructed in ancient Rome, David Watkin suggests that Hadrian's Villa at Tivoli can be considered an exception to this rule. In that it inspired 'the sixteenth-century intoxication with ruins', Watkin gives particular credit to Colonna's *Hypteromachia Poliphili,* 1499.[13] Set in a sylvan landscape through which lovers journey, the ruined temples and broken columns in Colonna's narrative are representative of love interlinked with time.

5 MacGregor, quoted in Jury, p. 23.

6 Summerson and Dorey, p. 125.

7 Millenson, pp. 134–146.

8 Chantrey was a fellow Royal Academecian; the bust was carved in 1828.

9 The Soane Museum Act of Parliament, quoted in Summerson and Dorey, p. 126.

10 Soane, 'Crude Hints', pp. 61, 65.

11 In *The Union of Architecture, Sculpture and Painting; Exemplified by a Series of Illustrations, with Descriptive Accounts of the House and Galleries of John Soane*, 1827, John Britton repeatedly refers to the picturesque. John Summerson describes 1806–1821 as Soane's picturesque period but this chronology is unlikely as Soane's concern for the picturesque was longstanding. Summerson, 'Soane: the Man and the Style', pp. 10, 14.

12 Soane, *Description of the House and Museum*, 1830, p. 30.

13 Watkin, 'Built Ruins', p. 5.

Joseph Michael Gandy, *The Dome Area at Night, Looking East*, 1811, 12–14 Lincoln's Inn Fields. Courtesy of the Trustees of Sir John Soane's Museum, London.

Hadrian's Villa, Tivoli, 2nd century AD. The Thermal Baths. Photograph, Jonathan Hill.

The first building known to have been constructed as a ruin was the Barchetto, *c.*1530, which Girolamo Genga created as a retreat for Francesco Maria I della Rovere, Duke of Urbino, in his park at Pesaro. At the same time, these themes were explored in Giulio Romano's Palazzo del Té, notably the dropped triglyphs in the courtyard frieze and the collapsing columns in the frescoes of the Sala dei Giganti, which Kent admired.

The concern for ruination came to fruition in the eighteenth century due to empiricism's attention to subjective experience, the heightened historical awareness in the Enlightenment's concern for origins and archaeology, and the value given to imagination, time and metaphor in the picturesque and romanticism. Whether found or fabricated, the ruin related the present to a particular past, imagined or real. It could evoke a lost idyll that would never be repeated, transfer gravitas and authority from one era to another, or suggest that the successes of the present would surpass those of the past.

For the many graduates of the Grand Tour, the ruin offered a parallel between imperial Rome and modern Britain and recalled the personal pleasures of an Italian sojourn. For an individual and a nation, the ruin also indicated fearful decay, evoking life and death in a single object. Diminishing an object physically but expanding its metaphorical potential, ruination drew attention to the environment. Weathered and overgrown, the ruin provided a means to negotiate between culture and nature – a principal theme of the time – as Anne Janowitz acknowledges:

> *What is true for the artefact is true for the nation: in the eighteenth-century ruin sentiment the cultural entity (Britain) was also forged as inextricable from the natural entity (the countryside), not merely superimposed but blended, and the nation came to be understood* as *nature.*[14]

In 1709, anticipating picturesque theory later in the century, Vanbrugh argued unsuccessfully that the medieval ruins of 'ancient Woodstock' Manor should be retained for their historical association and visual effect when seen from Blenheim Palace, Oxfordshire, then being constructed for the Duke of Marlborough.[15] Together the ruins and their setting 'wou'd make One of the Most Agreeable Objects that the best of Landskip Painters can invent'.[16] Clearly unappreciative, the Duchess of Marlborough dismissed Vanbrugh's request as 'ridiculous'.[17]

In *New Principles of Gardening,* 1728, Batty Langley proposed the fabricated classical ruin as a garden monument. A gothic ruin was equally viable as Rousham's Temple of the Mill attests. Publications such as Antoine Desgodtez's *Les Edifices antiques de Rome, dessinés et mesurés trés exactement*, 1682, Robert Wood's *The Ruins of Palmyra*, 1753, Julien-David Le Roy's *Les Ruines des plus Beaux Monuments de la Grèce*, 1758, James Stuart and Nicholas Revett's *The Antiquities of Athens*, vol. 1, 1762, and Robert Adam's *Ruins of the Palace of Emperor Diocletian at Spoleto*, 1764, furthered fascination for classical architecture. However, these works fall into two distinct categories: the analytical depiction of antiquities promoted by Desgodtez, Wood, Stuart and Revett, and the emotive evocation of ruins and the effects of time on architecture that concerned LeRoy and Adam.[18] While the former group was opposed to the picturesque, the latter celebrated it. In Rome, Adam studied under Charles-Louis Clérisseau, who was a pupil of Panini, the noted painter of ruins who Kent met in Rome. Soane became an avid collector of Clérisseau, who in 1766 designed a *trompe l'oeil* Ruin Room at SS Trinità dei Monti in Rome, with bushes and branches growing among broken walls and a coffered ceiling fractured by time. However, the primary

14 Janowitz, p. 5. Refer also to Baridon, pp. 93–94.

15 Vanbrugh, p. 231.

16 Vanbrugh, p. 232.

17 Duchess of Marlborough, quoted in Vanbrugh, p. 232.

18 Redford, pp. 44–82.

eighteenth-century influence on the emotive depiction of ruins was clearly Piranesi, who published his first engraved views of ancient ruins, *Prima Parte*, in 1743. Although the fascination for ruination was linked to a growing temporal awareness, a preserved or constructed ruin could have the opposite effect. Reducing decay to an aesthetic, it denied further change and prevented analysis of ruination's causes and effects.

Charles-Louis Clérisseau, *View or Capriccio of a Ruined, Vaulted Interior*, 1766. Courtesy of the Trustees of Sir John Soane's Museum, London.

Giovanni Battista Piranesi, *An Architectural Fantasy*, 1755. Courtesy of the Trustees of Sir John Soane's Museum, London.

Soane enrolled to study architecture at the Royal Academy in 1771, three years after its foundation. A successful student, he was awarded the King's Travelling Scholarship in 1777, which funded a tour of Italy: 'This was the most fortunate event of my life, for it was the means by which I formed those connexions to which I owe all the advantages I have since enjoyed.'[19] Offering guidance, Sir William Chambers gave Soane a copy of a letter he had prepared for another pupil in 1774: 'Seek for those who have most reputation, young or old, amongst which forget not Piranesi, whom you may see in my name; he is full of matter, extravagant it is true, often absurd, but from his overflowings you may gather much information.'[20] In 1778 Soane met Piranesi shortly before his death. Donating four engraved views of the ancient monuments and ruins of the city, the 'tutor' indicated his respect for the 'pupil'. Soane continued to collect Piranesi. Fifteen ink and wash drawings of the temples at Paestum hang on the hinged walls of the Picture Room at 12–14 Lincoln's Inn Fields, close to 'two Drawings of Ruins' by Panini.[21] Many of Piranesi's images refer to known places while others are fictive. But all are works of the

19 Soane, *Memoirs*, p. 12.

20 Chambers, letter to a pupil, 5 August 1774, quoted in Soane, *Memoirs*, p. 12.

21 Soane, *Description of the House and Museum*, 1832, p. 17.

imagination. Depicting multiple, discontinuous vistas of complex and fragmented spaces, they were a significant influence on Soane, who described part of 12–14 Lincoln's Inn Fields as 'one of those Carcerian dark Staircases represented in some of Piranesi's ingenious dreams for prisons'.[22] Christopher Thacker writes that Piranesi stimulated 'one of the main themes of romanticism, in which man, modern man, is saddened, frightened, or crushed by the strength and relentlessness of forces outside him – time, or nature, or simply "life"'.[23] According to Tafuri, Piranesi's ruinous world indicates that the eighteenth century condemned language to incoherence: 'a universe of empty signs is a place of total disorder'.[24] But ruins are not empty signs. Kames, in *Elements of Criticism*, and Whately in *Observations on Modern Gardening*, discuss ruins in relation to the association of ideas. Stating that the garden should stimulate the mind, Whately notes that ruins are particularly effective in this regard, more so than entire buildings, 'for imperfection and obscurity are their properties; and to carry the imagination to something greater than is seen, their effect'.[25] Richly suggestive because they are incomplete, ruins can imply potential as well as loss. To contemplate the past is also to imagine the future, and ruination is often a precursor to change.

Soane's concern for ruination was inseparable from his fascination for construction. Intrigued by a building's unfinished state, Soane required his pupils to further their education by drawing his buildings under construction.[26] For his drawing collection he purchased three engravings of Piranesi's 1794 rendering of Robert Mylne's Blackfriars Bridge, maybe the most famous eighteenth-century depiction of the construction process. Soane continued to alter 12–14 Lincoln's Inn Fields between the 1833 Act and his death in 1837 at the age of 84. If he had lived longer he would no doubt have made further changes. Visiting 12–14 Lincoln's Inn Fields today it is easy to ignore how different it was in Soane's lifetime. Rather than calm, composed and silent, 12–14 Lincoln's Fields was often a bustling building site where Soane remained while the three adjacent buildings were acquired, demolished, constructed, adjusted and rebuilt again.[27]

Demolition is essential to construction and building sites often appear ruinous. Richard Weston notes 'the feeling, widely shared amongst Romantic Classicists, such as Piranesi, that the full grandeur of architecture was revealed, rather than "softened", by partial ruination. Hence, in part, Sir John Soane's predilection for making presentation drawings of his designs as ruins'.[28] At Soane's request, in 1798 Joseph Gandy painted *The Bank of England, London: View of the Rotunda Imagined as a Ruin* in a manner reminiscent of Piranesi, depicting workers picking over the debris in a dark and foreboding light. At the Royal Academy in 1832 Gandy's painting was exhibited as *Architectural Ruins – A Vision*. In 1830 Gandy produced *A Bird's-*

22 Soane refers to Piranesi's etchings of imaginary prisons, the *Carceri*, 1750. Soane, 'Crude Hints', p. 63.

23 Thacker, p. 52.

24 Tafuri, *Architecture and Utopia*, p. 19.

25 Kames, vol. 2, p. 333; Whately, p. 131.

26 Richardson, *Building in Progress*, pp. 2, 7; Thornton and Dorey, p. 39.

27 After the death of his wife, Eliza, in 1815, Soane lived there alone with only his wife's terrier, Fanny. Soane's assistants and pupils were present during the working day and five staff and the housekeeper, Mrs Sarah Conduitt, maintained the house.

28 Weston, p. 122.

Joseph Michael Gandy, *The Bank of England, London: View of the Rotunda Imagined as a Ruin*, 1798, exhibited at the Royal Academy in 1832 as *Architectural Ruins – A Vision*. Courtesy of the Trustees of Sir John Soane's Museum, London.

Eye View of the Bank of England seemingly in ruins. But the painting is sometimes less poetically described as a cut-away perspective as decay is not obvious.[29]

Although the fashion was then on the wane, Soane fabricated ruins at two houses that he designed for his own use. At Pitzhanger Manor, Ealing, which he began to rebuild as his country residence in 1800, the ruins in the twenty-eight acre garden were of a Roman temple made from new.[30] Including thirteenth-century stonework from the Old Palace of Westminster, the ruins in the Monk's Yard at 12–14 Lincoln's Inn Fields are gothic, which Soane associated with English history as others had done before him.[31] In both instances Soane imagined that the ruins had been discovered, not recently built: 'to produce pleasing sensations there must be an appearance of truth and they must recall to the mind the idea of real objects and not be considered as mere pictures'.[32] Soane's memoirs describe the 'discovery' of Pitzhanger's ruins:

> *we perceived among the trees mutilated shafts of columns covered in ivy, wild roses, and briers. On removing some of the brambles and other obstacles, the ruins appeared to be of greater importance and extent than had at first been anticipated.*

29 Thornton and Dorey, p.98; Woodward, *In Ruins*, p. 164.

30 Dated 30 June 1802, and printed in 1833, Soane's *Plans, Elevations and Perspective Views of Pitzhanger Manor-House, and of the Ruins of an Edifice of Roman Architecture, Situated on the Border of Ealing Green, with a Description of the Ancient and Present State of the Manor-House, in a Letter to a Friend* was later absorbed into *Memoirs of the Professional Life of an Architect, between the Years 1768 and 1835. Written by Himself*, 1835.

Joseph Michael Gandy, *A Bird's-Eye View of the Bank of England*, 1830. Courtesy of the Trustees of Sir John Soane's Museum, London.

Geometrical elevations and a plan were made, from which the whole assumed the character of a regular composition. The ruins were afterwards represented in perspective, and an attempt made to restore the exterior to its original state.[33]

Whether classical or gothic, ruins developed the eighteenth-century discourse on nationhood and nature. But, ultimately, the attention given to the ruin reflected the attention given to subjectivity. The visionary ruins of Piranesi and Soane were appropriate to an era that valued self-expression, temporal awareness, multiple meanings and the potential for language's reinvention. Whether positive or negative, thoughts of change unavoidably led to thoughts of decay. As early as the end of the sixteenth century, English 'painters began to introduce ruins into the backgrounds of their society portraits. They were metaphors of the inevitability of the subject's death', remarks Christopher Woodward.[34] Soane linked the ruin of a building to the ruin of a life. In 'Crude Hints towards a History of My House in L(incoln's) I(nn) Fields', 1812, he imagines that his home is first occupied by lawyers and then left to decay. Assumed to be haunted, the house has no visitors until a future visitor, on finding it in ruins, attempts to decipher its earlier purpose and character.[35] In 'Crude Hints' Soane is obsessed by his future reputation and concerned that it will diminish and decay. Watkin concludes: 'What is surely exceptional is that since this melancholy document is dated 30 August, 7 September

31 Soane, 'Lecture X', in Watkin, *Sir John Soane*, p. 626. Refer to Dorey, 'Sir John Soane's Courtyard Gardens at Lincoln's Inn Fields', pp. 18–21.

32 Soane, 'Lecture X', in Watkin, *Sir John Soane,* p. 626.

33 Soane, *Memoirs*, p. 65.

34 Woodward, *In Ruins*, p. 95.

35 Soane, 'Crude Hints', p. 73.

and 22 September 1812, it was composed at exactly the moment when he was building no. 13 Lincoln's Inn Fields.'[36] In an era increasingly concerned with origins and memorials, Soane's concern for funerary monuments even surpassed that of his contemporaries.[37] Soane did not profess his religious beliefs and avoided Christian symbols in his buildings, but it is likely that he was a Deist like Shafesbury, acknowledging a distant, non-interfering God who leaves us to make our way as best we can.[38]

Conceiving 12–14 Lincoln's Inn Fields as a ruin, and ruining as much as he built, Soane collected, fabricated and remade ruins for over forty years. Soane established the 1833 Act to retain the grandeur of his architecture beyond the ruin of his life. Rather than a ruin open to actual decay, the Act conceived 12–14 Lincoln's Inn Fields as a fabricated and preserved ruin, a metaphor rather than a register of decay. Open to the past, present and future, the living ruin of Soane's lifetime is the better model for architecture's dialogue with time than the static ruin we see today.

36 Watkin, *Sir John Soane*, p. 81.

37 Watkin, 'Monuments and Mausolea', p. 9. Refer to Summerson, 'Sir John Soane', pp. 147–155.

38 Gittings, p. 50; Watkin, *Sir John Soane*, p. 80.

ABBOT WILLIAM, FATHER JOHN

In 1787 William Beckford commissioned Soane to transform a seventy-feet long second floor passage into a top-lit picture gallery at Fonthill Splendens, the Palladian house built by his father on the Fonthill estate in Wiltshire. But Soane only made minor alterations to Fonthill Splendens before its demolition in 1807. Beckford and Soane's working relationship was slight and their social meetings were infrequent. But they were kindred spirits and remained in contact throughout their lives, as 'Soane's Note Books' indicate.[39] Sharing an affinity for Piranesi, picturesque theory and French authors of the eighteenth century, their libraries contained many of the same volumes.[40]

Soane's evolving building work at 12–14 Lincoln's Inn Fields paralleled that of Beckford at Fonthill. Beckford's father created 'enchanting and frightening grottoes in the manner of the Savage Picturesque'.'[41] But reputedly the wealthiest man in eighteenth-century England, Beckford's ambitions were grander. Philippe Jacques de Loutherbourg, a painter and frequent visitor to 12–14 Lincoln's Inn Fields, transformed Fonthill into an oriental wonderland for Beckford's twenty-first birthday celebrations in 1781.[42] Beckford then commissioned an extensive picturesque landscape that was typical of the late eighteenth-century concern for wild and sudden variation, including an Alpine Garden, two grottoes and a hermitage. In 1793 he commissioned a wall around his estate, which extended for twelve miles

39 For example, Soane met Beckford in London on 5 and 17 December 1813. They met again on 14 May 1829. On 19 September 1829 Soane left his card at Beckford's home in Bath and visited two days later. Soane, 'Soane's Note Books', vol. 8, 1811–1813, pp. 121–122; vol. 13, 1829–1831, p. 20, p. 37.

40 Watkin, 'Beckford, Soane, and Hope', pp. 42–48.

41 Mowl, 'William Beckford', p. 18.

42 Eliza Soane, 'Mrs Soane's Note Books, 1804–1813', pp. 7, 33, 52 (3 May 1804, 23 and 26 June 1805, 24 March 1806).

and enclosed 1,900 acres. At the end of the eighteenth century he appointed James Wyatt to design a house appropriate to the setting. Construction began in 1796 and was complete in 1807; the design evolved as building work progressed. Built close to the site of a medieval priory, Fonthill Abbey's cruciform plan, high central tower and irregular composition recalled a monastic complex, furthering the fashion for the gothic in architecture and literature, which the picturesque had renewed and romanticism extended. Fêting 'this Gothick country' Kent regularly incorporated the gothic into his designs, illustrating Spenser's *The Faerie Queene* with castles and knights.[43] In 1750 Horace Walpole, the author of *The History of the Modern Taste in Gardening*, began his gothic revival house at Strawberry Hill, Twickenham, and in 1764 published his acclaimed novel *The Castle of Otranto*. A gothic tale set within a ruined building became a familiar literary form, the raw but highly charged surroundings reflecting the characters' emotions.

43 Kent, 30 January 1720, quoted in Hunt, *William Kent*, p. 51.

John Britton's *The Union of Architecture, Sculpture and Painting; Exemplified by a Series of Illustrations, with Descriptive Accounts of the House and Galleries*

James Wyatt, Fonthill Abbey, Wiltshire, 1796. *View of the South Front*, John Rutter, *Delineations of Fonthill and its Abbey*, 1823, plate 12.

of John Soane, 1827, was the first guide to 12–14 Lincoln's Inn Fields. But Soane had reservations about the result and decided to prepare his own publication. Following earlier editions in 1830 and 1832, Soane's *Description of the House and Museum on the North Side of Lincoln's Inn Fields*, 1835, includes sections by Barbara Hofland, his friend since at least 1811.[44] In one, she refers to 'the Prior of Alcobaça, described with such inimitable humour by the author of "Vathek"'.[45] No record remains of Beckford's original manuscript, which was written in French. Without mentioning the author, his literary adviser, Rev. Samuel Henley, first published *Vathek* in 1786 as an English translation with the title *An Arabian Tale, from an Unpublished Manuscript with Notes Critical and Explanatory*. Evoking the extravagant and atmospheric architecture of Samarah, the Caliph's capital, *Vathek* drew attention to the oriental as successfully as Walpole had to the gothic. Increasingly frequent encounters with peoples and places beyond Europe's classical heritage led to new sites for cultural and commercial exchange and exploitation, stimulating profits as well as poems. With objects and artefacts from Egypt, China and South America as well as Europe, Soane's collection was appropriately exotic, while Jamaican sugar plantations manned by slave labour were a source of the Beckfords' wealth.[46]

Beckford styled himself 'Abbot' of Fonthill, while Soane imagined a 'pious monk' among Pitzhanger's ruins and 'Padre Giovanni' – Father John – at 12–14 Lincoln's Inn Fields.[47] The pious monk is surely Father John, Soane himself. From the Monk's Parlour at 12–14 Lincoln's Inn Fields: 'the Ruins of a Monastery arrest the attention. The interest created in the mind of the spectator, on visiting the abode of the monk, will not be weakened by wandering among the ruins of his once noble monastery.'[48] Prophetically, the ruins in the Monk's Yard were completed in 1824, two years after Beckford sold the Abbey due to financial pressures, and one year before Fonthill's high central tower collapsed, turning the Abbey into a ruin. The landscape and a fragment of the building survive, fulfilling the picturesque sensibility for a ruin. In 1844 a visitor to the Abbey evocatively acknowledged the particular poignancy of the recently ruined:

> *Ruins that have been such for ages, whose tenants have long since been swept away, recall ideas of persons and times so far back that we have no sympathy with them at all; but if you wish for a sight of all that is melancholy, all that is desolate, visit a modern ruin. We passed through briars and brambles into the great octagon. Straight before us stands the western doorway of the noble entrance hall; but where is its oaken roof, with its proud heraldic emblazonments, where its lofty painted windows, where its ponderous doors, more than 30 feet high?*[49]

44 Written in 1835, Hofland's account of 12–14 Lincoln's Inn Fields first appeared in Soane's *Description of the House and Museum on the North Side of Lincoln's Inn Fields*, 1835. In 1919 it was published as *Popular Description of Sir John Soane's House, Museum and Library*. Hofland, p. 6.

45 Hofland, quoted in Soane, *Description of the House and Museum*, 1835, p. 28.

46 Neither Beckford nor Soane indicated an allegiance to one style. After selling Fonthill, Beckford commissioned a neo-classical tower in Bath.

47 Soane, *Memoirs*, pp. 65–66.

48 Soane, *Description of the House and Museum*, 1835, p. 26.

49 Lansdown. p. 40.

Joseph Michael Gandy, *The Monk's Yard Looking East*, 1825, 12–14 Lincoln's Inn Fields. Courtesy of the Trustees of Sir John Soane's Museum, London.

Introspective speculation on impending ruination can be debilitating, as Soane acknowledged: 'At home all day a prey to melancholy and gloomy reflections.'[50] Beckford and Soane were united in their admiration for the confessional literature of Jean-Jacques Rousseau and aimed for a comparable level of self-expression in their buildings and collections.[51] In 1770 Rousseau began private readings of his autobiographical *Confessions*, which was published posthumously in 1781.[52] Beckford and Soane 'identified with Rousseau as the victim of organized persecution and as a justification for self-obsession; psychologically, both suffered from perse-

50 Soane, 'Soane's Note Books', vol. 11, 1820–1822, p. 29, entry dated 22 November 1820.

51 Soane refers to Rousseau twice in his memoirs. Soane, *Memoirs*, pp. 19, 59.

52 Rousseau, *The Confessions*.

cution, real in Beckford's case, largely imaginary in Soane's' writes Watkin.[53] Recalling his unsuccessful application to be Surveyor to St Paul's Cathedral, Soane complained: 'I was represented as a man unqualified for the situation – ignorant of the principles of Architecture – brought up as a hack in Mr. Dance's office.' [54] Cataloguing a lifetime of criticism, Soane recalls:

> *the number of attacks on my professional and moral character; which commenced in the year 1786, on my appointment as Architect to the Governor and Company of the Bank of England, and which have been continued to the present time, through the medium of the public prints and anonymous letters. In some of these attacks I have been charged with suffering my nearest relatives to exist in a state of 'pauperism' whilst I am squandering my money by hundreds and thousands in the ostentatious gratification of pride and vanity.*[55]

Rousseau's romantic, uncompromising and persecuted self-expression was 'a turning point in the development of modern consciousness', an act of reinvention in which Rousseau created Rousseau.[56] Galvanised by the eighteenth-century preoccupation with the self, Fonthill Abbey and 12–14 Lincoln's Inn Fields are intensely personal autobiographies,[57] in which the author edited and reinvented his life as he reflected upon it. As Paul de Man remarks: 'We assume that life *produces* the autobiography as an act produces its consequences, but can we not suggest, with equal justice, that the autobiographical project may itself produce and determine the life.'[58] A writer metaphorically inhabits a book. But Soane literally lived in his autobiography. At 12–14 Lincoln's Inn Fields the evolving process of design and redesign, construction and demolition, was a means to deface as well as to elevate its architect.[59] Changing his name, Soane continued the tradition that Palladio and Kent had favoured and Ludwig Mies van der Rohe and Le Corbusier would continue.[60] The son of a bricklayer and the product of a poor and uneducated family that he never mentioned, Soan created Soane in 1783, even correcting all his earlier signatures to match his chosen name.[61]

THE LIVES AND OPINIONS OF TRISTRAM SHANDY AND JOHN SOANE, GENTLEMEN

An English literary parallel to Soane's work at Lincoln's Inn Fields is Laurence Sterne's *The Life and Opinions of Tristram Shandy, Gentleman,* published in nine volumes between 1759 and 1767. In the eighteenth century the influence of the

53 Watkin, 'Beckford, Soane, and Hope', p. 35.

54 Soane entered the office of George Dance the younger in 1768 at the age of fifteen. Soane, *Memoirs*, p. 29.

55 Soane, *Memoirs,* p. 60.

56 Watkin, *Sir John Soane*, pp. 7–8.

57 Watkin, 'Beckford, Soane, and Hope', p. 46.

58 De Man, p. 69.

59 De Man suggests that autobiography 'veils a defacement of the mind of which it is itself a cause'. De Man, p. 81.

60 Palladio was born Andrea di Pietro della Gondola; Kent was born William Cant; Mies was born Ludwig Miës; and Le Corbusier was born Charles-Édouard Jeanneret.

61 Du Prey, p. 4.

picturesque spread wide, to gardens, paintings and books. Sterne's highly self-conscious and meandering narration was 'the culmination of a decade of such experimentation' by lesser writers, writes Christopher Ricks.[62]

Tristram Shandy affectionately teases Locke, who criticised the inappropriate association of ideas and was noted for his promotion of reasonableness.[63] Recalling one of Uncle Toby's anecdotes, Tristram recounts the moment of his conception to explain a haphazard life. Tristram's father, a punctilious man of habit, would wind up a large clock on the first Sunday night of every month and then proceed to his wife's bed. But on one occasion, in a hurry, he failed to do so, with unfortunate consequences:

> *It was attended but with one misfortune, which, in a great measure, fell upon myself, and the effects of which I fear I shall carry with me to the grave; namely, that, from an unhappy association of ideas which have no connection in nature, it so fell out at length, that my poor mother could never hear the said clock wound up,—but the thoughts of some other things unavoidably popp'd into her head,—* & vice versâ*:—which strange combination of ideas, the sagacious* Locke*, who certainly understood the nature of these things better than most men, affirms to have produced more wry actions than all other sources of prejudice whatsoever.*[64]

Unaroused, she enquires: 'Pray my dear . . . have you forgot to wind up the clock?'[65] Distracted, he exclaims: *'Good G—!'*[66] Premature ejaculation 'scattered and dispersed the animal spirits, whose business was to have escorted and gone hand-in-hand with the *HOMUNCULUS*, and conducted him safe to the place destined for his reception'.[67]

The novel is surprisingly accepting of life's many accidents and failures, given that Sterne wrote *Tristram* Shandy quite late in his life, when his health was poor and after all but one of his children had died within days of birth. But the humour often turns black. Sterne attributes the playful misassociation of ideas to the effect of climate on character: 'that this strange irregularity in our climate, producing so strange an irregularity in our characters,—doth thereby, in some sort, make us amends, by giving us somewhat to make us merry with when the weather will not suffer us to go out of doors'.[68] Alongside a concern for climate Sterne echoes the new-found respect for natural life. Although Uncle Toby was once a soldier, he will not kill a fly. Letting it escape through a window, he exclaims: 'This world surely is wide enough to hold thee and me.'[69]

With storytelling now part of the story, Sterne profoundly influenced the course of literature. The narrator sets out to tell the story of his life but rarely gets beyond

62 Ricks, p. xii.

63 Locke, *An Essay concerning Human Understanding*, bk. 2, ch. 33, pp. 394–401.

64 Sterne, vol. 1, ch. 4, p. 9.

65 Sterne, vol. 1, ch. 1, p. 6.

66 Sterne, vol. 1, ch. 1, p. 6.

67 An idea that that was questioned in the eighteenth century, the animal spirits were supposed to account for the interaction of the mind and the body. The 'Homunculus', or little man, was the sperm. Sterne, vol. 1, ch. 2, p. 7; p. 599, n. 4; p. 600, n. 1.

68 Sterne, vol. 1, ch. 21, p. 57.

69 Ricks, p. xxvii.

his conception, birth and early childhood. Aware that no art form can fully describe a person and a life, Sterne turns this impossible task to creative advantage. As a person is a fluid accumulation of ideas, emotions and experiences and a life is not necessarily remembered, or even experienced, as a progressive sequence, the story does not develop chronologically but moves back, forward, around and sideways. Sterne remarks: 'Digressions, incontestably, are the sun-shine; they are the life, the soul of reading;- - -take them out of this book for instance,- - - you might as well take the book along with them'.[70] Through *Tristram Shandy*'s fractured narrative we actually acquire a more honest, detailed, nuanced and convincing portrait of a person than a linear narrative provides. Digressions occur in life as well as literature. Even the attention given to Tristram's formative years is an accurate representation of his concerns. As a metaphor of life itself, the final line of the book mocks the purposeless but pleasurable journey the reader has followed: 'A COCK and a BULL, said Yorick——And one of the best of its kind, I ever heard.'[71] In words that equally apply to the twists and turns of Kent, Soane and the picturesque, Primo Levi writes:

70 Sterne, vol. 1, ch. 28, p. 64..

71 Sterne, vol. 9, ch. 33, p. 588.

> *The clock is Shandy's first symbol. Under its influence he is conceived and his misfortunes begin, which are one and the same with this emblem of time. Death is hidden in clocks . . . Tristram Shandy does not want to be born, because he does not want to die. Every means and every weapon is valid to save oneself from death and time. If a straight line is the shortest distance between two fated and inevitable points, digressions will lengthen it; and if these digressions become so complex, so tangled and tortuous, so rapid as to hide their own tracks, who knows – perhaps death may not find us, perhaps time will lose its way, and perhaps we ourselves can remain concealed in our shifting hiding places.*[72]

72 Levi, in an introduction to an Italian edition of *Tristram Shandy*, quoted in Calvino, *Six Memos for the Next Millennium*, p. 47.

Tristram Shandy affirms the tradition of *ut pictura poesis*, which is so evident in the picturesque, and shares its fascination for fragmentation, incompletion and ruination as means to engage the reader or viewer. Noting 'Sterne's spirited awareness of the reader's imagination', W.B. Gerard remarks that *Tristram Shandy*'s 'highly reflexive narrator injects a sense of feeling (pathos or humour) into his descriptions that helps generate vivid images in the reader's mind, even in the absence of comprehensive description'.[73] An amateur painter, Sterne precisely controlled the visual quality of the printed page. Typographical devices indicate specific actions and images appear in place of words. A cross means that someone crosses himself and two small dots indicate that Colonel Trim snaps his fingers. Sterne's complex visual and typographical devices – 'tripping us up as we read'[74] – are the narrator's means to check that the reader is alert. Communicating in a manner that words

73 Gerard, pp. 175, 17.

74 Holtz, p. 88. Refer to Voogd, p. 386.

cannot, images call attention to the possibilities and limitations of both means of communication. Two black pages follow a reference to Yorick's grave.[75] A serpentine squiggle represents Corporal Trim's flourish of his stick,[76] which 'seems to resemble eighteenth-century illustrations of the motions of a spermatozoon'.[77] Elsewhere, enticing the reader into action and leaving the following page blank, Sterne asks the reader to imagine Widow Wadman: 'To conceive this right,—call for pen and ink—here's paper ready to your hand.——Sit down, Sir, paint her to your own mind——as like your mistress as you can——as unlike your wife as your conscience will let you—'tis all one to me——please but your fancy in it.'[78]

75 Sterne, vol. 1, ch. 12, pp. 31–32.

76 Sterne, vol. 9, ch. 4, p. 550.

77 Melvyn New, in Sterne, p. 726 (vol. 9, ch. 4, n. 1).

78 Sterne, vol. 6, ch. 38, p. 422.

In 1806 Soane was elected Professor of Architecture at the Royal Academy. Conceived as an elite, the academicians were limited to forty architects, painters and sculptors, who provided the Professors from among their number. Intended for students but also open to the public, the Professors were required to present lectures, which received wide attention and were reviewed in the press. Soane presented two series of six lectures, the first beginning in 1809, the second in 1815. He mentioned Sterne early in his first lecture and again in his two final lectures,[79] while a further reference appears in 'Crude Hints'.[80] Soane's narrative descriptions of 12–14 Lincoln's Inn Fields echo *Tristram Shandy* with architectural characters introduced alongside human ones. Picturesque, self-conscious, meandering narration was Soane's method as a designer and a writer.

79 Soane, 'Lecture I', 'Lecture XI' and 'Lecture XII', in Watkin, *Sir John Soane*, pp. 491, 647 and 653.

80 Soane, 'Crude Hint's, p. 63; Dorey, 'Crude Hints', p. 76, n. 16.

In his last lecture Soane echoed Sterne's affection for Locke.[81] He owned the four-volume *The Works of John Locke*, 1777, which includes *An Essay concerning Human Understanding* in the first volume, and mentioned the operations of the mind no less than 161 times in his lectures. A concern for the association of ideas runs through them, including a lengthy discussion of their relationship to gardens and ruins in the tenth lecture.[82] Porter notes that *Tristram Shandy*'s 'comedy made the new interiority of Lockean and Humean man – a creature of confused subjectivity – seem normal, and even sympathetic'.[83] But Soane took himself more seriously. His humour was less frequent and tinged with a deeper melancholy. Describing his home 'as a sort of portrait', Soane's desire to create a monument to his life was considerable even though, knowing *Tristram Shandy*, he must have accepted that it would always be illusory and incomplete.[84]

81 Soane, 'Lecture XII', in Watkin, *Sir John Soane*, p. 653.

82 Soane, 'Lecture X', in Watkin, *Sir John Soane*, pp. 624–626.

83 Porter, *Flesh in the Age of Reason*, p. 304.

84 Soane referring to Pitzhanger, quoted in Watkin, 'John Soane', p. 82.

A shared admiration for William Hogarth further connected Sterne and Soane. Arriving in London in 1760, Sterne asked for a Hogarth illustration to 'clap at the Front of my next Edition' of *Tristram Shandy*.[85] Hogarth's engravings appear in the frontispieces to the 1760 second edition of volumes one and two and the 1761 first edition of volumes three and four. In 1802 Soane acquired the eight paintings of *A Rake's Progress*, 1733–1734, from Beckford and in 1823 bought the four

85 Sterne, p. 598.

paintings of *An Election*, 1754, from the wife of the actor David Garrick. The following year the two series were displayed in Soane's newly completed Picture Room alongside other works that included Soane's own designs, Piranesi's drawings and two watercolour sketches of scenes from Sterne's *A Sentimental Journey*, 1768. Appreciating Hogarth's irreverent depictions, Sterne and Soane must have found their flawed heroes and black humour equally intriguing. In Tom Rakewell's decline from prosperity to Bedlam, Soane may also have seen the moral inverse to his own social rise and a fitting portrait of his elder son, George, who Soane refused to assist when he was imprisoned for debt and fraud in 1815. Critical of 12–14 Lincoln's Inn Fields, George disappointed and offended his father by publishing two anonymous articles in *The Champion*, which Soane blamed for the death of his wife, Eliza, in 1815:

William Hogarth, *A Rake's Progress, Scene VIII. The Madhouse*, 1733–1734. Courtesy of the Trustees of Sir John Soane's Museum, London.

The exterior, from its exceeding heaviness and monumental gloom, seems as if it were intended to convey a satire upon himself; it looks like a record of the departed, and can only mean that considering himself as deficient in that part of humanity – the mind and its affections – he has reared this mausoleum for the enshrinement of his body.[86]

86 Soane had four children but only two, George and John, survived childhood. John also died quite young in 1823. George Soane, *The Champion*, September 1815, quoted in Watkin, *Sir John Soane*, p. 419.

Disturbed by charges that he was squandering his money and concerned that his reputation would fall into disrepute, Soane may also have feared *An Architect's Progress*. In the 1830 and 1832 editions of *Description of the House and Museum on the North Side of Lincoln's-Inn-Fields*, he recalls the fate of his contemporary John Matthews:

This ingenious and indefatigable Artist, having failed in an attempt to gain the gold medal given in the Royal Academy in 1771, for the best Design of a Nobleman's Villa, felt the disappointment so poignantly, that he neglected his studies and passion for Architecture, became dissolute and sottish, and finally ended his days in a prison.[87]

87 Soane, *Description of the House and Museum,* 1832, p. 25. A slightly different version appears in the 1830 edition, p. 24.

4

the garden of architecture

(opposite) William Aislabie, Banqueting Hall, Hackfall, c. 1770, after Robert Adam, *Capriccio of Ruins*, c.1754–1758. Photograph, Jonathan Hill.

INTRODUCTION

A companion to the previous chapter, and concluding my investigation of Soane, this chapter analyses his fascination for the architectural potential of gardens, climate and weather, focusing in particular on 12–14 Lincoln's Inn Fields. The chapter is organised into four interconnecting sections, each with a specific theme. The first, 'A Picturesque Landscape', discusses the inspiration Soane acquired from the gardens and theories of the picturesque. The second, 'The Nature of Architecture', considers how the sensory appreciation of nature and weather informed the resulting analogy of architecture to poetry. The third, 'The Air of London', investigates Soane's reaction to the polluted atmosphere of the world's largest city. The concluding section, 'A Garden Climate', considers a building conceived as a garden and a climate.

A PICTURESQUE LANDSCAPE

The Father of Modern Gardening

The books in Soane's extensive Library eloquently express his concern for theories of the picturesque. But gardens were themselves an influence and fascination.[1] In 1816 and 1817 Soane visited Studley Royal in Yorkshire, which was laid out between 1722 and 1742 by John Aislabie, an original subscriber to Castell's *The Villas of the Ancients Illustrated*.[2] John's son, William, extended the garden, incorporating the adjacent ruins of Fountains Abbey for picturesque effect. Even if he did not visit a particular garden Soane may have known it through illustrations and descriptions. For example, his close friend since 1792, Joseph Mallord William Turner sketched Hackfall in 1816, close to Studley Royal.[3] Along a steeply wooded hillside flanking the River Ure, William Aislabie completed the garden in the 1770s. Built to look like a ruin and most likely copied from a Robert Adam watercolour, *Capriccio of Ruins*, *c*.1754–1758, a banqueting hall commands the top of the ridge and the views beyond. Adam's picturesque compositions were well known to Soane, who owned many of his drawings. Below the banqueting hall, Aislabie inserted winding paths, follies, waterfalls, pools and a stone seat dedicated to Kent.

In 1805, to house a collection of Saxon manuscripts, the first Marquis of Buckingham commissioned Soane to design the Gothic Library at Stowe, where he saw the garden contributions of Kent and Brown. Soane knew of Kames's

1 In addition to Pitzhanger, Soane created a garden at the new house of the Clerk of Works to the Royal Hospital at Chelsea, an appointment he had obtained in 1807. Palmer, 'Sir John Soane's Garden', pp. 14–20.

2 Soane visited Studley Royal on 31 July 1816 and 6 August 1817. Soane, 'Soane's Note Books', vol. 9, 1814–1816, p. 104; vol. 10, 1817–1819, p. 22.

3 Soane owned three of Turner's paintings, which he bought in 1804 and 1831. Soane rejected *Forum Romanum, for Mr Soane's Museum*, 1826, because the 'picture did not suit the place or the place the picture'. Eliza Soane. 'Mrs Soane's Note Books, 1804–1813', p. 7; Soane, quoted in Dorey, *John Soane & J.M.W. Turner*, p. 28.

criticism of Kent's emblematic monuments in Stowe's Elysian Fields.[4] Appointed the first Professor of Architecture at the foundation of the Royal Academy in 1768, Thomas Sandby repeated Kames's criticism in his lectures in the 1770s, which Soane mostly likely attended as a student and later included as transcripts in his Library.[5] In his own lectures, Soane places the gardens of Kent and Brown in a single line of development, praising Brown's landscapes but not his buildings because they are 'not very analogous to our customs and climate'. Maybe referring to Kent's designs as well as those of Brown, Soane dismisses 'miniature representations of Grecian or Roman temples . . . placed in our gardens without consulting the genius of the place'. [6]

Soane notably describes Kent as 'the father of modern gardening'.[7] The entries in 'Soane's Note Books' are cursory but he is very likely to have seen Rousham. He regularly visited nearby Oxford and Blenheim and also travelled on the road between Oxford and Banbury, which passes close to Kent's garden, only thirty miles

4 Kames, vol. 2, pp. 353. Refer to Watkin, *Sir John Soane*, p. 52.

5 Watkin, *Sir John Soane*, p. 30.

6 Soane, 'Lecture X', in Watkin, *Sir John Soane*, p. 625.

7 Soane, 'Lecture XI', in Watkin, *Sir John Soane*, p. 642. Refer also to Soane, *Description of the House and Museum*, 1830, p. 42.

William Kent, *Triumphal Arch with Donkey*, Holkham, *c.*1732. Courtesy of Viscount Coke and the Trustees of the Holkham Estate.

from Soane's birthplace.[8] Remarking that he had seen Kent's drawings 'a hundred times',[9] Soane owned forty-eight of them, including a design for an Arcadian Hermitage, *c.*1730, as discussed in Chapter 1. He also owned another preliminary design of the Richmond Hermitage from the same year, which is shown in plan, section and perspective.[10] Number 12–14 Lincoln's Inn Fields contains a number of pieces of furniture to Kent's designs. Describing Kent as 'a man of genius' and 'a great artist', Soane also remarks on his skill as an architect.[11] Holkham Hall is 'magnificent', especially the vestibule.[12] But criticising Kent's drawing for Holkham's Triumphal Arch, *c.*1732, Soane dismisses 'pyramids . . . introduced without any better reason'.[13] Remarking on the 'improper use of the ancient decoration, and . . . extravagant and ridiculous application of the orders of architecture', Soane affectionately teases Kent's indiscriminate commissions:[14]

> *Kent, who was respected for his architectural productions, was likewise consulted for designs for state coaches, city barges, and children's cradles. Nay, he was so far the oracle of the day, the arbiter of taste, that the very petticoats of the ladies were under the observation of the architect, and embroidered from his designs.*[15]

8 On 18 August 1817 he stayed at Banbury. On 29 January 1803 and 23 September 1828, he travelled on the road between Oxford and Banbury. Soane, 'Soane's Note Books', vol. 5, 1803–1804, p. 5; vol. 10, 1817–1819, p. 22; vol. 12, 1823–1828, p. 106.

9 Soane, *Description of the House and Museum*, 1830, p. 49.

A more austere personality than Kent, Soane had a lofty opinion of his worth and a keen sense of architectural propriety. But his assessment of Kent may have been unfair. In other gardens, Kent purposively employed references to life and death. For a family wishing to emphasise its ancestry, pyramids would have been a fitting symbol. A mile and a half to the north of the Triumphal Arch, a carriage arrived at Kent's Obelisk so that allusions to mortality and eternity marked each end of the axial avenue at Holkham.

The Mallet, Instead of the Chisel

The three key theorists of the late eighteenth-century picturesque were William Gilpin, Uvedale Price and Richard Payne Knight, who all favoured a wilder and more expressive landscape than was familiar in the early eighteenth century. Gilpin was best known for his guides to walking tours. The first was published in 1782, extending the picturesque aesthetic beyond gardens and encouraging the tourist economy of the expanding middle class.[16] Picturesque tours were further encouraged after 1793 when war with France reduced foreign travel, increasing nationalistic appreciation of British landscapes. According to Stephen Copley and Peter Garside: 'interest in the Picturesque appearance of the countryside is intimately involved with the . . . emergence of sections of society with the leisure and resources to cultivate an aesthetic of redundancy in those parts of the country least implicated in the economic changes from which their own prosperity derived'.[17] Depicting tiny figures in vast landscapes, Gilpin celebrated agricultural activities that depended on rural isolation, such as that of the shepherd.[18] But just as the early picturesque garden depended on parliamentary land enclosures that enlarged the surrounding estate, Gilpin relied on the industrial economy to leave certain areas fallow, generate a readership for his guides and provide cheap aquatint printing that made them commercially viable. Accompanying his concern for wild and discarded landscapes, Gilpin's appreciation of decay extended to buildings:

> *A piece of Palladian architecture may be elegant in the last degree . . . Should we wish to give it picturesque beauty, we must use the mallet, instead of the chisel: we must beat down one half of it, deface the other, and throw the mutilated members around in heaps. In short, from a* smooth *building, we must turn it into a* rough *ruin.*[19]

However, Soane only owned one of Gilpin's books and paid him little attention. Also in his Library were first and second editions of Price's *An Essay on the*

10 Harris argues that the drawing of the Arcadian Hermitage is a preliminary design for the Richmond Hermitage. Harris, *William Kent*, pp. 29–30.

11 Soane, 'Lecture VIII', in Watkin, *Sir John Soane*, p. 608.

12 Soane, 'Lecture IX', in Watkin, *Sir John Soane*, p. 618.

13 Soane, 'Lecture IV', in Watkin, *Sir John Soane*, p. 548.

14 Soane, 'Lecture XI', in Watkin, *Sir John Soane*, p. 643.

15 Soane, 'Lecture XI', in Watkin, *Sir John Soane*, p. 642.

16 Defined in the late eighteenth century, the term 'tourist' soon developed negative connotations.

17 Copley and Garside, 'Introduction', p. 7.

18 Gilpin, *Observations,* vol. 1, p. 197. Refer to Copley, p. 54; Copley and Garside, 'Introduction', p. 7.

19 Gilpin, *Three Essays*, pp. 7–8.

Picturesque, 1794, which Soane acquired the year it was published, influencing his sixth and ninth lectures. Paintings were important to Price's appreciation of the picturesque but his ultimate intention was to develop it into a category applicable to any art. Admiring *A Philosophical Enquiry into the Origin of our Ideas of the Sublime and Beautiful*, 1757, Price extended Burke's classificatory system to include the picturesque. Price concludes that each aesthetic category is distinct but the picturesque sits between the beautiful and the sublime and, therefore, 'is more frequently and more happily blended with them both than they are with each other'.[20] Roughness and variation are two qualities he attributes to the picturesque.[21] Introducing time as a means to define the differences between aesthetic categories, Price equates beauty with youth and the picturesque with age, which he associates with the effects of weather:

20 Price, *An Essay on the Picturesque*, p. 76.

21 Price, *An Essay on the Picturesque*, pp. 44–45.

> *Observe the process by which time (the great author of such changes) converts a beautiful object into a picturesque one. First, by means of weather stains . . . Next, the various accidents of weather loosen the stones themselves; they tumble in irregular masses upon what was perhaps smooth turf or pavement, or nicely trimmed walks and shrubberies, now mixed and overgrown with wild plants and creepers, that crawl and shoot among the fallen ruins.*[22]

22 Price, *An Essay on the Picturesque*, pp. 46–49.

Price's conception of the picturesque evokes English landscapes and its colours can be understood as English too, the product of a lively spring, gentle summer, drowsy autumn and mild winter, all in a damp climate:

> *Among these may be reckoned the autumnal hues in all their varieties, the weather-stains, and many of the mosses, lichens, and incrustations on bark and on wood, on stones, old walls, and buildings of every kind; the various gradations in the tints of the broken ground, and of the decayed parts in hollow trees.*[23]

23 Price, *Essays on the Picturesque*, vol. 1, pp. 169–170.

Countering the praise of Walpole and Whately, Price criticises the monotonous artificiality of Brown's gardens, which deny nature's liberty, he believes.[24] For similar reasons he also decides that Kent's gardens are not picturesque even though they differ significantly from Brown's gardens. Price refers to two characters in *Tristram Shandy* – 'Uncle Toby, under the direction of Corporal Trim, for they had converted this varied bank into a perfect glacis' – to dismiss the 'military style' of gardening that succeeds in 'spoiling a picturesque spot'.[25]

24 Walpole, *The History of the Modern Taste in Gardening*, p. 57; Whately, pp. 213–227; Price, *An Essay on the Picturesque*, pp. 9–16, 184–190.

25 Price, *Essays on the Picturesque*, vol. 1, pp. 32–33.

Excluding Kent from his criticism, Knight directs his attention at gardens that do not deserve to be called picturesque. In *The Landscape, A Didactic Poem*, 1794,

Nº 2

Nº 1

Richard Payne Knight, *The Landscape, A Didactic Poem*, 1794. Two comparative illustrations by Thomas Hearne. Courtesy of the British Library.

two comparative illustrations by Thomas Hearne indicate the differences between a Brownian garden and one promoted by Knight. In each illustration the architecture mirrors the landscape. In one, a meandering river lies in a broad, open lawn empty of planting. Traversed by a bridge, the river casually leads the eye towards a neo-classical house, before it curves to the right and continues into the distance. A few isolated trees emphasise the perspective and frame the view. The result is simply ordered and static; each element of the composition – river, lawn, bridge, house, trees – is distinct and separate. Knight describes such a Brownian landscape as the 'very reverse of picturesque; all subjects for painting instantly disappearing as they advance'.[26] In the other illustration, which depicts Knight's idea of a picturesque landscape, the river, bridge and house remain in the same positions, but the form and roofline of the house are now irregular. The trees are more numerous and verdant. The ground is overgrown with bracken, ferns and broken branches. Full of life, the varied types of vegetation intermingle, partially obscuring the river, bridge and house. The implication is clear. The picturesque landscape better encourages the association of ideas.

26 Knight, *The Landscape, A Didactic Poem*, p. 18.

Knight's and Price's criticisms were social as well as cultural. Whig Members of Parliament, they were landowners with a liberal education and extensive knowledge of paintings and treatises while Brown and his successor, Humphry Repton, were professionals who earned a living from garden design. As Brown was dead, Repton responded to the criticisms, commissioning William Coombe to write 'A Letter to Uvedale Price, Esq.' in 1794. Price rather than Knight was named because his text of that year was more obviously concerned with the landscape garden. Repton concluded that it was not Brown but Brown's inadequate imitators who were to blame. Questioning Knight's assertion that Brown was 'ignorant of painting' and had a formulaic disregard for nature's variety, Repton returned the criticism. Dismissing the 'wild neglect' of Knight's illustration of a picturesque landscape, he concluded that Knight saw 'no delight but in the scenes of Salvator Rosa'.[27]

27 Knight, *The Landscape, A Didactic Poem*, p. 43n; Repton, p. 101. Refer to Ballantyne, pp. 217–218; Hipple, p. 249.

Soane was less critical of Brown; while a student he worked in the partnership that Brown shared with Henry Holland; but he acknowledged Price's influence and his debt to Knight is more certain still. Purchased the year it was published, Knight's *An Analytical Inquiry into the Principles of Taste*, 1805, inspired extensive notes during Soane's preparation for his second series of Royal Academy lectures.[28]

28 Middleton, 'Soane's Spaces', pp. 32–33.

Price and Knight admire and promote the picturesque but disagree on its status. Price emphasises that a quality is intrinsic to an object and its effect on the senses is direct. Consequently, he assumes that a landscape can be designed to be inherently picturesque.[29] Instead, Knight quotes Hume's phrase that 'each mind

29 Price, *An Essay on the Picturesque*, pp. 45–46, 72.

perceives a different beauty'.[30] He follows Hume in valuing knowledge and learning but rejects Hume's support for the universal beauty of the educated mind and emphasises, instead, that standards of beauty are subject to cultural difference and change. Declaring that the beautiful, picturesque and sublime are generated in the mind, not simply by an object, Knight counters Price, concluding that they are not clearly distinct categories. Recognition that judgement is subjective as well as cultural does not deter him from defining and promoting a particular aesthetic: the picturesque is 'not sufficiently smooth to be beautiful, nor sufficiently rough and elevated to be sublime'.[31] Informed by Kames and Archibald Alison's *Essays on the Nature and Principles of Taste*, 1790, of which Soane owned several copies, Knight states that an extensive association of ideas indicates an active and knowledgeable mind and that richly varied picturesque effects may aid this process. Furthering the argument he presented in *The Landscape, A Didactic Poem*, Knight concludes:

> *As all the pleasures of the intellect arise from the association of ideas, the more the materials of association are multiplied, the more will the sphere of these pleasures be enlarged. To a mind richly stored, almost every object of nature or art, that presents itself to the senses, either excites fresh trains and combinations of ideas, or vivifies and strengthens those which existed before: so that recollection enhances enjoyment, and enjoyment brightens recollection.*[32]

Knight's illustration of a picturesque landscape achieves rich variation through more nature, not more architecture. Although Knight refers to 'every object of nature or art', Hearne's depiction does not contain the temples, statues and other emblematic devices associated with the early picturesque garden.

Price and Knight agreed that, wild and abundant, the picturesque requires time to reach fulfilment. But Knight's illustration of a picturesque landscape is deceptive. Giving the impression of dramatic contrast, it offers a static and particular vision instead, held in the appropriate degree of decay so that time is denied, not celebrated. Empiricism emphasised all the senses, which stimulated a concern for weather in the early picturesque. But empiricism's special attention to vision is particularly evident in late eighteenth-century theories of the picturesque, which mostly equate pleasure with sight. The concern for a more abundant nature was not necessarily accompanied by greater pleasure in the varied senses that it stimulated.[33] For example, Knight distinguishes the visual pleasure of decay from its effect on the other senses, which he finds offensive.[34] Equating the picturesque with vision was a means to keep less desirable conditions safely distant.

30 Hume, 'Of the Standard of Taste', pp. 136–137, 139; Knight, *An Analytical Inquiry*, pp. 16–17.

31 Knight, *An Analytical Inquiry*, pp 151–152.

32 Knight, *An Analytical Inquiry*, pp. 139–140.

33 Bermingham, 'The Picturesque', p. 89.

34 Knight, *An Analytical Inquiry*, pp. 71–72. Refer to Ballantyne, pp. 146–147.

In comparison to Knight's illustration of a picturesque landscape, Kent's garden drawings are inhabited and the pleasures of the garden are not exclusively visual. The differences between Kent's gardens and those of Price and Knight can be partly explained by their contrasting personalities and artistic sensibilities. Also the gregarious confidence of the earlier picturesque was less evident in the later picturesque because of the political, industrial and economic upheavals in the last decades of the eighteenth century. Furthermore, the patrons of the early eighteenth-century picturesque were of a different social status to those of the late eighteenth-century picturesque. Kent's clients were lords and generals. Price and Knight were lesser landowners. Ann Bermingham interprets the aesthetic theories of Price and Knight as a means to confirm the social status of their class: 'The picturesque emphasis on age is echoed in the increasing stress old country families placed on their ancestry to distinguish themselves from the new squires.'[35]

35 Bermingham, *Landscape and Ideology*, p. 74.

Beginning in the 1770s, Price and Knight developed and expressed their opinions on their Herefordshire estates, which were less rugged and more cultivated than the Lake District that Samuel Taylor Coleridge and William Wordsworth came to romanticise. Neither poet was an acknowledged influence on Price or Knight; nor were they mentioned in Soane's lectures.[36] Knight guided Coleridge around his collection of paintings and antiquities in 1804 but ignored the poet's high regard for Kant. A year later, in *An Analytical Inquiry,* Knight refers to 'Germany, where nonsense seems to have become the order of the day'.[37]

36 Soane, 'Lecture IV', in Watkin, *Sir John Soane*, p. 551.

37 Knight, *An Analytical Inquiry*, p. 391. Refer to Ballantyne, pp. 17, 141.

At Foxley, Price questioned the early eighteenth-century division of an estate into field and garden, labour and leisure, which Rousham had earlier helped to undermine. His criticism of the Brownian landscape concerned its lack of social diversity as well as its repetitive aesthetic. Price interpreted the picturesque broadly and emphasised the varied nature of his estate – from fields to farm cottages to woodland walks – as a means to establish social cohesion between landowner, tenant and farm labourer, maintaining the existing hierarchy and affirming the Georgic tradition. To this end, he commissioned the agrarian reformer Nathaniel Kent to propose improvements to Foxley in 1774 and published *Thoughts on the Defence of Property* in 1797.[38]

38 Daniels and Watkins, pp. 14–21.

In contrast, Knight restricted his concern to aesthetics and did not consider the management and social economy of his estate even though the possibility of political upheaval equally concerned him. In an extensive footnote at the end of *The Landscape, A Didactic Poem*, Knight recoils from the turmoil of the 1789 French Revolution.[39] A reference such as 'Walls, mellow'd into harmony by time' is a metaphor for the social benefits of continuity and compromise as well as a building description.[40] Valuing the existing character of a place, Knight remarks that 'the

39 Knight, *The Landscape, A Didactic Poem*, pp. 93–97. Refer to Whale, pp. 188–189.

40 Knight, *The Landscape, A Didactic Poem*, p. 34.

neglected style of forest scenery is preferable to all others' but regrets that scarcely 'any parts of our island are capable of affording the compositions of Salvator Rosa, Claude and the Poussins'.[41] *The Landscape, A Didactic Poem* depicts a topography unsuited to Salvator Rosa. Incorporating the steep banks of the River Teme, Knight's estate at Downton Castle contained a landscape closer to the one he admired, allowing him to follow his own advice to change little and enhance what was already there. In one illustration, Hearne shows the Alpine Bridge crossing the Teme where it is narrow and steep, framed by a heavy canopy of trees. A winding path leads to the bridge. Leaning inwards from each bank to meet at the centre, the bridge's two central supports are fallen trees still covered in bark; a filigree of uncut branches provides further bracing. Completing the bridge, the walkway is equally delicate and rustic. On the far side of the gorge, rising steps cut into the rock. Elsewhere on his estate, all linked by narrow winding paths, Knight created a cave, a mill, a rudimentary cold bath and a tunnel that frames views of the river where it changes from placid to torrid.

41 Knight, *The Landscape, A Didactic Poem*, pp. 44–45.

Exploiting the dramatic potential of an existing topography, Knight reflected growing interest in wilder landscapes as well as wilder gardens. Although he

Thomas Hearne, *The Alpine Bridge on the Teme at Downton Castle*, c.1786. Courtesy of the Victoria and Albert Museum, London.

questioned Burke's assumption that terror is essential to the sublime, Downton's landscape was sublime and romantic as well as picturesque, a combination that no doubt appealed to Soane.[42] Sharing Knight's respect for the architecture of classical antiquity Soane agreed that any architectural intervention should take account of the existing qualities of a place.[43] But he was not uncritical. Copying Knight's claim that 'variety, and intricacy of form, and light and shadow, may be carried to a degree' Soane questioned the neo-classical interior and castellated exterior of Downton Castle, 1778: 'Is not this buying into the picturesque at too dear a rate?'[44]

42 Knight, *An Analytical Inquiry*, p. 370. Refer to Ballantyne, pp. 245–280.

43 Watkin, *Sir John Soane*, pp. 237–245.

44 Knight, *An Analytical Inquiry*, p. 158; Soane, quoted in Watkin, *Sir John Soane*, p. 241.

THE NATURE OF ARCHITECTURE

Architecture's Natural Origins

Soane was equally interested in theories of the picturesque and Enlightenment architecture, which shared a substantial debt to the writings of Locke, Shaftesbury and Burke. Absorbed by the passage of time, Soane combined a concern for architecture's natural origins with a fascination for ruination and a desire to protect his future reputation. Written in the first century BC, Vitruvius' *De Architectura Libri Decem* (The Ten Books on Architecture) is 'the source of all the later speculation' on the primitive hut, writes Rykwert.[45] According to Vitruvius, the first shelter was a frame of timber branches finished in mud. The evolution of the primitive hut was the subject of Soane's first Royal Academy lecture and in his seventh lecture he remarked that 'The seeds of genius, the candidate for architectural fame must receive from nature.'[46] In the Renaissance, to acquire recognition as a mimetic art equivalent in status to painting, architecture had to convincingly represent nature, which it could not easily achieve.[47] The Enlightenment – the natural light of reason – offered a solution to this dilemma. In the frontispiece to the 1755 second edition of Marc-Antoine Laugier's *Essai sur l'architecture*, 1753, the primitive hut – four tree-trunks supporting a pediment of branches – is deemed to be perfect because it follows the reason inherent in nature and humanity alike. Enlightenment architects argued that architecture is superior to the other arts because it follows the principles of nature not merely its image.

Confidence in natural reason undermined the authority of the classical canon. Notably, in *Ordnance des cinq espèces de colonnes selon la méthode des anciens*, 1683, which was translated into English as *A Treatise on the Five Orders of*

45 Rykwert, *On Adam's House in Paradise*, p. 105; Vitruvius, pp. 38–39.

46 Soane, 'Lecture I', 'Lecture XII', in Watkin, *Sir John Soane*, pp. 492–499, 666.

47 Forty, pp. 223–224.

Marc-Antoine Laugier, *Essai sur l'architecture*, 1753. Frontispiece. Courtesy of the Conway Library, Courtauld Institute of Art, London.

Columns in Architecture in 1708, Claude Perrault questioned the authority of the architectural orders.[48] The established classical tradition was still revered and buildings were still designed in its image but its standards of taste and beauty were now open to question and no longer believed to be absolute and universal.

48 Middleton, 'Introduction', p. 19.

Soane admired Laugier, owning many copies of the various editions of *Essai sur l'architecture*, which was first published in English as *An Essay on Architecture* in 1755. Soane's reference to first garden design and then urban design in his tenth lecture is indebted to Laugier, who writes:[49]

49 Soane, 'Lecture X', in Watkin, *Sir John Soane*, p. 628.

> *The picturesque can be found in the pattern of a parterre as much as the composition of a painting. Let us carry out this idea and use the design of our parks as plan for our towns . . . Above all, let us avoid excessive regularity and excessive symmetry . . . a multitude of regular parts brings about a certain impression of irregularity and disorder which suits great cities so well.*[50]

50 Laugier, pp. 128–129.

In common with other architects who were inspired by Laugier's example, Soane's confidence in architecture's natural origins was sincere if unsubstantiated. He made little attempt to understand and investigate nature even though it was increasingly a subject of scientific research. Nature was but a useful concept, first to justify reason as natural, then to justify feelings as natural, and ultimately to make any human intervention appear natural, whether a building, garden or city. Soane's concern for reason and nature was stimulated rather than undermined by the ambiguity of these terms with regard to architecture. His ultimate concern was the architectural imagination: 'Painting and sculpture are arts of imitation and have always a model in nature before them which is only to be copied, whereas architecture being an art of invention has no such models to refer to.'[51] In *Observations on Modern Gardening*, which Soane acquired in 1778, Whately argues that 'the art of gardening aspires to more than imitation: it can create original characters'.[52] While preparing his tenth and eleventh lectures Soane made extensive notes in his copy of *Elements of Criticism*, focusing in particular on the chapter, 'Gardening and Architecture', in which Kames writes: 'Architecture and gardening cannot otherwise entertain the mind, than by raising certain agreeable emotions or feelings.'[53] However, in response to Kames's remark that 'gardening is not an inventive art, but an imitation of nature', Soane commented that it is 'therefore inferior to architecture'.[54]

51 Soane, 'Lecture III', in Watkin, *Sir John Soane*, p. 532.

52 Whately, p. 306.

53 Kames, vol. 2, p. 322. Refer also to Kames, vol. 1, pp. 120–130; Kames, vol. 2, pp. 321–354.

54 Kames, vol. 2, p. 329; Soane, quoted and referred to in Watkin, *Sir John Soane*, pp.51, 227–228.

The Sublime and Beautiful

The late 1750s were especially productive for ideas on nature, 'with a flood of writings coming so close together that it is often impossible to say which author influenced which at what point', writes Thacker. Rousseau and Burke 'had knowledge of Shaftesbury's writings; and . . . their interest was often communicated to friends before the actual production of their writings'.[55]

At Hume's invitation, Rousseau spent the winter of 1766–1767 in England, long enough to fall out with his host and confirm his influence on English romanticism. In *Émile*, 1762, Rousseau praises the primitive and natural state of humans, which he characterises as passionate, free and in contrast to society as it had developed. But Rousseau does not propose a return to primitive life. Instead, praising the influence of a temperate climate on well-being, he envisages a society that is closer to nature: 'Fix your eyes on nature, follow the path traced by her.'[56] In *Rêveries du promeneur solitaire* (Reveries of the Solitary Walker), written between 1776 and 1768 and published posthumously in 1782, Rousseau praises the solitary appreciation of untamed nature, which he equates with self-revelation and freedom of expression. But the Alpine landscapes he describes are the pastoral lower slopes, not the sublime mountains themselves.[57] Referring to Rousseau's island tomb at Ermenonville near Paris, Watkin remarks that 'Rousseau, the man of nature, was the first man to be buried publicly in a garden'.[58]

Written in the first century AD, published in England in 1554 and translated into English in 1652, Dionysius Longinus' *Peri Hupsos*, or *On the Sublime*, refers to oratory not nature. Acknowledging the influence of classical antiquity and Christian doctrine on later conceptions of sublime nature, Marjorie Hope Nicolson concludes that accounts in ancient Greece and the Old Testament were less dismissive of wilder, mountainous landscapes than ones in ancient Rome and the New Testament.[59] Sublime nature was acknowledged in earlier centuries but it did not receive extensive praise until the late seventeenth and eighteenth centuries. Influential evocations of sublime nature include Salvator Rosa's seventeenth-century paintings of rugged landscapes; Thomas Burnet's *Telluris Theoria Sacra* (The Sacred Theory of the Earth), 1681–1689; John Dennis's account of his 1688 journey across the Alps, published in *Miscellanies in Verse and Prose*, 1693; Defoe's *An Historical Narrative of the Great and Tremendous Storm Which Happened on Nov. 26th, 1703*; Shaftesbury's *The Moralists: A Philosophical Rhapsody*, 1709; Addison's 'The Pleasures of the Imagination', 1712; Thomson's *The Seasons*, 1730; John Baillie's *An Essay on the Sublime*, 1747; and Hogarth's *Analysis of Beauty*, 1753. Ascribing the Great Storm's 'wonderful effects' to divine intervention,

55 Thacker. p. 83.

56 Rousseau, *Émile*, p. 14.

57 Rousseau, *Reveries of the Solitary Walker*, pp. 62–63.

58 Watkin, 'John Soane', p. 80.

59 Nicolson, pp. 38–43.

Defoe describes the sublime more than fifty years before Burke: 'notwithstanding that pleasure may be mixed with terror, and astonishment!'[60] The natural sublime was a well-established concept by the time Burke published *Philosophical Enquiry into the Origin of our Ideas of the Sublime and Beautiful* in 1757. But his achievement was to compile the sublime and the beautiful into a system that provided a coherent argument for the sublime, influencing romanticism as well as the picturesque. Undermining the classical tradition that prioritises harmonious formal beauty, Burke equates the sublime with darkness, vastness and even deformity.[61] The beautiful is pleasant; but the sublime is magnificent. Its pleasure derives from initial terror and subsequent reassurance at safe distance:

60 Defoe, pp. 49–50.

61 Burke, pp. 144–147, 72–73, 102–104.

> *Whatever is fitted in any sort to excite the ideas of pain, and danger, that is to say, whatever is in any sort terrible, or is conversant about terrible objects, or operates in a manner analogous to terror, is a source of the* sublime; *that is, it is productive of the strongest emotion which the mind is capable of feeling . . . When danger or pain presses too nearly, they are incapable of giving any delight, and are simply terrible; but at certain distances, and certain modifications, they may be, and they are delightful, as we everyday experience.*[62]

62 Burke, pp. 39–40.

Burke identifies the sublime with a desolate and expansive landscape that is subject to the uncertain drama of natural forces but he also discusses it in relation to human constructions. Conceiving the sublime as reassuringly terrifying made it available for artistic reproduction and encouraged aesthetic speculations on the supernatural. Equally, it was a means to extend the safe management of nature, seen elsewhere in the picturesque garden and estate farm.[63]

63 Porter, *Enlightenment*, pp. 226–227.

Following Locke, *Philosophical Enquiry* focuses on the relations between objects, the senses and the mind. Although he does not entirely dismiss the mind's ability to associate ideas, Burke pays it little attention: it is 'absurd . . . to say that all things affect us by association only; since some things must have been originally and naturally agreeable or disagreeable'.[64] Burke confirms Locke's opinion that certain objects directly and consistently affect our senses: 'For sublime objects are vast in their dimensions, beautiful ones comparatively small.'[65] But with regard to architecture, Burke concludes that there is no direct relationship between an object and a perception. Although a building may not be vast, the eye and the mind may believe that it is:

64 Burke, pp. 130–131.

65 Burke, p. 124.

> *A true artist should put a generous deceit on the spectators, and effect the noblest designs by easy methods. Designs that are vast only by their dimensions, are always*

the sign of a common and low imagination. No work of art can be great, but as it deceives; to be otherwise is the prerogative of nature only.[66]

66 Burke, p. 76.

Consequently, Philip Shaw concludes that Burke avoids unequivocal conclusions:[67]

67 Burke's characterisation of gender is less thoughtful as he describes the sublime as masculine and the beautiful as feminine. But, citing the writings of Anne Radcliffe, Charlotte Smith and Ann Yearsley, Shaw notes that late eighteenth- and early nineteenth-century interpretations of the sublime were not always so simply gendered. Shaw, pp. 108–114.

Burke's account of the sublime raises serious questions about the relations between mind and matter: is the sublime a quality that resides within objects of natural grandeur, does it have purely subjective origins, or is it produced in some way from the interaction of mind and object? Still more radically, is the sublime a mere effect of language? Burke's unwillingness to present decisive answers to these questions is prompted in part by his instinctive emprîcism: a mode of thinking that restricts enquiry to that which can be verified by experience. Since a claim about the origins of the sublime cannot be proved, either by experiment or by reason, one must focus on its observable effects.[68]

68 Shaw, p. 53.

Tuveson describes Burke's treatise as 'the first really modern work on aesthetics' because he values 'the effect of things on the mind' more than 'a clear idea of the things in themselves'.[69] The appreciation of pleasure and pain in the shock of the sublime indicated an emerging romantic sensibility that is characteristic of modernity, which the heroic pretensions of the early twentieth-century avant-garde confirmed in their assumption that new means of production could inspire societal transformation.[70] But *Philosophical Enquiry* significantly differs from romanticism in that it pays little or no attention to some of romanticism's key concepts: the desire to protect and isolate nature, the role of subjective thoughts and emotions, and the imagination's ability to elevate the mind, influence society and engage the spiritual. Creating sublime effects, the romantic imagination could be equivalent to a force of nature and assume its divine mantle.

69 Tuveson, p. 174. Refer to Tuveson, pp. 166–170.

70 Refer to Crary, p. 143, n. 15; Benjamin, 'The Author as Producer', p. 230; Benjamin, 'The Work of Art', pp. 240–241; Lyotard, pp. 198–206.

The Architecture of Sensations

Watkin states that three books particularly informed Soane's understanding of the picturesque: Knight's *Analytical Inquiry*, Burke's *Philosophical Enquiry* and Kames's *Elements of Criticism*.[71] In emphasising the emotional impact of architecture and nature, Burke greatly influenced late eighteenth-century theorists of the picturesque. Kames was influenced by Locke's *An Essay concerning Human Understanding*, in which three sequential chapters are titled 'Of simple Modes; and first, of the simple Modes of Space', 'Duration, and its simple Modes' and 'Of Duration and

71 Watkin, *Sir John Soane*, p. 1.

Expansion, considered together'.[72] But in emphasising individual passions and emotions, Kames provides a more subtle appreciation of time and space that distinguishes between dimension and perception: 'travelling with an agreeable companion produceth a short computation both of the road and of time: especially if there be few objects that demand attention, or if the objects be familiar'.'[73]

72 Locke, *An Essay concerning Human Understanding*, bk. 2, ch. 13–15, pp. 166–204.

73 Kames, vol. 1, p. 126.

The influence of British writers soon spread to continental Europe. Burke's *Philosophical Enquiry* was first published in French in 1765. Soon after they were published in English, Kames's *Elements of Criticism* was translated into German and Whately's *Observations on Modern Gardening* appeared in both German and French. Kames and Whately focus more on the emotive power of a garden than a building.[74] Associating architecture with geometry, Whately argues that 'regularity can never attain to a great share of beauty, and to none of the species called *picturesque*; a denomination in general expressive of excellence'.[75] But together with Burke, Kames and Whately stimulated discussions on how architecture can evoke sensations comparable to those found in nature but specific to the discipline. Etienne-Louis Boullée, Nicolas Le Camus de Mézières, Claude-Nicolas Ledoux, Jean-Jacques Lequeau and Julien-David Le Roy in France and Soane in England all picked up on this theme. Attempting to establish a coherent but not universal discourse, these architects conceived architecture as an expressive language that can represent, respond to and influence the character of a person and a place. According to Watkin:

74 Kames, vol. 2, p. 323; Whately, pp. 146–150.

75 Whately, p. 146.

> *The relation between the philosophy of sensationalism in architecture and garden theory was well understood in France . . . One feels that this world of debate was really the intellectual setting for which Soane was made. Nothing like it existed in England, so that a quarter of a century later, he had to re-create it for himself, alone, in his cramped library at no. 12, Lincoln's Inn Fields.*[76]

76 Watkin, *Sir John Soane*, p. 213.

The attention given to subjectivity led to widespread concern for the futility of life. Louise Pelletier writes that 'A feeling of boredom (*l'ennui*) was identified as the sickness of the time (*le mal du temps*) in the eighteenth century. It afflicted the most brilliant minds with an unfolding awareness of the passing of time and their linear journey from life to death.' Confronting lethargy with energy: 'The various art forms that engaged this linearity of human experience were considered to be the most effective means to fight' back.[77] In *Le génie de l'architecture; ou, l'analogie de cet art avec nos sensations*, 1780, which was translated into English as *The Genius of Architecture; or, the Analogy of That Art With Our Sensations*, Le Camus

77 Pelletier, p. 194.

de Mézières describes the sensations evoked by a sequence of rooms in a grand town house:

> *Each room must have its own particular character. The analogy, the relation of proportions, decides our sensations; each room makes us want the next; and this agitation engages our minds and holds them in suspense. It is satisfaction in itself.*[78]

78 Le Camus de Mézières, p. 88.

Mirroring the increasing attention that the eighteenth century gave to the private individual, Le Camus de Mézières emphasises the particular purpose of each room and concentrates on ones for personal use. But his narrative has a public dimension in that it describes the *hôtel particulier* of the *Ancien Régime* and states that architecture should represent the social status as well as the personality of the owner.

Although he acknowledged neither author, Le Camus de Mézières was influenced by Locke and Étienne Bonnot de Condillac, who had an important role in interpreting Locke's empiricism for a French audience. *An Essay concerning Human Understanding* was translated into French in 1700 as *Essai concernant l'entendement humain* and Condillac owned a 1742 fourth edition. Confirming Locke's opinion that the mind is at first an empty cabinet, in *Traité des sensations* (Treatise on Sensations), 1754, Condillac compares the mind to a statue brought to life through the senses, which are acquired one by one in response to external stimuli. Accordingly, memory allows self-awareness and language to develop and stimulates the imagination. Condillac continues Locke's systematic appraisal of each of the senses but prioritises touch rather than vision because he considers it to be the most spatial of the senses. In *Essai sur l'origine des connoisances humaines* (An Essay on the Origin of Human Knowledge), 1746, he states that the sensory organs are consistent from person to person and, thus, taste has common standards. But he concludes that conditions and people vary too much for a particular object to guarantee a particular emotional response.[79]

79 Rather than *Traité des sensations*, Middleton suggests that Condillac's principal influence on Le Camus de Mézières was *Essai sur l'origine des connoisances humaines*, which was published in English in 1756. Middleton, 'Introduction', p. 55. Le Camus de Mézières, p. 74. Refer to Pelletier, p. 217, n. 7.

Le Camus de Mézières conceives architecture as a catalyst for a complete sensory experience in which weather plays a part. Echoing Burke's concern for the emotive power of objects and spaces, he gives particular emphasis to the modulation of light and shade, which may be beautiful when in harmony and sublime when in contrast. Also noting the importance of colour and smell, he offers the first detailed theoretical discourse on the architecture of sensations:

> *From the totality of the buildings known to us and the different sensations that they arouse in us, from their detail and from a description of the fabric and its masses,*

> *we shall extract principles that have been passed over, somewhat too lightly, by past writers on Architecture.*[80]

Alongside a concern for general principles he emphasises particular conditions, arguing that the architect must consider the location of a building, the orientation of rooms and façades and the changing light across days and seasons:

> *If a project, takes into consideration the time, place, nation and destination for which it is built, the proportion of masses and voids, of forms, ornaments, and all that is related to the art will vary infinitely.*[81]

Enjoying analogies to music and poetry, Le Camus de Mézières conceives architecture in terms of accumulative emotions. But ignoring Condillac's advice, he assumes that a specific object will generate a specific sensation, which will in turn lead to a specific emotion: 'in inanimate objects, it is their form that makes some pleasing to us, others unpleasing'.[82] Denying the diversity of possible responses to a situation, Le Camus de Mézières assumes that as the 'art will vary infinitely' so will its ability to orchestrate sensations.[83] For justification, he refers to the innate understanding of nature: 'The sensibility that almost all men share is enough to make them feel her influence to the full.'[84] Soane's judgement is subtler. Rather than an exclusively direct and causal relationship between matter and mind, he concludes: 'The mind receives pleasure or pain not only from the impulse of external objects, but also from the consciousness of its own operation and dispositions.'[85]

The Genius of the Garden

In *The Genius of Architecture* Le Camus de Mézières acknowledges his debt to the theatre, to which architecture was often compared in the eighteenth century. In accordance with the development of bourgeois art, eighteenth-century French theatre design increasingly emphasised the autonomy of the stage and its ability to create convincing images. Le Camus de Mézières mentions the architect and stage designer Jean-Nicolas Servandoni in particular, who conveyed plot development through optical effects rather than dialogue.[86] Servandoni even rejected sequential narrative in a 1738 production at the Salle des Machines, a theatre in the north wing of the Tuileries.[87] Rykwert notes that Servandoni's stage canvases were 'very much like those of his master, Giovanni Paolo Panini',[88] who so influenced Kent's multiple perspective technique and Soane collected in his Picture

80 Le Camus de Mézières, p. 105. Refer to Le Camus de Mézières, p. 95; Middleton, 'Introduction', pp. 51–54; Pelletier, pp. 131–137.

81 Le Camus de Mézières, p. 98.

82 Le Camus de Mézières, p. 70.

83 Le Camus de Mézières, p. 73.

84 Le Camus de Mézières, p. 74.

85 Soane's annotation to his copy of Alexander Gerard, *An Essay on Taste*, 1759, quoted in Watkin, *Sir John Soane*, p. 227.

86 Le Camus de Mézières, p. 71. Refer to Middleton, 'Introduction', pp. 31, 50, 55 and 62.

87 Pelletier, p. 28.

88 Rykwert, *The First Moderns*, p. 110.

Room. Inspired by one of Servandoni's designs, Le Camus de Mézières recognises that optical effects can trigger physical sensations, including ones associated with climate and weather:

> *The Camp of Godfrey was seen parched by the fires of the Dog days: almost no shadow, a reddish sky, an arid earth, an effect of light that suggested flames in the air, all this created an illusion to which no Spectator was immune. We supposed that we ourselves were suffering; we were in the power of Art. With equal success, he might have conveyed to our souls the idea of biting cold, by setting before us an image of those climes in which a few leafless birches are the only signs of inspiration to rise above the rocks covered with eternal snows; a sombre air, and a pale and featureless sky, would have betokened the onset of new frosts. Rivers frozen to a standstill, springs caught and arrested in their flight, would have shown us nature devoid of life and movement. That would have been a spectacle to make us shiver.*[89]

89 Le Camus de Mézières, p. 101. Refer to Le Camus de Mézières, p. 181, n. 3, where Middleton considers the performance to which Le Camus de Mézières refers.

Continuing the Italian Renaissance tradition, the relations between theatres and gardens fascinated Le Camus de Mézières, an amateur playwright. Created for the *Société dramatique de Charonne*, 1770–1781, the theme of Le Camus de Mézières' first play, *Les Dragons de Charonne*, is reminiscent of Rousseau.[90] The principal character, Colas, enjoys the country life of a gardener distant from the city. In a later novelistic tale, *Description des eaux de Chantilly et du hameau*, 1783, Le Camus de Mézières structures a narrative of desire around a garden created by Jean-François Le Roy in 1780, when the picturesque was increasingly popular in France. In that they share a sensory narrative and refer to gardens and mythological figures, Pelletier also notes similarities between *The Genius of Architecture* and Colonna's *Hypnerotomachia Poliphili*, which was translated into French by Jean Martin in 1546.[91] Soane, like Kent, admired *Hypnerotomachia Poliphili* and owned many copies, including the 1546 French translation.[92]

90 Rousseau, *Lettre à Monsieur D'Alembert*, p. 66. Refer to Pelletier, pp. 71, 72–73 and 207, n. 55.

91 Pelletier, pp. 177–191.

92 Watkin, *Sir John Soane,* p. 246.

Le Camus de Mézières dedicated *The Genius of Architecture* to his friend Claude-Henri Watelet, who began the garden of Moulin-Joli in 1754 and was the author of *Essai sur les jardins*, 1774, the first French treatise on the picturesque garden.[93] Full of praise for such a garden Le Camus de Mézières writes:

93 Lavin, pp. 16–33.

> *In it, all is sensed, all is foreseen, all is reasoned and dictated by delicacy. Every part affects us, and every part prompts the appropriate sensation . . . A beautiful dream, these ideas may be; but there is no denying that this is a dream that can be made to come true. Analyzed, these same ideas become still more delightful,*

and to develop them further can only spur our imaginations and place within our reach all the treasures of a mine in whose depths there lies the precious gift of exciting our emotions, gratifying our sensations, and suiting our dwellings to our tastes, to our desires, and to the various needs that luxury creates every day, both for our personal satisfaction and in relation to the customs and manners of the society to which we belong.[94]

94 Le Camus de Mézières, p. 101.

Jean-Marie Morel's *Théorie des jardins*, 1776, was another likely influence although Le Camus de Mézières fails to mention it. Confirming Whately's praise for the irregularity of a garden in comparison to the symmetry of a building, Watelet and Morel contrast the subtle and varied skills of the gardener to the rigid and limited techniques of the architect bound to geometry.[95] Watelet promotes gardens that acknowledge varied experiences and criticises geometric gardens in which 'The spectator surveys a part, guesses the rest, and feels only a mild desire to set out and explore.'[96] Including chapters on each of the seasons, Morel notes that in contrast to the painter or dramatist, the adept gardener takes subtle account of the changing effects of nature, time and weather, and recognises that the available sensations are temporal and uncertain. Watelet and Morel concentrate their discussions on picturesque gardens, which equally inspire Le Camus de Mézières: 'Those Gardens that we call English, although their true origin is Chinese, have furnished us with expedients drawn from nature herself.'[97] Drawing analogies between architecture, gardens and nature, and confirming the belief in architecture's natural origins, Le Camus de Mézières suggests that a house can be designed according to the same principles as a garden. Taking full account of all the senses, he implies that the architect should learn from the picturesque garden designer:

95 Whately, pp. 144–146; Watelet, p. 52; Morel, p. 6. Refer to Grillner, 'Nature's Lovers', pp. 64–67; Middleton, 'Introduction', pp. 48–51.

96 Watelet, p. 40.

97 Le Camus de Mézières, p. 74.

Now that we possess a number of treatises on Gardens that do honor to their authors, we have extracted from them a number of ideas: like the bee, we have tried to make then into an agreeable honey; happy if our efforts promote the progress of the Art on which we write.[98]

98 Le Camus de Mézières, p. 74.

The Poetry of Architecture

Number 12–14 Lincoln's Inn Fields differs from Le Camus de Mézières' *hôtel particulier* in that the interdependence of public and private is more fully expressed in Soane's house, office and museum, which were subject to constant change during his lifetime and designed without a prescribed narrative sequence. But *The*

Genius of Architecture influenced Soane considerably, encouraging him to consider a building as a poem and a garden, which he identified with the promotion of *ut pictura poesis* in the picturesque. Responding to Le Camus de Mézières' fusion of painting, sculpture, building and garden, Soane describes 12–14 Lincoln's Inn Fields as a 'union of the arts'.[99] Informed also by the analogy of architecture to theatre, Soane's preparatory notes for his fifth lecture may help explain the reserved front elevation of 12–14 Lincoln's Inn Fields:

99 Soane, quoted in Watkin, *Sir John Soane*, p. 81.

Sir John Soane, Exterior, 12–14 Lincoln's Inn Fields. Photograph, Martin Charles. Courtesy of the Trustees of Sir John Soane's Museum, London.

> *The front of a building is the prologue of a play. It prepares us for what we are to expect. If the outside promises more than we find in the inside, we are disappointed. The plot opens itself in the first act and is carried on through the remainder, through all the mazes of character, convenience of arrangement, elegance and propriety of ornaments, and lastly produces a complete whole in distribution, decoration and construction.*[100]

Conceiving a building as a garden led to the question of its climate and weather. Hippocrates influenced Vitruvius' chapter 'On Climate as Determining the Style of the House' in *The Ten Books on Architecture*, which was important to Soane and his Enlightenment predecessors including Laugier.[101] In 1804 Soane translated a passage from the second 1770 edition of *Les ruines des plus beaux monuments de la Grèce,* in which Le Roy discusses geography and climate and, aware of Piranesi, considers the Burkean sublime in nature and architecture.[102] In *Architecture, Essai sur l'art*, *c.* 1794, Boullée associates each season with a different mood and a different light, and imagines an architectural equivalent to poetry, an idea developed from Le Camus de Mézières. Soane did not know Boullée's *Essai* directly because it was then unpublished but he was familiar with Boullée's teachings.[103] Soane also noted de Piles's reference to a 'poetical whole' created 'from the combination of several objects'.[104] In *Description of the Residence of John Soane, Architect*, 1832, Soane describes the Breakfast Parlour at 13 Lincoln's Inn Fields and the Monument Court beyond, which is arranged with classical sculptures in the manner of the *cortile* of a Roman palazzo:

> *The view from this room into the Monument Court and into the Museum, the mirrors in the ceiling, and the looking-glasses, combined with the variety of outline and general arrangement in the design and decoration of this limited space, present a succession of those fanciful effects which constitute the poetry of Architecture.*[105]

Sophia Psarra concludes that 'architecture and language relate in the museum through the potential of meaning found in unexpected juxtapositions' while 'the multiplication of visual relations through the reflections work like the startling combinations of words in poetry, showing unusual angles of rooms and unexpected spatial relations'.[106] In conceiving a building as a poem in which emotional and discursive impact is more important than any specific meaning, architects influenced the development of poetry itself and informed wider cultural concerns. 'It is therefore undeniable that architecture was an important and vital factor in the creation of what has been called a pre-Romantic sensibility, a term which would be more accurately changed simply to Romantic', remarks Rémy Saisselin.[107]

100 Le Camus de Mézières, p. 74; Soane, quoted in Watkin, *Sir John Soane*, p. 188.

101 Vitruvius, pp. 170–171; Laugier, p. 84.

102 Le Roy's text first appeared in his *Histoire de la Disposition et des formes différents que les chrétiens ont données à leurs temples depius le règne de Constantin le Grand à nos jours*, 1764. Soane, referred to in Watkin, *Sir John Soane,* p. 201.

103 Boullée, pp. 212–213. Refer to Watkin, *Sir John Soane,* p. 203; Watkin, 'Soane and his Contemporaries', p. 41.

104 Soane, quoted in Watkin, *Sir John Soane*, p. 191.

105 Soane, *Description of the House and Museum,* 1835, p. 54.

106 Psarra, p. 130.

107 Saisselin, pp. 247–248.

This Strange Irregularity in Our Climate

The climate and weather were important to the architecture of sensations because the Burkean sublime depended on the drama of natural forces, and geography and climate were considered to be factors in the determination of architecture, culture and, even, character. The third approach to atmospheric phenomena in classical antiquity referred to the other two, in that like *Meteorologica* it offered a general theory, and like the weather signs tradition it offered a practical application. Its concern was the climate not the weather, the generic not the specific. Following principles devised by Parmenides in the fifth century BC, the world was divided into five unchanging zones arranged from north to south. In the second century AD Ptolemy divided the world into seven climatic zones, changing the number but not the principle. The term 'climate' derives from 'klima', as Lucian Boia remarks:

> *In Classical Greek,* climate *meant* inclination*, an association that does not exist in modern languages. The word defined the inclination of the Earth's axis on the plane of the horizon; the angle thus formed corresponded with the latitude of each area. In short, 'climate' was virtually synonymous with 'latitude'.*[108]

108 Boia, pp. 18–19.

Assuming that climate affects character, classical antiquity concluded that the temperate Greco–Roman world was bounded by zones that were either occupied by people of dubious character or largely unfit for inhabitation. For over two thousand years, the influence of climate on character was reaffirmed, notably by Charles Louis de Secondat, Baron de Montesquieu, in *Esprit des lois* (The Spirit of Laws), 1748.[109] Sterne attributed Englishness to 'this strange irregularity in our climate'.[110] However, not everyone accepted the influence of climate on character. Hume recognises human-induced – anthropogenic – climate change in 'Of the Populousness of Ancient Nations', 1742, but he dismisses climate's influence on humanity in 'Of National Characters', 1748, doubting 'that men owe anything of their temper or genius to the air, food or climate'.[111] However, Jan Golinski notes that Hume's eurocentricism 'left the door open to a degree of climatic influence to which he was reluctant to admit explicitly'.[112]

In *Decline and Fall of the Roman Empire*, 1776–1788, Edward Gibbon interprets the conflict between the Romans and Germans in terms of the effects of climate on character. Questioning the assumption that climate is consistent, he offers an early account of anthropogenic climate change. Gibbon attributes improvements in the European climate since classical antiquity to improvements in agriculture wrought by human ingenuity.[113] Gibbon was indebted to Georges-Louis

109 Montesquieu, *The Spirit of Laws*.

110 Sterne, vol. 1, ch. 21, p. 57.

111 Hume,'Of the Populousness of Ancient Nations', pp. 264–268; Hume, 'Of National Characters', p. 115.

112 Golinski, p. 178.

113 Gibbon, vol. 1, ch. 9, p. 238.

Leclerc, Count Buffon. Appreciating Evelyn's *Sylva,* Buffon was highly influential in addressing the human transformation of nature, and thus climate, as well as the influence of nature and climate on human character, notably in *Époques de la Nature*, 1778, and *Histoire Naturelle, Générale et Particulière,* which was published in forty-nine volumes between 1749 and 1804.[114] Although he questioned Buffon's dismissive assessment of the American landscape, which the Count attributed to the indolence of the American Indian, Thomas Jefferson similarly believed that nature could be modified and improved by agrarian developments, advocating systematic recording of the American weather as an aid to this process.[115]

114 Glacken, pp. 655–705.

115 Jefferson, *Notes on the State of Virginia*, p. 79; Jefferson, letter to Lewis E. Beck, 16 July 1824, in Jefferson, *The Writings of Thomas Jefferson*, vol. 15, pp. 71–72. Refer to Glacken, pp. 680–685.

No longer divided according to unchanging climatic zones, a static world was replaced by one that was never still, there to be managed and manipulated as well as measured. As character was acquired and supposedly subject to environmental influence, an improved climate might lead to an improved character.

Echoing Vitruvius and Laugier, Soane notes the effect of climate on character in his first lecture, concluding that as some climates are superior to others, so are some buildings:

> *Grecian architecture, which now claims our attention, owes its origin and perfection to causes very different from those already spoken of. The Greeks were the fathers of science and of art. Their climate, their laws, their mode of life, all contributed to gain them a superior rank in the higher walk of intellect.*[116]

116 Soane, 'Lecture I', in Watkin, *Sir John Soane*, p. 497.

Soane describes the architecture of classical antiquity as an invaluable model but criticises the literal transfer of architecture from one place to another and emphasises the influence of local conditions such as culture, climate and site.[117] Number 12–14 Lincoln's Inn Fields contained eleven instruments to measure time and atmosphere, including a late seventeenth-century barometer made by Daniel Quare. Alongside a concern for climate, Soane indicated an interest in the subtle variations and poetic effects of weather, reflecting the contemporary concern for the particularity of a person and a place. Soane asked Gandy to paint the recently completed Tyringham House, Buckinghamshire, at different times and in different weathers. *Tyringham Gate Lodge in a Storm*, 1798–1800, shows the façade raked by rain and illuminated by a thunderous sky. In *Design for a Sepulchral Church at Tyringham*, 1798, a gentle glow pervades the sky, illuminating the cupola. To accompany his lectures Soane's pupils produced extensive drawings. Indicating his admiration for Vanbrugh, one drawing sequence shows Blenheim Palace in different light conditions.[118] Through the mist, heavy with vapour, the north

117 Soane, 'Lecture I', 'Lecture VIII', in Watkin, *Sir John Soane*, pp. 492, 595. Refer to Lukacher, pp. 38–41.

118 Soane mentions visits to Blenheim on 25 July 1803, 7 August 1818 and 29 April 1827 but as the entries in his 'Note Books' are cursory, he may have visited more often. Soane, 'Soane's Note Books', vol. 5, 1803–1804, p. 34; vol. 10, 1817–1819, p. 63; vol. 12, 1823–1828, p. 70.

elevation of the Palace appears in pale silhouette between the sky and ground in watery greys. Referring to the picturesque convention of fore-, middle- and background Soane remarks:

> *there is a constant variety of outline that pleases from whatever point it is viewed (as are viewed ancient temples), whether at a distance wherein the great masses only are made out, or at a nearer approach when the prominent features are distinguished, or still nearer when the greater details are distinguished.*[119]

119 Soane, quoted in Watkin, *Sir John Soane,* p. 373.

THE AIR OF LONDON

A Hellish and Dismall Cloud

London's climate and weather were far less benevolent. Reports of the city's polluted skies were frequent even in the sixteenth and seventeenth centuries, when coal replaced wood as the principal domestic fuel. Evelyn's *Fumifugium: or The Inconvenience of the Aer and Smoak of London Dissipated*, 1661, was the first book to consider the city's polluted atmosphere as a whole. Opening with a dedication to King Charles II, Evelyn claims that he conceived *Fumifugium* in response to a 'pernicious Accident' in the royal palace of Whitehall. A 'presumptuous Smoake . . . did so invade the Court: that all the Rooms, Galleries, and Places about it were filled and infested with it; and that to such a degree, as Men could hardly discern one another'.[120] Remarking that a 'Hellish and dismall Cloud of SEA-COALE' blankets the city, Evelyn recalls the ancient Greek principle that the air – the breath – is 'the *Vehicle* of *the Soul*, as well as that of the Earth' and recounts Hippocratic opinion that the character of a people depends upon the character of 'the *Aer* of those *Climates*' they breathe.[121] Convinced that London's air is unhealthy, Evelyn proposes a medical 'Remedy' for 'this pernicious *Nuisance*'.[122] Noting the comparative clarity of the sky on Sunday when industries are idle, he mistakenly assumes that domestic fires contribute little pollution. Consequently, he proposes that coal-burning trades should be relocated east of the city so that the winds would carry the smoke away from London and the waters of the River Thames would be unsullied.[123] Evelyn further suggests that chandlers, butchers, slaughter-houses, fishmongers and graveyards should be moved beyond the city walls so that they do not contaminate the air and ground water. Prisons are also to be relocated, indicating that his purpose is moral as well as medical. In addition to practical

120 Evelyn, *Fumifugium*, pp. 1–2.

121 Evelyn, *Fumifugium*, pp. 11–13.

122 Evelyn, *Fumifugium*, pp. 3, 34, 35.

123 Evelyn, *Fumifugium*, pp. 34–37, 42–43.

measures Evelyn suggests poetic solutions. Taking the prevailing winds into account, he proposes 'That all low-grounds circumjacent to the City, especially *East* and *South-west*' should be forested and planted with 'such *Shrubs*, as yield the most fragrant and odoriferous Flowers and are aptest to tinge the Aer upon every gentle emission at a great distance' so that 'the whole City, would be sensible of the sweet and ravishing varieties of the perfumes'.[124] Evelyn's enduring fascination for gardens was influenced by Bacon's advice that the philosopher required a garden as well as a library and laboratory. In the seventeenth century, Evelyn's remedy – a perfumed botanical garden – would also have been associated with Heaven and the Garden of Eden and implied good health due to the known medical properties of certain plants and herbs.[125]

124 Evelyn, *Fumifugium*, pp. 47–49. Refer to Merchant, pp. 236–242.

125 Jenner, pp. 544–546.

Emphasising the allegorical as well as practical and poetic significance of Evelyn's treatise, Mark Jenner notes that contemporary imagery equated the monarch with the illuminating sun and the interregnum – between the execution of Charles I in 1649 and accession of Charles II in 1660 – as the obscuring cloud.[126] Recalling ancient Greece and an Old Testament verse, and making a clear distinction between pure and polluted air, Evelyn eulogises 'our Illustrious *CHARLES*, who is the very Breath of our Nostrils, in whose health all our happiness resides'.[127] Evelyn also considered the sun to be an appropriate emblem for the intellectual enlightenment of the Royal Society, of which he was elected a Fellow in 1661.

126 Jenner, pp. 542–543.

127 Jenner notes that this 'is a quotation from *Lamentations* 4.20 and refers to the Lord's Annointed'. Evelyn, *Fumifugium*, p. 44; Jenner, pp. 543–544.

In January 1662, at the King's request, Evelyn prepared a parliamentary bill to counter London's pollution but the legislation progressed no further.[128] Evelyn implicitly acknowledged the interdependence of nature and industry in London's climate and weather but *Fumifugium* had no practical effect. Later texts also recognised the detrimental effects of urban pollution on human health. Pope's physician and a friend of the poet, also a physician, authored two of the most notable treatises, respectively Richard Mead's *A Mechanical Account of Poisons*, 1702, and John Arbuthnot's *An Essay concerning the Effects of Air on Human Bodies*, 1733. But there was no significant demand for a reduction in urban pollution. Property rights and the economic intricacies of London's industries, as well as popular identification of a fire with a home – a private rather than a public space – made legislation unlikely.

128 Jenner, p. 549; Smith, 'John Evelyn and London Air', p. 186.

Transforming England during Soane's lifetime, industrialisation intensified in the final third of the eighteenth century alongside increased population growth and resulting consumer demand. Improved credit systems facilitated extensive investment in industrial production and a national distribution network, while agriculture expanded to cater for a booming population, which doubled between Soane's birth and death. Previously rural areas such as Lancashire and South Wales were most transformed by the new industries, affecting natural life as well as people. In Manchester, a strain of the moth Biston betularia – renamed Biston carbonaria – became increasingly familiar, its black wings offering camouflage against predators in the soot-clad city.

London was less exclusively an industrial city than the northern cities that developed in the second half of the eighteenth century. Nearly every industry was found there but London's economy also depended upon other factors, such as its port, government buildings and the social, cultural and culinary needs of its population. London consumed 800,000 tons of coal in 1700, 1,500,000 tons in 1750 and over 2,500,000 tons in 1790, when its population was ten times that of any other English city. Coals at this time had sulphur levels twice that of coals used centuries later. On combustion, the sulphur oxidised to introduce sulphur dioxide into the air and a secondary oxidation created sulphuric acid. Among the many industries in central London were glue and tallow manufacture, which boiled carcasses from Smithfield market. Fog, coal smoke and industrial fumes combined to turn the air into a darkly odorous smog. A new building had a shadow of soot even before the end of its construction.[129] Pollution coated yellow bricks black, corroded stones and metals, killed trees and flowers, stained clothes and furnishings, and caught in eyes, throats and lungs, making streets and squares at times unbearable and withdrawing everyday life into the interior. Crime levels added further cause for concern. The trustees of Lincoln's Inn Fields, who included Soane, struggled to protect the square from beggars, vagrants and rubbish. In 1790 it was remarked that 'The spot has the most uncouth and dismal appearance of any square in or about the metropolis.'[130]

129 An idea suggested to me by Adrian Petrenco. Refer to Brimblecombe, 'Interest in Air Pollution', p. 123; Brimblecombe, *The Big Smoke*, pp. 66, 74–75; Christianson, pp. 14–23; Edleston, p. 150; Porter, *English Society*, p. 187.

130 Anonymous letter, 1 November 1790, quoted in Palmer, 'From Fields to Gardens', p. 19.

The Contrivance of Mr A.M. Perkins

In contrast to his appreciation of the poetic potential of weather beyond the city, Soane decided that retreat was the appropriate response to London's heavy smog. Manipulating light and temperature, he created a benevolent internal climate in opposition to a malevolent external one. Indebted to Le Camus de Mézières' appreciation of the 'lumière mysterieuse', Soane's skilful manipulation of light is well known.[131] Referencing the yellow glass in Bernini's Rome and the light effects in Thomson's *The Seasons*, Watkin describes Soane as 'the heir to post-Newtonian poets . . . the golden light of yellow was the most luminous and beautiful of them all'.[132]

131 Le Camus de Mézières, p. 88; Soane, 'Lecture VIII', in Watkin, *Sir John Soane*, p. 598.

132 Watkin, *Sir John Soane*, p. 415. Refer to Watkin, 'John Soane', p. 82.

133 Soane, 'Lecture VIII', in Watkin, *Sir John Soane*, pp 595–598.

Soane dedicated a lengthy passage to heating systems in his eighth lecture.[133] But his concern for temperature control has received little discussion, no doubt because it is unfairly associated only with utility. An increasingly secular society emphasised its command of the natural world; whether domineering or thoughtful, humanity was conceived as an active agent of change, managing and manipulating the climate as well as the land. As these principles were applied at all scales and in all locations, greater demands were placed on building performance. The internal climate was subject to particular scrutiny. With rudimentary drainage, open fires and candle lighting, the eighteenth-century building was no more successful as a climate modifier than those of previous centuries. In contrast, the emergence of new technologies, such as central heating and water closets, ensured that the nineteenth-century house provided a more comfortable internal environment.

Alongside a concern for tradition, Soane experimented with new technologies just as he did with other architectural developments. Robert Adam and his brothers influenced Soane's fireplace designs but their 'inspiration, Roman architecture, was a culture, as Soane noted in his historical overview of heating, without a strong fireplace tradition. The Romans were known for the central hypocaust systems, not their fireplaces' writes Todd Willmert.[134] Recognising the importance of the fireplace in northern climates, Soane remarked that 'in England it is not sufficient that our houses are well warmed: we must see the fire, or no degree of heat will satisfy us'.[135] Soane understood that perceived warmth depends not just on the actual temperature but on all the senses, what is seen and heard, the flickering flame and the cracking ember. In his 1792–1793 design studies for the Bank of England Stock Office he proposed a stove decorated with a symbolic flame because the actual fire would be out of sight, contained within the stove for efficiency. For its symbolic association as well as practical purpose, a fireplace was also proposed for the same room.

134 Willmert, p. 50.

135 Soane, 'Lecture VIII', in Watkin, *Sir John Soane*, p. 596. Refer to Willmert, pp. 26–30.

In 1811 Sir Francis Bourgeois bequeathed a collection of paintings to Dulwich College, London. Bourgeois and his business partner, Noel Desanfans, had acquired many of the paintings for the King of Poland but Stanislaus Augustus was deposed before he could receive them. Bourgeois stipulated that the collection should be housed in England's first purpose-built public art gallery and that Soane should be its architect. Almshouses and a mausoleum accompanied the gallery, which opened in 1817.[136] Each space was heated in a different manner. The almshouses had fireplaces, the gallery had central steam heating and the mausoleum was unheated. Lighting, heating and materials accentuated the differing sensory realms. Bourgeois' tomb was placed at the centre of the mausoleum and those of Desanfans and his wife, Margaret, were to the sides. Proceeding from the gallery to the mausoleum,

136 Later, the gallery expanded into the almshouses.

Joseph Michael Gandy, *Interior view of the Dulwich Picture Gallery*, 1823. Courtesy of the Trustees of Sir John Soane's Museum, London.

the visitor passes from warm, quiet rooms with timber floors, rich red walls and an even light to echoes, pale stone surfaces, chilled air, defined shadows and an amber glow. Soane writes that 'a dull religious light shews the Mausoleum in the full pride of funereal grandeur'.[137] The effect of light and temperature is 'especially profound in winter, the season most closely allied with death'.[138]

137 Soane, *Memoirs*, p. 39.

138 Willmert, p. 57.

Due to his long residency, and its varied uses, Soane's most complex investigation of internal climate occurred at 12–14 Lincoln's Inn Fields.[139] Its inward focus is a reaction to London's polluted weather as well as a reflection of Soane's self-absorption. In the domestic rooms, vibrant colours differentiate mood. The ground floor Library–Dining Room is deep red and the first floor Drawing Rooms are primrose yellow. The museum and office are painted in pale colours so that the full effect of the skylights can be seen. Crimson glass to the west mirrors the evening light, conforming to Turner's conception of colour, while elsewhere there is a golden glow.[140] Soane also experimented with new lighting technologies, such as gas lamps, which were more consistent than candles and oil lamps. Coal stores under the pavement supplied the fireplaces in the domestic rooms facing onto the square. More delicate and less dominating than the ones that he replaced, Soane's fireplaces supplied hot coals for the bed-warming pans in winter. Willmert remarks: 'Although mirrors and decorative planes in these rooms make them spatially complex through illusion, they are actually simple, contained chambers easily heated by fireplace.'[141]

139 Refer to Lamb, p. 249; Palmer, *The Soanes at Home*, p. 23; Willmert, pp. 36, 49.

140 Turner associated yellow and grey with morning. Refer to Craddock, 'Sir John Soane and the Luminous Environment', referred to in Hawkes, p. 12; Wiedman, *Romantic Art Theories*, p. 144.

141 Willmert, p. 26.

As office hours were typically twelve hours a day, six days a week, Soane and his staff spent much of their time at work. At first the office was located in contained rooms at the rear of Number 12. When the office and museum were established in the rear of Number 13 in 1809, stoves heated the office while the museum, then separate, was at first unheated and later warmed by stoves, which ensured that smoke was contained and unable to spread elsewhere. Unusually cold weather added urgency to Soane's designs. High levels of volcanic activity combined with increased pollution to veil the atmosphere, ensuring that the decade from 1810 to 1819 was the coldest in London since the 1690s:

> *Two major families of heating systems – water systems dependent on pipes to distribute steam or hot water, and hot air systems employing ducts to deliver warmed air – gained currency in a relatively short time frame during the years of his practice. The sustained development of both steam and hot air heating started in the 1790s, and the major advancements were in place by the 1830s. Real innovations in hot water heating began in the 1810s and stretched through to the 1830s.*[142]

142 Willmert, pp. 26–27.

Soane was quick to experiment with heating developments, inserting a steam heating system at Tyringham in 1797. At 12–14 Lincoln's Inn Fields, the new heating systems had the potential to provide a more even heat than a fireplace or stove:

In 1824, hot air heating, originally employed in 1821 to serve the office, was used to heat all the professional spaces when they were enlarged from discrete rooms into the series of spaces that now characterize the rear portion of Lincoln's Inn Fields. This system, as well as others, proved inadequate. Soane installed other hot air systems and two types of hot water systems between 1825 and the early 1830s.[143]

143 Willmert, pp. 36–37.

Charles James Richardson worked for Soane between 1824 and 1837. In *A Popular Treatise on the Warming and Ventilating of Buildings: Showing the Advantage of the Improved System of Hot Water Circulation*, 1837, he notes that the heating systems inserted during the 1820s were only partially successful in creating a consistent temperature in 12–14 Lincoln's Inn Fields.[144] Willmert concludes:

144 Richardson, *A Popular Treatise*, pp. 51–52, quoted and discussed in Willmert, p. 36.

The professional spaces, because of their spatial complexity, were practicable only in light of modern building technologies . . . No other heating method would enable Soane to create such complex, layered spaces while simultaneously heating them adequately. The problem was waiting for the technological advancements to catch up with his spatial ideas.[145]

145 Willmert, pp. 26–36.

In 1832, just a year after it was patented, a hot water system was installed to heat the office and museum. Soane remarks that 'Amongst these ruins is placed the furnace that heats the water by which the Museum and part of the basement storey of the House is warmed, by means of an ingenious apparatus, the contrivance of Mr A. M. Perkins.'[146] After the failures of earlier systems Willmert assumes that the furnace's location in the Monk's Yard, a 'satire of Gothic antiquarianism, certainly leads to the conclusion that Soane thought that the Perkins system would soon be obsolete or replaced' but it remained in use until 1911.[147] In the early nineteenth century, hot water systems were uncommon because they required larger pipes than steam or air. But the Perkins high-pressure hot water system had a smaller bore and could be distributed unobtrusively so that Soane could even locate piping around the base of a skylight to counter cold air falling from the glass.

146 Soane refers to Angier March Perkins, who worked with his father Jacob Perkins. Soane, *Memoirs,* p. 27.

147 Willmert, p. 48. Refer to Breugmann, p. 148, p. 154; Richardson, *A Popular Treatise*, p. 51.

Soane understood that the heating systems of classical antiquity were of limited use in a northern climate. But he still cited ancient precedent whenever possible: 'The general application of steam to useful purposes has unquestionably been the work of the present age, but . . . its powers were not unknown to the ancients.'[148] Richardson noted that Soane liked the Perkins system because its pipes 'bore

148 Soane, 'Lecture VIII', in Watkin, *Sir John Soane*, pp. 595–596.

resemblance to the contrivance of the brass tube called Draco, mentioned by Seneca as used in supplying the warm water in the Piscina of the Thermae'. He also testified to its practical success according to the standards of the day:

> *The comfort and convenience of a moderate, warm, equalizing temperature can scarcely be understood or appreciated, without having been enjoyed. On entering from the open air, it may feel oppressive at a temperature of fifty-five or sixty degrees, but sitting quietly at sedentary occupations, no sensation is felt; we can move without being aware that the winter snow is outside, and we are not annoyed by being partially warmed on one side whilst we are chilled on the other.*[149]

149 Richardson, *A Popular Treatise*, p. 52, quoted in Willmert, pp. 47–48.

A GARDEN CLIMATE

A Garden

In his tenth lecture in 1815, Soane identifies gardening as an exception to the general superiority of 'the ancients over the moderns'. Discussing a building and its setting, he writes: 'Architecture being thus identified with gardening, it becomes a necessary part of the education of the architect that he shall be well acquainted with the principles of modern decorative landscape gardening.'[150] But his comparison of the building to the garden went further. Equally inspired by Enlightenment architecture and the picturesque, he responded to Le Camus de Mézières' claim that a house and a garden can be designed according to similar principles by conceiving 12–14 Lincoln's Inn Fields as a garden of architecture, and thus an art of invention not just imitation.

150 Soane, 'Lecture X', in Watkin, *Sir John Soane*, pp. 627–628, 624. Refer to Le Camus de Mézières, p. 88; Soane, quoted in Watkin, *Sir John Soane*, p. 228; Watkin, 'John Soane', p. 82.

Number 12–14 Lincoln's Inn Fields is Arcadian, self-contained and rich in classical iconography. Millenson writes that 'Soane's house-museum evokes the eighteenth-century landscape garden circuit' and offers Stourhead as an example.[151] But no particular didactic device and narrative sequence dominate Soane's garden. In that one can move 'infinitely through the museum and its contents' Psarra writes 'that it is not the visitors who walk in a circular route through history; it is time and history that circulate around them'.[152]

151 Millenson, pp. 109, 167.

152 Psarra, pp. 125–126.

Number 12–14 Lincoln's Inn Fields is so excessively emblematic that it is expressive. Even for a frequent visitor, learned interpretation of all the artefacts on view is impossible. Some objects in the collection were familiar and easy to decipher but little was known about ancient Egypt in the early nineteenth century. In March 1825 Soane held three candle-lit evening receptions for nearly 900 guests to view a recent acquisition, the thirteenth-century BC Sarcophagus of Pharoah Seti I, which Giovanni Belzoni had recently discovered in 1817. Lamps illuminated the façade to Lincoln's Inn Fields, while the interior flickered with candlelight and the sarcophagus was discovered in the crypt, alluding to its burial site. Turner and Coleridge were among the guests.[153] Hofland recalls the scene in Soane's *Description of the House and Museum on the North Side of Lincoln's Inn Fields*, 1835:

153 Benjamin Robert Haydon, in a letter to Mary Russell Mitford, referred to in Summerson and Dorey, p. 47.

> *Had any one of that gay company been placed* alone *in the sepulchral chamber, at the 'witching hour of night,' when 'Churchyards yawn, and graves give up their dead,' when the flickering lights became self-extinguished, and the last murmuring sounds from without ceased to speak of the living world, – it is probable that even the healthiest pulse would have been affected with the darker train of emotions which a situation so unallied to common life is calculated to produce.*[154]

154 Hofland, quoted in Soane, *Description of the House and Museum*, 1835, p. 39.

At 12–14 Lincoln's Inn Fields the poetry of architecture stimulated sensations and emotions and was designed to engender discourse as well as wonder – of specific elements and the whole ensemble – while acknowledging – as in Rousham's abundant allegories – that a coherent, overarching interpretation was neither necessary nor desirable. Soane valued architecture that can 'please generally and at first sight'. To sustain attention, he emphasised that a 'building often pleases from its variety and movement whereby the succession of interest is kept up'.[155] Displaying antiquities, statues, stones, shells and plants, the Italian Renaissance garden was conceived as a cabinet of curiosities alongside the collection housed within a villa or palace.[156] Soane continued this tradition, but the garden – as a cabinet of curiosities – became a building, and vice versa. Avid for acquisition and adjustment, Soane's inquisitive imagination guaranteed seasonal and yearly transformations. Sculptures and antiquities cover every surface like architectural foliage, recalling the shaggy aesthetic of the late eighteenth-century picturesque as well as Rousham's heavily wooded site. Like General Dormer's garden, Soane's garden includes clearings, pavilions and intricately interconnected alternative journeys, making it appear much larger than its actual dimensions. As objects and spaces cluster together, the Dome Area at the centre of the museum is a clearing while the Upper Drawing Office is a pavilion. Drawings, paintings and windows offer vistas and routes punctuated by monuments and ruins. The numerous and extensive skylights open the museum and office to the sky, enhancing the impression

155 Soane, quoted in Watkin, *Sir John Soane*, p. 194.

156 Hunt, *Garden and Grove*, pp. 73–82.

Sir John Soane, The Dome Area with Soane's bust, 12–14 Lincoln's Inn Fields. Photograph: Martin Charles. Courtesy of the Trustees of Sir John Soane's Museum, London.

of a garden. To disperse light and views, mirrors are positioned in every direction. Whether set into a surface or placed on a wall, many of the mirrors are flat and tinted or convex and round, collectively recalling the Claude Glass. The emblematic gardens of the early eighteenth-century picturesque were especially indebted to Claude. In the late eighteenth-century picturesque, reverence continued through the Claude Glass. A mirror – often convex, tinted and round or oval – named after Claude but never used by him, the Claude Glass alters nature according to picturesque conventions of composition and colour.[157] Associated with recollection and prediction, the mirror is an aid to self-reflection, especially a convex one because the viewer is part of the scene wherever he or she stands. But mirrors also distort, weather and age, as Helene Furján acknowledges: 'After all, the mirrors of Soane's time were, like Soane's own eyes, still prey to damage, their backings subject to moisture decay, dissolving and clouding the reflections.'[158] Elsewhere, glass was instrumental in weathering. In 1837 George Bailey, the first curator of Sir John Soane's Museum, noted the damage caused by the glass-fronted bookcases, which Soane no doubt appreciated for their reflective qualities: 'Many of the Books were found to have suffered from mildew; in many instances evidently from having being closed immediately after being bound up.'[159]

A Climate

Soane modulated environmental conditions, such as temperature and light, according to time and location but he may not have appreciated these weather anomalies because he designed a climate as much as a garden and a building. To create a meandering and habitable internal garden he required central heating, employing an invention of the industrial era to counter one of its by-products, intense pollution. Bathing his garden in a golden glow, Soane limited daytime visits to sunnier days when the contrast between light and shadow was strong. For a family member or employee, everyday experience was more varied, whether the garden was seen in moonlight, lit by candlelight or interrupted by tapping rain.

Conceiving a complex interior as a garden, Soane expanded the picturesque. Number 12–14 Lincoln's Inn Fields is a wonderfully eloquent advocate for the spatial, sensory and allegorical potential of the architectural garden in which foliage is built not grown. As an exotic collection, meandering garden and architectural paradigm, it is a microcosm of a larger world. But 12–14 Lincoln's Inn Fields is also typical of the picturesque in that its primary visual focus is internal. Although axes extend from the rear of the museum to the garden in the square, they are not

157 Identifying two devices available in the eighteenth century, Deborah Jane Warner and Arnaud Maillet distinguish between the Claude Mirror, a tinted convex mirror, and the Claude Glass, a flat filter of coloured glass sometimes presented as an array of separately tinted sheets. But I refer to the tinted convex mirror as the Claude Glass, which, as Maillet acknowledges, is an English convention. Warner, pp. 158–159; Maillet, pp. 31–32.

158 Furján notes that Soane suffered from cataracts and had one removed in 1825. Furján, p. 85. Refer to Psarra, p. 122; Steenbergen and Reh, p. 331.

159 Bailey, quoted in Harris, 'Sir John Soane's Library', p. 246.

drawn to eye-catchers such as Rousham's Temple of the Mill and Triumphal Arch. In the city, Soane's sensory appreciation did not extend beyond the boundaries of his house, office and museum. Distinguishing between a benign climate inside and a malign climate outside, Soane created a garden to exclude London. Conceiving 12–14 Lincoln's Inn Fields as a means of self-expression and morbidly concerned for his reputation, Soane displayed some of the characteristics of a romantic artist. But in denying the weather Soane departed from the picturesque and dissociated himself from the unmediated and self-revelatory engagement with nature that characterised romanticism. Only he was allowed to determine his garden's growth. Soane fabricated climate just as he fabricated ruins. But climate and weather are interdependent, as Soane's mildewed books attest.

5

pigments and pollution

INTRODUCTION

Concluding my investigation of picturesque and romantic attitudes to the environment in the eighteenth and early nineteenth centuries, this chapter concentrates on the latter era, when meteorology became a science and the arts increasingly eulogised the weather, which was considered to be as exceptional as the imagination. Focusing on the paintings, buildings and opinions of J.M.W. Turner, I compare his reaction to the hybridised weather of industrial London to that of Soane. Although they were friends for many years, and lived close to each other, their imagination drew them to contrasting conclusions and designs.

ENLIGHTENMENT AND ROMANTICISM

The end of the Enlightenment and beginning of romanticism are often associated with the advent of industrialisation and the violent aftermath of the 1789 French Revolution, which undermined faith in reason and reasonableness. But it is more accurate to recognise the Enlightenment and romanticism as representatives of two philosophical traditions, which evolved alongside each other and continue to inform the present. According to Richard Tarnas:

> *From the complex matrix of the Renaissance had issued forth two distinct streams of culture, two temperaments or general approaches to human existence characteristic of the Western mind. One emerged in the Scientific Revolution and Enlightenment and stressed rationality, empirical science, and a skeptical secularism. The other was its polar complement, sharing common roots in the Renaissance and classical Greco-Roman culture (and in the Reformation as well), but tending to express just those aspects of human experience suppressed by the Enlightenment's overriding spirit of rationalism.*[1]

1 Tarnas, p. 366.

But the distinction between them is not as certain as Tarnas maintains. Romanticism affirmed many of the principles associated with the Enlightenment, especially the British Enlightenment that is my concern in *Weather Architecture*. Romanticism conceived the world as a dynamic whole, eulogised nature and primitive origins, cherished a mythical past, denied immutable standards, questioned the authority of tradition and the classical canon, emphasised personal histories and individual experiences, and promoted personal liberty and the potential of the imagination. But, equally, there were significant differences. Focusing on the tangible and measurable, the Enlightenment ordered knowledge into distinct disciplines and practices as in the British Museum. In contrast to the particular focus of the Enlightenment specialist, the world as a whole was available to the romantic mind. As August Wiedman succinctly concludes, romanticism united 'the world in the self, the self in the world'.[2]

The romantic mind did not begin as a *tabula rasa*. In place of the empiricist concern for one idea leading to another, romanticism gave greater emphasis to the unconscious. A concern for the individual was combined with a concern for the community. On the one hand the value given to subjectivity focused attention on the viewer; on the other hand it celebrated the transformative power of the artist. Personifying romanticism's faith in the genius – which continued in modernism – the artist was understood to be both outside familiar society and able to redirect it through the appreciation of truths that only imagination and emotion can discover. Rather than discard reason, the search for complete understanding led the romantic mind to cultivate a dialogue between the rational and irrational, as Wiedman recognises:

> *Romanticism was the creative tension between a uniquely self-conscious intellect and an equally self-conscious anti-intellectualism which by its very nature precluded the pursuit of the thoughtlessly irrational.*[3]

Influential figures of the British Enlightenment such as Shaftesbury and Addison stimulated the concern for nature that romanticism deepened and expanded. Romantic art was understood as a self-organising creative force alongside the natural world – a second nature – and a means to establish a deeper understanding of the union of the human and the natural. But the romantic concern for wholeness led to a creative tension between the inner journey into the mind and the outer journey into the world. Romantics eulogised nature but in emphasising the imagination they sometimes allowed the natural world to be wilfully misrepresented. Within these broad principles, romanticism varied from person to person, country to country. The focus of this chapter is English romanticism and attitudes to weather in the early nineteenth century.[4]

THE SCIENCE OF METEOROLOGY

At first, Enlightenment science ignored the weather because it was deemed to be unreasonable and not subject to an obvious system. In gardens and mountains the

2 Wiedman, *Romantic Art Theories*, p. 102. Refer to Day, p. 76.

3 Wiedman, *Romantic Art Theories*, p. 11.

4 Only in the mid-nineteenth century were English artists and poets such as Turner, Wordsworth and Coleridge collectively described as romantics. Butler, p. 37.

weather was a pleasure to be enjoyed but varied weather conditions were not necessarily respected elsewhere, especially if they affected agricultural and industrial production. After being initially denied, the weather increasingly became an affront to reason and a challenging problem to be solved. If the weather could be categorised, then so could anything in nature.

More than sixty years after Linnaeus' *Critica Botanica*, standard classificatory systems for the weather were devised. Jean-Baptiste Lamarck categorised cloud types in *Annuaire Méteorologique*, 1802, but resistance to the French regime and language limited his influence. With greater precision and Latin terminology, Luke Howard's *On the Modification of Clouds*, 1803, provided the first widely accepted and systematic investigation of cloud formations.[5] Recognising that clouds are formed when water vapour cools and condenses in the atmosphere, Howard ordered clouds into three types according to their visual resemblance to either wisps of hair (Cirrus), a bulbous heap (Cumulus) or sheets layered together (Stratus). Combining the basic cloud types, he further identified the Cirro-cumulus, Cirro-stratus, Cumulo-stratus and the Nimbus, or Cumulo-cirro-stratus. Although other classificatory systems of the natural world used Latin terminology, there was some initial resistance to Howard's system because Latin was understood by only a small proportion of the population, confirming earlier fears that it would limit knowledge to specialists. Howard argued for Latin because it offered a 'universal language, by means of which the intelligent of every country may convey to each other without the necessity of translation'.[6] His phrase 'the intelligent of every country' indicates the class dimension to his classificatory system. But his influence was not limited to a single discipline and extended to painters and philosophers including Turner and Goethe, who admired Howard's schema because it relied on observation, indicating the union of art and science and the interconnectedness of the human and natural worlds.

5 In 1803 *On the Modification of Clouds* was serialised in the July, September and October editions of the *Philosophical Magazine* and was published as a single volume in the following year.

6 Howard, *The Climate of London*, p. xxxxii, quoted in Hamblyn, p. 156.

As in Enlightenment Britain, weather records were collected in German-speaking states, notably by medics and clerics once again. In 1717, a doctor in Breslau, Johann Kanold, and his colleagues, the naturalists Johann Christian Kundman and J.G. Braunschweig, began to collect information on the weather, while between 1781 and 1795, the court priest, Johann Jakob Hemmer, directed the Societas Meteorologica Palatina, which established the first network of weather stations.

Early attempts to categorise the wind included Hooke's 'Method for Making a History of the Weather', 1667, but there was then little understanding of its causes. In the mid-eighteenth century, George Hadley established that winds arise when the atmosphere attempts to equalise temperature and pressure differentials, which depend upon a complex set of interrelations between the land, sea and air at local, regional and global scales. Early in the nineteenth century, Gustave-Gaspard de Coriolis recognised that wind movement is further complicated by the earth's rotation, which may alter its direction. In 1806 Francis Beaufort devised the wind scale that takes his name, using English rather than Latin terms. The scale was initially graded from 0 (calm) to 13 (storm) but was soon revised so that a storm was rated 11 and a hurricane was 12, the highest designation. The Beaufort scale became mandatory on Royal Navy vessels in 1838 – nine years after its author had been appointed Hydrographer to the Navy – and in 1853 the first International Meteorological Conference in Brussels confirmed it as the universal standard. With only minor amendments, the Beaufort Scale and Howard's classificatory system remain in use today.

As science's influence increased, the study of the skies stopped being a theory of meteors in the Aristotelian tradition and developed into a science of weather based on systematic observation, measurement and analysis. Howard did not completely dismiss the weather signs tradition but considered the new science to be a superior alternative, which borrowed Aristotle's term even though its focus was quite different. Howard's influence led to the formation of the Meteorological Society of London in 1823, which became the British Meteorological Society in 1850 and Royal Meteorological Society in 1883. Meteorology affirmed the classical tradition in its concern for a comprehensive account of the atmosphere. But it emphasised reasoned explanation, not abstract theory or intuitive interpretation. Rather than coexistence with, and within, living nature, science placed the detached specialist outside the natural world, undermining Goethe's praise for Howard's classificatory system. Educated in the city and associated with its learned institutions and laboratories, the professional meteorologist favoured a rational system for an entire subject and appreciated local knowledge only so far as it furthered this aim. But in 1818 Howard remarked: 'Meteorology . . . is yet far from having acquired the regular and consistent form of a science.'[7] Its status was uncertain because the weather was uncertain.

7 Howard, *The Climate of London*, vol. 1, p. iii. Refer to Boia, pp. 85–88; Fleming, p. 37; Golinski, *British Weather,* pp. 74–75; Hamblyn, pp. 184–203; Jankovic, pp. 154–156.

LYRICAL WEATHER

Two attitudes to weather developed alongside each other in the late eighteenth and early nineteenth centuries, each offering a contrasting relationship between humanity and nature. In contrast to the sciences, the arts seemingly left nature to its own devices while associating it with subjective expression and moral virtue in a manner that united the spirits of a person and a world. Although mountain thunder and sea storms populate its images, romanticism did not exclusively focus on wild nature and unsettled weather. Rousseau praised the lower mountain pastures, while Coleridge and Wordsworth admired Thomson's *The Seasons*, which depicts the weather of farms and fields rather than sparsely populated mountains.[8] As exceptional as the imagination, the weather appears throughout the *Lyrical Ballads*, 1798, which Coleridge and Wordsworth created together while living in the Quantock Hills in Somerset. In the preface, Wordsworth writes that he chose 'rustic life . . . because in that condition of life elementary feelings co-exist in a state of greater simplicity, and, consequently can be more accurately contemplated, and more forcibly communicated'.[9] In 1804 he famously remarked: 'I wandered lonely as a Cloud That floats on high o'er Vales and Hills.'[10] Concern for nature and the weather was a means to unite the thoughts and perceptions of the author or artist to those of the reader or viewer. Wordsworth composed as he walked, echoing Repton's 1794 remark that 'the gardener surveys his scenery while in motion'.[11]

First in Somerset and then later in the Lake District, Wordsworth came to typify the English romantic poet, politically disillusioned by the violent repercussions of the French Revolution and retiring to rural life as an antidote to the modern, urban and mechanical. But Jonathan Bate questions the assumption that Wordsworth's romanticism exemplifies a reactionary retreat from political and social engagement: 'the Romantic ecology has nothing to do with the flight from the material world,

8 Rousseau, *Reveries of the Solitary Walker*, pp. 62–63.

9 Wordsworth, *Lyrical Ballads*, vol. 1, pp. vii–viii.

10 The poem is called both 'I Wandered Lonely as a Cloud' and 'The Daffodils'. Wordsworth, *William Wordsworth: The Major Works*, pp. 303–304.

11 Repton, *The Art of Landscape Gardening*, 1794, quoted in Bois, p. 43.

View towards Cat Bells, the Lake District. Photograph, Jonathan Hill.

from history and society – it is in fact an attempt to enable mankind the better to live in the material world by entering into harmony with the environment'.[12] To support his argument, Bate cites Wordsworth's *Guide to the Lakes*, which was published in 1810 as an introduction to Joseph Wilkinson's *Select Views in Cumberland, Westmoreland and Lancashire*. It first appeared independently as *A Description of the Scenery of the Lakes in The North of England*, 1822, and was reprinted numerous times with various titles and amendments in Wordsworth's lifetime. Bate's argument is valuable but he overstates his case. Romanticism includes both a 'flight from the material world' and 'an attempt to enable mankind the better to live in the material world by entering into harmony with the environment'.

12 Bate's *Romantic Ecology* is a riposte to Jerome J. McGann's *The Romantic Ideology: A Critical Investigation*, 1983. Bate, *Romantic Ecology*, p. 40.

Wordsworth's guide is holistic, discussing local history, buildings, climate, farming, forestry management, geology, tourism, water distribution and the relations between the land and its inhabitants. Wordsworth gives special attention to weather's contribution to the *genius loci* and provides a thoughtful discussion of the agricultural economy, undermining the assumption that he was necessarily opposed to mechanisation. Adjusting his language accordingly, Wordsworth indicates whether he considers his subject to be poetic or pragmatic:

> *Such clouds, cleaving to their stations, or lifting up suddenly their glittering heads from behind rocky barriers, or hurrying out of sight with speed of the sharpest edge, will often tempt an inhabitant to congratulate himself on belonging to a country of mists, and clouds, and storms, and make him think of the blank sky of Egypt, and of the cerulean vacancy of Italy, as an unanimated and even a sad spectacle.*[13]

13 Wordsworth, *A Description of the Scenery of the Lakes*, p. 36.

> *The family of each man, whether* estatesman *or farmer, formerly had a twofold support; first, the produce of his lands and flocks; and secondly, the profit drawn from the employment of the women and children, as manufacturers, spinning their own wool in their own houses (work chiefly done in the winter season) and carrying it to market for sale . . . But, by the invention and universal application of machinery, this second resource has been cut off; the gains being so far reduced, as not to be sought after but by a few aged persons disabled from other employment. Doubtless, the invention of machinery has not been to these people a pure loss; for the profits arising from home-manufactures operated as a strong temptation to choose that mode of labour in neglect of husbandry. They also participate in the general benefit which the island has derived from the increased value of the produce of land, brought about by the establishment of manufactories, and in the consequent quickening of agricultural industry. But this is far from making amends*

> *. . . The consequence, then, is – that, proprietors and farmers being no longer able to maintain themselves upon small farms, several are united into one, and the buildings go to decay, or are destroyed; and that the lands of* estatesmen *being mortgaged and the owners constrained to part with them, they fall into the hands of wealthy purchasers; and if they wish to become residents, erect new mansions out of the ruins of the ancient cottages, whose little enclosures, with all the wild graces that grew out of them, disappear.*[14]

14 Wordsworth, *A Description of the Scenery of the Lakes*, pp. 99–100.

Language keeps these subjects apart although they are interdependent and should be considered together. But they are at least adjacent in a single publication. *Guide to the Lakes* indicates that English romanticism's appreciation of the environment and weather could accommodate intellect as well as emotion and was not necessarily opposed to reason. The guide also undermines the familiar image of the lone romantic. Rather than the perfect product of a single mind it was a collaboration adjusted and adapted over time. Wordsworth's sister, Dorothy, contributed material to the 1822 and 1823 editions.[15] John Hudson edited and published the 1842 edition. Adam Sedgwick added sections on geology in the 1842, 1846 and 1853 editions, while Thomas Gough provided local plant knowledge.[16]

15 However, Dorothy Wordsworth did so without credit.

16 Sedgwick was the first Woodwardian Professor of Geology at the University of Cambridge. Bate, *Romantic Ecology*, pp. 42–45.

A PLACE AND A PERSON

While Wordsworth came to personify the English romantic poet, Turner held a comparable status as a painter. Before the eighteenth century, nature was most often presented as a comparatively static setting for mythological and human figures. The picturesque explored human activity in dialogue with an evolving natural world, which was usually mediated and appreciated in a garden. Favouring the direct and unmediated exploration of nature, romanticism focused attention on weather as a means to fully appreciate the qualities of a place and a person. In promoting the creative imagination, romanticism reduced the authority of the patron and increased that of the artist, who more often selected the subject and the site of an artwork. Interested in uncovering meanings encoded in a place, Turner's response was critical as well as personal. 'After scrambling over the rocks on the lee side of the island' to reach Fingal's Cave, he describes the return journey: 'The sun getting towards the horizon, burst through the rain-cloud, angry, and for wind; and so it proved, for we were driven for shelter into Loch Ulver, and did not get back to Tobermory before midnight.'[17] Hunt writes that Turner's 'notebooks especially reveal how careful he was to record landscape subjects from different points of view or

17 Turner, letter to James Lennox, 16 August 1845, quoted in Gage, *Collected Correspondence of J.M.W. Turner*, pp. 209–210.

in different weathers, times of day, or even the moods in which he painted, for only in this way does a particular place yield its fullest genius'.[18] Recognising the particular advantages that the British climate offered the landscape painter, many of Turner's paintings focus on changes in the weather and human response to those changes:

18 Hunt, *Gardens and the Picturesque*, p. 237.

> *In our variable climate the seasons are recognizable in one day . . . how happily is the landscape painter situated, how roused by every change in nature in every moment, that allows no langour even in her effects which she places before him, and demands most peremptorily every moment his admiration and investigation, to store his mind with every change of time and place.*[19]

19 Turner, quoted in Wilton, *The Life and Work of J.M.W Turner*, p. 107.

In the 1820s and 1830s, after the conclusion of the Napoleonic wars, the expanding bourgeois market favoured comforting domestic dramas and the sublime was less considered.[20] But Turner's interest in the sublime continued throughout his life to varying degrees. Turner disregarded Burke's preference for dark rather than light because they fascinated him equally. But he shared Burke's fascination for sudden shifts from one to the other.[21] Visits to remote and dramatic sites early in his career fuelled Turner's depiction of sublime nature and architecture, as in *The Pass of St Gothard*, *c.* 1803–1804, and *St Edmunds' Church, Salisbury*, *c.* 1800. In *Critique of Judgement*, 1790, Kant identifies two aspects to the sublime: the mathematical and the dynamic.[22] One is a result of magnitude, the other of might. Especially later in his career, when he increasingly depicted energies rather than objects, Turner tended towards sublime might but his attention to formlessness also involved a concern for magnitude. However, the sublime was but one of his concerns. Turner's romanticism was more subtle and complex than Burke's thesis. He addressed a variety of emotions, not just pleasure and terror, and gave greater attention to the imagination, which could itself be sublime but not necessarily threatening.

20 Wilton, *Turner as Draughtsman*, pp. 117–118.

21 Turner occasionally referred to the sublime. There is no indication that he read Burke's account of the sublime but he may have done so and must have known of it through conversations. Burke, pp. 73–74.

22 Kant, *Critique of Judgement*, part 1, pp. 94–117. Refer to Wiedmann, *Romantic Art Theories*, pp. 25–26.

AN IDEA OF CUMBERLAND

In 1798, two years into its lengthy construction, Wyatt commissioned Turner to paint *A Projected Design for Fonthill Abbey* to convince and delight Beckford, his patron. The painting was exhibited at the Royal Academy with only the architect credited. In the following year Beckford invited Turner to depict the Abbey under construction. In the now dismembered pages of the *Fonthill* sketchbook, Turner reveals the Abbey close-up. At different times and in different weathers, the completed watercolours show the distant Abbey set within the surrounding landscape.[23] As Turner no doubt intended, it is uncertain whether the Abbey is in ruin or under construction. Referring to one of the watercolours, a friend of Beckford remarked: 'The scenery there must be magnificent. The hills and beautiful lake give one an idea of Cumberland.'[24] But Beckford responded: 'It is a very fine drawing, but rather too poetical, too ideal, even for Fonthill. The scenery there is certainly beautiful, but Turner took such liberties with it that he entirely destroyed the portraiture, the locality of the spot. That was the reason I parted with it.'[25] Rather than the late picturesque landscape created by his client, Turner depicted something even wilder and more familiar to romantic painters and poets. Typically, Turner did not paint a literal scene but followed his knowledge, feelings and imagination to create a single work from a composite of times and places. Neither did he adhere strictly to perspective, remarking that 'Rules are the means, nature the end.'[26]

TURNERIAN TOPOGRAPHY

In volume one of *Modern Painters*, 1843, John Ruskin praises Turner by associating him with Wordsworth: 'the keenest-eyed of all modern poets for what is deep and essential in nature, illustrates Turner here, as we shall find him doing in all other points'.[27] But later, in volume three of *Modern Painters*, 1856, Ruskin accuses Wordsworth of the 'pathetic fallacy' in which nature is subordinated to the self, mocking the 'notion that Nature would not be able to get on well without Wordsworth'.[28] While Ruskin's opinion of Wordsworth diminished, his admiration for Turner remained constant. He first encountered the artist's work on his thirteenth birthday in 1833, when he received a copy of the 1830 edition of Samuel Roger's Byronic poem *Italy*, which includes Turner's engravings.[29] Although a generation younger, Ruskin became Turner's principal interpreter and advocate. Turner's response was cool, possibly because he recognised their differing values and opinions. Ruskin's influence continued after Turner's death. Originally one of eight executors he was later placed in charge of the bequest. Devising categories such as 'Fine', 'Interesting', 'Good for distribution', 'Bad', 'Rubbish' and 'Valueless', Ruskin even destroyed some works he disliked, such as those of a sexual scene.

In the first volume of *Modern Painters*, 1843, Ruskin claims that Turner's genius depends on his ability to represent nature.[30] When the frequent touches of blue, red and yellow in his paintings were questioned by a viewer, Turner retorted: 'Well, don't you see that in Nature? Because, if you don't, Heaven help you.'[31]

23 The number of watercolours is uncertain as Turner mentions seven and Beckford six. Gage, *J.M.W. Turner: 'A Wonderful Range of Mind'*, p. 245, n. 27.

24 Landsdown, p. 15.

25 Gage assumes that Beckford refers to the *Afternoon View*. Beckford, quoted in Landsdown, p. 15; Gage, *J.M.W. Turner: 'A Wonderful Range of Mind'*, p. 30.

26 Turner, quoted in Davies, *Turner as Professor*, p. 43.

27 Ruskin, *Modern Painters*, vol. 1, p. 174.

28 Ruskin, *Modern Painters*, vol. 3, p. 276.

29 While Kent and Soane visited Italy as young men, Turner first went there in 1819, when he was forty-four, partly because the wars with France had curtailed foreign travel until Napoleon's final defeat in 1815.

30 Turner's truth to nature is a constant theme in *Modern Painters*, vol. 1, with regard to chiaroscuro for example. Ruskin, *Modern Painters*, vol. 1, p. 180.

31 Turner, quoted in Thornbury, p. 292. Refer to Gage, *Colour in Turner*, p. 40.

Ruskin valued the accurate representation of nature because he believed it was faithful to God's creation but the Christian moral truth that he found in the natural world Turner did not see. In the fourth volume of *Modern Painters*, 1856, Ruskin refines his argument but not his moralism, recognising discrepancies between actual places and Turner's depictions. Rather than accurately represent physical topography, Ruskin states that 'Turnerian topography' truthfully depicts the impression of a place on an observer, taking into account memories of associated journeys, places and paintings.[32]

32 Ruskin, *Modern Painters*, vol. 4, pp. 27–47.

> *Any topographical delineation of the facts, therefore, must be wholly incapable of arousing in the mind of the beholder those sensations which would be caused by the facts themselves, seen in their natural relations to others. And the aim of the great inventive landscape painter must be to give the far higher and deeper truth of mental vision, rather than that of the physical facts, and to reach a representation which, though it may be totally useless to engineers and geographers, and, when tried by rule and measure, totally unlike the place, shall yet be capable of producing on the far-away beholder's mind precisely the impression which the reality would have produced, and putting his heart into the same state in which it would have been, had he verily descended into the valley from the gorges of Airolo.*[33]

33 Ruskin, *Modern Painters*, vol. 4, pp. 35–36.

Ruskin's appreciation of Turnerian topography informed his attitude to the picturesque, to which he was ambivalent but too committed to discard. He describes the 'lower picturesque' as 'heartless' because its advocate focuses on surface effects to the detriment of deeper social concerns:

> *All other men feel some regret at the sight of disorder and ruin. He alone delights in both; it matters not of what. Fallen cottage – desolate villa – deserted village – blasted heath – mouldering castle – to him, so that they do but show jagged angles of stone and timber, all are sights equally joyful. Poverty, and darkness, and guilt, bring in their several contributions to his treasury of pleasant thoughts. The shattered window, opening into black and ghastly rents of wall, the foul rag or straw wisp stopping them, the dangerous roof, decrepit floor and stair, ragged misery, or wasting age of the inhabitants, – all these conduce, each in due measure, to the fullness of his satisfaction.*[34]

34 Ruskin, *Modern Painters*, vol. 4, p. 19.

Similarly, he dismisses the tinted 'convex mirror, one of the most pestilent inventions for falsifying Nature and degrading art which was ever put into an artist's hand', because it intervenes between the artist and a direct appreciation of nature.[35] In

35 Ruskin, *The Elements of Drawing*, pp. 201–202.

contrast, Ruskin identifies the 'nobler', *'Turnerian Picturesque'*, concluding 'that the dignity of the picturesque increases from lower to higher, in exact proportion to the sympathy of the artist with his subject'.[36]

36 Ruskin, *Modern Painters*, vol. 4, pp. 24–26, 23.

THAT GOLDEN STAIN OF TIME

A concern for the noble picturesque continued in Ruskin's later work. *The Stones of Venice*, 1851–1853, owes it a significant debt. Also informed by German romantic thought – notably Goethe's 'Von Deutscher Baukunst' (On German Architecture), 1772 – Ruskin emphasises that 'art is valuable or otherwise, only as it expresses the personality, activity and living perception of a good and great human soul'.[37] Ruskin applied this principle of creative expression widely, recognising architectural authorship beyond that of the architect. Rather than the image of incremental accretion and decay in a picturesque ruin or the simple effects of contingency, he admires buildings that are conceived to accept changes in craftsmanship and use. Emphasising the social value of this theme in *The Seven Lamps of Architecture*, 1849, Ruskin extends the eighteenth-century theory of association to the politics of human labour, valuing 'not only what men have thought and felt, but what their hands have handled, and their strength wrought'.[38]

37 Goethe, 'On German Architecture', pp. 106–108; Ruskin, *The Stones of Venice*, vol. 1, pp. 35–45. Refer to Swenarton, pp. 1–8.

38 Ruskin, *The Seven Lamps of Architecture*, p. 169.

Ruskin reserves praise for ageing due to the effects of use and weather and regrets the effects of industrialisation, which he believes to be dehumanising: 'For, indeed, the greatest glory of a building is not in its stones, or its gold. Its glory is in its Age . . . it is in that golden stain of time, that we are to look for the real light, and colour, and preciousness of architecture.'[39] Analysing Ruskin's formative influences, Hunt identifies ruination as a recurring theme in his writings and traces its origins to his upbringing:

39 Ruskin, *The Seven Lamps of Architecture*, p. 177.

> *So that although picturesque ruin and its sentimental associations are specifically derided by the mid-1850s, the attraction to decay and incompleteness becomes the foundation of the whole work. The reason, I believe, is that his religious upbringing contrived to make ruin an essential feature of his spiritual landscape. His mother's evangelical training never ceased to insist upon the imperfections of human life and its achievements . . . For such a temperament as Ruskin's, the idea of ruin had a vital fascination. It seems furthermore to have permeated his whole psychology long after Ruskin ceased to subscribe to his mother's religious teaching; consequently, we find that he is ready to identify and discuss ruin even in contexts that do not otherwise declare any strong evangelical attitudes.*[40]

40 Hunt, *Gardens and the Picturesque*, p. 197.

Ruskin's concern for the effects of time on buildings had notable consequences, furthering the conservation movement, for example.[41] In 1877 William Morris founded the Society for the Protection of Ancient Buildings on the premise that each layer of a building's history should be retained. Unfortunately, rather than acknowledging the passage of time, such a conservation policy may lead to the denial of change. A further and even more significant consequence was to stimulate sustainable development:

41 Ruskin, *The Seven Lamps of Architecture*, pp. 184–186.

> *The idea of self-denial for the sake of posterity, of practising present economy for the sake of debtors yet unborn, of planting forests that our descendants may live under their shade, or of raising cities for future nations to inhabit, never, I suppose, efficiently takes place among publicly recognised motives of exertion. Yet these are not the less duties; nor is our part fitly sustained upon the earth, unless the range of our intended and deliberate usefulness include not only the companions, but the successors, of our pilgrimage. God has lent us the earth for our life; it is a great entail. It belongs as much to those who are to come after us, and whose names are already written in the book of creation, as to us; and we have no right, by anything that we do or neglect, to involve them in unnecessary penalties, or deprive them of benefits which it was in our power to bequeath.*[42]

42 Ruskin, *The Seven Lamps of Architecture*, p. 176.

Ruskin's analysis of the picturesque was beneficial in that it focused attention on human labour, which the picturesque had often ignored. But his assessment was a caricature, ignoring the range of social, cultural and environmental concerns that were essential to the picturesque since the early eighteenth century, whether Stowe's political agenda or Rousham's Georgic associations. Characterising much of the picturesque as mere visual gratification, Ruskin affirmed a particularly English morality that denigrates aesthetics if it lacks an overt and glaringly obvious social purpose. If the picturesque continues to be unrecognised or misunderstood it is in some degree due to Ruskin's influence.

THE STORM-CLOUD OF THE NINETEENTH CENTURY

Ruskin's concern for nature found vivid expression in his fascination for the sky, in which he recognised the heavenly light of Christian tradition. In his youth he measured its colour daily with the aid of a 'cyanometer'. Admiring Howard's *On the Modification of Clouds* Ruskin gives particular value to '*cloudiness*', which he describes as 'the most characteristic examples of modern landscape' painting.[43] In the first volume of

43 Ruskin, Modern Painters, vol. 3, p. 254. Refer to Fitch, p. 5.

Modern Painters he praises Turner's depiction of clouds: 'Show me a single picture, in the whole compass of ancient art, in which I can pass from cloud to cloud, from region to region, from first to second and third heaven, as I can here.'[44] In 1884, later in his life, Ruskin recognises an increasingly disturbing sky that fulfils his morbid fascination for ruination. Extending the age-old affiliation of human misadventure with environmental retribution, he characterises industrial pollution as 'the storm-cloud of the nineteenth century', which he associates with the spiritual abstinence of the modern world.[45] Coupling the growing storm to his declining sanity, Ruskin concludes that 'The curse on the sky is my chief plague – if only spring were spring! But it is too hard on me, this devil in the wind and clouds and light.'[46]

44 Ruskin, *Modern Painters*, vol. 1, pp. 233–234.

45 Ruskin, *The Storm-Cloud of the Nineteenth Century*, pp. 55–63.

46 Ruskin, *The Brantwood Diary of John Ruskin*, p. 228.

> *Raining in full drizzle, slow and steady; sky pitch-dark, and I just get a little light by sitting in the bow-window: diabolic clouds over everything: I found it one miserable mass of weeds gone to seed, the roses in the higher garden putrefied into brown sponges, feeling like dead snails; and the half-ripe strawberries all rotten at the stalk . . . In healthy weather, the sun is hidden behind a cloud, as it is behind a tree; and, when the cloud is past, it comes out again, as bright as before. But in plague-wind, the sun is choked out of the whole heaven, all day long, by a cloud which may be a thousand miles square and five miles deep.*[47]

47 Ruskin, *The Storm-Cloud of the Nineteenth Century*, pp. 58–59.

RAIN, STEAM, SPEED

The attention to nature and the effects of industrialisation furthered environmental awareness in the early nineteenth century. Many romantic painters and poets opposed industry to nature, which was defended from chemical and mechanical defilement. In his *Guide to the Lakes* Wordsworth does not dismiss agricultural machinery but in 1844 he opposed the proposed railway line between Kendal and Windermere because of the damage that he believed it would cause to the Lake District. Turner also cherished nature. But his romanticism was more inclusive. Whether natural, man-made or combinations of the two, the things around him were a stimulus to his feelings and imagination. Avoiding stereotypes, Turner painted the most mundane of tasks, whether agricultural or industrial. *Ploughing Up Turnips near Slough*, *c.*1809, is far removed from Claude's pastoral Arcadia. *Interior of an Iron Foundry*, *c.*1797, is equally direct. Turner admired de Loutherbourg, a painter with comparable concerns whose *Coalbrookdale by Night*, 1801, depicts smoking furnaces and discarded machinery parts alongside a horse-drawn wagon. But Turner's interest in new technologies and their effects was the most sustained and best known of his generation, extending the picturesque fascination for ruination to industrialisation. In 1841 Isambard Kingdom Brunel invited Turner to the speed trials of the newly constructed Great Western Railway between London and Bristol, where the steam engine reached 90 mph, epitomising technological advance. The resulting painting, *Rain, Steam, Speed – The Great Western Railway*, 1844, depicts a stretch of the Thames that Turner knew well and enjoyed. In a heavy storm, a steam engine rushes over Maidenhead Bridge as a hare flees along the track. Far below, the bridge's heavy arch dwarfs a small rowing boat as a horse-drawn plough works the fields and nearby figures gesticulate upwards. Ruskin remarked that Turner painted *Rain, Steam, Speed – The Great Western Railway* 'to show what he could do even with an ugly subject'.[48] But confusing his own opinions with those of the painter, Ruskin misinterpreted Turner's more subtle and nuanced response to mechanisation, which extended Turnerian topography to the industrial landscape. Depicting an animal in flight from a machine and agriculture surpassed by industry, Turner implies that technological advance

48 Ruskin, *The Works of John Ruskin*, vol. 35, p. 601.

J.M.W. Turner, *Rain, Steam, Speed – The Great Western Railway*, 1844. Courtesy of the National Gallery, London.

is not necessarily equivalent to social progress. But *Rain, Steam, Speed – The Great Western Railway* also reflects his fascination for complex combinations of the new and the old, the natural and the man-made; each has its respective energies and weathers, which inform and affect one another.

THE ENVELOPE OF ATMOSPHERE

Turner's concern for tradition and innovation is apparent in the painting's composition as well as its subject. *Rain, Steam, Speed – The Great Western Railway* references Nicolas Poussin, one of the seventeenth-century painters who influenced the eighteenth-century picturesque. According to Andrew Wilton:

> *The envelope of atmosphere – a wonderfully observed account of just those three 'abstractions' that Turner enumerates in his title – is founded on a design that pays tribute to that most draughtsmanly of Old Masters, Nicolas Poussin. The geometry of the receding perspective in the foreground viaduct and the firm horizontal that divides the whole composition in half is a reference to one of Turner's favourite pictures, the* Landscape with a Roman Road *that he had known for much of his adult life in the Dulwich Picture Gallery.*[49]

Devoted to the art of the past, Turner especially respected Claude, who two of his early patrons, Beckford and Knight, collected. His remark that a Claude painting is 'made up of bits' is praise, not criticism, because he admired the juxtaposition of images and allusions.[50] The association of ideas was a constant concern for Turner, who evoked the *genius loci* in two related paintings.[51] He painted *Pope's Villa at Twickenham* in 1808, the year after its demolition. Waiting boatmen in the foreground and the distant villa on the opposite bank of the Thames affirm the elegiac mood. Indicating his admiration for both poets, Turner painted *Thomson's Aeolian Harp* the following year, including Thomson's tomb and distorting the topography of the Thames to incorporate Pope's villa. According to Hunt:

> *Finally . . . the aeolian harp stands for or emblemizes the poet's responsiveness to the slightest influences of nature. Placed in the grove of Turner's painting it signals both the special spirit of place associated with Thomson and the especially responsive genius of the poet whom a sympathetic painter in his turn commemorates.*[52]

Turner admired many of the artists and poets who inspired the picturesque. He shared Price and Knight's concern for autumnal colours but considered their

49 This painting is dated 1648. Wilton, *Turner as Draughtsman*, p. 103. Refer to Gage, *Colour in Turner*, pp. 54–55.

50 Turner quoted in Gage, *J.M.W. Turner*, p. 108.

51 Gage, *Colour in Turner*, pp. 132–134.

52 The painting's title refers to Thomson's poem 'Ode on Aeolus's Harp'. Hunt, *Gardens and the Picturesque*, p. 229. Refer to Gage, *Colour in Turner*, pp. 54–55.

categorisation of the picturesque to be too narrow. Equally, his appreciation of the picturesque was more inclusive and less moralistic than that of Ruskin.

THE AUTHOR WAS IN THIS STORM

Turner's increasing reputation was influential not only in raising the status of landscape painting but also in expanding the types of landscape depicted. Previously, a landscape was often the background, not the subject, of a painting because historical, literary and biblical themes were held in the highest esteem. To acquire status before Turner's era, a landscape painting had to incorporate an established theme, as in the work of Claude.[53] Turner continued to depict grand narratives but did so with a new intensity. The paintings of Poussin and Claude place the painter and the viewer outside the scene, in which poised figures occupy a static landscape. In contrast, the vast, brooding sky dominates *Snow Storm: Hannibal and his Army Crossing the Alps*, 1812. Even the mountains are shrouded and the army occupies a thin line of ground at the base of the painting, representing humanity overwhelmed by the natural power of the impending storm. In the Royal Academy, a large painting was usually hung so that it was seen above the visitors' heads. But

53 Wilton, *Turner and the Sublime*, pp. 17–19.

J.M.W. Turner, *Snow Storm: Hannibal and his Army Crossing the Alps*, 1812. Courtesy of the Tate, London.

Turner demanded that *Snow Storm: Hannibal and his Army Crossing the Alps* was placed much lower so that the painting engulfed the viewers.

Rain, Steam, Speed – The Great Western Railway depicts fewer people but is even more absorbed by energy – the air is brooding and the train speeds forward – so that the viewer is drawn into the scene. In a further painting of natural and man-made forces, *Snow Storm – Steam-Boat off a Harbour's Mouth making Signals in Shallow Water, and going by the Lead. The Author was in this Storm on the Night the Ariel left Harwich*, 1842, no human figures are depicted because the painter was fully immersed in the scene. Turner remarks: 'I did not paint it to be understood, but I wished to show what such a scene was like: I got the sailors to lash me to the mast to observe it; I was lashed for four hours, and I did not expect to escape, but I felt bound to record it if I did. But no one has any business to like the picture.'[54] Turner's account is widely disputed. For example, Malcolm Andrews notes:

54 Turner, in a conversation recorded by the Rev. William Kingsley, published in Ruskin, *Modern Painters*, vol. 5, p. 445.

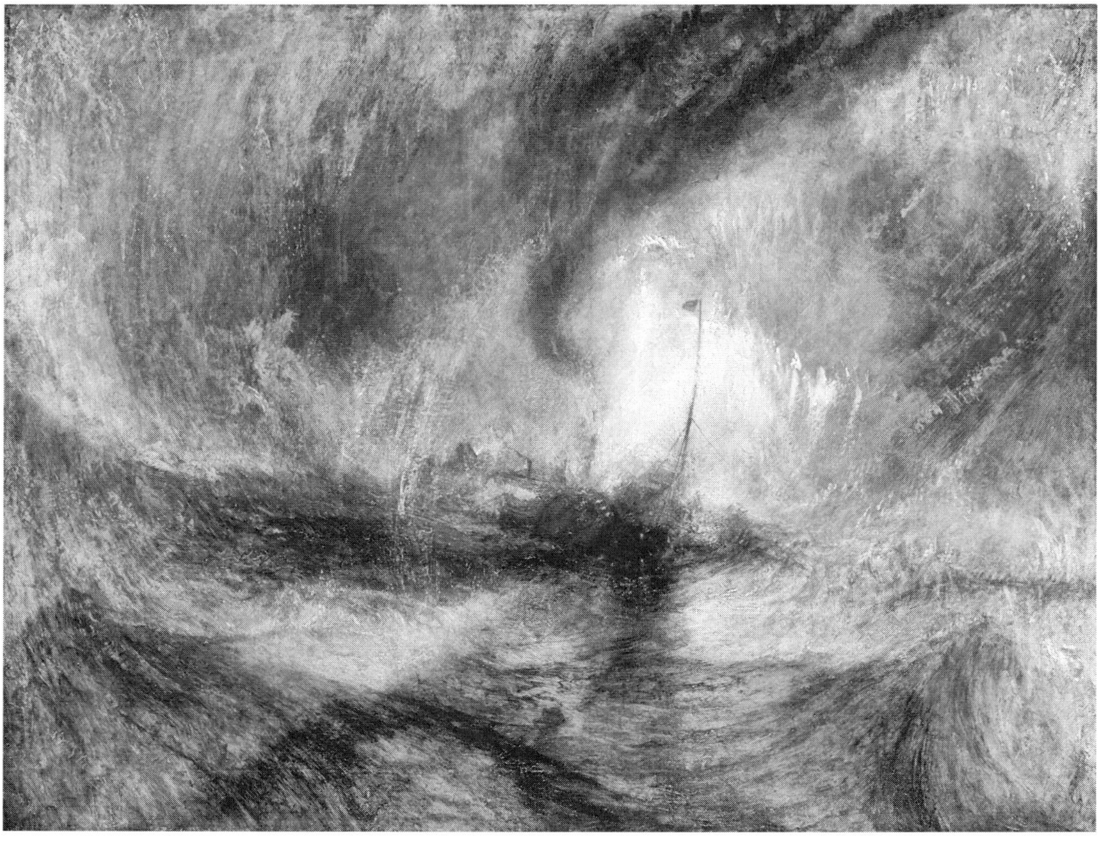

J.M.W. Turner, *Snow Storm – Steam-Boat off a Harbour's Mouth making Signals in Shallow Water, and going by the Lead. The Author was in this Storm on the Night the Ariel left Harwich*, 1842. Courtesy of the Tate, London.

> *The Ariel was a Dover, not a Harwich, paddle steamer, and Turner, as far as is known, had not been to that part of East Anglia for many years . . . given that Turner was in his late 50s at this time, one may be reasonably sceptical about his capacity to withstand the elements for as long as claimed.*[55]

55 Andrews, *Landscape in Western Art*, p. 177. Refer to Venning, pp. 123–124; Wilton, *Turner and the Sublime*, pp. 17–19; Wilton, *Turner as Draughtsman*, p. 103.

An avid traveller who experienced storms on land and at sea, Turner did not need to be lashed to a ship's mast to produce the painting. Its lengthy title adds drama and detail, indicating that he wanted to convey the experience within the storm, not the view from a distance. Turner's remark – 'I wished to show what such a scene was like' – further invites the viewer and confirms Ruskin's description of Turnerian topography. Absorbed in atmosphere, the author and viewer are overwhelmed by nature's majesty. But the 'Author' in the title, the reference to heroic dedication ('I got the sailors to lash me to the mast'), and disregard for the viewer's response ('no one has any business to like the picture') indicate a conception of authorship that is typical of romanticism. David Blayney Brown remarks:

> *No earlier painter would have centred himself in the experience of his picture in quite this way, insisted so much on the uniqueness of his interpretation and his mission to present it at all costs, and been so proudly heedless of whether it was liked or understood.*[56]

56 Brown, *Romanticism*, p. 21.

STORM AND STEAM

Turner's artistic fascination for industry and energy paralleled scientific and climatic research. In 1781 the Royal Academy, Royal Society and Society of Antiquaries moved to Sir William Chambers's Somerset House in London, remaining there until 1837. On leaving the Strand, the visitor passed into the portico, which framed the expansive central courtyard beyond. Within the portico, and to the left, was the entrance to the Royal Society, which promoted the sciences. Directly opposite, and to the right, was the entrance to the Royal Academy, which promoted the arts. Their proximity encouraged the members of one institution to attend the meetings of the other. Turner was a regular visitor to the Royal Society and conversed with a number of eminent scientists there and elsewhere. His acquaintances included Sir Humphry Davy, Professor of Chemistry at the Royal Institution, which was founded in 1799 to complement the more theoretical concerns of the Royal Society; Sir Michael Faraday, Davy's successor; Charles Babbage, creator of the Difference

Engine; and the mathematician Mary Somerville. Davy climbed the Lake District with Wordsworth in 1805, while in 1808 Coleridge lectured on 'Poetry and the Imagination' at the Royal Institution at his invitation. Davy admired Thomson's *The Seasons*, which inspired his own poems on energy in nature. Drawing parallels between the scientific and artistic minds, he remarks:

> *The perception of truth is almost as simple a feeling as the perception of beauty; and the genius of Newton, of Shakespeare, of Michel Angelo, and of Handel, are not very remote in character from each other. Imagination, as well as the reason, is necessary to perfection in the philosophical mind. A rapidity of combination, a power of perceiving analogies, and of comparing them by facts, is the creative source of discovery. Discrimination and delicacy of sensation, so important in physical research, are other words for taste; and love of nature is the same passion, as the love of the magnificent, the sublime and the beautiful.*[57]

57 Davy, quoted in Holmes, p. 276. Refer to Hamilton, *Turner and the Scientists*, p. 12; Holmes, pp. 243, 295–300.

The respect was mutual. In the preface to the 1802 edition of *Lyrical Ballads*, Wordsworth considers the convergence of poetry and science, with Davy as the likely model:

> *If the labours of men of Science should ever create any material revolution, direct or indirect, in our condition, and in the impressions which we habitually receive, the Poet will sleep no more than at present, but he will be ready to follow the steps of the man of Science, not only in those general indirect effects, but he will be at his side, carrying sensation into the midst of the objects of science itself. The remotest discoveries of the Chemist, the Botanist, or Mineralogist, will be as proper objects of the Poet's art as any upon which it can be employed.*[58]

58 Wordsworth, *Lyrical Ballads*, p. xxxviii.

Turner owned few scientific books but had a first edition of Somerville's *Mechanism of the Heavens*, 1831, and admired her experiment on the magnetising properties of certain colours of light, notably violet and indigo.[59] She, in turn, admired his paintings. Turner also knew David Brewster – the inventor of the kaleidoscope in 1815 – who in 1839 published 'Statistics and Philosophy of Storms' in the *Edinburgh Review*, a journal that Turner regularly consulted. It is likely that Faraday and Turner first became acquainted due to their mutual friendship with the physician James Carrick Moore and his eldest daughter, Harriet, who gave the painter a nickname he enjoyed: 'Mr Avalanche Jenkinson'. Sharing Turner's concern for the detailed observation of nature, Faraday describes a sublime natural event:

59 *Mechanism of the Heavens* was a translation and interpretation of Pierre Simon Laplace's *Traité de Mécanique Céleste*, 1798–1827. Refer to Gage, *Colour in Turner*, p. 107; Hamilton, *Faraday*, p. 277.

The sound of these avalanches is exceedingly fine and solemn. It is the sound of thunder known to be caused by a fall of terrestrial matter, and conveys the idea of irresistible force. To the sight the avalanche is at this distance not terrible but beautiful. Rarely is it seen in the commencement, but the ear tells first of something strange happening, and then looking, the eye sees a falling cloud of snow, or else what was a moment before a cataract of water changed into a tumultuous and heavily waving rush of snow, ice, and fluid, which, as it descends through the air, looks like water thickened, but as it runs over the inclined surfaces of the heaps below, moves heavily like paste, stopping and going as the mass behind accumulates or is dispersed.[60]

A member of a sect that adhered strictly to the Bible, Faraday considered nature to be divine.[61] He offered Turner advice on colour formation and admired his depictions of sea storms, hanging one – most likely an engraving or a copy – in his study in the Royal Institution. But his research on electricity was probably his principal influence on Turner. In 1831 Faraday submitted his seminal paper on electromagnetic induction to the Royal Society, the first of a series of over thirty papers that he produced during the following decades with the collective title 'Experimental Researches in Electricity'. Indicating that magnetism in motion can guarantee a consistent current, Faraday's discovery heralded the future demise of steam power and the rise of the electrical age.

Aware of the earth's magnetic force, in 1842 Faraday conducted an experiment into terrestrial electromagnetic induction in the Thames at Waterloo Bridge, stimulating romantic fascination for scientific understanding of the earth's forces. Noting Turner's friendship with scientists, James Hamilton suggests an interpretation of *Snow Storm – Steam-Boat off a Harbour's Mouth* that refers to the research of Somerville and Faraday:

In Snow Storm – Steam-Boat off a Harbour's Mouth *Turner is giving graphic expression to the very real lines of force that his scientist friends had showed were being emitted from all points of the earth's surface at all times . . . Turner subtly links the imagery of iron filings on paper in an invisible magnetic field with energised sea water surrounding and acting upon a magnetic iron ship.*[62]

Produced just two years apart, *Rain, Steam, Speed – The Great Western Railway* and *Snow Storm – Steam-Boat off a Harbour's Mouth* depict the complex interweaving of intense natural energy with that of the era's most formidable machine, the steam engine. On land, the train appears most powerful, surpassing older

60 Faraday, 5 August 1841, quoted in Hamilton, *Faraday*, pp. 301–302; refer to pp. 241–242.

61 The Sandemanian sect was named after Robert Sandeman.

62 Hamilton, *Turner and the Scientists*, p. 128. Refer to Hamilton, *Faraday*, pp. 240, 359–361, 375–377; Jones, *The Life and Letters of Michael Faraday*, vol. 1, p. 378; Rodner, pp. 80–83; Wiedman, *Romantic Art Theories*, p. 8.

technologies and the weather's energies. At sea, the boat is vulnerable to the greater power of nature: storm and steam are drawn into a single vortex so powerful that Turner 'did not expect to escape', evoking a parallel passion for life and death. Typically romantic, Turner combined a desire to live life to the full with a profound pessimism.

THE BIG SMOKE

Londoners, and the inhabitants of other industrial cities, were well aware of the man-made atmospheres they inhabited. But scientific understanding of industrialisation's influence on climate developed very gradually during the nineteenth century and without public debate. In 1816 and again in 1822, Jean Baptiste Joseph Fourier likened the atmosphere to a greenhouse that captures heat from the sun, stars and earth, which it radiates back to the earth.[63] A later article in 1824, which was republished in 1827, less explicitly mentions the greenhouse effect but was most effective in disseminating Fourier's idea.[64] Subsequently, at the Royal Society in 1859, John Tyndall presented his research into the absorption and transmission of thermal radiation through water vapour and gases.[65]

In the decade following his systematic investigation of cloud formations, Howard focused on the ways in which the city creates its own clouds, fulfilling the implications of Evelyn's earlier research. *The Climate of London* appeared in two volumes in 1818 and 1820 and as an expanded edition in 1833 with *On the Modification of Clouds* as the introduction. Previous attempts to curb pollution had focused on particular points of origin, creating a 'black catalogue' of offending polluters as in the preface to the 1772 edition of Evelyn's *Fumifugium*.[66] But Howard recognised that pollution generated throughout London led to the formation of city-wide fogs, which stagnant days failed to dissipate.[67] Severe fogs were common in the sixteenth century and their frequency noticeably increased after 1750. Due to intense atmospheric pollution, London acquired the nickname the 'big smoke'. Enveloping the city that produced it, the smoke even entered interiors. In 1832 'The Duke of Devonshire's ball was held in the clouds: so thick was the fog in the drawing-room that you could not recognize people at the other end of the room.'[68]

Ruskin traced Turner's fascination for detritus and decay to his childhood next to Covent Garden market: 'Turner devoted picture after picture to the illustration of effects of dinginess, smoke, soot, dust, and dusty texture; old sides of boats, weedy roadside vegetation, dung-hills, straw-yards, and all the soilings and stains of every common labour.'[69] A Londoner throughout his life, Turner's reaction to the polluted

63 Fourier, *The Analytical Theory of Heat*, p. 9; Fourier, 'Théorie de la chaleur', pp. 350–376.

64 Fourier, 'Remarques générales sur la températures du globe terrestre et des espaces planétaires' ('General Remarks on the Temperature of the Terrestrial Globe and Planetary Spaces'), pp. 153. Refer to Christianson, pp. 11–12; Fleming, pp. 55–64.

65 Tyndall, p. 37.

66 Samuel Pegge, in Evelyn, *Fumifugium*, p. iii. Refer to Brimblecombe, *The Big Smoke*, pp. 96, 113.

67 Howard, *The Climate of London*, vol. 2, pp. 288–289.

68 Extract from a letter of 25 February 1832, from Dorothea, Princess Lieven, to Lady Cowper.

69 Ruskin, *Modern Painters*, vol. 5, p. 318.

air of the world's largest industrial city was fascination rather than repulsion. Its light and colour effects especially intrigued him, extending to the city the romantic concern for colour's emotive impact. Noting the smog's predominantly yellow tinge, Peter Brimblecombe concludes 'that fine smoke particles in the atmosphere could absorb the blue wavelengths from the sunlight above the fog in such a way that the fog at ground level was illuminated by a yellow light . . . It is also possible that the colour might have been the result of tarry compounds present in fog droplets'.[70] Depicting a myriad of colours alongside dominant yellows, *The Thames above Waterloo Bridge*, *c.*1830–1835, depicts the city as a heady haze.[71] In *Snow Storm – Steam-Boat off a Harbour's Mouth* and *Rain, Steam, Speed – The Great Western Railway* the various energies are intense but somewhat distinct. *The Thames above Waterloo Bridge* is thicker, heavier, slower. Monuments, buildings, barges, figures, fluids and fumes are all absorbed into a single atmosphere in which divisions between the natural and man-made are indistinct. Here, the city is the weather. Turner was not

70 Brimblecombe, *The Big Smoke*, p. 125.

71 The painting was not exhibited during Turner's lifetime.

J.M.W. Turner, *The Thames above Waterloo Bridge*, *c.*1830–1835. Courtesy of the Tate, London.

alone in his passion for the big smoke. Charles Dickens opens *Bleak House*, 1852–1853, with an atmospheric account of 'Smoke lowering down from chimney-pots, making a soft blank drizzle, with flakes of soot in it as big as full-grown snow-flakes – gone into mourning, one might imagine, for the death of the sun.'[72]

72 Dickens, *Bleak House*, p. 11.

THE PLEASURE OF BEING YOUR OWN ARCHITECT

Turner is known principally as a painter but he also pursued an architectural career. As weather was one of his fascinations its influence on his designs is worthy of discussion. Turner studied and worked in the offices of the architectural draughtsman Thomas Malton Junior and the architect Thomas Hardwick before entering the Royal Academy Schools in 1789 when he was fourteen. He initially continued his career as an architectural draughtsman alongside his work as an artist.

Soane became the Professor of Architecture at the Royal Academy in 1806 and in the following year he argued that a new Professor of Perspective should be appointed. Of particular relevance to the education of architects the post was less prestigious than that of the Professor of Painting. Sir Joshua Reynolds recounts Sir William Chambers's opinion 'that any one qualified, in all points, to be an Academician, would never condescend to teach an inferior and mechanick branch of the art'.[73] Soane's illustrator, Gandy, put his name forward to teach the subject but was not qualified for the Professorship as he was only an associate Academician. The only candidate, and a full Academician since 1802, Turner was appointed Professor later in 1807.

73 Reynolds, p. 107.

In 1826 Turner remarked to the painter and collector James Holworthy, who was then building a house at Hathersage, Derbyshire: 'you talk of mountains high as the moon . . . but consider the pleasure of being your own architect day by day, its growing honors hour by hour, increasing strata by strata'.[74] Turner's largest completed design was Sandycombe Lodge, 1812, his country villa at Twickenham, then a fashionable country town associated with Pope's villa, which Turner fondly recalled. It is assumed that Soane influenced Turner's design, in which Grecian brick corbels and deep Italianate eaves surmount restrained, compact, symmetrical elevations. Helen Dorey remarks that the entrance hall is 'like a miniature version of Soane's Pitzhanger with its pair of segmental headed arches and small, winding stair with a rounded headed niche on the turn of the stairs. A telling detail is Turner's use of the roll mouldings which seem to be unique to Soane'.[75] The Twickenham air was less polluted than London's and there is no indication that it was an impor-

74 Turner, letter to Holworthy, 7 January 1826, in Gage, *Collected Correspondence of J.M.W. Turner*, p. 96.

75 Dorey, *John Soane & J.M.W. Turner*, p. 26. Refer to Dean, p. 183.

tant design consideration for Turner. Beyond the normal requirements of shelter, the weather did not inform the design of Sandycombe Lodge.

A COLD WET DAY IN AUTUMN

Artistic convention favoured oil paintings over drawings and watercolours, which Turner painted for a decade before he completed his first oil painting in 1796. Drawing in situ was an important feature of his artistic practice, both as an end in itself and as an aid to studio painting. Turner sketched wherever and whenever he could, including from a slow-moving horse-drawn carriage. But only a small number of his watercolours and even fewer oil paintings were made outdoors. *House beside the River, with Trees and Sheep*, *c.*1806–1812, is splattered with raindrops. More often Turner painted in his studio. In 1799 he moved to 64 Harley Street. Three years later he bought a lease on the property and designed a first floor gallery for the display of his paintings, which was completed in 1804. In 1810 he moved to 47 Queen Anne Street West close by, where he completed a second gallery in 1822, again to his own design, which Dorey concludes was 'surely inspired by Soane's celebrated Dulwich Picture Gallery of 1811 and perhaps by Soane's own Library and Study, also painted Pompeiian red'.[76]

Relying on repeated experiences of a place, Turner's painting practice paralleled the familiar experience of architecture. Painting requires concentration while use is often associated with absent-minded distraction.[77] However, use is an intuitive intelligence acquired over time, and can either deviate from familiar behaviour or estabish, affirm or develop a habit that is itself creative. Reassociation, misuse and physical transformation are some of the ways in which the user can make a building or space anew.[78]

Turner's transformation of 47 Queen Anne Street West occurred by use as much as by design. An early visitor, the Rev. William Kingsley, admired the elegant house and 'best lighted gallery I have ever seen'.[79] From the adjacent studio, Turner could watch 'his visitor's every move from the small peephole in the dividing wall'.[80] After a visit in 1842 the painter William Leighton Leitch describes a quite different scene, which Walter Thornbury, Turner's first biographer, confirms:

> *The house had a desolate look. The door was shabby, and nearly destitute of paint, and the windows were obscured by dirt . . . The hall was not like that of an ordinary London house. It had a square empty appearance; no furniture in it, a dingy brown colour on the walls, and some casts from the Elgin marbles inserted in the upper*

76 Dorey, *John Soane & J.M.W. Turner*, p. 13. Refer to Finberg, *The Life of J.M.W. Turner*, pp. 267–269; Gage, *Colour in Turner*, p. 134; Gage, *J.M.W. Turner*, p. 68; Townsend, *Turner's Painting Techniques*, p. 58.

77 Benjamin, 'The Work of Art in the Age of Mechanical Production', p. 239.

78 Hill, *Actions of Architecture*, pp. 63–89.

79 Kingsley, quoted in Gage, *Colour in Turner*, p. 162.

80 Hamilton, *Turner*, p. 213.

part. Everything was covered with dust, and had a neglected look. When I entered the gallery and looked at the pictures I was astonished, and the state in which they were shocked me. The skylights on the roof were excessively dirty, many of the panes of glass were broken, and some were awanting altogether. It was a cold wet day in autumn, and the rain was coming through the broken glass, on to the middle of the floor, and all the time I was there – fully an hour – I had to keep my umbrella up over my head . . . two of the finest (of the pictures), 'The Rise of Carthage' and 'Crossing the Brook' were in anything but good condition.[81]

81 A. MacGeorge, quoted in Gage, *J.M.W. Turner*, pp. 152–153.

Backward stretched a large unfurnished room filled with unfinished pictures; then a larger and drearier room yet; lastly, a back room, against the walls of which stood his unfinished productions, large full canvasses placed carelessly against a wall, the damp of which had taken off the colours altogether, or had damaged them.[82]

82 Thornbury, p. 362.

Decay must have begun much earlier for the house, gallery and studio to reach such a level of decrepitude by the early 1840s, when Turner painted *Snow Storm – Steam-Boat off a Harbour's Mouth* and *Rain, Steam, Speed – The Great Western Railway*. Historians cite Turner's old age and curmudgeonly character to explain the decay. David Blayney Brown describes Turner as 'a profound pessimist' and 'depressive whose resolve, in old age, has so far flagged that he could not be bothered to look after the works he intended for posterity'.[83] Turner familiarly worked on a number of paintings at the same time and often left an unfinished painting in his studio for an extended period before returning to it later. Finished paintings also remained in the decrepit studio and gallery:

83 Brown, *Romanticism*, p. 161. Refer to Gage, *Colour in Turner*, p. 171.

Turner's tendency to keep his unfinished and unsold works in a damp studio which had rain leaking in, and was possibly poorly heated when he worked there (since his indifference to extreme and unpleasant weather was remarked on in his lifetime) promoted such damaging mould growth, perhaps before the paint dried.[84]

84 Townsend, 'Turner's Use of Materials', p. 6.

There are many examples among the unfinished paintings of damages caused by Turner's stacking canvasses together, where both priming and paint has been transferred to an adjacent stretcher.[85]

85 Townsend, 'Turner's Use of Materials', p. 6.

As unfinished paintings were left in the studio they acquired a layer of dirt and grease, which Turner should have cleaned away before adding further paint. But he did not. The layer of dirt became part of the painting, decreasing adhesion between the old and new layers and causing flaking.[86]

86 Hackney, pp. 53–54.

> *The finished paintings . . . frequently suffer from moisture sensitivity, disfiguring mould growth, flaking of priming from canvas, flaking of paint from paint, wrinkled and cracked paint, discoloured glazes and shadows, loss of texture as a result of early lining treatments, extreme temperature sensitivity and extreme solvent sensibility. These problems are far from unknown in works by other nineteenth century artists, but it has been discovered that Turner's choice of media for both paint and priming, and his ways of applying paint, serve to make the problems worse than those usually encountered.*[87]

In these descriptions, the painting conservationists Joyce Townsend and Stephen Hackney identify a number of reasons for the poor condition of Turner's paintings today, all significantly due to his working practices, including the dilapidated state of his studio. Confirming Ruskin's opinion that 'First, he receives a true impression from the place itself . . . and then he sets himself as far as possible to reproduce that impression on the mind of the spectator',[88] Townsend concludes that 'the impression he had sought to record was more important than the painting itself'.[89] But it is likely that Turner identified the progressive decay and gradual ruination of a painting as a means to convey the impression of a place in relation to time and weather. A successful and wealthy artist, Turner could have had his studio repaired if he wished.[90] Instead of indicating pessimism and disinterest, it is probable that Turner's treatment of his paintings was deliberate and necessary.

87 Townsend, 'Turner's Use of Materials', p. 5.

88 Ruskin, *Modern Painters*, vol. 4, pp. 21–22.

89 Townsend, *Turner's Painting Techniques*, p. 70.

90 He considered doing so in 1844. Turner, quoted in Finberg, *The Life of J. M. W. Turner* p. 397. Refer to Gage, *Colour in Turner*, p. 171.

MILES APART

Soane and Turner were close friends for over forty years. They regularly dined together, attended each other's lectures, went fishing on the Thames and shared a concern for the effects of light and shade, atmosphere and weather. Indicating the depth of their friendship, they spent Christmas Eve together after the death of Soane's wife, Eliza, in November 1815.

Soane and Turner lived and worked barely a mile apart. But their attitudes to London's weather were distant. Soane established a clear division between a benign internal environment and a malign external one, which his fascination for new technologies maintained. In contrast to 12–14 Lincoln's Inn Fields, Turner allowed London's polluted air to infiltrate his studio through the broken roof. Soane wished to control ruination while Turner accepted decay. Soane recognised the architectural potential of a climate while Turner acknowledged the weather as a significant authorial voice that complemented his own. To some extent, their differing professions determined their differing attitudes. Creating a comfortable environment, the architect has a responsibility to everyday use that need not concern the painter. But Soane and Turner also represent differing attitudes to architecture and authorship. There is a fundamental difference between an isolated interior in which the designer aims for complete control and a complex and interrelated environment in which the designer accepts other influences.

Whether at sea or in the city, Turner painted what he experienced. In London, his dilapidated studio enabled him to paint in situ. His subject literally entered his work. The dirt and rain that landed on unfinished canvases, and Turner left there, combined with pigments that were also composites of the natural and industrial. In the early nineteenth century, concerns that old and new pigments were incompatible mirrored wider fears of industrialisation.[91] In contrast, reflecting his concern for the past and the present, Turner readily combined traditional and newly manufactured pigments: 'the earliest verified uses of cobalt blue, chrome yellows, viridian, barium chromate and emerald green in the Tate's British paintings have all been by Turner'.[92] Subject to seasons and industries, the fusion of atmospheres and energies that defined early nineteenth-century London entered his work in pigments and pollution. Turner's subject, site and painting practice were perfectly aligned and 'a quintessentially Romantic piece of rule-breaking'.[93] But rather than rejecting industry and retreating to nature, Turner's romanticism acknowledged the full complexity of his time, its climate and weather, which nature and industry together created, offering an early indication of human-induced – anthropogenic – climate change.

91 Townsend, *Turner's Painting Techniques*, p. 39.

92 Townsend, 'Turner's Use of Materials', p. 5.

93 Powell, p. 60.

The hybridised weather depicted by Turner paralleled a transformation in physical nature that we increasingly experience today. It is no longer possible to experience the first nature as an independent entity devoid of human intervention, while the second increasingly refers to infrastructure as well as agriculture, and the third is as likely to be a garden of concrete as much as clay. Their distinct characters are powerful conceptual tools but the three natures are interdependent and equally subject to human and natural influences.

6

the weather of our houses

INTRODUCTION

Analysing recurring attitudes to the environment, the second half of this book, which includes this chapter and the following three, considers the picturesque and romantic thread that was revived in the mid-twentieth century as a means to reassess and revise modernism. As before, creative architects looked to the past to imagine the future, using the weather as their principal means to recognise and represent time. This chapter is organised into three interconnecting sections, each with a specific theme, which together consider Mies's attitudes to the weather and the weather's reactions to his architecture. The first, 'The *Genius Loci* in German', analyses Mies's relationship to modernism and acknowledges his debt to Romano Guardini and Karl Friedrich Schinkel. The second, 'Reflections on Nature', considers the relations between architecture and weather in the Barcelona Pavilion, 1929–1930, and Farnsworth House, 1951. As a contrast to these designs, the concluding section, 'Owning the Weather', analyses the technological bombast of mid-twentieth-century America, when computation aimed to transform meteorology into an exact science, the military funded research into climate modification and attention was drawn to anthropogenic climate change.

THE *GENIUS LOCI* IN GERMAN

The Function of Modernism

Indicating that evolution occurs through varied mutations, Charles Darwin's *The Origin of Species*, 1859, undermined environmental determinism, which includes the determination of character by climate.[1] But architectural determinism, which is indebted to environmental determinism, did not wither, as Bill Hillier recognises:

1 Darwin, p. 109.

> *There were probably three reasons for this improper survival. First, environmental determinism was a scientific error, and therefore refutable, whilst architectural determinism was a more diffuse cultural paradigm, often below the level of conscious thought, and not exposed therefore to direct refutation. Second, because it was a cultural belief, it tended to become institutionalised. If you spent money on architecture as moral engineering, then you had to believe in it. Third, the Darwinian revolution left many of the cultural by-products of environmental determinism behind because the metaphorical impact of Darwinism on culture lay*

elsewhere, in the survival of the fittest and the descent from monkeys, with the reformulation of the form-function problem in nature only in the small print read by the specialist.[2]

2 Hillier, p. 299.

Functionalism is familiarly associated with early twentieth-century modernism and flavours its later interpretations. The prime concern of functionalist theory is the relationship between a form and the behaviour it accommodates. One of its principles is determinism, which assumes that every event has a cause and that the actions and needs of the user are predictable, consistent and universal. Edward De Zurko defines functionalist ideas in terms of three analogies – the organic, mechanical and moral – which were all evident in the early twentieth century.[3] He identifies the origins of functionalist theory in classical philosophy and medieval theology but recognises that it first became important to architects in the nineteenth century. Referring to Jean-Nicholas-Louis Durand, Alberto Pérez-Gómez writes: 'The architect's only concern should be . . . the most convenient and economical "disposition". Here is the direct precedent of twentieth-century functionalism . . . The architecture of the Industrial Revolution owed to Durand the first coherent articulation of its principles and intentions.'[4] Alongside the extensive classification of buildings by type, industrialisation gave increasing emphasis to the quantification of space and labour. Following this lead, early twentieth-century modernists mostly ignored visual references to the body, focusing on actions instead. Concerned that social unrest would follow the turmoil of the First World War, Fordism and Taylorism were proposed as models for the regeneration of architecture and society. Named after Henry Ford, Fordism is a highly centralised, rationalised and rigid means of production that generates a limited range of products through the use of special-purpose machinery, market research, experimental prototypes and the standardisation and fragmentation of labour according to principles established by Frederick W. Taylor. In *The Principles of Scientific Management*, 1911, Taylor advocates the expert analysis of labour to calculate the optimal efficiency of each task in the production process. In 1928, based on research he conducted for a German housing agency, Alexander Klein proposed the Functional House for Frictionless Living. A vehement advocate of the scientific management of labour, Klein assumed that a one-to-one compatibility of a function and a space is possible, necessary and beneficial. Considering the house to be a machine, he contrasted the complex intersection of everyday paths of movement through a typical nineteenth-century house to their separation in his own design, which he assumed to be superior because it reduced the possibility of accidental encounters and, thus, social friction.

3 De Zurko, p. 45. Refer to Ligo, p. 9.

4 Pérez-Gómez, pp. 302–311.

Taylor was soon translated into French and Le Corbusier was an early and influential advocate of his ideas in relation to architecture.[5] Le Corbusier's *Vers une architecture*, 1923, was translated into English as *Towards a New Architecture*, 1927. Taken literally, his statements that a house is 'a machine for living in' and 'one can be proud of having a house as serviceable as a typewriter' are accurate descriptions of functionalist sensibilities in that the human is integral to the machine.[6] Later he remarked: 'What did I mean by "a machine for living"? Simple: the optimum return in terms of function and furnishings.'[7] But with regard to Le Corbusier's 'machine for living in', Hillier remarks:

5 Taylor, *The Principles of Scientific Management*. Refer to McLeod, p.133; Weber, p. 140.

6 Le Corbusier, *Towards a New Architecture*, pp. 10, 241.

7 Le Corbusier, quoted in Brassaï, p. 86. Refer to Weber, p. 581.

> *On the face of it, this seems to assert a direct analogy between buildings and machines. In fact, a closer reading quickly suggests this is not to be taken seriously. Nothing like this conception is to be found in Le Corbusier's text . . . It is clear that his preoccupation is not with the machine as formal analogue for the organisation of the dwelling, but with the machine as metaphor for a style uncluttered with the decorative detritus of the past.*[8]

8 Hillier, p. 292.

Dismissive of past habits and past architectures, modernists denounced domesticity, which they characterised as bourgeois. Discomfort with comfort was a familiar theme, as was continuing unease with a home abundant in possessions, memories and traces. In the Bauhaus publication *Von Material zu Architektur*, 1928, which appeared as *The New Vision: From Material to Architecture* in 1930, László Moholy-Nagy provides a subtle and complex discourse on the interdependence of spaces and bodies. But he still criticises people 'who look for the essence of architecture in the meaning of the conception of shelter'.[9] In 1927 Mies curated the Weissenhofsiedlung, a Stuttgart housing development that was part of *Die Wohnung* (The Dwelling) exhibition organised by the Deutsche Werkbund. In an accompanying poster a large red 'X' obliterates a photograph of an interior that is full of the daily clutter of domestic life.[10] Functionalism's debt to Taylorism and Fordism ensured that modernist architects' response to bourgeois capitalist society was neither categorical nor consistently critical. But just as the early twentieth-century artistic avant-garde conjoined a new art and a new life, architects wished to change society not merely to reflect it. For early modernists concerned with images as much as instruments, function followed form as much as form followed function.[11] Functionalism was without doubt a useful concept for early twentieth-century modernists but there was no coherent theorisation of architectural determinism at the time and little indication that it was rigorously applied to a design. In 'The Fiction of Function' Stanford Anderson concludes:

9 Moholy-Nagy, p. 59.

10 Willi Baumeister, *Die Wohnung Werkbund Ausstellung*, 1927. Refer to Friedman, pp. 143–44.

11 The phrase 'form follows function' is attributed to Louis Sullivan. Sullivan, p. 207.

Architecture is, among other things, a bearer of meaning . . . Yet this was no less so in modernism than in other periods. Furthermore, it is surely not unique to modern architecture that part of the story it tells is about function. It may be sustainable, however, that modern architecture, more than that of any other time, emphasized stories about function.[12]

12 Anderson, p. 21.

Mies and Modernism

Mies is familiarly cited as a principal modernist architect but his opinions frequently diverged from modernist orthodoxy. In 'Build Beautifully and Practically! Stop This Cold Functionality', 1930, he dismisses functionalism: 'And what finally is beauty? Certainly nothing that can be calculated or measured. It is always something imponderable, something that lies between things.'[13] In 1958 he further questioned the value of functional specificity: 'The purposes for which a building is used are constantly changing and we cannot afford to tear down the building each time.'[14] For much of the twentieth century, Mies's high reputation was associated with the tectonic order that his advocates identified in his architecture. In *Mies van der Rohe: The Art of Structure*, 1994, which was first published in German in 1965, Werner Blaser writes that 'Mies has evolved his ideas from the basic principles of construction: hence the form of his buildings is the expression of their structure.'[15] But Mies did not simply express structure and construction. The cruciform columns of the Barcelona Pavilion, 1929–1930, are too delicate to perform much structural purpose and consist of a number of material layers. In the Lange and Esters Houses, Krefeld, 1930, no indication is given that the structural loads are frequently transferred on beams above window openings.[16] Mies's noted aphorisms 'less is more' and 'almost nothing' do not refer to structural efficiency alone. Emphasising perception and experience, Mies's intention was to achieve 'the greatest effect using the meagerest of means'.[17] In his foreword to *The Art of Structure* Mies describes technology as 'a civilizing force' but not an end in itself:[18]

What Ford wants is simple and illuminating. His factories show mechanization in dizzying perfection. We agree with the direction Ford has taken, but reject the plane on which he moves. Mechanization can never be goal, it must remain means. Means towards a spiritual purpose.[19]

In contrast to the simple faith in progress that often characterised early modernism, Mies concludes: 'I felt that it must be possible to harmonize the old and the new

13 Mies, 'Build Beautifully'.

14 Mies, in Norberg-Schulz. 'A Talk with Mies van der Rohe', p. 339.

15 Blaser, *Mies van der Rohe: The Art of Structure*, p. 11.

16 The Barcelona Pavilion is included in *Mies van der Rohe: The Art of Structure*. The Lange and Esters Houses are not.

17 Mies, quoted in Savi and Montaner, p. 12.

18 Mies, in Blaser, *Mies van der Rohe: The Art of Structure*, p. 5.

19 Mies, 'Lecture, 19 June 1924', quoted in Neumeyer, *The Artless Word*, p. 250.

in our civilization. Each of my buildings was a statement of this idea.'[20] Fritz Neumeyer notes Mies's particular debt to the Catholic theologian Romano Guardini, who promoted a questioning engagement with modernity that neither rejected Platonic order nor ignored contemporary technology and existential philosophy.[21] Mies studied Guardini's *Die Technik un der Mensch: Briefe von Comer See* (*Letters from Lake Como: Explorations in Technology and the Human Race*), 1927, while he designed the Barcelona Pavilion and Tugendhat House, Brno, 1930. Born in Verona, Guardini praised the harmonious interdependence of architecture and nature that he found in the villas around Lake Como, which were similar to those that Kent had appreciated elsewhere in Italy. Noting the 'Villa Pliniana, a serious work of Renaissance art', which was built in 1577 and named after Pliny, who was born in Como and owned two villas there, Guardini remarks:

20 Mies, in Blaser, *Mies van der Rohe: The Art of Structure*, p. 5.

21 Guardini, pp. 80–83, 97–98. Refer to Neumeyer, *The Artless Word*, p. 213.

> *Hence all the things that were made – works, buildings, furnishings, clothes, along with movements, orders, customs and usages – could fit easily into nature. Even now they do not disturb nature in any ultimate sense. They do not break it open. They are always natural. Even if there is no mingling, for nature and culture remain different things and have to remain different, the things which culture has made can relate to nature. The two notes can ring out harmoniously together.*[22]

22 Guardini. pp. 67–68.

In his 1927–1928 notebook, Mies quotes Guardini:

> *There is totally untouched nature, and the longing for it, is itself a cultural result. Nature is truly affecting only when it begins to be dwelled in; when culture begins in it. Piece by piece nature is formed. Man creates in it his own world, not only out of a natural need, but with a deliberate purpose, serving spiritual ideas.*[23]

23 Guardini, *Briefe von Comer See*, copied by Mies and translated in Neumeyer, *The Artless Word*, p. 281.

The Ambiguous Object

Mies dismissed functionalism and acknowledged the changeability of use, enjoyed the appearance of tectonic order more than its literal expression, promoted continuity as well as innovation, appreciated nature and prioritised spiritual needs. So what sort of modernist was he? And what of the past did he recognise in the present?

Modernist architecture is widely described as didactic. But Tafuri offers an alternative modernism: 'What joins together the entire Modern Movement is . . . the concept of architecture as *ambiguous object* . . . The observer becomes more and more the user who gives meanings to the *object* or to the *series*.'[24] Tafuri identifies

24 Tafuri, *Theories and History of Architecture*, p. 84.

the origin of the ambiguous object in the picturesque, which furthered the value given to subjectivity in the eighteenth century. Citing Kent, Soane and Le Camus de Mézières, he concludes: 'Architecture, from absolute object, becomes in the landscaped context, relative value: it becomes a medium for the description of an edifying play.'[25] No object is completely ambiguous. Rather, as Tafuri suggests, it is relatively so. Although he does not mention *Observations on Modern Gardening*, his argument recalls Whately's praise for gardens that, in allowing the imagination to roam, 'insensibly lead to subjects, far distant perhaps from the original thought'.[26]

25 Tafuri, *Theories and History of Architecture*, p. 82.

26 Whately, p. 154.

The ambiguous object does not apply to the entire modern movement because there are many modernisms not one; functionalism intends no ambiguity, for example. But the origins of modernism's ambiguous objects are found in the ideas, buildings and gardens of the eighteenth century, as Tafuri suggests. For example, eighteenth-century fascination for the illusions of parallax – the perceived differences in an object's position when seen from different locations – were important to the development of a discontinuous and temporal conception of space.[27]

27 Refer to Giedion, pp. 14, 432–443.

Tafuri's remarks have a critical edge: 'the disappearance of the *object* hasn't been replaced by a critical behaviour . . . The critical attention is absorbed by involving the observer in a sort of mere game'.[28] Denying the liberating potential that Walter Benjamin identifies in the shock of mechanical production, Tafuri dismisses the early twentieth-century avant-garde because it exalted the 'mechanical universe' of bourgeois capitalism: 'The public had to be provoked. Only in this way could it be actively introduced into the universe of precision dominated by the laws of production.'[29] Denying shock and ambiguity any critical effect, Tafuri's conclusions are unconvincing because they are so conclusive. Shock may help to promote new ideas and spaces. However, it wears off quickly and is comparatively ineffective as most buildings are experienced not once but repeatedly when they are not the focus of attention. Enduring ambiguity – the ability to resist resolution and continually stimulate the imagination – is more appropriate to architecture because it both depends upon and questions repeated experience, emphasising weather's role in changing perception.

28 Tafuri, *Theories and History of Architecture*, pp. 94–96.

29 Benjamin, 'The Work of Art in the Age of Mechanical Production', p. 239; Tafuri, *Architecture and Utopia*, pp. 91–95

Englischer Garten

The landscape that Tafuri identifies as the inspiration for modernism's ambiguous objects was readily available to Mies due to the collaboration of Karl Friedrich Schinkel and his 'kindred spirit', the garden designer Peter Joseph Lenné, on the Prussian royal estates at Potsdam, south-west of Berlin.[30] In 1826 Schinkel

30 Neumeyer, 'Search for Reflection', p. 159.

Karl Friedrich Schinkel, Schloss Glienicke, 1824. Antique fragments set into exterior wall. Photograph, Adrian Forty.

travelled extensively around Britain, studying buildings at the request of his government. Interrupting his journey from Berlin to Calais he visited Goethe in Weimar for their fourth meeting.[31] In London, Schinkel visited 12–14 Lincoln's Inn Fields, praising the collection, which 'contains a great number of casts, fragments of

31 Schinkel, pp. 21–22.

antique sculptures and buildings, vases, sarcophagi, little panels and bronzes, all exhibited in the most ingenious way'. In conclusion he identifies 'Everywhere little deceptions.'[32] Consequently, it is sometimes assumed that he did not approve of Soane.[33] But the antique fragments set into the cloister of Schinkel's Schloss Glienicke, 1824, are comparable to 12–14 Lincoln's Inn Fields. Both architects admired Goethe, and respected the gothic as well as the classical. In Schinkel's account of Soane's buildings positive remarks outnumber critical ones. Even 'Everywhere little deceptions' is not necessarily a criticism. A talented set designer, Schinkel indicates his fascination for John Nash's highly theatrical Royal Pavilion, Brighton, 1815–1821, describing the interior as 'magnificent'.[34] Schinkel also expresses his admiration for Hogarth, visits Fingal's Cave, which Turner had enjoyed, and commends picturesque compositions of architecture and nature on numerous occasions.[35] In Derbyshire he identifies 'The bathing huts of Matlock extremely picturesque on the slope opposite the cliff.'[36] At Warwick he commends:

32 Schinkel, p. 114.

33 Bindman, pp. 15–16.

34 Schinkel, p. 114.

35 Schinkel, pp. 92, 101, 114, 119, 123, 137 and 145.

36 Schinkel, p. 134.

> *Magnificent vegetation. At the entrance through the gate there is a path hewn in the rock leading to the park, the walls are covered in ivy and wonderful plants, above is a most beautiful south-facing wood. You emerge in front of the castle, a splendid courtyard, the old towers and walls half concealed by tall trees wound about with climbing plants. Across a bridge and through a gate one arrives at a courtyard with a lawn; all around stands the ancient castle building, in perfect preservation, everything is covered in ivy and ancient trees grow high above the castle walls.*[37]

37 Schinkel, p. 124.

Informed by a visit to England in the early 1820s, Lenné's influences were the English picturesque and the German picturesque, which was inspired by English examples. Lenné's tutor, Ludwig Skell, designed Munich's Englischer Garten, 1789. Commissioned by Prince Leopold Friedrich Franz of Anhalt-Dessau and developed between 1764 and 1800, the richly emblematic gardens at Wörlitz pioneered the German picturesque. English ideas had been a significant influence on German states since the mid-eighteenth century. The Prince appreciated the picturesque's association with personal and political liberty and visited England at his garden's inception and during its construction. Rousham was one influence, where the Prince and his architect, Friedrich Wilhelm von Erdmannsdorff, and garden designer, Johann Friedrich Eyserbeck, stayed for three days on their first visit.[38] Rousseau was a further influence, to whom the Prince dedicated an island that recalls Rousseau's tomb in the gardens at Ermenonville near Paris.

38 Hunt, *The Picturesque Garden in Europe*, pp. 158–163.

In 'On German Architecture', 1772, Goethe eulogises 'the genius of Erwin von Steinbach' at Strasbourg's gothic cathedral.[39] Advocating idealism, Goethe states

39 Goethe, 'On German Architecture (1772)', p. 108.

that art is the expression of creative spirit and is endowed with that spirit: 'For in man's nature there is a will to create form which becomes active the moment his survival is assured.'[40] Praising von Steinbach, Goethe states that art is another nature, which learns from nature but is distinct from it:

40 Goethe, 'On German Architecture (1772)', p. 109.

> *Yet what need you a memorial! You have erected the most magnificent one for yourself, and although your name does not bother the ants who crawl around it, you have the same destiny as that Architect who piled up his mountains to the clouds . . . Just as in the eternal works of nature, everything is perfectly formed down to the meanest thread, and all contributing purposively to the whole.*[41]

41 Goethe, 'On German Architecture (1772)', pp. 104–108.

Echoing Laugier in *An Essay on Architecture*, 'On German Architecture' dismisses the rococo.[42] But the picturesque was readily absorbed into garden design in German-speaking territories because its concerns – irregularity, temporality and the pleasures of nature – were already characteristic of the rococo, which was contemporary with the early picturesque in England. Schloss Sanssouci at Potsdam is a notable example, which Johann Boumann completed in 1747 after Frederick the Great quarrelled with the original architect, Georg von Knobelsdorff.

42 Laugier characterises the rococo as fanciful. Laugier, p. 56; Goethe, 'On German Architecture (1772)', pp. 108–110.

After a visit to Paestum in 1787, Goethe's appreciation of classicism became as romantic and nationalistic as his earlier promotion of gothic. Accompanied and encouraged by Goethe, a visit to Wörlitz inspired Duke Karl August to commission a picturesque garden in Weimar, the city most associated with the German Enlightenment. Identifying the temples and landscapes of the picturesque as settings for the revival of the humanist ideals of classical antiquity, Goethe assisted in the remodelling of the park along the River Ilm. At first Goethe occupied a cottage in the park, which later became his summer retreat. On the opposite bank he contributed to Johann August Arens's design of the Roman House, 1798, the ducal summer retreat. Set on the cusp of a ridge just as it begins to fall to the river, the location exaggerates the building's scale, ensuring that it commands the valley. Elsewhere, a carved stone inscription – 'Genio huis loci' (Genius of this place) – indicates the park's debt to the English picturesque as well as its concern for associations and symbols specific to German-speaking territories.[43]

43 Opposed to the objective and quantifiable investigation of colour in Newton's *Opticks*, Goethe later extended his fascination for the unfolding experiences of the picturesque to consider the temporal perception of colour in *Farbenlehre*, 1810, which was published in English as *Theory of Colours*, 1840. Goethe removed his criticism of Newton from the second edition.

Johann August Arens, Roman House, Weimar, 1798. Photograph, Jonathan Hill.

The Land of the Free

Napoleon once quipped that Germany was always 'becoming, not being'.[44] To counter French influence, romanticism in German-speaking territories combined with nationalism to an extent not seen in Britain. At the Berlin Academy in 1797, Friedrich Gilly's monument to Frederick the Great attracted considerable attention.[45] Surmounting a dark-stoned acropolis that rises above the Prussian plain, Gilly

44 Napoleon, quoted in Davies, *A History of Europe*, p. 733.

45 The design began as a competition entry the previous year, for which it gained no prize. Frederick the Great was Friedrich II, King of Prussia.

Friedrich Gilly, Monument to Frederick the Great, 1796–1797. Courtesy of the Bildagentur für Kunst, Kultur und Geschichte, Berlin.

remarked that the sombre Doric temple was 'of a lighter material in order to make striking the noble effect of its gleam against the sky'.[46]Although the monument is nationalistic, its inspirations were not. Barry Bergdoll writes that 'Gilly was familiar with a wide range of architectural theory; with French sensationalist aesthetics, outlined in Le Camus de Mézière's *Genius of Architecture*; and with contemporary romantic theories of art as a vehicle for channelling private emotions towards collective experience.'[47] David Watkin and Tilmann Mellinghoff note the originality and influence of Gilly's design and depiction:

> *An environmental concern had been familiar in England as an aspect of the Picturesque sensibility which began with Vanbrugh in the early years of the eighteenth century. However, it had rarely been applied, even in England, to public monuments or urban architecture . . . In accounting for the quite extraordinary impact of Gilly's design one should not, moreover, forget its quality as a Romantic architectural drawing. Though garden buildings and monuments were occasionally represented in perspective and natural settings, it was extremely unusual, if not unique, for a major public building to be represented in this pictorial fashion. Gilly's large watercolour, showing a monumental building in its setting, viewed from an angle and bathed in light and shadow, must have come as a revelation.*[48]

Schinkel decided to become an architect while standing in front of Gilly's design, which he inherited in 1800 after the early death of his tutor and mentor in romantic classicism.[49] Adjacent to one of Schinkel's most noted works:

46 Gilly, quoted in Watkin and Mellinghoff, p. 68.

47 Bergdoll, *Karl Friedrich Schinkel*, p. 14.

48 Watkin and Mellinghoff, p. 69.

49 Schinkel made this claim after the event. Refer to Bergdoll, *Karl Friedrich Schinkel*, p. 16; Neumeyer, 'Search for Reflection', p. 165; Waagen, p. 317.

Allées cut through the trees to either side, flanked by portrait busts, in the guise of antique herms, Italians to one side (Ariosto, Tasso, Dante, Petrach), Germans to the other (Goethe, Schiller, Herder, Wieland). They express the polarities between north and south that run through German romanticism and resound in the plantings and images of Charlottenhof.[50]

50 The busts were appropriate to his concerns but not placed there by Schinkel. Bergdoll, *Karl Friedrich Schinkel*, pp. 148–149.

In 1825, to celebrate the marriage of Crown Prince Friedrich Wilhelm of Prussia to Princess Elizabeth of Bavaria, Friedrich Wilhelm III presented a wedding gift to his son. The one hundred-hectare Charlottenhof estate lies adjacent to the royal palaces and gardens of Sanssouci. Having acquired its name in the mid-eighteenth century when the Prussian court was Francophile, Sanssouci offered a 'carefree' existence distinct from the formality and obligations of government in the capital city.

Flat and marshy, Charlottenhof was not immediately promising. But between 1826 and 1835 Lenné integrated it into Sanssouci, which he had begun to transform in 1816. Indicating a particular debt to Repton, Lenné's design for Charlottenhof incorporates slowly winding paths and wide lawns that have neither the intimacy of the early eighteenth-century English picturesque nor the savagery of the late eighteenth century. An active client, the Crown Prince described his sketches as '*malerisch*', meaning picturesque.[51] The later development of the picturesque in German-speaking territories helps to explain its conjunction with romanticism, which Soane shared to some extent. Nearly a century after Kent and decades after Gilpin, Price and Knight, Lenné's sensibility echoed that of his collaborator, Schinkel, and client, the Crown Prince, who collectively conceived Charlottenhof as a landscape for romantic self-reflection. The Crown Prince described his estate as 'Siam' – 'the land of the free' – having been introduced to Rousseau's appreciation of nature by his tutor, Friedrich Delbrück. According to Rand Carter:

51 Crown Prince Friedrich Wilhelm, quoted in Watkin and Mellinghoff, p. 105.

Without the burden of archaeological evidence, these little-known lands on the far side of the earth, which at the time had only begun to be subjected to philological scrutiny of western scholars, stirred in the German humanists somewhat freer speculation. For them, 'Siam' could signify a world of natural freedom. The high-minded Delbrück sought to realize his idyllic world in the special ambience of Potsdam. Likewise, the Crown Prince thought of his private retreat at Potsdam as an ideal landscape in which Utopian reveries might not only be dreamt but actually lived.[52]

52 Carter, 'Gartenreich Potsdam'. p. 74. Refer to Whyte, p. 5.

At Stourhead the house is distant from the garden. At Stowe, and even Rousham, the house is at the garden's edge. At 12–14 Lincoln's Inn Fields the garden is in the house. But at Charlottenhof the house is in the garden. In 1833 Schinkel completed Schloss Charlottenhof for the Crown Prince, a comparatively modest villa that recalls a significant influence on the picturesque and romantic classicism. 'The model for Siam, of course, was not Siam, but Italy', writes Iain Boyd Whyte.[53] Praised in the Italian Renaissance, Pliny's gardens were neither picturesque nor romantic but they inspired both movements. At Charlottenhof, Schinkel intended to make the debt explicit by recreating the gardens of Pliny's Tuscan villa but the project was never completed. Schinkel also relied on sketches of country houses from his visit to Italy in 1803–1804. The Italian influence continues in the interior of Schloss Charlottenhof. The Crown Prince's study is decorated with engravings after Raphael, the artist he wished to be prominent in Schinkel's Altes Museum, 1830, in the centre of Berlin. As the architect of the Villa Madama – an earlier evocation of Pliny – and the painter of *Madonna dell'Impannata,* Raphael depicted the social proximity that once influenced Kent and later infected Charlottenhof.

53 Whyte, p. 8.

Karl Friedrich Schinkel, Schloss Charlottenhof, 1833. The central rill on the upper terrace. Photograph, Sophia Psarra.

When figures appear in Schinkel's drawings they are in animated conversation. Virtually without precedent in a royal residence, Friedrich Wilhelm and Elizabeth shared a bedroom and a bed.[54]

In 1804, in a letter to David Gilly, Friedrich's father, Schinkel appreciates the ancient monuments he observes in Italy: 'the sight of these works in their natural setting holds a surprise which comes not only from their size, but also from their picturesque grouping'.[55] Schloss Charlottenhof is picturesque in that the paths of the eye and the body often diverge. The approach through the gardens is on the oblique and the central rill interrupts axial movement on the upper terrace. Visible through the trees, Schinkel designed a collection of buildings in which the debt to the picturesque, and to Italy, is more explicit. Built incrementally between 1829 and 1840 in collaboration with Lenné and Ludwig Persius, the complex of the Court Gardener's House includes the Tea Pavilion and Roman Baths. Richly varied, movement occurs not on axis, as in classical architecture, but through shifts in direction, as in the picturesque. Emphasising time's role, Schinkel remarks:

> *Thus this complex forms a whole, grouped picturesquely, offering manifold pleasing views, secret resting places, comfortable rooms and open spaces for the enjoyment of rural life, by nature capable of continuing expansion and enrichment, so that a ceaseless pleasure in production is preserved.*[56]

Plants envelop pergolas, stairs and walls. Water is everywhere. A lake encircles the complex on two sides and the fountain in the sunken court is the focus of the whole design. At the heart of the Roman Baths is the monumental bathtub of green jaspar, its heavy veins mirroring rippling water. Elsewhere, water pours from the mouth of a flat fish, a playful reference to the Crown Prince, who acquired the nickname 'der Butt' – the flounder – and signed drawings 'Fritz-Siam-Butt'. The waterspout has

54 Refer to Bergdoll, *Karl Friedrich Schinkel*, p. 149; Vogtherr, p. 75.

55 Schinkel, quoted in Watkin and Mellinghoff, p. 86.

56 Schinkel, *Sammlung Architektonischer Entwürfe*, 1841–1843, translated and quoted in Whyte, p. 13.

Karl Friedrich Schinkel with Ludwig Persius, Court Gardener's House, Potsdam, 1829–1840. Perspective of the principal elevation before the addition of the Roman Baths. Courtesy of the Bildagentur für Kunst, Kultur und Geschichte, Berlin.

Karl Friedrich Schinkel with Ludwig Persius, Court Gardener's House, Charlottenhof, 1829–1840. Water spout. Photograph, Sophia Psarra.

a further, darker meaning in that it is both 'fons vitae' – 'the source of all life' – and a metaphor for the passage of time, pouring into a stone trough that resembles a sarcophagus.[57]

The designated occupants of Schinkel's design – the court gardener and his assistant – signify the dialogue between architecture and nature that is the subject of the complex, which a regular visitor further emphasised. At first a guest at Schloss Charlottenhof, Alexander von Humboldt later occupied a room at the Court Gardener's House. Frequent collaborators, Schinkel and Humboldt knew each other well. In 1817 Humboldt devised one of the first meteorological maps, which he covered with lines – isotherms – that connect places of the same temperature. Previously, weather data were often described in tabular form but Humboldt's intervention was significant and by the end of the century the map was accepted as the principal means to describe and analyse the weather.[58] In 1844 and 1847

57 Whyte, p. 18.

58 Nebeker, pp. 19–20.

Humboldt published the two volumes of *Cosmos: A Sketch of the Physical Description of the Universe*, in which he argues that natural history and human history must be considered together because the underlying order of natural creation is common to them both. Humboldt refers to historical sources such as Pliny and praises the picturesque compositions of Claude.[59] Travelling widely, he also promoted detailed observation and, in a manner that showed some allegiance to romanticism, emphasised that the natural world is in constant transformation. Recalling 'the ancient bond that unites natural science with poetry and artistic feeling', Humboldt concludes that 'a distinction must be made in landscape painting, as in every branch of art, between the elements generated by the more limited field of contemplation and direct observation, and those which spring from the boundless depth of feeling and from the force of idealizing mental power'.[60] Writing to Goethe, his friend and early mentor, he remarks that 'Nature . . . must be felt.'[61]

59 Humboldt, pp. 94–100.

60 Humboldt, p. 95.

61 Humboldt, 'Letter to Goethe', quoted in Bergdoll, *Karl Friedrich Schinkel*, p. 148.

The Sea and the Mountain

Rather than consistently advocating a particular philosophical position, Schinkel was informed by the evolving ideas of German nationalism, idealism and romanticism. In *Critique of Pure Reason*, 1781, Kant writes 'that all our knowledge begins with experience' but adds that 'it does not follow that it all arises out of experience'.[62] As empirical investigation without a priori concepts is impossible, we cannot simply see objects as they are. Kant concludes that we can gain certain knowledge not of reality but aspects of *our* reality. Idealism's influence led German romanticism to emphasise the mind's ability to construct reality, placing less emphasis on the direct experience of wilder nature, which fascinated English romanticism. On the recommendation of his close friend Karl Wilhelm Ferdinand Solger, a philosopher who taught aesthetics in Berlin, Schinkel studied Friedrich von Schelling, one of the most romantic of the idealist philosophers due to the attention that he gave to the union of the human and the natural in *Ideen zu einer Philosophie der Natur* (Ideas for a Philosophy of Nature), 1797. Solger also recommended the more adamantly idealist Johann Gottlieb Fichte. In *Die Bestimmung des Menschen* (The Vocation of Man), 1800, which Schinkel studied during his visit to Sicily in 1804, Fichte denies any reality independent of the human subject, concluding that the natural world is there to be manipulated at will. During the Napoleonic occupation of Berlin between 1806 and 1813, Fichte galvanised nationalism in *Reden an die Deutsche Nation* (Addresses to the German Nation), 1807–1808.[63]

62 Kant, *Immanuel Kant's Critique of Pure Reason*, p. 41.

63 In 1809 Schinkel also became closely allied with the German romantic poets, Achim and Bettina von Arnim and Clemens Brentano, who were regular visitors to his apartment and studio on Alexanderplatz. Refer to Bergdoll, *Karl Friedrich Schinkel*, pp. 19, 31; Watkin and Mellinghoff, p. 91.

Caspar David Friedrich, *Monk by the Sea*, 1809. Courtesy of the Bildagentur für Kunst, Kultur und Geschichte, Berlin.

Keen to express national identity, Caspar David Friedrich exhibited *Monk by the Sea*, 1809, at the Berlin Academy in 1810. Many visitors were disturbed by the painting's emptiness but Schinkel expressed his admiration. Rather than the sequential arrangement of fore-, middle- and background that is characteristic of the picturesque, only the foreground and background are present. The dark sea and drifting sky dominate the painting. Standing on the jagged coastline at its furthest point, the small figure of a single monk looks out towards the distant horizon, willing the sky closer.[64] But the monk's head does not quite reach the horizon, which appears tantalising near and woefully distant. *Monk by the Sea* indicates the search for the supernatural in the natural and the possibility of transcendence, confirming Friedrich's Lutheran conviction that the path to God is personal: 'The painter should not paint merely what he sees in front of him, but also what he sees within himself.'[65] Friedrich's concern was the poetic imagination, not the union of art and science that Goethe favoured. Rejecting enthusiasm for Howard, Friedrich dismissed any attempt 'to force the free and airy clouds into a rigid order and classification'.[66] But *Monk by the Sea* also displays the concern for classical composition that pervades German romanticism even when the theme is anti-classical and questioning of human authority.

64 X-rays have revealed that Friedrich painted over several boats, which he had originally intended to include. Rosenblum, p. 13.

65 Friedrich, quoted in Koerner, p. 74. Refer to Rosenblum, p. 28.

66 Friedrich, quoted in Hamblyn, p. 221. Refer to Robson-Scott, p. 271; Wiedman, *Romantic Art Theories*, p. 128.

In 'What is Romanticism', Charles Baudelaire concludes that northern Europe is most attuned to romanticism because its weather generates opacity: 'Romanticism is a child of the North, and the North is a colourist; dreams and fairy tales are children of the mist.'[67] Nature was the focus of German and English romanticism, while there was less concern for the dialogue with natural forces in French romantic art. Affirming Kant's classification of the sublime, Friedrich tended towards magnitude, Turner to might.[68] The great exponents of German and English romantic art shared a concern for a unified world but depicted a different nature and a different humanity. In *Monk by the Sea*, transcendent nature is still and distant, as is the painter. In *Snow Storm – Steam-Boat off a Harbour's Mouth*, dynamic nature is energetic and immediate, as is the painter. Informed by empiricism and not known to be religious, Turner placed the painter within nature, not at its edge.

67 Baudelaire, p. 53.

68 Kant, *Critique of Judgement*, part 1, pp. 94–117. Refer to Rosenblum, pp. 35–36; Wiedmann, *Romantic Art Theories*, pp. vii, 25–26.

Differentiating monuments, buildings and cities from plants, rivers and mountains, Schinkel describes architecture as 'complete in and of itself'.[69] But architecture is like nature in that it develops according to a purpose: 'Architecture is the continuation of nature in her constructive activity. This activity is conducted through that natural product: Mankind.'[70] Schinkel was concerned to promote the poetic and constructive co-dependence of the human and natural worlds within an overriding natural order. In his buildings, paintings and set designs, an architectural foreground frequently frames a natural background and the intervening landscape is absent. In *Landscape with Gothic Arches*, 1812, two figures stand on a high terrace, viewing a distant landscape that is shrouded in mist. Potsdam is too flat to readily permit such a dramatic contrast. Its closest equivalent is the Grosse Neugierde at Schloss Glienicke, 1837, which Schinkel placed on a wooded slope above the River Havel. Maintaining this arrangement even when the landscape was unrelentingly flat, Schinkel raised Schloss Charlottenhof on a podium, along which he placed a pergola. At the Court Gardener's House, staircases lead to raised terraces on the principal façade, which pergolas complete. But Schinkel did not adhere to the transcendental nature depicted in *Monk by the Sea*. In 1804, on reaching the summit of Mount Etna, Sicily, after an overnight climb, he expressed neither sublime terror nor spiritual fulfilment: 'all of it lay below me so easily surveyable, that I felt myself almost larger'.[71] Schinkel further emphasised the subjugation of the natural world in 1825:

69 Schinkel quoted in Bergdoll, 'The Nature of Mies's Space', p. 75.

70 Schinkel, quoted in Bergdoll, *Karl Friedrich Schinkel*, p. 208.

71 Schinkel, quoted in Bergdoll, *Karl Friedrich Schinkel*, p. 23.

> *An overall view of a land on which no human has ever set foot can have a quality of awesome beauty; but the viewer becomes uncertain, uneasy and unhappy because what a human being most wants to experience is the way fellow human beings tame nature, live within her and enjoy her beauty.*[72]

72 Schinkel, quoted in Börsch-Supan, p. 10.

73 Kent, *The Soul of the North*, pp. 58–59; Vogtherr, p. 75.

74 Rousseau, *Reveries of the Solitary Walker*, pp. 62–63.

Schinkel's vision was devoid of Friedrich's melancholy.[73] As metaphors of human decay and spiritual longing, ruins are familiar in Friedrich's paintings. In the *Ruins of Eldena*, *c.*1825, the overgrown Cistercian monastery looms over a rural building. But there are no ruins – found or imagined – at Charlottenhof. Communion with nature occurred in a cultivated garden, not at the summit of a windswept peak or the edge of a brooding sea. Such a landscape may appear distant from the arduous journeys and rugged mountains that are often associated with romanticism, but Charlottenhof affirms German romantic philosophy and recalls the Crown Prince's initial inspiration. The landscapes praised by Rousseau in *Reveries of the Solitary Walker*, 1782, are the pastoral lower slopes, not the sublime mountains themselves.[74]

REFLECTIONS ON NATURE

The Garden House

75 The original exhibition title was *Modern Architecture: International Exhibition*, with a catalogue of the same name. The book, *The International Style: Architecture Since 1922* also appeared in 1932. Westheim, pp. 55–62; Johnson, *Mies van der Rohe*, p. 58.

76 Mies, quoted in Blake, p. 94.

77 Eisenman, pp. 12–13.

78 Johnson, 'Schinkel and Mies', pp. 165–177.

79 Schulze, *Philip Johnson: Life and Work*, p. 196.

In 1927 Paul Westheim was the first critic to recognise Schinkel's influence on Mies, an opinion that Henry-Russell Hitchcock and Philip Johnson repeated in *The International Style*, 1932, and which Johnson made a feature of his writings on Mies.[75] For much of the twentieth century Schinkel and Mies were identified with a shared concern for tectonics, with some justification. Mies remarks: 'His buildings were an excellent example of classicism – the best that I know . . . I think Schinkel had wonderful constructions, excellent proportions, and good detailing.'[76] Peter Eisenman notes that Johnson's specific intention was to undermine functionalism and emphasise, instead, the art of building.[77] Writing in 1961, Johnson describes Schinkel and Mies as 'Romantic Classicists'. Within this categorisation he implies that some designs are more 'Classical' and others are more 'Romantic'. Schinkel's Altes Museum, Berlin, 1830, and Mies's Seagram Building, New York, 1957, tend towards the 'Classical', while the Court Gardener's House and Barcelona Pavilion are more 'Romantic'. Johnson refers to the Court Gardener's House as 'the creation of emotional space, by such casual and eclectic means'.[78] But he disregards the dialogue between architecture and nature and recognises only the podium of the Barcelona Pavilion as a significant debt to Schinkel. Johnson's omission is somewhat surprising as he associated the location of his Glass House, 1949, with Schinkel's Casino at Glienicke, 1825.[79] But even though his New Canaan estate is indebted to romantic classicism and the picturesque, nature is relentlessly manicured and not allowed to intervene with architecture in any manner that Kent, Price, Knight or Schinkel advocated.

In 1934 Raymond McGrath described the Pavilion as a 'Garden House'.[80] But more often nature's role in Mies's design has been actively ignored because it is seen to compromise the Pavilion, whether it is understood as an exemplar of architecture as contemplative artwork or tectonic expression.[81] This process of denial is as old as the Pavilion. The plan in *The International Style* omits all planting and ignores the path that leads to the garden to the rear of the Pavilion. More recently, Bergdoll and Neumeyer have acknowledged the lessons that Mies learnt from the relations between architecture and nature at Charlottenhof.[82] Themes that Mies explored throughout his career were evident in his first building, a house in Potsdam-Neubabelsberg, which Alois Riehl commissioned in 1906 when Mies was just twenty. To expand his architect's education, Riehl sponsored Mies's six-week tour of Italy in 1908. Travelling to Florence, Rome and Vicenza, Mies visited the Villa Rotonda and admired other villas by Palladio in the Veneto. But, missing Germany's grey 'heavens', the Mediterranean sun gave him less pleasure.[83] The Riehl House is raised on a long retaining wall, which creates an architectural foreground – the loggia – to view a natural background – the park at Glienicke – which Lenné and Schinkel had designed. A year after completing the Riehl House, Mies began working in the Neubabelsberg studio of Peter Behrens, who promoted the architectural garden in 'Der moderne Garten', 1911, and encouraged his assistants to study Schinkel's designs around Potsdam.

80 McGrath, *Twentieth Century Houses*, p. 167.

81 Between 1929 and 1930 it was an exhibit, between 1930 and 1986 it was only known through photographs, and since 1986 the reconstruction's status as a historical monument discourages everyday use. Hill, *Actions of Architecture*, pp. 18–24.

82 Hitchcock and Johnson, p. 182. Refer to Bergdoll, 'Mies and Schinkel', pp. 125–135; Bergdoll, 'The Nature of Mies's Space', pp. 67–105; Neumeyer, *The Artless Word*, pp. 76–78; Neumeyer, 'Search for Reflection', pp. 148–171.

83 Schulze, *Mies van der Rohe*, p. 30.

The Picturesque Pavilion

The Barcelona Pavilion's debt to the picturesque, and also to romantic classicism, is evident in the dialogue it constructs between architecture, nature and perception. Connections between the Pavilion and the picturesque have been frequently noted, as Caroline Constant attests:

> *The term 'pavilion' was first associated with garden structures for temporary shelter in the late seventeenth century, such buildings provided the architectural leitmotif of the English landscape garden, which emerged in the following century as a vehicle of the new sensibility.*[84]

Three pedestals are shown in the Pavilion's earliest plan, drawn in 1928.[85] One pedestal is at the end of the larger pool, another terminates the axis from the rear

84 Constant, 'The Barcelona Pavilion as Landscape Garden', p. 46, with reference to *The Compact Edition of the Oxford English Dictionary*, p. 572.

85 The pedestals were designed to receive sculptures by Wilhelm Lehmbruck.

garden, and a third is placed in the smaller pool, acting as a further eye-catcher. Consistent with romantic classicism as well as the picturesque, Mies designed local symmetries within an asymmetrical composition, which Schinkel had earlier promoted.[86] Mies's final design reduced the pedestals to one, supporting Georg Kolbe's sculpture *Dawn*.[87] 'By eliminating these sculptural focal points, he rejected pictorial means,' Constant concludes.[88] But this is surely incorrect. Surfaces rather than sculptures – a wall of red onyx or green alpine marble – punctuate journeys around the Pavilion.[89] Views are framed across water and along vistas to create alternative routes that affirm the self-reflection and personal liberty associated with the picturesque. Movement often occurs on the oblique and by shifts in direction.

86 Psarra, p. 50.

87 Solà Morales, Cirici and Ramos give the name of the sculpture as *Dawn* but Dodds suggests that it has been variously titled *Morning*, *Dawn* and *Evening*. Solà Morales, Cirici and Ramos, p. 21; Dodds, p. 18.

The Pavilion shows a specific debt to the Court Gardener's House. Rejecting an alternative location, Mies selected a site at one end of the elongated Gran Plaza de la Fuente Mágica at the centre of the Barcelona Universal Exposition, of which the Pavilion formed a part. His first plan shows the Pavilion surrounded by vegetation on three sides and open on the other, facing the square. Reminiscent of the Court Gardener's House, this combination of the verdant enclosing garden and the open view continued in the final design. On the principal façades of the

Ludwig Mies van der Rohe, Barcelona Pavilion, 1929–1930, reconstruction, 1986. Exterior from the Gran Plaza de la Fuente Mágica. Photograph, Adrian Forty.

Court Gardener's House and Barcelona Pavilion, a flight of stairs – placed in a similar location – leads up to a podium, which generates the open view. The Court Gardener's House offers picturesque views within and beyond its boundaries, while a romantic vista is available from the podium. Here Mies departed from Schinkel, presumably because the distinctly formal Gran Plaza could not be identified as wilder nature. If the view across the square has a precedent it is the one beyond the picturesque garden not a romantic vista. The contrast between the picturesque pleasure garden, within the Pavilion and the productive landscape beyond was especially evident when the Exposition opened in 1929:

> *The system adopted in Barcelona consisted of a series of independent buildings devoted to different branches of production – Steel-making, Transport, Textiles, Agriculture, Graphic Arts, Electricity, etc. – and subdivided internally into areas occupied by the industries of the different exhibiting nations.*[90]

But as visitors approached the Pavilion with their backs to the square, the views across the Gran Plaza were rarely noticed and appear in none of the Berliner Bild-Bericht photographs from Mies's personal collection, which established the Pavilion's reputation.[91] Adhering to the principles of the picturesque, the focus is mostly inward. However, the Pavilion also contains within its boundaries two lengthy views respectively associated with the picturesque and the romantic. The view along the rear of the podium follows the picturesque convention of fore-, middle- and background, with Kolbe's water-bound sculpture as a visual punctuation and the green Alpine marble signifying distant mountains. Taking into account Evans's assumption that the Pavilion's horizontal symmetry generates an internal horizon,[92] Mies's abstract architectural vocabulary excludes the intermediary landscape and generates romantic vistas, which opaque glass cloaks in a northern mist.

In conception and setting the Court Gardener's House and Barcelona Pavilion hover between the north and south. Built for a Prussian prince, the Court Gardener's House imagines the Mediterranean. The Barcelona Pavilion was conceived in Berlin but many of its optical effects required a bright sky. Psarra describes the Pavilion as a 'temple of light'; the Mediterranean sun provides strong shadows but also dematerialises surfaces in myriad reflections, which the northern climate could not achieve. In the darkest pool, suspended between clouds and water, Kolbe's *Dawn* faces south not east, alone resisting the destructive light. Her body stoops, leaning back, while her face turns away, looking down. Raised hands shield her face from the harshest sun.[93]

88 Constant, 'The Barcelona Pavilion as Landscape Garden', p. 47.

89 The 1986 reconstruction is not the same as the 1929 Pavilion. But as the reconstruction approximates to the original, I mostly use the present tense to describe the Pavilion except when discussing an element in the original that is missing from the copy.

90 Solà Morales, Cirici and Ramos, p.7.

91 The photographs were bequeathed to the Museum of Modern Art in 1969. Photographs of those parts of the design that were either compromised by economic restrictions or never completed do not remain and may not have been taken. Solà Morales, Cirici and Ramos, pp. 14, 15 and 29.

92 Placed two panels high, the dimensions of the red onyx determined the Pavilion's height and may have suggested the horizontal symmetry. Evans, 'Mies van der Rohe's Paradoxical Symmetries', p. 258.

93 Sophia Psarra proposed the ideas in this paragraph in conversation with the author, 31 July 2009.

At Charlottenhof and Barcelona, the materials were cultivated as well as crafted. Mirroring the Court Gardener's House, the Pavilion's focus is a sunken court completed by water. Each building has a second pool. The green jaspar tub in the sombre Roman Baths is equivalent to the Pavilion's dark inner pool, itself enclosed by green Alpine marble. The Pavilion's travertine floors, onyx wall and red curtain all recall surfaces and colours in the Roman Baths. Mies was keen to incorporate nature into the Pavilion throughout the design process, furthering the association with Schinkel. His first plan shows the perimeter wall adjacent to the larger pool as dense vegetation, which was replaced by travertine in the constructed Pavilion. But nature reappeared in the same location in a different form. Contemporary aerial photographs indicate that concealed high-level planters were incorporated into the travertine wall, a decision confirmed in a later model.[94] Circular plant pots in the Berliner Bild-Bericht photographs are reminiscent of those in Schinkel's engravings of the Court Gardener's House. Water lilies, familiar in picturesque gardens, were planted in the larger pool to contrast with the placid second pool.[95] As changes in the daily and seasonal weather were immediately evident, repeated visits yielded varied experiences. The large pool and two flags – one German, one Spanish, flying from masts placed symmetrically in front of the Pavilion and each measuring 9m × 6m – immediately drew attention to any change in wind direction and strength.[96] The water lilies expanded to cover the entire surface of the pool, even causing maintenance problems. Also unintended, muddy rainwater poured down the slope of Montjuic, frequently flooding the site. The one figurative element – Kolbe's sculpture – further expands the dialogue between architecture and nature. Its serpentine line and female form affirm the Pavilion's familiar association with beauty. But *Dawn* – as nature – may alternatively be understood as a counterpoint to architecture.

The Pavilion's man-made surfaces suggest a further allegiance to the picturesque. In 1922 Mies countered the familiar association of modernist architecture with visual transparency. Emphasising reflections instead, he concludes: 'My experiments with a glass model helped me along the way and I soon recognized that by employing glass, it is not an effect of light and shadow one wants to achieve but a rich interplay of light reflections.'[97] In the Berliner Bild-Bericht photographs, nature is seen in the Pavilion's many reflective surfaces: water, chrome, red onyx, two green marbles, yellow travertine when wet and glass that is either clear, white, grey or green. In 1932, and then in 1937, McGrath was the first critic to relate Mies's 'metaphysical pavilion' to the picturesque, comparing its stereoscopic effects to those of the Claude Glass.[98] The Pavilion's surfaces are not immediately equivalent to a tinted convex mirror as most are flat. But many are coloured and some

(opposite top) Ludwig Mies van der Rohe, Barcelona Pavilion, 1929–1930, reconstruction, 1986. Travertine wall framing the view to Kolbe's *Dawn*. Photograph, Adrian Forty.

(opposite below) Ludwig Mies van der Rohe, Barcelona Pavilion, 1929–1930, reconstruction, 1986. Interior looking towards Kolbe's *Dawn* and the small pool. Photograph, Adrian Forty.

94 Bergdoll, 'The Nature of Mies's Space', p. 93, p. 375, n. 95.

95 Solà Morales, Cirici and Ramos, p. 19.

96 The Berliner Bild-Bericht photographs show the flags but not the water lilies and there is little indication of the high-level planters.

97 Mies, 'Skyscrapers', p. 240.

98 McGrath's comments refer to the photographs as he never visited the Pavilion. McGrath, 'Looking into Glass', pp. 29–30. See also McGrath and Frost, *Glass in Architecture and Decoration*, p. 370. Refer to Dodds, pp. 79–80.

are uneven or distorting: heavily veined stones, water rippled by the breeze, the curved corners of the chrome column facings. Creating an image of nature to suit picturesque conventions, the Claude Glass may offer detachment rather than engagement. Can the same be said of the Pavilion?

The Political Pavilion

Familiarly known as the Barcelona Pavilion, the German Pavilion at the Barcelona Universal Exposition was commissioned by the Weimar Republic. The Pavilion's purpose was to praise Germany. Dr Georg von Schnitzler, the German representative, and Alfonso XIII, King of Spain, attended the opening ceremony on 26 May 1929. Each described the Pavilion as a model of German endeavour and industry.[99] But the Pavilion was unheated, empty apart from a few chairs and had no everyday function. The only electric lighting was located within the opaque glass light well, which glowed with natural light in the day and artificial light at night.

In removing two of the three pedestals, Mies mirrored the transfer from the emblematic to the expressive garden in the mid-eighteenth century, when immediate and intuitive experiences were favoured to the extent that associations were less specific and narratives less apparent.[100] But the expressive garden can still be read emblematically. Analysing the Pavilion, Tafuri recognises stoic resistance in Mies's silence and concludes: 'Even the empty spaces of Mies are symbols; as ghosts of European intellectualism they have, in fact, become emblems.'[101] Whether emblematic or expressive, picturesque gardens are often accused of ignoring the world beyond their boundaries. Evans associates the Pavilion with such a denial: 'I would argue that Mies is holding the world at arm's length, less to contemplate its absurdity than to avoid its odour.'[102] Identifying the Pavilion with its client – the ineffective Weimar Republic – and noting Mies's later collaboration with the Nazis, Evans analyses its aesthetic:

> *The abstraction, the silence, the vacancy of the pavilion makes it hard to determine what has been removed . . . I would make two guesses about what the Barcelona Pavilion helped Mies and his contemporaries forget: politics and violence.*[103]

Mies's political opportunism deserves criticism but Evans's accusation is too broad, damning abstraction by association. Earlier in his essay, Evans remarks that 'We believe that Mies's buildings exhibit a sublime rationality because so many people

99 Solà Morales, Cirici and Ramos, p. 20.

100 Whately, p. 153.

101 Tafuri, *Architecture and Utopia*, p. 148; Tafuri, *Theories and History of Architecture*, p. 91.

102 Evans does not discuss the Pavilion with regard to the picturesque. Evans, 'Mies van der Rohe's Paradoxical Symmetries', p. 266.

103 In 1934 Mies was one of five architects invited to submit a design for the German Pavilion at the 1935 International Exposition in Brussels. Evans, 'Mies van der Rohe's Paradoxical Symmetries', pp. 268–269, and refer to p. 266.

have reported seeing it there. These sightings are only rumours.'[104] As Evans indicates here, and eighteenth-century advocates of the picturesque knew well, associations are uncertain.

In another essay, referred to in the first chapter of this book, Evans further undermines his criticism of the Pavilion when he praises the open plan, an architectural arrangement that is evident in Mies's design. Offering the Villa Madama as an example, Evans considers the matrix of interconnected internal and external rooms in the Renaissance villa, which inspired Kent, Schinkel and Mies. In contrast to the gregarious social proximity of the Villa Madama, Evans equates modernism with attempts to order social behaviour and deny the unpredictability of everyday life. But because it is permeable to movement, Evans describes the matrix of interconnected rooms as an open plan, a term commonly applied to modernist architecture.[105] The modernist open plan is familiarly associated with visual transparency and spatial continuity, which permit free-flowing movement. Sigfried Giedion, the secretary of CIAM (Congrès Internationaux d'Architecture Moderne), concluded in 1929: 'Consequently, this open house also signifies a reflection of the contemporary mental condition: there are no longer separate affairs, all domains interpenetrate.'[106] Endless visibility tends to repress rather than encourage gregarious behaviour. But all is not visible within the Pavilion. Reflections concerned Mies more, as he made clear. Rooms and routes in the Renaissance villa can be easily opened or closed, revealed or concealed, an arrangement that is necessary and stimulating even in a gregarious society.[107] As Roland Barthes remarks, a naked body is less erotic than the spot 'where the garment leaves gaps'.[108] The Pavilion is less adaptable than a Renaissance palazzo but it is worth repeating Evans's description of the Villa Madama because it equally describes Mies's design, which could comfortably incorporate similar inhibition even though it was not designed for gregarious behaviour:

> *Although most spaces within the villa were symmetrically composed, there were no duplications; every room was different. Uniformity was restricted to the parts where it could be immediately apprehended; the building as a whole was diverse. Yet, despite this striving to create a singularity of place, it is very difficult to tell from the plan which parts are enclosed, and which are open, as the relationship between all the spaces is much the same throughout. The chambers, loggias, courts and gardens all register as walled shapes – like large rooms – which add up to fill the site. The building seems to have been conceived as an accumulation of these enclosures, with the component spaces being more regular than the overall pattern.*[109]

104 Evans, 'Mies van der Rohe's Paradoxical Symmetries', p. 244.

105 Evans, 'Figures, Doors and Passages', pp. 64–65, 88.

106 Giedion, *Beifreites Wohnen*, p. 8; quoted and translated in Heynen, p. 36.

107 Evans, 'Figures, Doors and Passages', p. 88.

108 Barthes, *The Pleasure of the Text*, p. 9.

109 Evans, 'Figures, Doors and Passages', p. 60.

The picturesque garden's debt to the Renaissance villa's matrix of interconnected rooms continued in the Barcelona Pavilion, in which specific spaces were not ascribed specific uses. Demolished in 1930 and recreated as a museum exhibit in 1986, the Pavilion has not been tested by everyday use. A proposal in 1930 to retain and reuse the original Pavilion as a restaurant was neither successful nor appropriate. The Pavilion is a creative stimulus to use precisely because it has no specific function and lacks many of the familiar environmental characteristics of a building, such as adequate heating and lighting. The Pavilion should be occupied like a picturesque garden, in which uses are seasonal and the weather is always apparent.

The Ambiguous Pavilion

The architects of the 1986 reconstruction – Ignasi de Solà Morales, Christian Cirici and Fernando Ramos – aimed to faithfully complete the 1929 Pavilion. Emphasising the original design rather than the original building, they improved construction where necessary and built those parts of the design either compromised by economic restrictions or never built. For example, the roof is thicker than the original building, which required temporary reinforcement to hold it steady. Clad in green Alpine marble and travertine, the exterior side and rear walls follow Mies's design, not the plastered brickwork painted green and yellow in the 1929 building.[110] However, Solà Morales, Cirici and Ramos ignored some elements that Mies had intended, such as the water lilies, planters and circular plant pots. The flags are also absent in all the photographs in their book on the reconstruction. I assume that Solà Morales, Cirici and Ramos denied elements that would introduce life, weather and decay to the Pavilion because they wished to emphasise its aura as an object of artistic contemplation preserved in a pristine state and protected from decay, thus affirming architects' status as visual artists. Associated with the gallery but not exclusive to it, contemplation is a reverential mode of visual awareness in which sound, smell and touch are mostly ignored.[111] Their words – gaze, drawn, enmeshed, envelop, move, contemplate – describe a viewer absorbed by an artwork:

110 Solà Morales, Cirici and Ramos, pp. 14, 29.

111 Benjamin, 'The Work of Art in the Age of Mechanical Reproduction', p. 240.

> *It is necessary to go there, to walk amidst and see the startling contrast between the building and its surroundings, to let your gaze be drawn into the calligraphy of the patterned marble and its kaleidoscopic figures, to feel yourself enmeshed in a system of planes in stone, glass and water that envelops and moves you through*

Ludwig Mies van der Rohe, Barcelona Pavilion, 1929–1930, reconstruction, 1986. Large pool and travertine walls without the plants that appeared in the 1929 Pavilion. Photograph, Adrian Forty.

space, and contemplate the hard, emphatic play of Kolbe's bronze dancer over water.[112]

The 1929 original and 1986 copy were designed to be unheated, empty and without function. But the two buildings are not the same. The dialogue between architecture and nature is absent from the copy. A garden building as well as a garden, the 1929 Pavilion was abundantly planted and subject to the weather, recalling a ruin. Incomplete, the eighteenth-century ruin was a stimulus to the imagination and emotions, indicating both potential and loss. Ascribing evocative silence to the Pavilion, Evans and Tafuri seem to affirm its status as a ruin but we do not know if this was Mies's intention. There are no ruins at Charlottenhof, his likely inspiration.

Even more than other garden buildings the ruin is subject to the weather, literally and metaphorically. In *A Theory of /Cloud/ Toward a Theory of Painting*, 1972, Hubert Damisch places the cloud between forward slashes to indicate that his concern is the /cloud/ as signifier not the actual cloud. Recognising that the dialectic between linear perspective and the /cloud/ has been crucial to the history of painting, and arguing that linear perspective cannot accommodate all visual

112 Solà Morales, Cirici and Ramos, p. 39.

experience, Damisch concludes that the /cloud/ identifies the limits of the system. Consequently, he criticises Ruskin for attempting to depict the sky in linear perspective.[113] Quoting Damisch – 'the /cloud/ has no meaning that can be properly assigned to it; it has no value than that which comes to it from those serial relations of opposition and substitution that it entertains with the other elements of the system' – Rosalind Krauss wonders whether 'it is accurate or relevant to read the Barcelona Pavilion in terms of the /cloud/'.[114] George Dodds extends this discussion further:

113 Damisch, pp. 190–193; Ruskin, *Modern Painters*, vol. 5, pp. 144–161.

114 Krauss's translation is slightly different from the English edition of Damisch's book. Krauss, pp. 45, 146.

> *Rethinking the Barcelona Pavilion in terms of Brunelleschi's mirror, it may be productive to think of the pavilion as being assigned not only to the zone of architecture, but the zone of the silver leaf as well. Understanding that the pavilion is both 'sky' and 'mirror' – both the object and the* surface *of reflection – may explicate the nature of the collective desire that is fixated on but never fulfilled by the photographs of this building.*[115]

115 Dodds, p. 84.

In an early fifteenth-century demonstration of linear perspective, to which Damisch, Krauss and Dodds refer, Filippo Brunelleschi depicted the square around the Baptistery in Florence.[116] But rather than draw the sky he silvered part of a wooden panel so that it was seen in reflection, and a different sky was always present. Brunelleschi's demonstration seems to confirm the opinion that weather is outside architecture and outside architectural representation. But an alternative interpretation indicates the importance of weather to architecture. Locating architecture in a specific time and place, and encouraging its coexistence with the immediate and wider environments, the weather also makes architecture more ambiguous, unpredictable and open to varied interpretation, questioning established uses. Architecture is not just a mirror to the weather but can be like the weather in its subtle variety. Building and garden, mirror and sky, the Pavilion is picturesque, romantic and modernist: an ambiguous object.[117]

116 The Baptistery sits in the Piazza del Duomo. In another demonstration Brunelleschi depicted the Piazza della Signoria. Both were completed before 1420. Damisch, pp. 121–124; Krauss, pp. 141–142; Dodds, p. 84.

117 Philip Steadman suggests that Brunelleschi may have drawn both perspectives onto mirrored surfaces. If this were the case, the essential importance of weather to architecture would have been further emphasised.

A Picture of Nature

In 1937 a commission from Helen and Stanley Resor for a vacation house near Jackson Hole, Wyoming, first brought Mies to the United States. At the time of his visit to Wyoming, Mies spoke no English and his clients did not understand German. He admired the mountain views and changing light conditions but Mies's design affirmed his concerns in Europe. Recalling an arrangement that appeared in many of his previous designs, the Resor House creates a raised architectural foreground to view a natural background. Two drawings show the views from the house, which was to straddle Mill Creek, a tributary of the Snake River. One shows a 1928 Paul Klee painting owned by the Resors – *Bunte Mahlzeit* (Colourful Meal) – a timber wall in colour and pencil lines demarcating a column and window frame, all set against a black-and-white photograph of a rugged landscape.[118] The only colour is within the house and there is a clear distinction between the smooth interior and the rough landscape. Architecture and nature are kept apart. Their relationship is purely visual and nature is reduced to a picture. 'The exterior never manages to be present, to be perceived as material reality, not even at its most imposing, as in the mountains of Wyoming – only its representation is permitted', writes Jose Quetglas.[119]

But the drawing asks questions of the viewer that undermine this initial and familiar interpretation. The perspective is flattened and the drawing has no single focus. Forming understanding through movement, the eye roams backwards and forwards, up and down, between and across the fragments in a manner analogous to the picturesque as well as twentieth-century experiments in collage and montage. Each fragment is provocatively misrepresented, depicted on its own terms for meaningful effect, not visual accuracy. Klee's painting is shown much larger than its actual dimensions, reflecting Mies's affinity for an artist he collected and later displayed in his Chicago home. Within *Bunte Mahlzeit*, vibrant forms barely touch as they float against a black background, affirming the flattened perspective of Mies's drawing and further animating its composition. The monochrome landscape is not the actual one adjacent to Mill Creek; two riders look back towards the house, emphasising that a view may follow more than one direction. At the vertical edges of the drawing – to the left and the right – the landscape is cropped, as is the window, questioning the architectural enclosure. The floor and ceiling are represented by absence and two other architectural elements – the column and window frame – are insubstantial in comparison to the drawing's other fragments. Rather than a strict separation, it is possible to conclude that Mies's drawing depicts a continuous and unfolding environment in which architecture and nature are interrelated. In 1943, nature intervened forcefully. The project was abandoned due to extensive site damage caused by a spring flood.[120]

118 It is likely that George Danforth and William Priestley produced the drawing in 1939 but Terence Riley suggests that it may have been produced for Mies's 1947 retrospective exhibition at the Museum of Modern Art. Riley, 'Making History', p. 15. Refer to Dodds, p. 22, fig. 1.17b; McAtee, pp. 160, 180; Mies van der Rohe, *Drawings from the Collection of the Museum of Modern Art, New York*, fig. 18.

119 Quetglas, p. 134.

120 McAtee, p. 180.

Edith and Margaret in the Bathroom

In 1951 Mies completed a weekend house for Dr Edith Farnsworth at Plano, Illinois. A Midwest town built around a railway station, Plano is an untypical weekend base for prosperous Chicago residents, who tend towards the shores of Lake Michigan to the east. Consisting of one principal room glazed on four sides, the Farnsworth House is designed for a single occupant.[121] But the two bathrooms in the central core indicate that guests are expected, either during the day or also overnight.[122] The long kitchen confirms that the house is intended for entertaining as well as retreat. As social events in 1950s America often centred on family life and a single person was unlikely to be invited, some critics have focused on the personality and gender of the original owner. Alice T. Friedman gives particular importance to Mies's comment that the addition of a guest bathroom prevented visitors from 'seeing Edith's nightgown on the back of the bathroom door'.[123] But rather than the suppression of a specific gender, a wider disinterest is implied, which invites no personal expression other than that of the architect.

121 Mies, in *The Listener*, p. 620.

122 The alternatives are to share the double bed or sleep on the sofa.

123 Mies, as reported to Alice T. Friedman in April 1988 by Myron Goldsmith, Mies's associate on the Farnsworth House. Friedman, p. 143.

In other projects, such as the Barcelona Pavilion and the Tugendhat House, Mies designed furniture to accompany the building. He intended that the Farnsworth House would also contain only his furniture but the architect and client fell out before the project was furnished. Farnsworth, who claimed that she found the house uncomfortable but still lived there for twenty years, placed her objects and furniture around the house. Photographs suggest that they added little to the design. Peter Palumbo, a great admirer of Mies and the house's second owner in 1970, included furniture designed by the architect and in 1972 employed Mies's grandson, Dirk Lohan, to supervise the renovation. In the 1997 visitor guide, which he commissioned from Mies's biographer Franz Schulze, Palumbo perches uneasily on the edge of a Mies daybed. A valued memento, a signed photograph from Margaret Thatcher thanking Palumbo for his support, was displayed in a bathroom. The Farnsworth House does not readily accept its occupant's possessions, memories and traces. Despite Mies's disavowal of functionalism, the owner is not expected to express his or her identity because the architect's vision and control are complete. In 2003 Palumbo sold the Farnsworth House. Owned by the National Trust for Historic Preservation and managed by the Landmarks Preservation Council of Illinois, it is now a historical monument open to the public for hourly visits and unperturbed by daily life.

The Color of Our Houses

The comfortably bourgeois character of Mies's Chicago home suggests that he can be accused of hypocrisy: 'He lives in an old fashioned apartment . . . On the walls glow large pictures by Paul Klee. The maid serves on a low Chinese table.'[124] But

124 Norberg-Schulz, 'A Talk with Mies van der Rohe', p. 339.

if the Farnsworth House is not intended for domestic paraphernalia, what can it accommodate? In the grand house of an eighteenth-century estate, paintings, furniture and heirlooms accumulated. Adjacent, the picturesque garden housed pleasures rather than furnishings. Family and guests visited a garden pavilion occasionally, to start or conclude an extensive dinner, for example. Maintaining another house in Plano as his principal weekend residence, Palumbo often visited the Farnsworth House in a similar manner. On my visit with two friends, the house immediately brought to mind a favourite pleasure: a steak, a smoke, a glass of wine. When the house was empty, and before surveillance cameras were installed, its terraces were known as a favourite picnic site. Rather than accommodate objects, the Farnsworth House accommodates pleasures.

The appreciation of nature is one such pleasure. Affirming Mies's debt to Guardini, Neumeyer places a photograph of the Farnsworth House alongside a quotation from *Letters from Lake Como*:

> *When one ties up at San Giovanni on the lakeshore, on a terrace on which a stonemason has now set up his shop, one sees a beautifully built stair climb up toward the land . . . toward the Villa Giulia. How delightful was this climbing and how indescribably wonderful the walking! Surrounded by greatness, by width, by sky and sun . . . all illuminated by the power of form-giving . . . A large garden space opens up . . . within it, nothing . . . only space. But the villa of such simplicity that you marvel . . . The entire layout so that man can stride through sunlight, over heights, in fully formed greatness.*[125]

Close to the north bank of the Fox River and next to a black sugar maple – one of the most venerable in the area but now sadly dying after a lightning strike – the Farnsworth House is sited in meadow and deciduous woodland. Mies's design has 'such simplicity that you marvel' but differs from a Renaissance villa in that it is asymmetrical and not approached on axis. Also, its site is uncultivated and unlike any Renaissance or picturesque garden, apart from its waterfront site, countering Mies's quotation of Guardini: 'Nature is truly affecting only when it begins to be dwelled in, when culture begins in it.'[126] The Farnsworth House is as aloof from its site as it is from its occupant. Twelve steel columns raise the floor and roof planes above the meadow. Welded, ground smooth, then primed and finished in three coats of white paint, the structure seems to be cut from a single material without detail and weight. The height and detailing of the structure confirm the conceptual and physical detachment of architecture from nature, which Mies acknowledges:

125 The comparison is apt but Neumeyer edits Guardini's description to fit the Farnsworth House. Guardini, *Briefe von Comer See*, translated in Neumeyer, *The Artless Word*, p. 212.

126 Guardini, *Briefe von Comer See*, copied by Mies and quoted and translated in Neumeyer, *The Artless Word*, p. 281.

Ludwig Mies van der Rohe, Farnsworth House, Plano, Illinois, 1951. View from across the Fox River. Photograph, Yeoryia Manolopoulou.

Nature, too, shall live its own life. We must beware not to disrupt it with the color of our houses and interior fittings. Yet we should attempt to bring nature, houses, and human beings together into a higher unity. If you view nature through the glass walls of the Farnsworth House, it gains a more profound significance than if viewed from outside. This way more is said about nature – it becomes a part of a larger whole.[127]

The final line recalls Schinkel's influence. But Mies also emphasises that the visual experience of nature from within architecture is superior to the actual experience of nature within nature. Architecture and nature are not poetically interrelated as in the Court Gardener's House and Barcelona Pavilion. Recognising a metaphorical connection rather than an actual one, Neumeyer notes the influence of Mies's Bauhaus colleague Siegfried Ebeling, who in *Der Raum als Membran* (Space as Membrane), 1926, conceived architecture in terms of a protective barrier equivalent to the bark of a tree.[128]

Viewing nature from a sealed glass enclosure was a familiar theme in early modernist architecture, which developed in conjunction with new technologies. In

127 Mies in Norberg-Schulz, 'A Talk with Mies van der Rohe', p. 339.

128 Neumeyer, *The Artless Word,* p. 175.

129 Huguet Silk Mills, Wayland, NY. Banham, *The Architecture of the Well-tempered Environment*, p. 275.

1907 the pioneer of air-conditioning, Willis Havilland Carrier, guaranteed the environmental conditions within a building for the first time.[129] The term 'air-conditioning' was devised not by Carrier but by a competitor, Stuart W. Cramer, in 1904. For many years, Carrier used a more poetic term: man-made weather.[130] But man-made climate is more appropriate because Carrier's concern was consistency not poetry. In detaching the interior from the exterior, the tightly sealed and heavily insulated house ensures the occupant has no means to experience, appreciate and understand the surrounding environment. As early as 1915 Le Corbusier proposed a universal 'neutralising wall' to isolate inside from outside, its materials either transparent or solid as required.[131] Depending on the external conditions, hot or cold air was to circulate in the gap between a double membrane, maintaining a consistent internal temperature wherever a building was located:

> *At this moment of general diffusion, of international scientific techniques, I propose: only one house for all countries, the house of exact breathing . . . In winter it is warm inside, in summer cool, which means that at all times there is clean air inside at exactly 18°. The house is sealed fast!*[132]

Ludwig Mies van der Rohe, Farnsworth House, Plano, Illinois, 1951. View from the north bank of the Fox River with the black sugar maple. Courtesy of the Farnsworth House, a National Trust for Historic Preservation site.

130 Banham, *The Architecture of the Well-tempered Environment*, p. 172. Refer to Bhatia, pp. 239–241.

131 First devised for the Villa Schwob, La Chaux de Fonds, 1915. Banham, *The Architecture of the Well-tempered Environment*, pp. 156–163.

132 Le Corbusier, *Precisions*, pp. 65–66.

Profligate with energy consumption, the fully glazed modernist house typically requires air conditioning and central heating. Even today, when a sealed enclosure and substantial insulation are combined to limit energy consumption and heat loss, it is usually an inappropriate means to address environmental issues because its occupants are encouraged to be ignorant of the external world.

Accommodating a family and a private life in cosy domesticity during a booming consumer economy, the seventeenth-century Dutch house was the model home, establishing principles that were affirmed in the following centuries. But the apparent safety of the home was also the sign of its opposite, a fear of the tangible or intangible dangers inside and outside. Domesticity and cleanliness went hand in hand. Home was a powerful concept that society deployed to domesticate all its citizens in preparation for the public realm as well as the private one. Cleansing extended outwards from the surfaces of the home to the pavement. Seeking comfort in the moral force of a sweep of water, Dutch cities were noted as the cleanest in Europe. Due to the Netherlands' precarious geography and struggle for nationhood, fear focused on the vagrant and the flood tide, the most disturbing natural force in the Dutch landscape.[133] As the sea was the source of the Netherlands' growing prosperity as a trading nation, the flood tide was understood as both destructive and a means of moral redemption. In a culture that both enjoyed wealth and felt guilty about it, the flood tide eased the moral ambiguity of commercial success and initiated a period of rebuilding compatible with a society driven by market forces. The modernist house was less accepting of the objects and traces of domestic life. But no less than the Dutch seventeenth-century house, if by different means, it established precise boundaries between interior and exterior, confirming the long-held conflation of dirt, disorder and weather: 'The house is sealed fast!' Dismissive of weathering as well as weather, Le Corbusier also argued that whitewash is morally superior to other surfaces.[134]

133 The United Provinces of the Netherlands were founded in 1609. Refer to Sarti, p. 111; Schama, pp. 38, 47–49, 570–572, 587.

134 Le Corbusier, 'A Coat of Whitewash', pp. 185–92. Refer to Leatherbarrow and Mostafavi, pp. 72–6.

The Fox River House

Unlike the Barcelona Pavilion, the Farnsworth House does not create multiple reflections that entangle the viewer in self-reflection. Directed towards uncultivated nature, the raised view across the Fox River is romantic but for the glass enclosure. Mies's statement – 'If you view nature through the glass walls of the Farnsworth House, it gains a more profound significance than if viewed from outside' – suggests a concern for the visual and a disinterest in the complete experience of nature, which many critics recognise in his designs.[135] But the dialogue between architecture and nature at the Barcelona Pavilion has often been ignored and there is

135 Quetglas, pp. 134–35. Tafuri and Dal Co, p. 157. Evans, 'Mies van der Rohe's Paradoxical Symmetries', p. 258.

also another way to understand the Farnsworth House. Nature is seen on all sides as in a panorama rather than a picture. But rather than commanding, the viewer feels exposed. Since the Farnsworth House was first occupied, nature has regularly intervened to emphasise the vulnerability of the interior.

At first the damp meadow grass was left long and uncut, allowing mosquitoes to proliferate in summer.[136] In the 1947 model exhibited at the Museum of Modern Art, New York, a mosquito screen enclosed the upper terrace. But it did not please Mies and was not in place in early 1951. Farnsworth added a screen later that year after her relationship with her architect deteriorated.[137] With delicate silk curtains and the foliage of the maple tree the principal protection from the sun, the Farnsworth House is often uncomfortably warm in summer. Aided by an electric fan in the floor, some cross-ventilation is possible when the entry doors to the west and hopper windows to the east are open and the wind is blowing in the right direction. In winter the underfloor heating is insufficient, while excessive condensation collects on the single-glazed walls and stains adjacent surfaces. Given the size of the kitchen and principal room, the Farnsworth House can comfortably accommodate between one and twenty people. In winter such a crowd may be an asset, providing extra warmth, while in summer it interrupts airflow, making the internal temperature even more uncomfortable. Attempting to defend the design, Schulze notes that domestic air conditioning was unusual in the 1940s and people in the Midwest 'were long accustomed to enduring summer heat in their homes'.[138] But they lived in brick or timber houses with small windows; not a glass house.

At certain times of the year the Fox River is benign. Palumbo decided to celebrate his purchase by swimming across the river to the house: 'but I didn't realize that during the summer months, the water level in the Fox River falls quite dramatically. If it comes up to one's waist that's as far as it goes! . . . Swimming the Fox became instead, fording the Fox.'[139] As the architects' enquiries suggested a maximum flood of 0.9m above the meadow, the upper terrace was placed at 1.6m. Standing in the meadow, the visitor's eye level matches that of the terrace, creating a new horizon. The undercroft is more apparent than photographs suggest, and a black service stack is visible in the shadow. For much of the year the undercroft is barren, while in autumn the wind forms eddies of leaves. At other times, waves are watery and a greater threat. In 1954 the Fox River flood peaked at 2.8m above the meadow and 1.2m above the internal floor, ruining carpets and furniture. Faced in primavera wood-veneer, the central core fortunately survived. In 1996 the river rose 0.3m higher still, cracking two of the glass walls and destroying the wood-veneer, carpets, furniture and fittings. In 1997 a second renovation by Lohan was commissioned, which allows the wood-veneer panels to be dismantled

136 Today the meadow is cut to a lawn to reduce mosquitoes.

137 The screen was designed by an assistant in Mies's office, William Dunlap, with Mies offering advice without Farnsworth's knowledge. Schulze, *The Farnsworth House*, p. 17.

138 Schulze, *The Farnsworth House*, p. 15. Refer to Vandenburg, pp. 15, 21.

138 Palumbo, in Goldberger and Palumbo, p. 23.

and stored high within the house. Floods above the internal floor-level are now a common occurrence. Submerging the upper and lower terraces, the flood creates a further horizon that parallels the Barcelona Pavilion's horizontal symmetry.[140] Evans acknowledges that a reflection may disrupt or complete an image. The flood destroys the building fabric but restores the Farnsworth House, which is reflected in its mirrored surface.

Myron Goldsmith, Mies's employee on the Farnsworth House, claims responsibility for not placing the floor above the flood.[141] But Maritz Vandenburg partly attributes the rising flood to 'the outward expansion and paving over of Chicago's environs, the volume of water run-off increased and flood-levels began to rise dramatically in the 1950s'.[142] The Fox River flood undermines distinctions between the human and natural worlds, as well as those between the urban and rural.

A Difficult Beauty

Farnsworth made clear her criticism of her architect and her house. In 1951 she sued Mies and he sued her. Citing the house's constructional and environmental failings, she claimed that Mies had falsely represented himself as 'a skilled, proficient and experienced architect'.[143] Sixty-five at the completion of the Farnsworth House and the architect of many buildings in Europe and the United States, Mies was indeed an experienced architect, knowledgeable in construction and services. The Barcelona Pavilion was unheated but the Tugendhat House had a sophisticated and unobtrusive heating and ventilation system. Noting that 'the air-heating device worked wonderfully' Grete Tugendhat remarked: 'technically the whole building was planned by Mies down to the last detail, quite perfect', an opinion confirmed by her daughter.[144]

Mies failed to predict the rising flood. But he most likely knew that the Farnsworth House would suffer from condensation, glare, overheating and excessive cold,[145] and that the absence of a hearth to the fireplace would have 'the unhappy effect of creating a wild circulation of ash throughout the interior'.[146] Mies may not have cared, conceiving the Farnsworth House as an unyielding Platonic form and allowing daily life no influence on his design. Alternatively, he may have considered its environmental 'failings' to be necessary to the experience of the Farnsworth House, contradicting his statement that architecture and nature should be kept apart.[147] Certainly, many architects have said one thing and done another. The soft browns of timber and travertine affirm Mies's request not to disrupt nature 'with the color of our houses and interior fittings'. But the pink suede Barcelona chairs

140 Evans, 'Mies van der Rohe's Paradoxical Symmetries', pp. 261–266.

141 Goldsmith, interview with Keith Harrington, quoted in Lambert, 'Mies Immersion', p. 508.

142 Vandenburg, p. 26.

143 The case was finally settled out of court to Mies's advantage but Farnsworth paid him less than he demanded. Kendall County Circuit Court, Yorkville, Illinois, summary of the case proceedings, quoted in Friedman, p. 140.

144 Tugendhat, p. 7; Hammer-Tugendhat, 'Is the Tugendhat House Inhabitable?', pp. 29–34.

145 Another failing was caused by roof insulation placed below the waterproof membrane, common practice at the time of the Farnsworth House's construction. Warm, moist air rising to meet the cold surface of the waterproof membrane caused staining, mould growth and diminished insulation. This failing was one of those addressed in the 1972 restoration.

146 To alleviate the problem, Lohan added a raised travertine hearth in his 1972 restoration. Schulze, *The Farnsworth House*, p. 14.

he intended for the Farnsworth House would have made 'the house look like a Helena Rubenstein studio', as Farnsworth remarked.[148]

Like the Barcelona Pavilion, the Farnsworth House is one of the best-known examples of the modernist open plan, for which the traditional Japanese house is identified as a precedent.[149] A flexible and flowing spatial organisation is often cited as their principal similarity. As important but less recognised is the low level of thermal and sound insulation that their open internal volumes and delicate elevations provide. In the traditional Japanese house, windows are faced in opaque rice paper, oiled to become waterproof. Paper accentuates senses other than the visual but condensation on the glass walls of the Farnsworth House may have a similar effect, to be made, adjusted and erased by the user. In both houses, the heat source and thermal insulation are equally ineffective. The warmth of the stove in the traditional Japanese house is as limited as the Farnsworth House's underfloor heating.[150] Acknowledging Mies's interest in Japanese architecture, Arthur Drexler remarks that in the traditional Japanese house 'Winter was held to offer an experience of difficult but rewarding beauty.'[151] These words are as applicable to the Farnsworth House except that a 'difficult but rewarding beauty' is not only found in winter.

Is beauty the only appropriate term, however? Recalling the evening she first discussed the house with Mies, Farnsworth concludes that 'the effect was tremendous, like a storm, a flood, or other act of God'.[152] The Farnsworth House's vulnerable interior heightens awareness of nature's sublime effects, as in Palumbo's recollection of 'an electric storm of Wagnerian proportions illuminating the night sky and shaking the foundations of the house to their very core'.[153] But when the Fox River becomes a roaring torrent and bursts its banks nature is less docile, putting the sublime in such danger that a safe distance may be replaced by the sheer proximity of terror.

The Nature of Ambiguity

Baudelaire associates romanticism with the north, with 'intimacy, spirituality, colour, yearning for the infinite . . . the mist'.'[154] Equating the horizon in Friedrich's *Monk by the Sea*, 1809, with Mark Rothko's *Green on Blue*, 1956, Robert Rosenblum recognises a northern romantic tradition in painting, which he characterises as 'the search for transcendence in a secular world'.[155] In architecture, there is a parallel northern romantic tradition of which romantic classicism is a part. Although Rosenblum cites Friedrich, transcendence in northern romantic art and architecture is more often devoid of religiosity.

147 Elsewhere, as at Haus Esters, Krefeld, 1930, Mies designed oblique views that blur the relationship between architecture and nature.

148 Edith Farnsworth, 'Memoirs', ch. 13, unpaginated, quoted in Friedman, p. 143.

149 Gropius, p. 120.

150 The traditional Korean house, which was less well known to early modernists but has similar spatial qualities and papered windows, uses underfloor heating. Social cohesion in Japan and Korea, informed by the prevalence of Confucian values, ensures that a social boundary need not necessarily be physical.

151 Drexler, *The Architecture of Japan*, p. 11 and p. 41.

152 Schulze, *The Farnsworth House*, p. 18.

153 Palumbo, p. 8.

154 Baudelaire, p. 53.

155 Rosenblum, p. 218.

Johnson described the Kempner House, 1922, as Mies's 'last Romantic design' in the catalogue to the 1947 exhibition at the Museum of Modern Art, New York.[156] In later describing Schinkel and Mies as 'Romantic Classicists', Johnson acknowledged that his assessment was inaccurate but 'it was a position that Mies endorsed, at least tacitly, as it served to draw a polemical line between his work of the teens and his work of the 1920s', remarks Terence Riley.[157]

Mies's romanticism was established in Germany. Later collaborations increased his awareness of North American romanticism. For example, while Mies was Director of the School of Architecture at Illinois Institute of Technology (IIT), Alfred Caldwell taught landscape architecture and contributed landscaping to Mies's designs, including the IIT campus begun in 1940. In the 1920s Caldwell was an assistant to the landscape architect Jens Jensen, who emphasised native plants and nature's integrity in the tradition of Henry David Thoreau, the nineteenth-century American author who advocated the benefits of living in harmony with nature in *Walden, or Living in the Woods,* 1854.[158]

Nature is a recurring theme of northern romanticism. The Farnsworth House does not subtly mediate between architecture and nature in the manner of the Court Gardener's House and Barcelona Pavilion. But it does not keep them apart. The environmental conditions outside so temper and intrude on those inside that the relationship between architecture and nature is by no means visual alone. Within its vulnerable interior the full effects of weather and weathering are amplified and experienced, from the pleasant beauty of sunlight to the painful beauty of cold and condensation, from the majesty of thunder and lightning to the fearful flood when immediate danger overcomes the sublime. Rather than subtle mediation, the Farnsworth House exemplifies the more fully romantic immersion in nature that is less familiar to German romanticism, emphasising engagement as much as transcendence. We do not know if this was Mies's intention. One response to this dilemma is to recognise the architect's debt to romantic classicism, acknowledge his experience of the American landscape, and speculate that his purpose at the Farnsworth House was a more extreme interaction between architecture and nature. Another is to focus less on the architect's intentions and more on the building's fate, recognising the weather's role in affirming the northern romantic tradition. Ambiguous because of the weather as much as the architect, the Farnsworth House is a hinge between the early modernist control of nature and the later modernist accommodation of nature.

156 The design of the Kempner House began in 1919 and the building was completed in 1922. Johnson, *Mies van der Rohe*, p. 20.

157 Johnson, 'Schinkel and Mies', pp. 165–177; Riley, 'Making History', pp. 16–17.

158 Lambert, 'Mies Immersion', p. 589.

OWNING THE WEATHER

The Meteorological Project

Mies's commissions for corporate headquarters, federal offices and private houses are frequently cited as personifications of post-war American confidence. But the Farnsworth House was vulnerable to nature and out of step with the technological bombast of the time. Between the first meeting of its architect and client in 1945 and the first flood in 1954, American scientists introduced new means to order and affect the weather, radically transforming meteorology.

In principle the roles of observer, theorist and forecaster were fundamental to the meteorological profession as it was established in the early nineteenth century. In practice an empirical science based on statistics was separate from a theoretical science based on physics. Forecasting was further isolated from observation and theory because it was considered to be less scientific. Only in the twentieth century were the three roles fully combined. Early in the century, the Norwegian physicist Villhelm Bjerknes and his colleagues in Bergen utilised theories from physics and mathematics alongside a detailed network of weather observation. The meteorological profession's resistance to computation delayed their influence for two decades but, in time, the principles and practices of the Bergen School became the basis of modern meteorology. Technology was a further reason for delay. In *Weather Prediction by Numerical Process*, 1922, Lewis Fry Richardson writes: 'Perhaps some day in the dim future it will be possible to advance the calculations faster than the weather advances. But that is a dream.'[159]

159 Richardson, *Weather Prediction by Numerical Process*, p. 291. Refer to Nebeker, p. 1; Stevens, pp. 84–89.

Meteorological science has always depended on the accuracy of its instrumentation. In the second half of the seventeenth century, the first systematic weather records relied on the invention of the thermometer and barometer. In the nineteenth century, daily weather analysis and prediction became possible because the telegraph allowed faster communication between weather stations and the laboratory, while radio had a similar impact in the twentieth century. The increase in air travel in the first half of the twentieth century furthered demand for accurate weather forecasting, which was developed for military purposes in the Second World War, when radar became an invaluable tool.

In the second half of the twentieth century, meteorology underwent a further technological transformation, which established its present form. To secure long-term funding for his computational research, the mathematician John von Neumann needed a challenge that science was yet to solve. He turned to weather forecasting as 'the most complex, interactive, and highly nonlinear problem that had ever been conceived of – one that would challenge the capabilities of the fastest computing devices for many years'.[160] With US Navy funding, von Neumann established the Meteorological Project at Princeton University's Institute of Advanced Study in 1946 and two years later appointed another mathematician, Jule Charney, as its director. The Meteorological Project continued the ambitions of the Bergen School. Early in the 1940s Charney had met two of its members, Jacob Bjerknes and Carl-Gustaf Rossby, who were by then conducting research in the USA. Aware of their military sponsors' demands for efficient weather prediction and modification, in 1950 von Neumann and Charney created the first computer-based weather simulation on the first electronic computer – ENIAC – at the US Army's Ballistic Research Laboratory in Aberdeen, Maryland. Two years later, research continued on the Meteorological Project's own computer, which was by then complete. By the mid-1950s computational power had increased sufficiently to allow for the preparation of General Circulation Models (GCMs) of the atmosphere. In 1955, reaffirming the Enlightenment's ambition to establish human authority over nature, von Neumann remarked that 'intervention in atmospheric and climatic matters will come in a few decades and will unfold on a scale difficult to imagine at present . . . what power over our environment, over all Nature, is implied!'[161]

160 Von Neumann, quoted in Stevens, p. 95.

161 Von Neumann, quoted in Hulme, p. 348.

A parallel research project, which focused on weather modification and also acquired military support, began at the research laboratories of the General Electric Company (GEC) in the 1940s. Historical examples of weather modification include cannon fire to prevent hail damage, while Jefferson's enthusiasm for the effects of agriculture on climate was synonymous with the American self-image, civilising nature.[162] At GEC, Irving Langmuir, Vincent Schaefer and Bernard Vonnegut discovered that precipitation increases when pure silver iodide is sprinkled into clouds. Intended to disperse fog, suppress hail or encourage rain, 'cloud seeding' can have an agricultural purpose. But in 1947 the US government began to fund the research, later transferring 'Project Cirrus' to the Naval Weapons Center in China Lake, California. The CIA subsequently attempted to destabilise the Cuban economy by encouraging clouds to rain on the sea before they reached the island's sugar crop and, beginning in the mid-1960s, the US Department of Defense supported a seven-year cloud seeding programme during the Vietnam War. In 1996 the Chief of Staff of the US Air Force received a report – *Weather as a Force Multiplier: Owning the Weather in 2025* – which proposed techniques to control the weather for military purposes. Referring to 'localised and short-term forms of weather modification' the report was carefully worded to remain within the 1977 'Convention on the Prohibition of Military or Any Other Hostile Use of Environmental Modification

162 Jefferson, letter to Lewis E. Beck, 16 July 1824, in Jefferson, *The Writings of Thomas Jefferson*, vol. 15, pp. 71–72; Jefferson, *Notes on the State of Virginia*, p. 79.

Techniques' (ENMOD), which banned practices that could result in 'widespread, long-lasting or severe effects'.[163]

163 House et al., quoted in Pretor-Pinney, p. 266; ENMOD, quoted in Pretor-Pinney, p. 266.

The Greenhouse Effect

Numerous technological advances have first had a military purpose. In the 1940s and 1950s, the armed forces' demand for specific military applications helped to ensure that weather prediction and modification continued to receive more scientific attention than climate change, a more widespread transformation of the atmosphere. Citing Fourier and Tyndall's research on thermal radiation, Svante Arrhenius – a Swedish physicist and friend of Villhelm Bjerknes – published 'On the Influence of Carbonic Acid in the Air upon the Temperature of the Ground' in 1896.[164] Identifying an effect comparable to a greenhouse, he concluded that intensive fossil fuel consumption could increase the amount of heat-absorbing gases in the atmosphere, raising its temperature. But Arrhenius recognised only positive benefit and a more equable climate. The greenhouse effect received little further attention until Guy Stewart Callendar published 'The Artificial Production of Carbon Dioxide and its Influence on Temperature' in 1938.[165] Collating fifty years of weather data, Callendar identified an increase in global temperature but foresaw no significant dangers to the environment. Gradually this optimistic prognosis was undermined. Beginning in the late 1950s, Charles David Keeling's detailed measurements confirmed a steady increase in carbon dioxide in the atmosphere. The 'Keeling curve' confirmed the upward trajectory identified in Callendar's research.[166] However, despite the burgeoning environmental movement exemplified in Rachel Carson's *Silent Spring*, 1962,[167] scientists in the 1960s still familiarly assumed that 'the climate for all practical purposes could be treated as constant'.[168] Climate change remained of marginal interest even in the mid-1970s, when less than 100 scientific papers were published on the subject each year worldwide.[169] But the mid-1970s were a turning point as research increasingly focused on human influences on global warming. Chlorofluorocarbons (CFCs), such as refrigerants and aerosol propellants, had previously received little scientific investigation but new research indicated that they linger in the atmosphere for centuries, stimulating a chemical reaction that diminishes the ozone layer and removes protection from harmful ultraviolet rays.[170] Further investigation noted that CFCs are effective heat-absorbers, contributing to global warming as well as to ozone depletion.[171] Attention to methane came later because its level in the atmosphere is low in comparison to carbon dioxide. But its greenhouse effect per molecule is twenty times greater.

164 Arrhenius, pp. 237–276. Refer to Christianson, pp. 105–115, 141; Fleming, pp. 74–82.

165 Callendar, pp. 223–240.

166 Keeling, pp. 200–203.

167 Carson's principal concern is the effect of pesticides on wildlife. Carson, pp. 277–297.

168 Climatic Research Unit, University of East Anglia, http://www.cru.uea.ac.uk/cru/about/history (10 October 2010).

169 Stanhill, p. 396. Refer to Weart, p. 94.

170 Molina and Rowland, pp. 810–812.

171 Ramanathan, 'Greenhouse Effect', pp. 50–52. Refer to Christianson, pp. 158–171,189.

Methane's influence on the atmosphere increases as gases are released from the melting ice cap and agriculture expands to serve a rising population.[172] Deforestation also increases global warming because there are fewer trees to absorb carbon dioxide in the atmosphere. The reduction of the rainforest may have a secondary influence in that the cooling effect of evaporation is reduced. Air travel further contributes to global warming by carbon dioxide emissions and contrails, high-altitude condensation trails that develop into thin Cirriform clouds – Cirrus, Cirro-stratus and Cirro-cumulus – that impact on temperatures on the ground. Cloud cover may help maintain temperatures, especially in cities at night, but the overall effect of most cloud types is to cool rather than warm because they block the sun's radiation. Cirriform clouds have the opposite effect because they allow sunlight through and prevent some warmth departing, re-radiating it back to earth.

172 Ramanathan et al., 'Trace Gas Trends', pp. 5547–5566.

In the late 1970s and early 1980s, global warming became a subject of political and public debate rather than one limited to the scientific community. As recognition increased, discussion focused on the means to monitor, predict and reduce climate change. The first weather satellite was launched in 1960 and in 1979, during Jimmy Carter's US Presidency, the National Academy of Sciences appointed a panel to consider a GCM's capability to evaluate changes in the atmosphere. Chaired by Charney, the panel concluded in the affirmative, in principle at least.[173] But the accuracy of a GCM cannot be guaranteed as 'The Charney Report' recognises: 'Of course, we can never be sure that some badly estimated or totally overlooked effect may not vitiate our conclusions. We can only say that we have not been able to find such effects.'[174] If we assume a GCM to be true and respond with corrective measures that seem appropriate to our needs we may cause more harm than good, creating an ever more vicious circle. In 1818 Howard remarked: 'Meteorology . . . is yet far from having acquired the regular and consistent form of a science.'[175] Meteorology is now more of a science but it remains inexact.

173 'Charney Report', p. 12.

174 'Charney Report', p. 17. Refer also to Cotton and Pielke, p. 247.

175 Howard, *The Climate of London*, vol. 1, p. iii.

Anthropogenic Climate Change

Meteorologists distinguish between 'climate variability' from one year to the next, 'climate fluctuation' from one decade to the next, and long-term 'climate change', which may indicate temperature fluctuations up or down.[176] Climate always changes, whether by human agency or other means, but the term is sometimes used to imply that the current climate is an ideal that must be preserved. In arguing for the means to limit global warming and sustain the current climate, critics of

176 Glantz, pp. 23–24.

anthropogenic climate change are not so far removed from other advocates of climate modification.

As an idea, 'nature' is a human construction. But the places, species and phenomena that we include within 'nature' are real and not only subject to our imagination and will. Just because we have named something does not mean that we have made it, whatever our influence on the natural world. Instead, Steve Rayner offers the term 'coproduction' to categorise nature–culture relations.[177] As an idea, and the contemporary means to consider the relations between nature and culture, climate change has allowed criticism to focus on the free-market economy and the isolationist policies of countries and corporations. Rather than 'coproduction', critics of climate change tend to affirm the tradition of the biblical flood, in which environmental catastrophe is the punishment for human failing. According to Mike Hulme, a noted climate change researcher:

177 Rayner, p. 287.

> *Climate change is increasingly discussed using language borrowed from religion, theology and morality. Those in the West hear of 'penances' being paid for 'carbon sins' through the purchase of emission offsets, read of the personal 'guilt' associated with flying, and are challenged to 'repent' of their profligate consumption and to 'convert' to low-carbon lifestyles.*[178]

178 Hulme, pp. 173–174.

In the 1970s, concerns at first focused on global cooling but in current debates, due to current fears, climate change is conflated with global warming induced by human action. Other causes and consequences of climate change – anthropogenic or not – need to be acknowledged as well. For example, William R. Cotton and Roger A. Pielke Sr state the 'main effect of humans on the global climate system, as it impacts society, is not from the globally averaged increase in surface temperature, or even in ocean heat content'. Instead, they emphasise how humans 'alter atmospheric and ocean circulation patterns, such as the position of the polar jet stream'.[179]

179 Cotton and Pielke, p. 253.

In 1988 the World Meteorological Organisation (WMO) and United Nations Environment Programme (UNEP) established the Intergovernmental Panel on Climate Change (IPCC) with the purpose to provide a comprehensive and objective assessment of contemporary research. The IPCC publishes regular reports on the subject; the first appeared in 1990. Hulme recognises the dangers to human and natural life posed by a changing climate but argues that the contemporary definition of climate change is intrinsically problematic:

> *By constructing climate change as the 'mother of all problems' . . . perhaps we have outmanoeuvred ourselves. We have allowed climate change to accrete to*

> *itself more and more individual problems in our world – unsustainable energy, endemic poverty, climatic hazards, food security, structural adjustment, hyper-consumption, tropical deforestation, biodiversity loss – and woven them together using the meta-narrative of climate change.*[180]

180 Hulme, p. 333, refer to p. xxxiii.

Adopting Horst Rittel's definition of a 'wicked problem', Hulme concludes that climate change is now so complicated that it is beyond our ability to comprehend and solve.[181] But just as von Neumann recognised weather prediction as a challenge, the difficulty and significance of the problem draws funding to climate change research. Leigh Glover associates anthropogenic climate change with the project of modernity, which began in the Renaissance, promoted scientific reason and led to industrialisation. The proposed scientific 'solutions' to anthropogenic climate change – large scale, heavily funded and monolithic – reaffirm a faith in technological progress that is consistent with the conception of modernity that caused anthropogenic climate change.[182] Blinded by its confidence in human progress, science largely failed to recognise anthropogenic climate change until recently. Its ability to offer convincing and appropriate predictions and conclusions is equally open to doubt. The tendency to offer top-down, global solutions is itself a problem, as Hulme acknowledges:

181 Hulme, p. 334. Refer to Rittel and Webber, pp. 155–169.

182 Glover, pp. 22–23, 28–30, 86–88, 246–251.

> *If we pursue the route of seeking ever larger and grander solutions to climate change we will continue to end up frustrated and disillusioned: global deals will be stymied, science and economics will remain battlegrounds for rearguard actions, global emissions will continue to rise, vulnerabilities to climate risks will remain. And we will end up unleashing ever more reactionary and dangerous interventions in our despairing search for a solution to our wicked problem: the colonisation of agricultural land with energy crops, the colonisation of space with mirrors, the colonisation of the human spirit with authoritarian government.*[183]

183 Hulme, p. 359.

Instead, Hulme proposes that 'we construct our problems in such a way as to make them fit our capabilities for solution-making rather than imagine that our human ingenuity can find solutions to whatever problems we casually invent'.[184] Questioning the effectiveness of an organisation dominated by scientists – the IPCC – Hulme also argues that climate change is not just a physical phenomenon and neither is it exclusively a scientific concern.[185] Unlike the weather, which we can see and feel, we cannot directly experience climate because it is an idea aggregated over time – at least thirty years according to the World Meteorological Organisation. Neither the weather nor the climate can be comprehended by science alone because

184 Hulme, p. 338.

185 Hulme, p. 4.

our knowledge and understanding of any subject is dependent on who we are, where we live and what we believe. Stating that 'climate change has more potency now as a mobilising idea than it does as a physical phenomenon' Hulme convincingly argues for a complex, creative and contextual engagement with climate change that is not solely driven by fear:

> *As a resource of the imagination, the idea of climate change can be deployed around our geographical, social and virtual worlds in creative ways. The idea of climate change can stimulate new thinking about technology. It can inspire new artistic creations in visual, written and dramatised media. It can invigorate efforts to protect our citizens from the hazards of climate. The idea of climate change can provoke new ethical and theological thinking about our relationship with the future. It can arouse new interest in how science and culture interrelate. It can galvanise new social movements to explore new ways of living in urban and rural settings. And the idea of climate change can touch each of us as we reflect on the goals and values that matter to us. These are all creative applications of the idea of climate change, but they are applications that do not demand agreement. Indeed, they may be hindered by the search for agreement. They thrive in conditions of pluralism and hope, rather than in conditions of universalism and fear. Nor are they applications that will lead to stabilising climate – they will not 'solve' climate change.*[186]

186 Hulme, p. 363, refer to p. 328.

Climate change, whether by natural or human means, was of little concern to scientists in the mid-twentieth century when the Farnsworth House was designed and built. Equally, there is no indication that it concerned Mies. But a project may have a life beyond its original author. The Farnsworth House's vulnerability to anthropogenic climate change, exemplified in the Fox River flood, furthers the romantic immersion in the hybridised weather of nature and industry that Turner consciously engaged in the nineteenth century.

7

submitting to the seasons

INTRODUCTION

Neumeyer's *The Artless Word* examines Mies's many influences. But Mies is still known for saying little about his ideas and interests. Consequently, this chapter focuses on Alison and Peter Smithson, who often stated their admiration for Mies. Their designs and writings help to locate the Farnsworth House in relation to an architectural movement committed to an appreciation of the environment and weather, which they further developed and creatively theorised as a reappraisal of the picturesque and critique of consumer society.

THE MODERNIST PICTURESQUE

Claims that modernism is utterly new or reassuringly old are alternative means of validation and promotion. Countering the myth that modernism has no history, historians have resorted to different periods to give it a past.[1] In *Modern Architecture: Romanticism and Regeneration*, 1929, Hitchcock remarks that although late eighteenth-century buildings were 'often absurd' they 'indicated an aggravated sensibility to architectural effects judged pictorially. This was certainly uncritical but it was healthy'. In Le Corbusier's League of Nations, 1927, and Ernst May's 1920s housing in the Nidda Valley, Hitchcock notes a similar pictorial sensibility: 'Uvedale Price, the great authority on the picturesque, would have approved both terraces and ribbon windows.'[2]

Admiring Christopher Hussey's *The Picturesque: Studies in a Point of View*, 1927, Nikolaus Pevsner promoted the picturesque as an editor of *The Architectural Review* in the 1940s and 1950s. Alongside building reviews the magazine included articles on 'Fonthill Abbey', 'The Lure of Rusticity' and related themes.[3] Unlike Hitchcock, Pevsner's argument was social and cultural as well as aesthetic. Defining the genius of a people and a place, he identifies the picturesque as the personification of Englishness: 'the theory of the flowing line, the more general aesthetic theory of surprise and concealment, the way the Picturesque is tied up with English outdoor life and ultimately even the general British philosophy of liberalism and liberty'.[4] Pevsner's promotion of the picturesque culminated in 'The Englishness of English Art', the 1955 BBC Reith Lectures, which eulogised Hogarth, Soane, Sterne and Turner and appeared as a single volume in 1956. The first chapter – 'The Geography of Art' – provides 'a whole string of facts from art and literature tentatively derived from the climate' and suggests that a stoic pleasure in unreliable weather is particularly English.[5] Pevsner accepts that 'an atmospheric view of the world'

1 For example, Colin Rowe discusses ideal proportions in the designs of Palladio and Le Corbusier and links the Miesian to the Palladian. Rowe, 'The Mathematics of the Ideal Villa', pp 1–27; Rowe, 'Neo-"Classicism" and Modern Architecture I', pp. 119–138; Rowe, 'Neo-"Classicism" and Modern Architecture II', pp. 139–158.

2 Hitchcock, pp. 12, 220.

3 Bronkman, pp. 149–157; Pevsner, 'The Lure of Rusticity', p. 27.

4 Pevsner, 'The Genius of the Place', p. 232.

5 Pevsner, *The Englishness of English Art*, p. 14.

represents 'a European not merely an English development' and recognises that national character is 'far from permanent' but attributes two English traits – moderation and imagination – to a mild and misty climate:[6]

> *That moisture steams out of Turner's canvases . . . and lays a haze over man and building, dissolving their bodily solidity. It thus links up with the incorporeal tradition of English art. And it makes the English, to return to the business in hand, the creators of landscape gardening and of the Picturesque.*[7]

Concluding that moderation has tended to prevail over imagination in the English visual arts, Pevsner identifies the picturesque as the means to address this imbalance because it 'belongs as much to the side of fantasy as to the side of intelligently understood function'.[8]

The picturesque came to fruition in England. But given its precedents in classical antiquity, Chinese landscape drawings and seventeenth-century continental paintings, compatibility with French and German rococo and varied development internationally, it cannot be described as exclusively English. Indeed, its diverse origins were important in the eighteenth century and again in the mid-twentieth century because the picturesque was synonymous with liberalism, British or otherwise. In response to Britain's diminishing status before the Second World War and, then, to bolster the nation in response to military aggression and its aftermath, a burgeoning British neo-romanticism celebrated national identity. During the Blitz, Kenneth Clark – director of the National Gallery and chairman of the War Artists Advisory Committee – even stated that 'Bomb damage is itself Picturesque'.[9] On 15 August 1944, *The Times* published a letter in which noted figures including Clark, T.S. Eliot, H.S. Goodhart-Rendell and John Maynard Keynes claimed that a ruined church was an appropriate and evocative memorial to the devastation.[10] In a subsequent publication, *Bombed Churches as War Memorials*, Hugh Casson argued that ruins could become a place of remembrance, contemplation and prayer when incorporated into a garden:[11]

> *It will not be many years before all traces of war damage will have gone, and its strange beauty vanished from our streets. No longer will the evening sky be reflected in the water-pools which today lie dark and quiet between torn and gaping walls. Soon a pockmarked parapet or a broken cornice will be to future generations the only sign of former shock and flame. The shabby heap of stones, flowering with willow-herbs as pink and lively as the flames which earlier sprouted from their crevices, will disappear, and with their going the ordeal which we passed will seem remote, unreal, perhaps forgotten.*

6 Pevsner, *The Englishness of English Art*, pp. 18–19, 185–187.

7 Pevsner, *The Englishness of English Art*, pp. 163–164.

8 Pevsner, *The Englishness of English Art*, p. 186. Refer to Lang and Pevsner, p. 392.

9 Clark, quoted in Woodward, *In Ruins*, p. 212.

10 Reprinted in Casson, Colvin, and Groag. p. 4. Refer also to Jellicoe and Conder, pp. 139–146, with an introduction by the Dean of St Paul's Cathedral, London.

11 The architectural consequences of the war were a recurring theme for Casson. In September 1944 *The Architectural Review* published his article 'Art by Accident: The Aesthetics of Camouflage'.

> *Save us, then, some of our ruins, not as moral warnings, not as symbols of vengeful memory, but as places of rest and worship, and above all as reminders of the sacrifices, the gallantry and the faith of those who fought and died, many thousands of them among these very stones whose existence to-day is a testament that they did not die in vain.*[12]

12 Casson, 'Ruins for Remembrance', p. 22.

No doubt contemplating his personal history, the liberalism that Pevsner associated with the English and their gardens was intrinsic to his affection: 'England has indeed profited just as much from the un-Englishness of the immigrants as they have profited from the Englishing they underwent.'[13] For all its special relationship with England, Pevsner did not characterise the picturesque as exclusive to one nation. To further cohesion at a time of uncertainty he made no distinction between English and British and in 1944 he described the picturesque as England's principal contribution to European architecture, later editing *The Picturesque Garden and its Influence Outside the British Isles*, 1974.[14]

13 Pevsner, *The Englishness of English Art*, p. 185.

14 Pevsner, 'The Genesis of the Picturesque', p. 139.

Aware of inter-war resistance to a new architecture, Pevsner saw the picturesque as a means to make modernism familiar to England. Associating one with the other, he concluded that the picturesque and 'the modern revolution of the early twentieth century . . . had all the fundamentals in common'.[15] His concern was modernism's future as well as its history. Identifying the picturesque with 'the modern revolution' as well as a later modernism, and associating the picturesque with England while affirming its wider relevance, Pevsner attempted a delicate balance of ideas. Noting an increasing sensitivity to place and 'a new faith in nature' that recalled Thomson, Pevsner drew attention to the picturesque in order to question one modernism – international, mechanical and insensitive – in favour of another – local, emotive and environmentally aware.[16] As he associated the picturesque with a particular climate, one question left unanswered was the geographical limits of the modernism he advocated.

15 Pevsner, 'Twentieth-Century Picturesque: An Answer to Basil Taylor's Broadcast', p. 229. Refer to Pevsner, *The Englishness of English Art*, p. 183; Pevsner, 'The Genesis of the Picturesque', p. 139.

16 Pevsner, 'The Lure of Rusticity', p. 27.

REVENGE OF THE PICTURESQUE

Pevsner's praise for the picturesque met fierce criticism. Defending modernism as an architecture 'proper to the twentieth century', Alan Colquohoun claimed that Pevsner had focused on aesthetics to the detriment of function and other concerns, which Pevsner denied.[17] Due to their close association Reyner Banham was Pevsner's most notable critic. At the Courtauld Institute of Art, London, Pevsner had supervised Banham's PhD, which was completed in 1958 and published with

17 Colquohoun, p. 2; Pevsner, 'Twentieth Century Picturesque: Reply to Alan Colquohoun', p. 2.

some additions as *Theory and Design in the First Machine Age* in 1960. The acknowledgements begin with Banham's dedication 'to Nikolaus Pevsner for the original impulse, and for guidance constantly and ungrudgingly given'.[18] *Theory and Design in the First Machine Age* is a response to Pevsner's *Pioneers of the Modern Movement*, 1936, which was reprinted as *Pioneers of Modern Design* in 1949 and revised in 1960.[19] The books share a concern for machine age modernism although they focus on different architects. Pevsner begins with the mid-nineteenth century and William Morris while Banham places greater emphasis on technology and the Futurists, who Pevsner largely ignores. In no edition does Pevsner refer to the picturesque although Banham notes that he places 'a very high valuation on the English contribution to the rise of Modern Architecture'.[20] Pevsner's praise for the picturesque shocked Banham. In *Concerning Architecture*, 1968, a collection of essays that honours Pevsner's contribution to architectural history, only one chapter is critical. In 'Revenge of the Picturesque' Banham declares Pevsner's support for the 'empiricism and compromises' of the picturesque to be a denial of his life's work.[21]

THE NEW BRUTALISM

In the December 1955 issue of *The Architectural Review* Banham discusses a new architectural movement, which he opposes to the picturesque.[22] As precedents for 'The New Brutalism' he cites the anti-formal and non-hierarchical tendencies in Jean Dubuffet's Art Brut and Michel Tapié's concept of *Un Art Autre*, 1952, which he applies to Brutalism as *Une Architecture Autre*.[23] Banham concludes that the principles of Brutalism are '1, Memorability as an Image; 2, Clear exhibition of Structure; and 3, Valuation of Materials "as found".'[24] The second and third principles affirm the modernist concern for truthful and unadorned structures and materials. The first principle is less expected given modernism's supposed aversion to aesthetic discussions and Banham's conclusion to *Theory and Design in the First Machine Age*:

> *The architect who proposes to run with technology knows now he will be in fast company, and that, in order to keep up, he may have to emulate the Futurists and discard his whole cultural load, including the professional garments by which he is recognised as an architect.*[25]

But the image Banham advocates is not applied. It is the direct result of structure and materials, function and technology:

18 Banham, *Theory and Design in the First Machine Age*, p. 2.

19 Pevsner, *Pioneers of the Modern Movement*.

20 Banham, *The New Brutalism*, p. 14.

21 Banham, 'Revenge of the Picturesque', p. 267.

22 In 'The New Brutalism' Banham does not refer to the picturesque directly but to Basil Taylor's criticism, to which Pevsner responded. In *The New Brutalism*, 1966, Banham details his attack on the picturesque. Banham, 'The New Brutalism', p. 355; Banham, *The New Brutalism*, p. 43, Pevsner, 'Twentieth-Century Picturesque: An Answer to Basil Taylor's Broadcast', pp. 227–229.

23 Banham. 'The New Brutalism', pp. 356, 358 and 361.

24 Banham, 'The New Brutalism', p. 361.

25 Banham, *Theory and Design in the First Machine Age*, pp. 329–330.

> *Basically, it requires that the building should be an immediately apprehensible visual entity, and that the form should be confirmed by experience of the building in use. Further, that this form should be entirely proper to the functions and materials of the building, in their entirety.*[26]

Banham identifies Alison and Peter Smithson as Brutalism's key architects and praises the directness of their first significant building: Hunstanton Secondary Modern School, 1954, 'is almost unique among modern buildings in being made of what it appears to be made of . . . Water and electricity do not come out of unexplained holes in the wall, but are delivered to the point of use by visible pipes and manifest conduits'.[27] Recognising the influence of Rudolf Wittkower – author of *Architectural Principles in the Age of Humanism*, 1949 – Banham's one criticism is the school's formal composition.[28]

The Smithsons claimed that Alison Smithson was the first person to use the term 'Brutalism' in 1953; Banham's article on the subject was a response to their one-page statement in the January 1955 issue of *Architectural Design* in which they describe 'The New Brutalism' as 'the only possible development *for this moment* from the Modern Movement'.[29] As precedents the Smithsons cite Le Corbusier's use of 'béton brût' (raw concrete) in the early 1950s, which Banham also mentions.[30] They also praise traditional Japanese architecture, which, they argue, was misunderstood by earlier modernists who focused only on its aesthetic:

> *But for the Japanese their FORM was only a part of a general conception of life, a sort of reverence for the natural world and, from that, for the materials of the built world. It is this reverence for materials – a realisation of the affinity which can be established between building and man – which is at the root of the so-called New Brutalism.*[31]

The Smithsons conclude that 'Brutalism tries to face up to a mass production society, and drag a rough poetry out of the confused and powerful forces which are at work. Up to now Brutalism has been discussed stylistically, whereas its essence is ethical.'[32]

HA-HA

Banham extended his discussion in *The New Brutalism: Ethic or Aesthetic,* 1966. The Smithsons' response was a page-by-page, often critical review with few

26 Banham,'The New Brutalism', p. 358.

27 Banham, 'The New B rutalism', p.357.

28 Banham notes that the Smithsons disputed the timing of that influence. Banham, 'The New Brutalism', pp. 357–361. Refer to Wittkower, *Architectural Principles in the Age of Humanism.*

29 Alison and Peter Smithson, 'Banham's Bumper Book on Brutalism', p. 1590; Alison and Peter Smithson, 'The New Brutalism', p. 1.

30 Banham, 'The New Brutalism', p. 356.

31 Banham notes that the Smithsons had not visited Japan at that time. Alison and Peter Smithson, 'The New Brutalism', p. 1; Banham, *The New Brutalism*, p. 46.

32 Alison and Peter Smithson. 'The New Brutalism: Alison and Peter Smithson Answer the Criticisms on the Opposite Page', p. 113.

moments of praise: 'Our generation's relationship to *The Architectural Review*, after about 1947, Banham gets dead right on p12.'[33] There, noting Pevsner's research into 'the origins and practice of English picturesque planning' and its twentieth-century relevance, Banham writes:

> *Such an approach, which 'judges every case on its merits', etc, stands on a firm tradition of British Liberalism, democracy and common law, but it seemed of absolutely trivial value to a younger generation to whom the given elements of the planning situation seemed to be social chaos, a world in ruins, the prospect of nuclear annihilation, and what appeared to be a complete abandonment of architectural standards on the part of their elders.*[34]

After this initial opposition, Banham documents the Smithsons' increasing engagement with the picturesque. Characterising it as a 'purely visual discipline' he identifies 'the re-appearance of Picturesque Method' in the 1950s.[35] The union was soon complete:

> *Symbolically, the gap between the Brutalists and the Picturesque Townscape movement may be said to close in 1962, when the Smithsons employed Gordon Cullen, greatest of* The Architectural Review's *'Townscape' draughtsmen to prepare the perspectives of their Economist building.*[36]

In 1966 Banham dismissed much of his 1955 article: 'In retrospect it reveals only too clearly my attempt to father some of my pet notions on the movement.'[37]

> *For a short period, around 1953–55, it looked as if an 'other architecture' might indeed emerge, entirely free of the professional preconceptions and prejudices that have encrusted architecture since it became 'an art'. It looked for a moment as if we might be on the threshold of an entirely uninhibited functionalism.*[38]

Banham had misjudged the Smithsons and Alison's response was mockingly abrupt: 'Poor Peter (Banham), he's forever condemned to be disappointed, don't you know.'[39] Banham even underestimated the speed and extent of the Smithsons' conversion to the picturesque. He cites their competition design for Coventry Cathedral 1951 as 'still almost the last secure point in history on which the opponents of Picturesque compromise can rely'.[40] But at Hunstanton School, first designed in 1949, there are references to the English landscape garden, which the Smithsons acknowledge: 'The school's approach had the indented verge to the ha-ha, by which the school territory was separated from the road.'[41]

33 Alison and Peter Smithson, 'Banham's Bumper Book on Brutalism', p. 1590.

34 Banham, *The New Brutalism*, p. 12.

35 Banham, *The New Brutalism*, pp. 12, 74.

36 Banham, *The New Brutalism*, p. 75.

37 Banham, *The New Brutalism*, p. 134.

38 Banham, *The New Brutalism*, p. 135.

39 Alison Smithson, quoted in Whiteley, p. 133.

40 Banham, 'Revenge of the Picturesque', p. 273.

41 Alison and Peter Smithson, *Alison and Peter Smithson: The Shift*, p. 36.

Rather than simple nostalgia, the Smithsons saw the picturesque as a found condition relevant to the present. Alison Smithson remarked: 'I work with memory, and it allows me to make connections to the past, interpolations of the present and gives foresight – a most valuable facility for an architect – as to a possible future.'[42] Rather than an untainted technological futurism, they favoured the continuity of modernism with earlier centuries. Rather than ethics or aesthetics, their concern was the means to combine them. In eighteenth-century England, the genius of the place was made as much as found, the fusion of new ideas, forms and spaces with those already in place, which were often the results of earlier migrations. The same was true of Brutalism.

42 Alison Smithson, 'Patio and Pavilion', p. 11.

YESTERDAY, TODAY AND TOMORROW

At the 1956 *Daily Mail Ideal Home* exhibition in London, the Smithsons displayed the House of the Future, which imagined the home of a young, urban and childless couple in 1981. Walls, floors and ceilings were sculpted into a single, smoothly flowing surface. The internal temperature was constant and maintained automatically. At the press of a button the adjustable living room table would sink into the floor, typifying a technological Pop sensibility. Peter Cook writes:

> *For those of us in the next generation, the puzzlement remained as to why the Smithsons chose not to continue on the line of exploration started by the House of the Future: and in the projects by my friends David Greene and Warren Chalk (the Pod and the Capsule respectively), homage is offered quite openly to them.*[43]

43 Cook, p. 40.

Also in 1956, Theo Crosby organised *This is Tomorrow*, an exhibition at the Whitechapel Gallery, London. Group Six – Nigel Henderson, R.S. Jenkins, Eduardo Paolozzi and the Smithsons – created Patio and Pavilion, one of the twelve exhibits.[44] The House of the Future contained a courtyard, a relationship that Patio and Pavilion inverted. Their gardens were very different. The House of the Future encircled a gentle scene of grass, flowers and willowy trees, while the Patio was rough and rustic. The Pavilion was a shed of reused timber boarding with a corrugated plastic roof and limited thermal comfort, adorned with decayed and discarded objects. Responding to intellectual, emotional and physical needs in a simple and direct manner that was reminiscent of the primitive hut and appropriate to post-war austerity, Patio and Pavilion was astutely described as 'a frugal pastoral' by Lawrence Alloway.[45] But Banham criticised it as 'submissive to traditional

44 Group Six's members belonged to the Independent Group, which was active and influential in the mid-1950s.

45 Alloway, quoted in Lippard, p. 36.

Alison and Peter Smithson, House of the Future, *Daily Mail Ideal Home*, London, 1956. Living room with sunken table, looking towards the patio and kitchen. Courtesy of the Smithson Family Collection.

Alison and Peter Smithson with Nigel Henderson, R.S. Jenkins and Eduardo Paolozzi, Patio and Pavilion, *This is Tomorrow*, Whitechapel Gallery, London, 1956. Photograph, Nigel Henderson. Courtesy of the Smithson Family Collection.

values'.[46] He failed to realise that the House of the Future and Patio and Pavilion were not mutually exclusive, just as Cook failed to recognise the House of the Future in the Smithsons' later work. Alison Smithson later remarked that 'The change in thinking, in attitude, that both of these 1956 exhibition buildings effected – and still represent – was our beginning of a response to climate.'[47] Their influence is apparent in the Smithsons' principal contribution to the twentieth-century re-evaluation of the picturesque.

46 Banham, 'This is Tomorrow', p. 187.

47 Alison Smithson, 'Patio and Pavilion', p. 10.

FONTHILL FOLLY

The Smithsons knew Fonthill well. As a second home to their one in London, they bought a small cottage in 1958, which was part of a complex of former farm buildings in the south of the estate. Close to the top of rising farmland, a garden wall wraps the rectangular site, forming the cottage's northern boundary. The Smithsons removed much of the cottage, which was subject to a demolition order due to its dilapidated condition. But – combining new and old – they added a two-

Alison and Peter Smithson, Upper Lawn Pavilion, 1959–. The house is already occupied although the lower glazing is yet to be installed and the upper glazing is partially complete, autumn 1961. Courtesy of the Smithson Family Collection.

storey house of similar volume and incorporated existing fragments such as the garden wall, chimney, paving and well. Accessible up a steep climb, more a ladder than a staircase, the glazed first floor room looks in all directions:

> *The gazebo – to experience fully during short visits, the country from the first floor spaces: to the north and west the Fonthill Woods, to the east and south the Wardour Woods set against the skyline of the Downs.*[48]

48 Alison and Peter Smithson, 'Folly at Fonthill, Wilts.', p. 482.

On the ground floor, set within the garden wall, two retained cottage windows afford long views to the undulating fields and woods beyond, which shutters can obscure when necessary. Creating ambiguities between inside and outside and home and garden, the position of the new house does not quite match that of the old cottage. One retained cottage window is inside the new house and the other is outside adjacent to a patio.

Aligning their practice with the picturesque, the Smithsons described their new home as a '"folly" implanted within the bounds of the original "lawns" of Beckford's folly at Fonthill'.[49] To commemorate the sale of his estate, Beckford commissioned John Rutter to produce *Delineations of Fonthill and its Abbey*, 1823:

49 Alison and Peter Smithson, *The Charged Void*, p. 238.

> *The grounds of Fonthill exhibit the true spirit of English gardening, carried to its utmost extent of a bold and varied simplicity. Every tree, every shrub, and every flower, has contributed to the production of one unequalled effect of wild profusion.*[50]

50 Rutter, p. 84.

In Rutter's map of the 'Fonthill Domain' the Smithsons' site is part of 'West Lawn Farm House'.[51] Fonthill Abbey is only a mile away, due north. The Smithson's house – Upper Lawn Pavilion – is 165m above sea level. The land dips and undulates between them but the Abbey's site is just 10m higher. In 1823 the 55m tower of Fonthill Abbey would have been visible above the surrounding woods. In 1958 its ghostly spirit could be imagined in the autumn mist.

51 Rutter, following p. 100.

The Smithsons knew that their fascination for Fonthill would have been abhorrent to an earlier generation of modernists. In *Modern Architecture: Romanticism and Regeneration*, Hitchcock writes: 'The most important Romantic monument of the eighteenth century in England, Wyatt's Fonthill Abbey, was so shoddily built that it fell within a generation after its erection and is known to us only from contemporary books and prints. It is doubtless better so'.[52]

52 Hitchcock, p. 9.

AS IN DS

The Smithsons travelled to Fonthill by Citroën.[53] The DS was their favourite, designed by the architect Flaminio Bertoni in 1955. *La Déesse* – the Goddess – 'marks a change in the mythology of cars . . . it is now more *homely* . . . conceived as comfort rather than performance', remarked Roland Barthes in 1957.[54] Panoramic windows, pneumatic suspension, front wheel drive, 3125mm between the front and rear axles and a chassis-cloaking body combine to create a smooth and spacious ride: Alison Smithson's 'private room on wheels'.[55]

53 The Smithsons interest in driving extended to urban design. Multiple urban centres were connected by motorways in 'Cluster City', which they first presented at CIAM's tenth conference at Dubrovnik in 1956. Alison and Peter Smithson, 'Cluster City', pp. 332–336. Refer to Fraser with Kerr, p. 178.

54 Barthes, 'The New Citroën', p. 89.

55 Alison Smithson, *AS in DS*, p. 111.

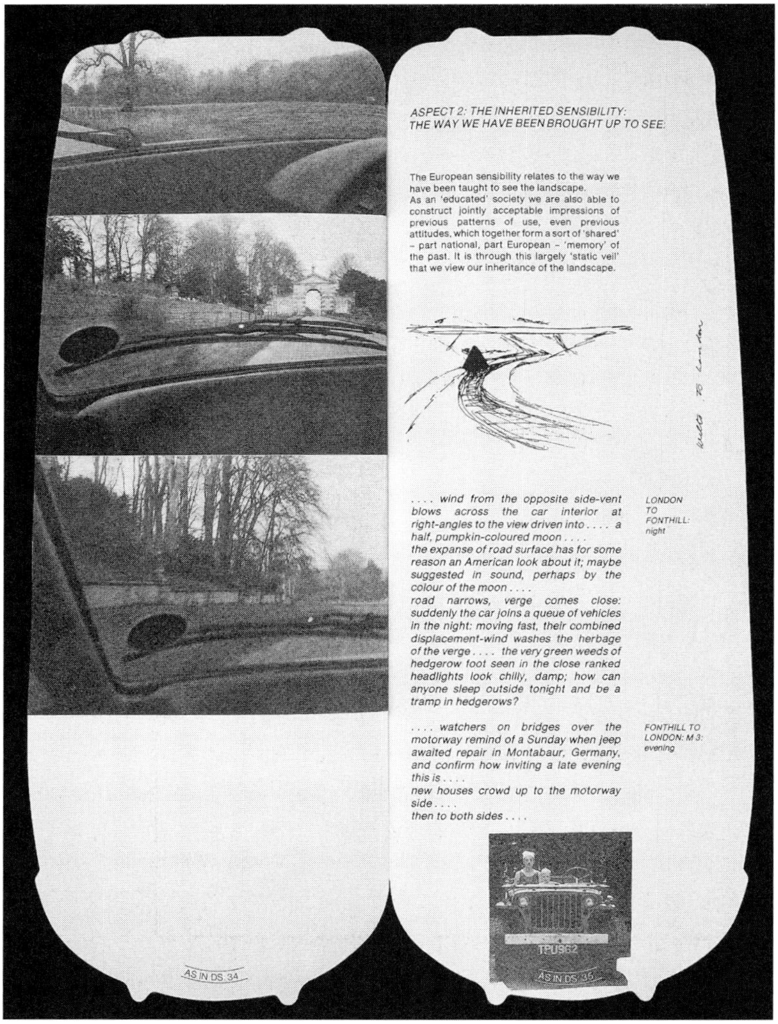

Alison Smithson, *AS in DS: An Eye on the Road*, 1983, pp. 34–35. First published in 1983 by Delft University Press, reprinted in 2001 by Lars Müller Publishers, Switzerland. Courtesy of the Smithson Family Collection.

The Smithsons worked collectively but specific responsibility for Upper Lawn Pavilion was credited to Alison Smithson.[56] As a passenger rather than a driver, *AS in DS: An Eye on the Road*, 1983, is her account of journeys around England in the early 1970s. The book is cut to the plan-shape of the car that made it possible, at 1:18 scale and a size common to toy cars and architectural guide-books.[57] In his introduction, Peter Smithson describes *AS in DS* as a 'Primer' for the 'sensibility resulting from the moving view of landscape'.[58] Comforted in 'our own-climate-cell', Alison Smithson concludes that observation at a distance and at speed can be detached but engaged:[59]

56 Alison and Peter Smithson, *The Charged Void*, p. 238.

57 Citroën paid for the book to be cut to this size and shape.

58 Peter Smithson, 'A Sensibility Primer', p. 1; Alison Smithson, *AS in DS*, p. 47.

59 Alison Smithson, *AS in DS*, p. 47.

> *The car is operative in all moods of the European climate, day or night. To be within ones own surfaces, with ones things, perhaps enjoying a picnic seated in armchair comfort, looking at a view we chose, when we chose . . . this is the freedom given by technology, satisfying the delicate balance between togetherness/apartness. Our sensibilities have been affected by our use of our 'room on wheels' but also, there comes a new awareness of the responsibilities inherent in our comfortable view of just anywhere. Our idea of quality of place, our will to bring through quality in all things, these should also be affected by our possession of a cell of perfected technology.*[60]

60 Alison Smithson, *AS in DS*, p. 111.

Rather than characterise this sensibility as completely new, she locates its origins in the eighteenth-century picturesque, which was also explored through movement:

> *With landscape, we are most encumbered by established English sensibilities; and so deeply involved we have in front of our eyes almost a pre-formed vision, the where-with-all to relive the whole spirit of the English picturesque.*[61]

61 Alison Smithson, *AS in DS*, p. 151.

AS in DS is about the picturesque and of the picturesque: it affords many views literally and in interpretation. In words, drawings, maps and photographs – many produced in the DS – diary entries describe the weather and its effects and refer to travels, peoples and events in the past and present from Beckford to Apollo 13. Each diary entry describes an 'as found' condition in a vivid and immediate manner that is typical of Brutalism and the late eighteenth-century picturesque:

> *a brush-stroke of duck-egg blue setting-off aggressive grey clouds; a foretaste of the stupendous water-sharp-colours of the view that never fails to please . . . the sun behind and to the right, shows to perfection massed bare woods and ivy clad trunks.*[62]

62 Alison Smithson, *AS in DS*, p. 39.

the colours of the country by day in this strangely late autumn have all been Gainsborough browns, as if allowing a sight of an historic country-side.[63]

p. 33.

well ahead of the car, dead sticks and torn, summer-grotty leaves fall straight down, join a straw storm that swirls twistingly towards this car, swooshing over the bonnet, up and over the windscreen.[64]

64 Alison Smithson, *AS in DS*, p. 52.

Alison Smithson does not mention the differing opinions of Gilpin, Knight and Price. Instead, she creates a broad amalgam of late eighteenth-century attitudes to the picturesque, favouring a shaggy aesthetic as well as the association of ideas. With regard to whether beauty is intrinsic to an object or an experience – a question central to the eighteenth century – she tends towards experience but her aesthetic responses suggest an affinity for both sides of the argument. Describing the picturesque as an English tradition, she recognises that perception is cultural and social as well as personal.

As a 'teaching document' Alison Smithson intends *AS in DS* to improve understanding of specific landscape conditions, such as weather, topography, natural history and use, and to encourage designs that respond with thoughtful invention. She notes the delicate adjustments of an old road to site and seasons. In contrast,

Alison and Peter Smithson, Upper Lawn Pavilion, 1959–. View of the north façade and Citroën DS, 1962. Courtesy of the Smithson Family Collection.

'a modern road might lead a passenger to suspect that the road's engineer has no long knowledge of the route, nor the tricks of micro-climate, nor sufficient interest to have travelled "his" route to discover its seasonal weather mutations'.[65] In the subtlety of the old road, she identifies a model for building as well as road-making.

In *AS in DS*, photographs appear as often as drawings and maps and are as important to the narrative. The landscape, road and car are the main characters. Thirty-two photographs show views taken from the DS, while in twelve the car is the subject, either moving or static. When a home is illustrated it is a backdrop to the car. In five photographs the DS is outside the London home and just three show it at Fonthill.[66] But each photograph of the DS at Upper Lawn Pavilion is a version of the iconic image regularly chosen for publication and indicative of the architects' intentions.[67] Photographed from the road, the DS is parked outside the garden wall, directly in front of the patio window.

Another well-known image, taken from within the garden wall, shows the view through the patio window to the woods beyond. The car is absent because the photograph was taken in 1983 after the Smithsons left Fonthill. But parked in its

Alison and Peter Smithson, Upper Lawn Pavilion, 1959–. View through the patio window to the Fonthill woods to the north, 1995, taken after the Smithsons left Fonthill. Photograph, Georg Aerni.

65 Alison Smithson, *AS in DS*, p. 91, refer to p. 11.

66 One photograph appears on p. 31 and two on p. 106.

67 Only the distinctive number plates – 9 FGK and 93 DLT – differ.

iconic location, the DS would have transformed the view from the garden to the landscape beyond, which passed through three layers of glass, first the patio window and then the side windows of the DS's bulbous body, recalling a famous instrument of the picturesque. In a Thomas Gainsborough sketch, c.1750, a seated artist holds the Claude Glass in his left hand and sketches with his right. Praising 'the *general effect*, the *forms of the objects*, and the *beauty of tints*, in one complex view' Gilpin even describes the merits of using the Claude Glass at speed:

> *In a chaise particularly the exhibitions of the convex-mirror are amusing. We are rapidly carried from one object to another. A succession of high-coloured pictures is continually gliding before the eye. They are like the visions of the imagination; or the brilliant landscapes of a dream.*[68]

Views through side and rear view mirrors appear frequently in *AS in DS*. Mobile, the DS recalls Gilpin's picturesque tours and a Claude Glass on the move. Static, the DS refers to Gainsborough's artist. Parked in front of the patio window the DS altered the view out and further enclosed the garden. Depending on light and weather conditions, the view north was either reflected back, romantically filtered by glass overlaid with dew, or composed into fore-, middle- and background, recalling Claude's paintings as well as the Claude Glass.

The Claude Glass was just one instrument carried by an eighteenth-century picturesque tourist. Others included pens, pencils, watercolours, sketchbooks, guides, a pedometer, water-flask, telescope and barometer. Together, they equate to the instrumentation available in the DS. A car driver looks forward through the windscreen and backwards through mirrors. But a Claude Glass draws the eye to the reflected landscape, not the path ahead. In 1805 a Lakeland traveller who stumbled near the summit of Helvellyn was found with a Claude Glass by his side, becoming 'the first man to die in search of the picturesque'.[69] As a passenger Alison Smithson could concentrate on the view and not worry about the road.

Alongside associations with the picturesque, *AS in DS* establishes connections to modernism. Photographs of the DS at Upper Lawn Pavilion pay homage to Le Corbusier's 1921 mass-production house: '"Citrohan" (not to say Citroën). That is to say, a house like a motor-car', and his habit of photographing a favoured car, the Voisin, in front of his houses of that period.[70] But at Fonthill the house and the car are neither exclusively similar nor just opposed. They exemplify the picturesque incorporation of difference that is also characteristic of Brutalism. The house recalls the rustic Patio and Pavilion while the DS recalls the sleek House of the Future, which the Smithsons likened to their car.[71] Especially today, with increasing fears

68 Gilpin, *Remarks on Forest Scenery*, vol. 2, p. 225.

69 Hamblyn, p. 172. Refer to 'The Story of Gough and his Dog' in Rawnsley, pp. 153–208; Maillet, p. 271, n. 5.

70 Le Corbusier, *Towards a New Architecture*, p. 222.

71 Beatriz Colomina notes that they associated the DS with House of the Future in hindsight and argues that a more likely influence was the Volkswagen Beetle, which they owned when they designed the *Ideal Home* exhibit. Colomina, 'Unbreathed Air 1956', p. 36; Alison and Peter Smithson, *Changing the Art of Inhabitation*, p. 115; Peter Smithson, 'Conglomerate Ordering', p. 186.

Thomas Gainsborough, *Sketch of an Artist with a 'Claude Glass'*, *c.*1750. Courtesy of the British Museum.

of environmental catastrophe, we may recognise Patio and Pavilion as futuristic and the House of the Future as nostalgic. But as an equivalent to Bertoni's car, which the Smithsons characterised as Brutalist, the House of the Future is not obsessed with technology but sculpted and homely.[72]

Le Corbusier's appreciation of cars has further relevance to Fonthill. In *Vers Une Architecture*, 1923, which was published in English as *Towards a New Architecture*, 1927, he places photographs of ancient Greek temples next to

72 Alison and Peter Smithson, 'Banham's Bumper Book on Brutalism', p. 1591.

photographs of cars. 'Paestum, 600–550 BC' is on the same page as 'Humber, 1907'. 'The Parthenon, 447–434 BC' is next to 'Delage, "Grand-Sport", 1921'. Le Corbusier 'ennobles the automobile' by placing it alongside a temple. The caption to 'Voisin, Sports Torpedo, 1921' even discusses other temples not other cars.[73] In *Towards a New Architecture* the car is a temple. In Le Corbusier's early twentieth-century experiments with purism in art and architecture and his neo-Platonist description of architecture as the play of primary forms in light, there is an echo of Plato's praise for the beauty of 'solids produced on a lathe or with ruler and square'.[74] As Karsten Harries remarks, 'We get here a hint why this perennial Platonism should so easily have allied itself with the machine aesthetic.'[75]

If a car can be a temple the DS easily qualifies.[76] Away from Fonthill, the DS was a temple in a twentieth-century picturesque landscape. At the end of their journey, the Smithsons turned onto a minor road before crossing the entire estate north to south to reach Upper Lawn Pavilion. Once the DS passed under the arched gateway at the estate's northern boundary, it became a temple in an eighteenth-century picturesque landscape. Parked in its iconic position outside the patio window the DS was not just a temple or a car. It was also a home. The DS is as much a part of Upper Lawn Pavilion as the house and the garden, the wall and the well. And when the car is absent, Upper Lawn Pavilion is incomplete.

73 Le Corbusier, *Towards a New Architecture*, pp. 124, 125, 130, 135.

74 Le Corbusier, *Towards a New Architecture*, p. 31; Plato, *Philebus*, p. 51.

75 Harries, p. 229.

76 Barthes, 'The New Citroën', p. 89.

JEROME-ING

Critical of suburban sprawl, the Smithsons wished to express the differences between the city and the country while recognising their interdependence. Acknowledging the tradition from classical antiquity to the picturesque and modernism that conceives nature as a place of retreat, contemplation and study, Alison Smithson described life at Upper Lawn Pavilion as 'Jerome-ing'.[77] A fourth-century monk who translated the Bible from its original languages into Latin, Saint Jerome was a favoured subject of Renaissance artists. Simply furnished and set within a cloister that frames views to the landscape beyond, the best-known depiction – Antonello da Messina, *Saint Jerome in his Study*, c.1475 – is a model for Upper Lawn Pavilion:

> *The timelessness of the ideal is in many images of the Study of Jerome. The Study depicted by the painters contains all conveniences . . . cooled water, shapely wash bowl, fresh towel, growing flowers, birds and animals as man's companions, books, writing materials, cupboards, oriental carpet, warm clothes, wine.*[78]

77 As this lecture was given many years after the design of Upper Lawn Pavilion, Alison Smithson's interpretation may, in part, be due to hindsight. Alison Smithson, 'At the time of the Presentation of Upper Lawn Book: Barcelona', unpublished lecture, December 1986, quoted in Risselada, p. 54,

78 Alison Smithson, 'Saint Jerome', p. 227.

Antonello da Messina, *Saint Jerome in his Study*, *c.* 1475. Courtesy of the National Gallery, London.

Discussing paintings and sculptures in which Saint Jerome is shown in either the desert or study, Alison Smithson remarks that these 'habitats can also be thought of as allegories for the restorative place in nature and the energising cell supported by human order'.[79] Rather than opposites, desert and study are complementary means to learning: 'In Saint Jerome's life, withdrawal to Desert and asceticism becomes an integral part of a productive, academic life. Jerome's books went with him to the desert.'[80] In a number of the desert paintings Saint Jerome seeks the protection of a cave. A regular feature of the eighteenth-century picturesque, the grotto recalls the cave and the desert beyond:

79 Alison Smithson, 'Saint Jerome', p. 225.

80 Alison Smithson, 'Saint Jerome', p. 228.

> *Under the influence of travel, paintings, literature, Saint Jerome's Desert habitat of Renaissance imagery continued life in Europe as the impression of the* Wild *place found in untamed nature –* 'the awfulness of rocks' *– reconstructed for the European landscape garden.*[81]

81 Alison Smithson, 'Saint Jerome', p. 228.

Where Beckford commissioned the hermitage, grotto and rocky outcrop, Alison Smithson discovered the habitats of Saint Jerome's life – the study, cave and desert – nurturing them in her house and garden, and even her car.[82] The DS was her study on wheels, a home from home. It was also a grotto full of gleaming surfaces because a visit to the Caves Les Baux de Provence in 1953 had inspired the House of the Future, the Smithsons' car-home.[83] In Saint Jerome's life and the eighteenth-century picturesque, the cave-grotto and desert-wilderness had positive connotations. But conscious of Hiroshima and the Cold War, the Smithsons extended the analogy: 'All the food is bombarded with gamma rays – an atomic byproduct to kill all bacteria.'[84] The House of the Future was a bunker as well as a cave, 'a kind of bomb shelter', as Beatriz Colomina concludes.[85] Where there is a cave there is often a desert. But where there is a bunker there is the fear of devastation and a nuclear desert. The DS evoked a nihilistic refuge as well as a comforting home and elegant temple.

82 Alison Smithson, 'Saint Jerome', p. 228.

83 Colomina, 'Unbreathed Air 1956', p. 43.

84 Alison and Peter Smithson, 'House of the Future', p. 99.

85 Colomina, 'Unbreathed Air 1956', p. 43.

LETTER TO AMERICA

The faith in technological solutions that ultimately led to the atom bomb also underpinned much of early modernism. Searching for Saint Jerome and an alternative modernist history, Alison Smithson describes Upper Lawn Pavilion as the 'New Brutalist grandchild' of the Barcelona Pavilion, which she discusses as a covered study, travertine desert and forest glade.[86] As further examples of environmentally sensitive '*light touch* inhabitation' in the tradition of Saint Jerome, she mentions the Farnsworth House and Charles and Ray Eames's 1949 home at Pacific Palisades, which she concludes are modernist, order views ordered according to picturesque convention and equivalent to Upper Lawn Pavilion.[87] She distinguishes the Barcelona Pavilion from the others in that none of its territory is 'as found', while I question her assumption that the landscape at the Farnsworth House is picturesque.[88]

The Smithsons revered Mies, as Peter Smithson acknowledged: 'My own debt to Mies is so great that it is difficult for me to disentangle what I hold as my own thoughts, so often they have been the result of insights received from him.'[89]

86 Alison Smithson, 'Mies' Barcelona Pavilion, Myth and Reality', pp. 35–36; Alison Smithson, 'Territory of the Pavilion', p. 33.

87 Alison Smithson, 'Saint Jerome', p. 225; Alison Smithson, 'Territory of the Pavilion', pp. 33–34.

88 Alison Smithson, 'Territory of the Pavilion', p. 34.

89 Peter Smithson, in Alison and Peter Smithson, *The Heroic Period of Modern Architecture*, p. 61.

Architecture's potential to engage and enable life particularly fascinated the Smithsons:

> *A building today is interesting only if it is more than itself; if it charges the space around it with connective possibilities – especially if it does this by a quietness, that up to now our sensibilities have not recognized as architecture at all . . . Schinkel used the neutralizing skin of columns . . . Mies got the message.*[90]

90 Alison and Peter Smithson, 'Mies van der Rohe', pp. 363–364.

But their admiration had limits. The Smithsons especially enjoyed the Eames's conjunction of a delicate enclosure and the 'fresh, pretty, colourful ephemera' of daily life, which they did not find in Mies's designs.[91] In *Without Rhetoric,* 1973, alongside two photographs of Upper Lawn Pavilion, they praise 'the *Eames Aesthetic* – the *select and arrange* technique which we have used in the designing and equipping of our own houses . . . This, of course, as a design method, is close to flower arrangement'.[92] Their analogy is a knowingly witty affront to the aloof ambitions of early modernism. After a visit to the Farnsworth House in 1958, Peter Smithson divides blame between the architect and the user and suggests a cathartic solution appropriate to the picturesque and romanticism:

91 Alison Smithson, 'And Now Dhamas are Dying Out in Japan', p. 447.

92 Alison and Peter Smithson, *Without Rhetoric*, p. 47.

> *The house then was lived in carelessly; that is, without affection between occupier and building. This had depreciated the spirit of the fabric. When a building is in complete dereliction or ruin, and only the air, the trees, the animals and the birds live there, its spirit recovers.*[93]

93 Peter Smithson, 'Going Back, Workpoints', p. 31.

Although the Farnsworth House was completed just seven years before the Smithsons began Upper Lawn Pavilion, Alison Smithson associates the two designs with different times and conditions:

> *Mies could take quietness for granted in the first half of the century. He could be sure of the individual rights of the undisturbed, inhabited place situated away from industry until almost at the end of his life, when the new state highway was built directly opposite his last pavilion, the Farnsworth house . . . Starting to work in the 1950s we never could make the innocent assumptions available to the* Heroic Period of Modern Architecture. *In the American magazines of the 1940s and 1950s we could foresee the consumer-orientated society that would, through advertisements, change all our lives. But, primarily, World War II had acted as the great divide between ourselves and our grandparent architects, who built for the few tall cars and for the genteel who shopped for rarely replaced objects.*[94]

94 Alison Smithson, 'Patio and Pavilion', pp. 10–11.

Alison and Peter Smithson, Upper Lawn Pavilion, 1959–. Kitchen with ladder to first floor, June 1962. Courtesy of the Smithson Family Collection.

The carefully composed collections of the Eames and Smithsons also recalled an earlier society in which the domestic still life was a highly favoured artistic genre. Private, intimate, particular to a family and abundantly adorned with possessions, the seventeenth-century Dutch house was a model home that influenced domestic architecture in the UK and USA.[95]

After fifteen years' regulation, rationing in the UK finally ended in 1954, leading to rising prices.[96] But the mid-1950s consumer boom was soon so buoyant that in 1957 the incoming Conservative Prime Minister Harold Macmillan famously remarked: 'people have never had it so good'.[97] In 'Letter to America', 1958, Peter Smithson patronisingly dismisses American architecture as 'aluminium folk-art . . . of metal working peasants'. In contrast, 'throw-away' images and appliances receive fascination and praise.[98] The true results of mass production, such as cars and refrigerators, 'are simply staggering'.[99] But 'Letter to America' also indicates the Smithsons' growing disenchantment with wasteful 'consumer-orientated society'.[100] They attributed post-war consumerism to one country in particular when

95 Hill, *Immaterial Architecture*, pp. 6–14.

96 Zweinger-Bargielowska, pp. 234–242.

97 Macmillan, quoted in Fisher, p. 192.

98 The article was reprinted and credited to Alison and Peter Smithson in *Ordinariness and Light,* pp. 135–143. Peter Smithson, 'Letter to America', p. 95.

99 Peter Smithson, 'Letter to America', p. 102. Refer also to Alison Smithson, 'And Now Dhamas are Dying Out in Japan', p. 443.

100 Alison Smithson, 'Patio and Pavilion', p. 11. Refer to Fraser with Kerr, pp. 365–366.

it was a global phenomenon but their concern for local and sustainable responses was genuine. Rather than celebrate the new abundance, they continued the philosophy of 'make do and mend' that prevailed during rationing. Departing from the Eames House, Upper Lawn Pavilion avoided the shiny services and surfaces found in mid-century modernism. Avid collectors, the Smithsons regularly replaced one Citroën for another but the objects displayed at Upper Lawn Pavilion were often found not bought, aged not pristine. At Fonthill, a courtyard setting maintained the tradition of domestic intimacy, which Peter Smithson later suggested was a conscious alternative to the more open American interiors of the Eames House and Farnsworth House.[101] Upper Lawn Pavilion's construction also differs from its American 'models'. At the Eames House, the standard industrial components of the steel structure are straightforward and delicate, implying potential rearrangement. At the Farnsworth House, careful detailing conceals junctions, drawing attention to the object, not its construction. Louisa Hutton, who worked for the Smithsons in the 1980s, notes their enjoyment of adjustments made on site:

101 Peter Smithson and Derek Sugden, 'The Sugden House, Farm Field, Watford', Twentieth Century Society conference on the 'Post War Private House', Courtauld Institute, London, 18 November 2000. Refer to Fraser with Kerr, p. 371.

> *Peter always had a great respect for those who actually constructed the building. He was once really distraught to discover that one particular concrete wall had been executed so badly that it had been twice demolished out of shame before he was allowed to see it. I found his acceptance of errors in building very generous, human and heartening. He saw the act of building as an accumulative process in which mistakes are integrated into the final product in an organic way.*[102]

102 Hutton, p. 52.

Upper Lawn Pavilion's design and construction are ad hoc, reflecting the anecdotal assemblage of *AS in DS* and the Smithsons' other writings, which reused and adapted words and images, whether their own or others.

CAMPING OUT

As a further precedent for Upper Lawn Pavilion Alison Smithson writes: 'The Study as "*the machine for living in*" was recognised in those writings of the Heroic Period of the Modern Movement in Architecture concerned with again raising the minimal *cell* into an art.'[103] But the hermetic living unit of the early twentieth century is not her obvious model. In Renaissance paintings she identifies a 'conspicuously perfected functionalism' and a rewarding precedent for the modernism she admires.[104] Saint Jerome's study and Upper Lawn Pavilion are minimal cells but they do not rigorously separate inside from outside. The first floor 'gazebo' rests on the garden

103 Le Corbusier, *Towards a New Architecture*, pp. 10 and 241; Alison Smithson, 'Saint Jerome', p. 227.

104 Alison Smithson, 'Saint Jerome', p. 227.

wall, chimney and two new concrete columns so that the ground floor interior is open to the courtyard when the glazed doors are folded back. Located on the ground floor, services were limited when the Smithsons lived at Fonthill. The kitchen had a sink and dishwasher but no fridge, oven or hob. Cooking occurred outside. Bedrooms were not defined; at night mattresses were unrolled and placed on the floor. A wood-burning stove provided limited warmth. The single-glazed expanse caused overheating in summer and condensation and heat loss in winter, which was particularly apparent because the winter of 1962–1963 was the coldest since 1740, when Rousham was being remodelled. But these 'failings' were important to the experience offered by Upper Lawn Pavilion, questioning familiar notions of domestic shelter and privacy. 'Camping out' at a 'primitive' 'Solar Pavilion Folly' the Smithsons tested the assumption that some loss in environmental comfort is amply compensated by, and even necessary to, a more complete experience of nature and weather.[105] Their design recalls the 'reverence for the natural world' in Japanese architecture, which the Smithsons describe as the 'root' of Brutalism.[106] Peter Smithson remarks that 'Upper Lawn was placed in an eighteenth century English landscape with the conscious intention of enjoying its pleasure . . . submitting to the seasons'.[107]

Largely ignoring its international ancestry and influence, the Smithsons discussed the picturesque as an English phenomenon and in relation to an English climate. The weather is a familiar means to express nostalgia.[108] In *AS in DS* there are many references to the virtues of a moist and misty climate. But just as the Smithsons valued the picturesque for its continuing relevance, they accepted eighteenth-century levels of thermal comfort and energy consumption as a means to engage the present through the past. The contemporary domestic environment is a significant contributor to national and global energy consumption. But energy efficiency does not necessarily lead to a reduction in energy use because comfort standards may rise as a result. Dismissing a sealed and insulated interior because it detaches the occupant from the environment, the Smithsons submitted to the seasons to know them better. Active rather than sedentary, they accepted less heating and a lower temperature. Encouraging a sustainable culture of repair and reuse that diminished consumption and waste, they recognised that the earth's resources are limited, predicting later concerns for anthropogenic climate change.

105 Peter Smithson, in conversation with Bruno Krucker, 28 September 2001, quoted in Krucker, p. 40; Alison and Peter Smithson, *The Charged Void*, p. 238; Alison and Peter Smithson, 'Folly at Fonthill, Wilts', p. 482.

106 Alison and Peter Smithson, 'The New Brutalism', p. 1.

107 Peter Smithson, in Alison and Peter Smithson, *Upper Lawn, Solar Pavilion Folly*.

108 Refer to Harley, pp. 109–113.

CLIMATE REGISTER

The Farnsworth House immerses the user in nature but we do not know if this was Mies's intention. At Upper Lawn Pavilion we can be certain that immersion was deliberate due to the architects' statements, and gentle due to the mild climate. The Smithsons enjoyed the seasons but had no wish to see their buildings unliveable. Rather, they wanted to establish a balance between weather and architecture. In the sectional drawing of Upper Lawn Pavilion, the house is small against one horizontal register – the garden wall – and two vertical registers – the deep well and the high trees – which have an environmental purpose that is aesthetic as well as practical, a combination the Smithsons explored in other projects. Describing the glass-walled Yellow House at an Intersection, 1976, the Smithsons write: 'The trees in the private garden are acacia whose light leafage filters the sun in summer and blows away golden pennies in winter.'[109] The façades of the Garden Building, St Hilda's College, Oxford, 1970, are completed by a heavy timber trellis covered with ivy so that 'their gentle skin modulation seemed to offer themselves in various sorts of ways for the contribution of the seasons, and, passively, to the arts of inhabitation'.[110]

The Smithsons described the moulded forms of churches such as Nicholas Hawksmoor's St George's, Bloomsbury, 1731, as London's 'climate register', their surfaces marked by sun, wind, rain and pollution.[111] In 1994 the Smithsons' former employee, Peter Salter, and then assistant, Lorenzo Wong, adopted the term as the title of an Architectural Association exhibition and publication on four of the Smithsons' buildings, including the London headquarters of *The Economist*, which was designed at the same time as Upper Lawn Pavilion and occupied a few years later.[112] Elsewhere, Salter describes the Smithsons as 'our greatest modern readers of context'.[113] As a register of climate and weather, a building is a means to understand, expose and develop the nuances of regional and local contexts, especially when and where they impact on conditions of use.

In the second half of the nineteenth century and first half of the twentieth century, extensive legislation was introduced to monitor and reduce London's airborne pollution. But on Thursday 4 December 1952 a slow-moving anticyclone settled over London. In the following days the smog became progressively heavier. 'By Friday night the treatment of respiratory cases was running at twice its normal level and the anticyclone had stalled completely . . . Gradually, with visibility near zero, the transport system began to grind to a halt.'[114] Sir Donald Acheson, once the Chief Medical Officer, recalled: 'I lost myself in a street in London which I knew like the back of my hand. I couldn't see anything, had no idea where I was.'[115] In a single day, the filters to the National Gallery's air conditioning system 'clogged at 26 times the normal rate and in one four-hour period they clogged at 54 times the normal rate'.[116] The worst incident of air pollution ever recorded anywhere in the world, and the cause of twelve thousand deaths, the Great Smog of 1952

109 Alison and Peter Smithson, *The Charged Void*, p. 394.

110 Alison and Peter Smithson, *Alison and Peter Smithson: The Shift*. p. 66.

111 Alison and Peter Smithson, 1986, quoted in Salter and Wong, p. 9. Refer to Salter in Salter and Wong, pp. 40–41.

112 Salter worked for the Smithsons between 1980 and 1983, initially for just one day a week during his final year at the Architectural Association School of Architecture and later as a full-time assistant. Relating climates to peoples and places, Alison Smithson's *Imprint of India*, was published as a parallel volume to *Climate Register*. Elsewhere, Salter refers to a 'weather register'; Salter, quoted in Steel, p. 30.

113 Salter, 'Peter Smithson Obituary', p. 25.

114 Brimblecombe, p. 166.

115 Acheson, quoted in Simons, p. 219.

116 Brimblecombe, p. 168, refer to pp. 170–171.

was a catalyst for the Clean Air Act of 1956, which was the first UK legislation to address pollution from domestic as well as industrial sources. The Act did not address the true pollutant – sulphur dioxide – but sulphur emissions were reduced because all domestic and most industrial consumption was transferred to electricity, gas and smokeless fuels.

The Smithsons' attitude to London's atmosphere recalled Turner in his studio. *The Economist* building was designed with precedent and pollution in mind, as Salter acknowledges:

> *Influenced by the use of Portland Stone on the façades of London's churches, the Smithsons decided to use Roach Bed Portland stone for the spandrels and column cappings of the façades of the Economist Building. This white stone is extracted from the highest bed of the sedimentary limestone series close to the surface at Portland Bill. It is very hard and therefore lends itself to machine-cutting. It also contains large fossil fragments and indentations or pockets. Used on the façade of the Economist, it absorbed and collected from the air the final soots from London's fireplaces. Anticipating the deep staining from the pollutants, the façade was detailed to channel rainwater from window sills to the column gutters, at which point the stone was scoured by the effects of rain and up-draught winds and its whiteness renewed. As a consequence the façade, which originally had little modulation of its structure, acquired great visual depth, understood through the control of the shadows of soot and the scouring of the stone. The recent washing of the stone has sadly diminished this effect.*[117]

117 Salter, in Salter and Wong, p. 40.

Soot accumulating in fossil-indented stone is an absorbing metaphor for the interdependence of the human and natural worlds. Agriculture has been industrialised as much as other areas of production but rural life has retained its allure. The Smithsons understood that 'the Virgilian dream' has always been conceived and 'enjoyed with the self-consciousness of the city dweller'.[118] Their photographs of Upper Lawn Pavilion evoke rustic and relaxed habits: 'old iron implements dug up, apples picked or dried, fragments of glass and china, table settings, displays of flowers, petals and berries, wasps' nests and cedar cones'.[119] Weathered and worn, the found objects they assembled and displayed at Upper Lawn Pavilion are a mirror image of the building as it ages. Clad in reflective aluminium and rich teak, the contrast between old and new was obvious in 1961 when it was first occupied. Further building works continued until 1962 but Upper Lawn Pavilion could not then be described as complete because it was designed with ageing in mind, unlike the Farnsworth House.[120] The Smithsons revealed artifice more often than is typical

118 Alison and Peter Smithson, *Without Rhetoric*, p. 14.

119 Padovan, p. 205.

120 The Smithsons list the dates of Upper Lawn Pavilion as 1959–1982, from the year that they began building work to the year that they left Fonthill. Alison and Peter Smithson, *The Charged Void*, p. 238.

Alison and Peter Smithson, *The Economist* Building, London, 1964. Column detail. Photograph, Murray Fraser.

in the picturesque, and enjoyed the ways in which use and weather may draw further attention to the means of construction. But over the years, weathering has reduced the visual contrast between concrete, stone, teak and aluminium, materials that – aged to soft greys – provide a background to the changing colours of nature

– yellow, brown, green, red and gold. Understanding the importance of Upper Lawn Pavilion's weathered condition, the architects of the 2003 renovation, Sergison Bates, appointed 'a specialist restoration contractor who normally works with 16th-century barns rather than 1960s modernist icons'.[121] Improving the building's thermal performance, the renovation was less sensitive to the pleasures of 'submitting to the seasons'.

121 Jonathan Sergison in Allison, pp. 97–98.

RUSTIC MACHINE

Upper Lawn Pavilion is difficult to reconcile with functionalism. But functionalism still cast a long shadow in the 1950s. To develop but temper the modernist project, functionalism was often questioned but rarely discarded. The classification of buildings by function in planning applications and building regulations also helped to keep thoughts of functionalism close at hand even though the mid-century witnessed changes in production and consumption that emphasised diversity rather than standardisation. To maintain the social and economic value of their skills, architects continued to claim expert knowledge of use as well as design while they attempted to avoid accusations of determinism. In 1947, citing modest, modernist, vernacular houses by Sven Markelius, Sture Frolen and Ralph Erskine, Pevsner and the other editors of *The Architectural Review* praised 'The New Empiricism: Sweden's Latest Style' as an attempt to 'humanise' functionalism.[122] No doubt enjoying the irony, Pevsner described the Smithsons' buildings as 'entirely unbrutal'.[123] But the eighteenth-century picturesque did have a certain brutality given its concern for decay and the Smithsons were equally accepting of ageing; for them Brutalism meant honest and direct, not insensitive. In 1957 they described themselves as functionalists but not in the early modernist sense: 'today the word functional does not merely mean mechanical, as it did thirty years ago. Our functionalism means accepting the realities of the situation, with all their contradictions and confusions, and trying to do something with them'.[124] Rather than imposing a universal model on behaviour the Smithsons promoted empirical observation of the physical fabric and patterns of inhabitation already on site. Consequently, Peter Smithson appreciated the 'Picturesque not as picture, but people in the centre, sensitiveness and feeling; the Picturesque as a root of our thoughts.'[125] Elsewhere, he likened their practice to 'an organisational Picturesqueness . . . it expresses in direct architectural terms the way of life that these people have chosen'.[126] But rather than ordering a building according to a way of life that is bound to vary, Upper Lawn Pavilion suggests a loose fit between architecture and daily life that

122 Richards, Pevsner, Lancaster and Hastings, p. 199.

123 Pevsner refers to Hunstanton School and *The Economist* Building. Pevsner, 'The Anti-Pioneers', p. 298.

124 Alison and Peter Smithson, 'Cluster City', p. 332.

125 Peter Smithson in conversation with Bruno Krucker, 3 June 1995, quoted in Krucker, p. 17.

126 Peter Smithson, in discussion with Wendell H. Lovett, in Newman, p. 52.

accepts the inevitability of change. Equally, it is picturesque in its aesthetic as well as its organisation.

Detaching the functional from the mechanical seems to contradict Alison Smithson's praise for the 'machine for living in', even if her inspiration was the fifteenth century as much as the twenitieth. But as the Smithsons identify another functionalism, maybe Upper Lawn Pavilion is another machine. Alison Smithson proposes that 'a society becoming more climate, nature, energy-resource responsive . . . will allow us to begin to think of a new form of restorative habitat for a future *light touch* inhabitation of the earth'.[127] In a similar spirit, and affirming the 'Virgilian dream', Peter Smithson wishes 'to build like a farmer', drawing on local knowledge of a place 'not only the visual, but what a place smells like, how the wind hits it'.[128] Simple and adaptable, submitting to the seasons, Upper Lawn Pavilion is a rustic machine.

127 Alison Smithson, 'Saint Jerome', p. 225.

128 Peter Smithson, *Conversations*, pp. 48–49.

Alison and Peter Smithson, Upper Lawn Pavilion, 1959–. North façade, taken recently. Photograph, Jonathan Hill.

A MODEL HOME

Occupying the site while building occurred and making adjustments over twenty years, the Smithsons made a life as well as a house. In choosing a site and a name, retaining fragments, creating a 'half-building/half-ruin', allowing ivy to grow inside and out, and enjoying weather and weathering, their approach was characteristic of the picturesque, in which design, construction and use are potentially interdependent and open-ended, as at Rousham and 12–14 Lincoln's Inn Fields.[129] Rather than Banham's *tabula rasa* – a fascination for technology and disposability that serves a market-led economy – Upper Lawn Pavilion recognises no rupture between the past, present and future. Brutalist, modernist and picturesque, attuned to the environment and its limited resources, employing ad-hoc construction and arranged with objects of emotional rather than financial value, Upper Lawn Pavilion is increasingly relevant.

129 Alison and Peter Smithson, 'Tisbury', p. 212.

8

fog, glare and gloom

INTRODUCTION

A parallel to the Smithsons' picturesque modernism, Sigurd Lewerentz and Sverre Fehn shared their concern for history, nature, context and poetic and ethical construction, which opposed the wastefulness of consumer society. But the harsher climate they evoked led to a romantic modernism, which drew on architectural and artistic traditions and new developments alike.

NATIONAL ROMANTICISM

The north is an idea as much as a place.[1] Northern character, geography and weather are imagined as much as they are found. A formative influence on German and Nordic romanticism, Johann Gottfried Herder combined nationalism and romanticism in opposition to French influence. In *Ideen zu einer Philosophie der Geschichte der Menschheit* (Outlines of a Philosophy of the History of Man), 1784–1791, he argued that nations have different identities due to the influence of climate on character. Conceiving a dynamic interaction between a people and an environment, Herder influenced the national identity of Nordic countries. Affirming the romantic concern for primitive origins, he considered the farmer, rooted in nature and folklore, to be a model for the peoples of northern Europe.[2] Continuing this tradition into the early nineteenth century but opposed to German influence as well as French, the Danish theologian Nikolai Frederik Severin Grundtvig proposed the Folk High School movement for rural education, a system that was later adopted throughout the Nordic countries.[3] In the same era, the painter and writer Johan Christian Clausen Dahl painted isolated farmsteads and promoted the farmer as the model Norwegian. Dahl credited Claude, who 'taught me disposition and harmony in the foreground and a gradually disappearing foreground'.[4] But Dahl's subject was a much wilder landscape, initiating a Norwegian painting tradition. In *Winter at Sognefjord*, 1827, a stone sentinel – an ancient Norse monument – stands close to a precipice, silhouetted against the rugged mountains beyond. The landscape between them is absent, absorbed by the canyon. Dahl was a devout Lutheran but he was less concerned to express religious meaning than Friedrich, his friend. In Friedrich's *Arctic Shipwreck*, c.1823–1824, no life is seen among the wreckage of a ship crushed and splintered by an iceberg. Due to the name inscribed on the ship, the painting was once known as *Wreck of the Hope*, adding to the sense of foreboding. Dahl purchased the painting after Friedrich's death but in contrast he depicted nature in dramatic

1 Davidson, p. 9.

2 Herder was a pupil of Kant and contemporary of Goethe. Herder, pp. 172–177, 561.

3 Norse mythology preoccupied Grundtvig but he questioned romanticism when it undermined Christian traditions. Kent, *The Soul of the North*, pp. 59–60, 187.

4 Dahl, quoted in Kent, *The Triumph of Light and Nature*, p. 61. Refer to Lane, pp. 22–28.

dialogue with humanity. *Shipwreck on the Coast of Norway*, 1832, is comparable to Turner's *Snow Storm – Steam-Boat off a Harbour's Mouth* except that the painter is on the shore not in the storm. Furthering the romantic appreciation of the past and the mnemonic potential of ruins, Dahl was influential in the foundation of the Society for the Preservation of Norwegian Ancient Monuments in 1844. A similar society was founded in Denmark as early as 1807. The romantic landscape tradition continued into the second half of the nineteenth century. The Norwegian artists August Cappelen and Peder Balke, who studied under Dahl, depicted the awesome power of seas and rivers. In Sweden, Markus Larsson painted remote and brooding forests while the poet and author Verner von Heidenstam was particularly influential in promoting a popular affinity for the Nordic landscape and architecture. Extending these traditions, national romanticism flourished across the arts in Germany and Scandinavia in the late nineteenth and early twentieth centuries, which in each country was accompanied by nostalgia for an earlier era when it was most powerful.[5] Not simply regressive, national romanticism was questioning and inventive, proposing poignant and resonant images, forms and texts.

5 Other countries influenced by national romanticism include Hungary and Scotland. Wrede, pp. 23–24.

Johan Christian Clausen Dahl, *Winter at Sognefjord*, 1827. Courtesy of the National Museum of Art, Architecture and Design, Oslo.

(right) Caspar David Friedrich, *Arctic Shipwreck*, c.1823–1824. Courtesy of BPK, Bildagentur für Kunst, Kultur und Geshichte, Berlin.

(below) Johan Christian Clausen Dahl, *Shipwreck on the Coast of Norway*, 1832. Courtesy of the National Museum of Art, Architecture and Design, Oslo.

FLAMES OVER WORMS

National romanticism dominated the early architectural education and practice of Sigurd Lewerentz, Mies's contemporary. In Munich he worked in the offices of Theodor Fischer and Richard Riemerschmid, where he contributed to the designs of Hellerau, the garden city near Dresden begun in 1909. In 1910 he enrolled to study architecture at the Academy of Fine Arts in Stockholm but transferred to the Klara Skola – Free School – formed by students disaffected by the Academy's conservatism. His tutors were Ragnar Östberg and Carl Westman, two of the best-known exponents of Swedish national romanticism, which was indebted to local medieval and vernacular architecture as well as the English arts and crafts movement. In Westman's office Lewerentz assisted on the home of the writer Claes Fähraeus, the Villa Högberga on Lidingö, a prosperous residential island in the archipelago surrounding Stockholm. Lewerentz soon established his own practice, initially with Torsten Stubelius. Influenced by the Villa Högberga, and on a nearby site in 1912, he completed the Villa Ericsson in a manner and materials typical of national romanticism. The walls are rough stone at the lowest level and orange-red brickwork above. A smooth stone dresses the entrance level doorways and projecting bays. Flush with the wall, windows diminish in size floor by floor, exaggerating the volume's mass and height. Sited on the brow of a ridge, the villa affords long views of the coastline. Seen from the water, the steeply gabled roof rises above the surrounding woods, creating an archetypal profile.

Lewerentz was to become best known for public not private projects. Support for cremation increased in the second half of the nineteenth century due to public health concerns that cemeteries were overcrowded and expanding. Reviving an ancient funeral custom in Scandinavia, the Cremation Society of Sweden was founded in 1880 to the rallying cry of 'flames over worms' even though bacteria in the human body are the principal cause of decomposition after death.[6] In 1915 Lewerentz and Stubelius were commissioned to design the new cemetery at Valdemarsvik. In a heavily wooded valley close to Bronze Age burial mounds, the entrance chapel is reminiscent of a fairy tale illustration. Built of stone excavated on site and roughly hewn, the chapel's circular wall – now overgrown – is one metre deep at the base and swells further still around the arched doorway and single window. A deeply recessed wall plate surmounts the wall, from which an eleven-metre high spire rises. Covered in over fifteen thousand tarred pine shingles, the spire curves inwards and upwards, rising steeply and culminating in an eight-pointed gold star. Internally, under a shallow wooden dome painted grey, the floor is grey limestone and the wall is plastered, whitewashed and decorated with

6 Ahlin, *Sigurd Lewerentz, Architect*, p. 35.

candleholders. Outside, a stepped walkway winds downward around the chapel to meet the main cemetery path, signifying an archaic journey into the earth that is appropriate to cremation as well as burial. Also in 1915, Lewerentz and Erik Gunnar Asplund won the competition for the extension to the Stockholm South Cemetery at Enskede. To foster contemplation of life and death, the architects exploited the Nordic affinity for nature. Paths at the 'Woodland Cemetery' weave through the pine forest. Graves appear small against massive trees and sculpted hills allude to primitive burial mounds. The darkly intense pencil drawings of the competition entry refer to the romantic appreciation of the forest, leading Stuart Wrede to suggest a possible influence:

Gunnar Asplund and Sigurd Lewerentz, Woodland Cemetery, Stockholm, 1915–. Gravestones among the trees. Photograph, Jonathan Hill.

Friedrich, seeking to revitalise the experience of divinity in a secular world, had been a wellspring of the Northern Romantic sensibility in painting, bringing into conscious usage for the first time certain archetypal Nordic landscape images, the deep evergreen forest, the endless sea, the dolmen on the heath surrounded by oaks, and the wayfarer's cross as an element in the landscape.[7]

7 Wrede, p. 32. Refer to Constant, *The Woodland Cemetery*, p. 1.

As Asplund and Lewerentz did not mention Friedrich, Wrede concludes that his influence was most likely indirect, through the work of nineteenth-century Swedish and Norwegian landscape painters who continued his themes. In 1939 Lewerentz suggested a further precedent for the Woodland Cemetery:

The cemetery may, in fact, be regarded as a garden, but of a very special kind, because, as well as possessing the typical characteristics of this kind of open-air space – trees, shrubs, paths and lawns – it is, above all, a monument suitable for a burial ground . . . From the eighteenth-century onwards, those who concerned themselves with the 'art of the garden' have stressed the limits imposed by the use of vertical monuments . . . For the design of cemeteries with horizontal tombstones, I suggest a burial ground dotted with plaques or tombstones amidst the plants and flowers that are capable of instilling visitors with a sense of tranquillity.[8]

8 Lewerentz, 'Modern Cemeteries: Notes on the Landscape', pp. 44–45.

Picturesque gardens appeared in Sweden and Norway in the late eighteenth century, notably those designed by Fredrik Magnus Piper, who twice undertook

Gunnar Asplund and Sigurd Lewerentz, Woodland Cemetery, Stockholm, 1915–. Sculpted mound. Photograph, Jonathan Hill.

prolonged garden tours of England and created gardens for the Swedish king, Gustavus III, at Haga and Drottningholm in the early 1780s. Piper was sensitive to the local topography and gave woodland particular prominence in his gardens. Echoes of an Italian climate and garden were even less likely than in England. In his manuscript, 'Description of the Idea and General Plan for an English Pleasure Park', Piper mentions 'a discriminating love of Nature's romantic and often, in their wildness, enchanting scenes'.[9] Equally, the picturesque influence on the Woodland Cemetery was absorbed into a wider fascination for the Nordic landscape.

9 Piper, quoted in Hunt, *The Picturesque Garden in Europe*, p. 143. Refer to Phibbs, pp. 60–61.

SCANDINAVIAN SYNTHESIS

In the 1920s Lewerentz was influenced by Schinkel, avidly studying his drawings.[10] Along with many other Swedish architects Lewerentz produced austere neo-classical designs such as the Chapel of the Resurrection at the Woodland Cemetery, 1925, before working in a modernist idiom at the 1930 Stockholm Exhibition, to which he contributed a number of small buildings. All traces of national romanticism were seemingly discarded. But Barbara Miller Lane and Christian Norberg-Schulz argue that modernism owes a significant debt to national romanticism, especially in Scandinavia:

10 Ahlin, 'Sigurd Lewerentz', p. 380.

> *Quite soon, Scandinavian modernists reasserted aspects of nationalism in their modern work, such as attention to site, materials, and national traditions. They were prompted partly by the continuing good reputation of National Romanticism in the Scandinavian countries, partly by their dislike of Nazi architectural policies in Germany, and partly by well-founded fears of German aggression. The result was a 'Scandinavian synthesis' in architecture and design, a synthesis that has persisted in various ways up until the present day.*[11]

11 National romanticism in Germany was damned by its association with the Nazi regime. Lane, *National Romanticism and Modern Architecture*, p. 8.

> *Therefore . . . certain Nordic values managed to survive the tabula rasa of the thirties, namely, the sense of dwelling and the desire for contact with nature. Both were brought forth under the light of national romanticism, and for that reason, it is not unjustified to call Nordic architecture romantic modernism . . . It was this romantic undercurrent that laid the basis for postwar regionalism, and that represents the North's greatest contribution to contemporary architecture.*[12]

12 Norberg-Schulz, *Nightlands*, p. 154.

Neither international nor revolutionary, Scandinavian modernism absorbed vernacular traditions and new developments alike. Lewerentz was one of the first

Sigurd Lewerentz, Chapel of the Resurrection, Woodland Cemetery, Stockholm, 1925. Photograph, Murray Fraser.

Swedish architects with a connection to the Deutsche Werkbund. Peter Behrens, Herman Muthesius, and Fischer and Riemerschmid – Lewerentz's employers in Munich – were among its founders in 1907. The Werkbund's aim was to improve the standard of everyday design, especially industrial products. In 1929 Lewerentz founded two companies in which he was principal designer. Stockholm Ljusreklam specialised in illuminated signage and IDESTA created steel windows and doors. Lewerentz's first designs were manufactured by others. But between 1943 and 1956 he assumed this responsibility, establishing a factory to manufacture IDESTA products at Eskilstuna. Living in an attic apartment above the factory and working alongside his thirty employees, Lewerentz diminished the gap between thought and action. Design decisions were often made in situ, in response to materials and techniques, defining a personal ethic and practice, which Janne Ahlin describes:

> *His clothes were elegant, but worn. The obligatory white socks were mended many times over and his work smock was baggy. Clothes were to be used as long as they*

> *lasted. That is how it was in the workshop as well. In the evenings he rummaged around in the waste basket, stuffing his pockets full of metal scraps and other waste which he considered to be of use . . . For him, to be thrifty was a deeply ethical question. That it might be less expensive, for technical reasons of production, to discard the scraps, did not influence him.*[13]

13 Ahlin, *Sigurd Lewerentz, Architect*, pp. 139–140.

A concern for expressed construction is evident in national romanticism as well as modernism, indicating their shared debt to the arts and crafts movement. The Villa Edstrand, 1937, was Lewerentz's first modernist building to celebrate the unadorned materials and techniques evident at Valdemarsvik. Owners of a firm that acted as agents for IDESTA products, the Edstrand family asked Lewerentz to design a small holiday house at Falsterbro, a coastal town in southern Sweden. Reminiscent of Le Corbusier's 1920s villas, Lewerentz's first design in 1933 was finished in smooth stucco. But his final design in 1935 discarded adornment for asceticism:

> *The stuccoed skin disappeared, leaving the yellow brick exposed. Lewerentz allowed steel lintels and joists to remain visible above openings and under terraces. Welded joints were not to be ground down but were to be left visible. Where it was suitable he allowed the electrical wiring to run exposed on the walls.*[14]

14 Ahlin, *Sigurd Lewerentz, Architect*, p. 122.

ANCIENT AND MODERN

Increasingly, found conditions and the materials and means of construction informed Lewerentz's designs, which developed incrementally, whether through addition or subtraction. His later buildings are as archaic as the national romantic cemetery chapel at Valdemarsvik and also recall his experiments in Nordic classicism. Equally, they exude the luscious austerity sometimes associated with modernism, for example in Adolf Loos's 1896 assertion that each material has its own formal language and the 'as found' character of Brutalism.[15] The Smithsons appreciated Lewerentz, including him in the first generation of 'silent architects of the Modern Movement' who were 'non-polemical – non-political and nothing-to-do with packaging'.[16] Lewerentz's concern for the ethics of site-specific construction, in which materials are reused and waste is limited, paralleled the Smithsons' intentions at Fonthill, as did his interest in the effects of weather on architecture. Faced with an ever-faster world, they wished to make time seem slower and more apparent. Faced with an ever-changing world, they wished to recognise the ancient

15 Loos, 'The Principle of Cladding', p. 66; Banham, 'The New Brutalism', p. 361.

16 The other architects of the first generation are Dimitri Pikonis and Konstantin Melnikov. The second generation is Charles and Ray Eames, José Antonio Coderch and Max Bill. The third generation includes Ralph Erskine. Alison and Peter Smithson, 'The Silent Architects', p. 5.

as well as the modern, the natural as well as the man-made. Associating Lewerentz with the Scandinavian sensitivity to nature, Alison Smithson writes:

> *Our interest in Lewerentz is his inventing a language we might call trees that became buildings . . . a grove of column trunks truncated, some still growing, some made building . . . We find variations of light as we move through this part built, part still growing forest.*[17]

17 Alison Smithson, 'The Landscape that Can Survive', p. 374.

In 1930 Lewerentz designed a speedboat, *Ewa*, in which for nearly thirty years, until it was destroyed in an autumn storm, he explored the extensive Stockholm archipelago, which includes the island of Utö where he maintained a summer home. On journeys, he studied 'nature's details: the water, the plants, the stones, the play between land and water, the worn tones of umber and ochre of the rocks and the wild-swept vegetation'.[18]

18 Ahlin, *Sigurd Lewerentz, Architect*, p. 99.

In 1956 Lewerentz entered the competition for the church and parish offices of St Mark's at Skarpnäck, Björkhagen, on the edge of Stockholm, as Ahlin recalls:

> *Among the five entries was one proposal, lightly drawn on sketch paper, clipped in a makeshift manner to cardboard. It was difficult to interpret, even for those professionals on the diligent jury, and contained several alternatives, most particularly with regard to the interior design, and seemed to be fraught with contradictions.*[19]

19 Ahlin, *Sigurd Lewerentz, Architect*, p. 152.

Awarding the commission to Lewerentz, the jury recognised an enquiring and evolving design practice in which drawings were suggestive not definitive. Lewerentz's attitude to construction was equally questioning. In response to a metalworker's request for a site instruction he remarked: 'All I know is that you are not going to do it the way you normally do.'[20] Visiting the construction site every working day, he gradually articulated a language for St Mark's – frameless windows and rough brickwork with coarse mortar joints internally and externally – that he refined in his next church design. Arguing that such asceticism makes the invisible visible, Sverre Fehn remarks that the dark bricks and pale mortar form a dialogue with the dappled trunks of the surrounding birch trees, causing visitors to exclaim: 'What an amazingly lovely birch wood. I never noticed it until the church was built.'[21] In a section of *The New Brutalism* titled 'Hard Cases: the Brick Brutalists', Banham refers to St Mark's, which was completed in 1964:

20 Lewerentz, quoted in Ahlin, *Sigurd Lewerentz, Architect*, p. 9.

21 Fehn quoted in Jormakka, p. 34.

> *When one observes how this 'other' architecture is the work of a man firmly grounded in the Scandinavian traditions of neo-Classical order and picturesque*

Sigurd Lewerentz, St Mark's Church and Parish Offices, Skarpnäck, 1964. Photograph, Murray Fraser.

sensibility, one cannot help wondering if Hans Asplund, in coining the term 'Neo-Brutalist' was not identifying a trend that might have emerged anyhow, without any assistance at all from Le Corbusier, Louis Kahn or the British.[22]

In 1963 Lewerentz won the commission for the church and parish offices of St Peter's, Klippan, a small town near Helsingborg in southern Sweden. His competition motto was a composite of two words – *mellan* meaning 'between' and *spel* meaning 'play' – confirming Fehn's opinion that Lewerentz's 'intuitive and dual-natured' architecture is distinctly Nordic.[23] Fehn identifies the northern sky as the key to the character of a people, culture and architecture:

Here in the north you are moving in the fog, you are moving in a way where the shadows do not define anything . . . It is another light in which you walk. And that also makes architecture more mysterious, more romantic, more undefined.[24]

You become totally alone with yourself.[25]

22 Asplund first used the term 'Neo-Brutalist' in 1950 but Banham elsewhere distinguishes it from 'The New Brutalism' in that one is an aesthetic, the other is an ethic. Banham, *The New Brutalism*, pp. 10, 125.

23 Wilson, 'Sigurd Lewerentz', p. 16; Fehn, in Lavalou, p. 85.

The light of the north is horizontal and shadows are long. Its mobile scale makes architecture periodically invisible, the envelope is often a sort of mist. It is a flickering, sensitive light that offers an infinite number of variations. It leads to romanticism. The dramaturgy of Nordic countries is never either exact or direct. Situations are not cut and dried . . . Lewerentz's work could not have been designed anywhere else.[26]

24 Fehn, in Norri, p. 250.

25 Fehn, in Petri, p. 251.

26 Fehn, in Lavalou, p. 85.

Fehn's appreciation of the northern sky mirrored Baudelaire and Pevsner in associating a misty climate with a fecund imagination.[27] The sky equally affected Lewerentz but his inspiration was not the fog but the gloom. One has no shadow; the other is all shadow. In *Nightlands*, Norberg-Schulz associates the Nordic countries with dark mid-winter days when the sun barely rises. In mid-summer the low sun barely sets, creating a continual glare even at midnight. Fog, gloom, glare; each light condition is distinct. But their effects are similar. Objects are only gradually revealed as the eye slowly adjusts. None offers clarity. Rather, ambiguity results.

27 Baudelaire, p. 53; Pevsner, *The Englishness of English Art*, pp. 18–19, 163–164, 185–187.

The retina has two types of light-receptor cells. The cones are mostly at the centre and function in the light. The rods are mostly at the periphery and function in the dark.[28] The cones and rods 'adapt at different rates: cone adaptation is completed in about seven minutes, while rod adaptation continues for an hour or more'.[29] In the fog, time stands largely still. But Richard Gregory equates the slow adjustment to the gloom to a journey back in time:

28 Gregory, p. 55.

29 Gregory, p. 85.

It might be said that whenever we look from the central fovea towards the periphery we travel back in evolutionary time – from the most highly organized structure in nature to a primitive eye barely capable of detecting movements of shadows. The very edge of the human retina does not even give a sensation when stimulated by movement. It provides unconscious reflexes, directing the highly developed foveal region to where it is likely to be needed, to use its high acuity and massive brain power for establishing what might be there.[30]

30 Gregory, pp. 55–56.

At St Peter's the gloom predominates. But amidst the dark, the glare of unframed openings stands out even brighter, recalling a divine luminosity. Passing from gloom to glare to gloom, the eye repeatedly adapts as the visitor moves around the church, further delaying the process of acclimatisation.

Lewerentz designed the buildings for which he is best known late in his life, completing St Peter's when he was 81, which Colin St John Wilson describes as 'an old man's building' even though the elderly are rarely so open to

Sigurd Lewerentz, St Peter's Church and Parish Offices, Klippan, 1966. Interior. Photograph, Chris Davy.

experimentation.[31] Wilson's characterisation relies on Lewerentz's lifetime of experience and willingness to accept what was at hand. It also depends on St Peter's solemn atmosphere and concern for the archaic, evident in Lewerentz's fascination for ancient Persian architecture and Hadrian's Villa at Tivoli, which he visited early in his career and photographed extensively.[32] St Peter's is as archaic as its gloom. Rather than made *as new* the church was made *as old*:

> *The old brick factory at Helsingborg was a model. It was there . . . that he found the remains of an old brick wall which fascinated him. It was dilapidated, attacked by frost and partially overgrown with moss. The wall was partially sintered together in a strange symbiosis . . . He searched among the bricks and picked out a few dozen. They contained the imperfections of rejected bricks and it was this quality which pleased him.*[33]

Norberg-Schulz states that St Peter's expresses a typically Nordic concern for 'the unitary use of materials'.[34] The undulating floor, internal and external walls, altar, pulpit and vaulted roof are all made of the same purple-brown Helsingborg brickwork. Reflecting the ethical construction that Lewerentz developed in the IDESTA factory, bricks are uncut and none are specials. Joints are deep and textured; the mortar is a dry mix with ground slate, wiped with an old sack to further

31 Wilson, 'Sigurd Lewerentz', p. 23.

32 Ahlin, *Sigurd Lewerentz, Architect*, p. 172; Flora, Giardiello and Postiglione, 'Journey to Italy', pp. 35–43.

33 Ahlin suggests that the Helsinborg brick factory, which supplied the bricks for St Mark's and St Peter's, was a model for the materiality and lighting of both churches. Ahlin, *Sigurd Lewerentz, Architect*, p. 172.

34 Norberg-Schulz, *Nightlands*, p. 186.

roughen the surface and scatter mortar debris across the bricks. To create an upstand, the mortar is simply packed high. Openings are rectangular; the reveals, sills and lintels are brick. A sealed glazing unit – a comparatively new technology in the 1960s – covers each opening, held in place top and bottom by brackets screwed directly into the exterior brickwork. As the glazing unit is larger than the opening, a thick line of mastic – another rather new technology at the time of construction – seals brick to glass. The window's construction can be understood as modern as well as primitive, as can the harsh light emanating from each window. Other components and materials are treated in an equally direct manner. Welds are not ground down or polished, services are surface mounted, the central column is Cor-ten 'weathering' steel coated in rust, timber doors are left rough on the outside and sanded smooth on the inside. A similar distinction is made on the main west front where water disposal is unseen; on the lesser elevations water is visibly dispersed through copper gutters and downpipes. The heating system is concealed. From the basement boiler, hot air circulates in the wall cavities, entering the interior through open joints in the brickwork walls and window sills. Ventilation occurs in a similar manner.

In 1969, six years before his death, Lewerentz completed his last building – the Flower Kiosk at the Malmö Eastern Cemetery – where he had worked since his competition success in 1916, adding the chapels of St Knut and St Gertrud in 1943. The Flower Kiosk's walls are concrete. Affecting the concrete as it set, the

Sigurd Lewerentz, St Peter's Church and Parish Offices, Klippan, 1966. Mortar detail. Photograph, Jonathan Hill.

Sigurd Lewerentz, St Peter's Church and Parish Offices, Klippan, 1966. Window detail. Photograph, Jonathan Hill.

weather informed the construction process and its product. Cast against untreated plywood with chamfered edges, a grid of delicate ridges runs across each façade.[35] A copper monopitch roof slopes steeply from north to south, creating a deep overhang towards the road, which protects the long picture window on the south elevation. With no gutter or downpipe, water pours unhindered from the monopitch. In heavy rain a visitor can stand between a curtain of glass and a curtain of water, each altering the view and creating a sense of enclosure. To the sides the edges of the roof are flush with the walls; rainwater stains the concrete, emphasising the ridges. High on the north elevation to the rear, two further windows each consist of a sheet of glass set into a notch in the concrete. The outer face of the glass is flush with the outer surface of the concrete. At each edge, the glass is held in place by two rusted steel clips; the joint between glass and concrete is finished with black sealant. The timber doors are left rough and painted black. Internally, electrical wiring is nailed to untreated concrete walls and the floor is tiled. The ceiling is clad in aluminium, casting a heavenly light onto the flowers, newly cut and dying. Celebrating the weather and the seasons, the story of its construction and decay, the Flower Kiosk cherishes life and acknowledges that death is at hand.[36] Given Lewerentz's earlier reference to the eighteenth-century garden, the Flower Kiosk's internally reflective surfaces, high light and watery cascades suggest a grotto, which derives from the Latin *crypta*, evoking the spirits that reside there.[37]

35 A detail suggested by Bernt Nyberg, Lewerentz's friend and companion late in his life. Ahlin, *Sigurd Lewerentz, Architect*, p. 175.

36 A cumbersome side extension and shelving casually arranged inside and out undermine the purity of Lewerentz's design, which copes badly with these disruptions.

37 Lewerentz, 'Modern Cemeteries: Notes on the Landscape', pp. 44–45. Refer to Worn, pp. 35–36.

(top) Sigurd Lewerentz, Flower Kiosk, Malmö Eastern Cemetery, 1969. Front façade in early morning. Photograph, Alan Worn.

(left) Sigurd Lewerentz, Flower Kiosk, Malmö Eastern Cemetery, 1969. Rear door detail. Photograph, Alan Worn.

Sigurd Lewerentz, Flower Kiosk, Malmö Eastern Cemetery, 1969. Weathered concrete ridge detail. Photograph, Jonathan Hill.

After his wife's death, Lewerentz moved to Lund in 1970. Klas Anselm designed a one-room studio, which he hoped would appeal to his tenant. Its blackened walls were wood-composite sheeting coated externally in asphalt and internally in aluminium foil. The floor was pine. There were no windows but three acrylic rooflights were set into the aluminium-clad roof. Two rusty radiators provided heating. A single door opened onto the garden.[38] The studio recalled the language and purpose of the Flower Kiosk. But rather than flowers, dying and displayed, it contained living nature alongside Lewerentz's slow demise:

> *One day a tender plant forced its way up between the floorboards in the middle of the black box. It awakened Lewerentz' wonder and captured his interest. He helped it along, letting it climb up the cord to his drafting lamp and further, and one day saw it reach the ceiling. Thus a bindweed had bored through the black box. Lewerentz was proud that it wanted to live there and he tended it with tenderness*

38 Ahlin, *Sigurd Lewerentz, Architect*, p. 178.

and care. A hope for continuation of life had been grafted onto the room, now when he felt his own life slowly running out . . . The epiphany of the bindweed evoked the certainty that he was something very small within something very large.[39]

39 Ahlin, *Sigurd Lewerentz, Architect*, p. 183.

DREAMS OF NATURE

A generation younger than Lewerentz, Fehn was born in the 1920s like the Smithsons. But Fehn and Lewerentz designed their best-known buildings in the 1960s and Banham included them alongside each other in *The New Brutalism*.[40] Norwegians and Swedes share a common history and understand each other's language. But Stockholm recalls an imperial power to which Oslo cannot compare. The Swedish landscape is varied, including lakes, mountains and lowlands. But Norway is largely mountainous and less than one-twentieth of its landscape is cultivated. Norway's population is small in comparison to its size, generating the lowest population density in Europe. Industrialisation and prosperity arrived late.

40 Banham mentions Fehn's 1959 museum extension at Lillehammer, Norway, designed with Geir Grung.

Due to the harsh winters, traditional Norwegian buildings are solid, protective and introverted. The massive timber construction of a rural farm is a response to its isolation and vulnerability. But the all-encompassing landscape and climate also demand a dialogue with nature. 'Nature is never far away, and plays a large part in people's dreams and concepts', acknowledges Norberg-Schulz.[41] 'The Norwegian *vær* (weather) is furthermore related to *å vær* (to be)', helping to explain why Bjerknes and the Bergen School were instrumental in the development of twentieth-century meteorology.[42]

41 Norberg-Schulz, *Modern Norwegian Architecture*, p. 80.

42 Norberg-Schulz, *Nightlands*, p. 6.

Norway's long subjection to its neighbours intensified the degree to which Norwegians identify their independence and character with a landscape and climate. In 1814, after 400 years of Danish rule, Norway prepared to declare independence but instead entered into an uncomfortable union with Sweden. At the very end of the nineteenth century a political and cultural movement unsuccessfully tried to replace the official state language with an amalgamation of local peasant dialects. Around the same time, and especially after independence from Sweden in 1905, national romantic architecture incorporated '*motifs* derived from Norwegian nature'.[43] When Norwegian modernism flourished in the 1920s it emphasised local conditions more often than a didactic functionalism, a situation repeated after the end of the German occupation in the Second World War.

43 Norberg-Schulz, *Modern Norwegian Architecture*, p. 80.

POETIC STORIES

I have never thought of myself as modernistic . . . or, one might say, that modernism's conception has been extended.[44]

44 Fehn, in Petri, p. 250.

I have all my life tried to run away from the Nordic tradition. But I realize that it is difficult to run away from yourself.[45]

45 Fehn, in Yoshida, 'Interview', p. 17.

Ambivalence characterises Fehn's reaction to both modernism and the Nordic tradition. When he was a student at the Oslo School of Architecture in the 1940s two of the best-known Norwegian modernists – Knut Knutsen and Arne Korsmo – were influential tutors. Knutsen responded more to the local vernacular while Korsmo was most aware of developments internationally. But both pursued a poetic, regional modernism. In an issue of *A+U* devoted to Fehn the final image shows his home, a villa designed by Korsmo, his principal tutor and a significant influence who emphasised an essential romanticism:

Objects become real to us when seen and when touched in the fresh and fragrant air of song and light, close to the center of being, like catalysts between the dreams of humanity and the relentless metamorphosis of time, like memories of the pulsating dramatization of time itself, in that slither of time between life and death.[46]

46 Korsmo, quoted in Norberg-Schulz, 'The Poetic Vision of Sverre Fehn', p. 38.

'I don't believe that my work reflects Korsmo's architecture, but I became very attached to his intuitive world of thinking',[47] remarks Fehn, who concludes: 'I see materials as letters we use to write our poetic thoughts . . . We work with letters, an alphabet, we write a story.'[48]

47 Fehn, in Petri, p. 251.

48 Fehn, in Yoshida, 'Interview', p. 17.

THE STORY OF RUIN

The greatest mental construction of all – the one that strikes me as being the most poetic – is the idea mankind has of a possible life after death. To me it seems to have been the motor of the great architectural innovations. All the great structures deal with the problem of death – the pyramids, gothic architecture – but much more modest constructions do so too.[49]

49 Fehn, in Lavalou, p. 85.

Fehn complains that the nature of existence no longer receives the attention it deserves. Instead, 'Today's religion is the refusal of death. Thus even objects are not allowed to die, and are conserved.'[50] But he recognises that societal attitudes to death are reflected in his own work: 'I am sick of the sentimental way of dealing with these matters. On the other hand, if you look at my buildings and their surroundings, you can easily see that I have tried to preserve every single tree. It is a love–hate story.'[51]

A metaphor for time, the ruin is a recurring theme in Fehn's architecture. Left to decay, a ruin indicates what we wish to forget. Preserved, it shows what we wish to remember. But a preserved ruin may have other purposes, either retaining an uncomfortable memory or cultivating an imaginary past. Exploiting the ruin's long association with loss and potential, Fehn imagined his designs as ruins and incorporated actual ruins whenever possible.[52]

In the 1977 competition for Trondheim public library Fehn exposed buried medieval vaults, which were incorporated into the main reading room. Connecting the building to the city and the nation, the principal route through the library followed the ancient route to the south out of Trondheim, which is the most northerly of Norway's major cities. In 1982 Fehn entered the competition for the museum to house the *Wasa*, which sank in 1628 during the reign of King Gustavus Adolphus when Sweden became a European power. Recognising that it combined melancholic failure and glorious success, Fehn proposed that the ship should be placed as though it had just been discovered. Around the *Wasa* he designed a protective shell.

In 1567 the Swedish army destroyed much of the medieval fortress at Hamar. A nineteenth-century barn was built on its ruins. Completed in 1979, the Archbishopric Museum incorporates the medieval ruins and the remains of the later barn. The north and west wings exhibit medieval and ethnographic collections, including objects excavated or found on the site, while the south wing houses the administration, lecture hall and travelling exhibitions. Only the south wing is heated. Visits are restricted to the summer months but the ruins are most evocative when the air is chilled, emphasising past decay and coming thaw. Fehn identifies 'four temporal layers' among the ruins, which are as essential to the museum as the other exhibits:[53]

> *The ruins are not restored to the state they were in before destruction. Each time layer is not detached from the next, but rather floats across its neighbour. The manifestation of their presence is an effort to inhabit a mystery. The museum embraces the remains so as to allow the ruined element to live as a thought.*[54]

Fehn describes each architectural layer as 'timeless' not because it is appropriate to all times but because it echoes across time, creating a dialogue between past

50 Fehn, quoted in Giardiello, p. 265.

51 Fehn, 'An Architectural Autobiography', p. 246.

52 Dal Co, p. 12.

53 Fehn, 'An Architectural Autobiography', p. 246.

54 Fjeld paraphrasing Fehn, in Fjeld, p. 133.

Sverre Fehn, the Archbishopric Museum, Hamar, 1979. Exterior with ramp. Photograph, Catherine Harrington.

and present and offering future relevance.[55] His respect for each historical layer is compatible with established conservation policy. But Fehn applies a further temporal layer to draw attention to each previous layer: 'Only by manifesting the present can you make the past speak.'[56] The materials of the present are precisely finished concrete, timber and glass. Creating fragments of a building rather than a complete structure, Fehn adds a contemporary ruin to the earlier ruins. Bridges weave through the barn. A hairpin concrete ramp slides over ruined walls, connecting an upper floor to the courtyard formed by the three wings. Over the outer face of the heavy stone walls, a regular glass plane covers each irregular opening. Together, the contemporary ruin and the earlier ruins form a new imagined ruin, alluding to a life after death.

55 Fehn, in Norri, p. 250.

56 Fehn, in Yoshida, *A + U*, p. 45.

THE STORY OF THE HORIZON

The horizon is a familiar motif in Fehn's buildings, representing the evolving quest for understanding: 'at Hamar, where the whole history of the place was to be found in the ground below, you have to respect the surface in your design and give the structure of the construction a suspended character. By walking on the bridges you in a way find your own horizon'.[57] In the romantic landscape tradition of Friedrich and Dahl, the horizon means the sea and the illumination of a low sun. Ships are prevalent in Fehn's sketches. Their type and size differ but the vertical line of the mast and the horizontal line of the sea recur. However, Fehn contends that voyages of discovery are devoid of purpose and pleasure once nature is no longer mysterious:

> *In order to see beyond the horizon, we had to conquer the sea. The immensity of the sea inspired boat-building . . . The secret of the boat was to fight the horizon*

57 Fehn, in Yoshida, 'Interview', p. 19.

Sverre Fehn, the Archbishopric Museum, Hamar, 1979. Interior with bridge. Photograph, Catherine Harrington.

. . . Nature with her enormous scale was no longer the uncharted, since the unknown had been usurped by man.[58]

58 Fjeld paraphrasing Fehn, in Fjeld, pp. 26–27.

Fehn concludes that the bounded horizon of the flat earth offered the reassuring image of the edge and the poetic mystery of the unknown, while the endless horizon of the globe undermines any sense of scale, limit and enclosure.[59] Reducing vertical elements, which refer to the mast, he emphasises horizontal elements, which refer to the bounded horizon between earth and sky.

59 Fjeld paraphrasing Fehn, in Fjeld, p. 26.

THE STORY OF THE PLACE

A further story concerns the *genius loci*, the genius of the place, which the most influential twentieth-century Norwegian architectural theorist, Norberg-Schulz, made the focus of his research.[60] A visit to Morocco in 1952 allowed Fehn to better appreciate the interdependence of culture, climate and architecture. From a distance he 'obtained a better understanding of the Nordic atmosphere: trees, grass, rain, winter, snow – they all acquired a new meaning':[61]

60 Norberg-Schulz, *Genius Loci: Towards a Phenomenology of Architecture*.

61 Fehn, 'An Architectural Autobiography', pp. 246–247.

The globe is divided in longitude and latitude degrees. And each crossing point has its certain climate, its certain plants and winds. As an architect, you have to try to understand the difference of life in each point.[62]

62 Fehn, *The Pritzker Architecture Prize*, unpaginated.

Accordingly, the 'walk through nature' is the 'first step towards architecture'. Cutting a path is 'like writing on the surface of the earth. The crushing of grass and brushwood is an interference with nature, a simple definition of man's culture'.[63] Consequently, building begins with destruction even when an architect is highly attuned to the natural environment. Confirming the dual-nature that he considers to be distinctly Nordic, Fehn asks architects to 'Never consider nature in a romantic way. Always try to create a tension between nature and your intervention.'[64] But his request is romantic. As depicted by Turner and Dahl, the northern romantic tradition is an encounter with nature as much as it is a eulogy to nature. Faced with the severe drama of the Nordic landscape and weather, the relationship between architecture and nature can have little of the benign accord of Italy.

63 Fehn, *The Pritzker Architecture Prize*, unpaginated.

64 Fehn, in Lavalou, p. 85.

THE STORY OF CONSTRUCTION

During his visit to Morocco, 'a very simple way of building' inspired Fehn, which the first modernists had also admired in Mediterranean vernacular architecture.[65] Fehn's handling of space and construction are also reminiscent of Mies, a significant influence on Norwegian architects in the 1950s and 1960s, especially after Norberg-Schulz returned from working in his office. Fehn remarks that 'The rationalism of modern architecture is always in danger of forgetting construction. But without construction, architecture is meaningless.'[66] Construction is a means to define the genius of the place both in the ways that elements are made and the manner in which they are brought together. Combining elements directly but delicately, Fehn referred to Norwegian vernacular architecture. In stave construction the individual elements are expressed, in contrast to Swedish vernacular architecture, which emphasises the continuous surface that Lewerentz exploited.[67] Fehn favoured a densely articulated roof canopy as in stave construction but his emphasis was horizontal rather than vertical. Instead of timber he used concrete, which carries the imprint of the surface against which it is cast and effect of the weather as it dries.

Fehn admired Carlo Scarpa, who shared his interest in weather's impact on architecture and its potential as a building 'material'. In 1963 Carlo Scarpa completed his reworking of the ground floor and courtyard garden of the Querini Stampalia Foundation, Venice, which floods regularly. Rather than introduce measures to exclude the high tide, Scarpa created a layered terrain of steps and troughs to allow water to enter the interior in a specific manner: the 'high tide inside the building, the same as the rest of the city. Only we must contain and control it, use it as a source of light and reflection. Wait and see the light playing on the yellow and purple stuccoes on the ceilings'.[68] Fehn's concern for articulated construction, and combination of the ancient and modern, further emphasise his affinity for Scarpa. The Archbishopric Museum at Hamar notably recalls Scarpa's Castelvecchio Museum in Verona, 1964, in which historical artefacts and concrete bridges weave through an old structure. But Fehn emphasises that building construction and social life are less elaborate in Norway:

> *Scarpa has a richness concerning detailing that only a man from Venice is able to create, with his background in the architectural tradition. If you look at Norway we have a different background, much simpler both in our architecture history and in our way of living.*[69]

65 Fehn, 'The Primitive Architecture of Morocco', p. 41; Fehn, 'An Architectural Autobiography', pp. 246–247.

66 Fehn quoted in Yoshida, 'Editor's Preface', p. 4.

67 Norberg-Schulz, *Nightlands*, p. 65.

68 Scarpa, quoted in Manzelle, unpaginated.

69 Fehn, in Yoshida, 'Interview', p. 19.

Sverre Fehn, the Archbishopric Museum, Hamar, 1979. Interior with bridge and door. Photograph, Catherine Harrington.

THE STORY OF LIGHT

In 1962 the Pavilion of the Nordic Nations opened in the gardens of the Venice Biennale. Serving Finland, Norway and Sweden, the Nordic Pavilion is located between the American and Danish Pavilions and next to a small hill. It is a single rectangular room. The north and west walls, respectively adjacent to the hill and the American Pavilion, are boarded concrete; those to the south and east are sliding glass. The roof consists of two layers of deep and slender concrete beams closely spaced. The upper layer is aligned east to west. The lower structural layer extends from the north wall to double beams on the south elevation, which rest on the double column at the south-east corner of the Pavilion. The articulated structure recalls stave construction as well as Mies's designs.

Fehn describes architecture as an intervention in nature but the Nordic Pavilion limits the destruction. Large trees are abundant throughout the Biennale gardens: 'In union with nature the structure offers no resistance . . . The building stops where the trees are too many and the hill too steep for a building to follow it naturally.'[70]

70 Fjeld paraphrasing Fehn, in Fjeld, p. 112.

Sverre Fehn, Pavilion of the Nordic Nations, Venice Biennale, 1962. East façade. Photograph, Jonathan Hill.

Trees that coincide with the Pavilion are incorporated within it. Gaps between the roof beams allow the trunks to grow unhindered while the two wings of the double column bifurcate at 45 degrees to frame a particularly large tree. Pale concrete beams and walls, clear fibreglass roof panels and sliding glass doors make the Pavilion appear unusually delicate, focusing attention on the dark tree-trunks.

The Nordic Pavilion intervenes in nature in that it intervenes in light. Especially in summer, the high Venetian sun creates a warm, sharp light with strong shadows that emphasise the solidity and mass of buildings. In contrast, the typical Nordic light is diffuse and cool with soft shadows that flatten and diminish matter. 'There are few national galleries which when you enter engulf you in an iridescent fog-light that quickly determines one's state of mind; at once chilling and irresistible', remarks John Hejduk.[71] Rather than gloom or glare, the fog fascinates Fehn:

> *If you are building, for example, in Greece, then it is the light that is creating the greatest part of your architecture. You only need to scratch the marble with your fingernail and the scratch is visible. Up here in the Nordic light, it just wouldn't be visible at all. These factors render our architectonic world shadowless.*[72]

71 Hejduk, quoted in Fjeld, p. 156.

72 Fehn, in Petri, p. 251.

Sverre Fehn, Pavilion of the Nordic Nations, Venice Biennale, 1962. Bifurcating column. Photograph, Jonathan Hill.

To represent Nordic culture, the Nordic Pavilion creates a Nordic light. Designed according to the trajectory of the sun in the Venetian summer, the two layers of concrete beams exclude direct sunlight and create a light that is soft and diffuse, transforming Venetian light into Nordic light. Emphasising that the 'shadow of stone is not the same as that of a brittle autumn leaf' Fehn manipulated each building material to minimise its shadows.[73] For example, the concrete is smooth, and is a mix of white cement, white sand and crushed white marble.

73 Fehn, 'Has a Doll Life?', p. 244.

Nordic paintings depict a Nordic light. A diffuse light is also found in the modern art gallery. But the Nordic Pavilion questions the isolation of the gallery and its light. Extending beyond the glass walls – left open in summer – the concrete floor is flush with the gardens that surround it, diminishing the threshold between inside and outside, which is marked not by a physical barrier but by a shift from Venetian light to Nordic light. Blurring the boundary between gallery and garden, the Nordic Pavilion invites casual movements that undermine the aura of art, which the other national pavilions affirm.

Sverre Fehn, Pavilion of the Nordic Nations, Venice Biennale, 1962. Interior. Photograph, Jonathan Hill.

THE STORY OF RAIN

Even more than light, in Venice the context is water, whether in the canal or lagoon, mist or rain. Built in a marshy landscape, the sea is the source of the city's wealth. First, because intricate navigational routes through the shallow lagoon protected the city from attack and allowed the development of sea-bound trade. Second, because tourists are drawn to the precarious beauty of a watery city under threat from the rising sea. Evidence and experience of decay is key to Venice's romantic appeal.

Protecting the interior, the Nordic Pavilion's transparent roof panels 'pay homage to the rain'.[74] But in a downpour, water trickles down the trees and into the gallery. One photograph, enjoyed by Fehn, shows the doors absent and the concrete floor shiny after a rainstorm. Norwegian architecture confronts the cold and Venetian architecture confronts the flood. But the milder Venetian climate

74 Fjeld paraphrasing Fehn, in Fjeld, p. 112.

allows Fehn to blur architecture and nature to a degree that is unlikely in a Nordic country. As its name suggests, the Nordic Pavilion combines traditions from the north and the south: the encounter with sublime nature and the embrace with cultivated nature. Accommodating trees and rain, transforming Venetian light into Nordic light, the Nordic Pavilion expands the dialogue between architecture and nature: 'This honouring of sun and rain . . . is the beginning of a search for a higher order of architecture.'[75]

75 Fjeld paraphrasing Fehn, in Fjeld, p. 112.

THE STORY OF GAPS

In *Theory of the Avant-Garde* Bürger distinguishes between two concepts of art. In the organic work of art the individual parts are subordinate to, and in harmony with, the overall composition, while in the non-organic work of art the parts, arrangement and context are distinct and non-hierarchical. 'The organic work of art seeks to make unrecognisable the fact that it has been made.' But the non-organic work of art declares its artifice: 'To this extent, montage may be considered the fundamental principle of avant-gardist art.'[76]

76 Bürger, p. 72.

Benjamin identifies Baroque allegorical drama as an inspiration for early twentieth-century montage because its meaning was open to discursive and critical interpretation.[77] The picturesque also shares characteristics with montage: the formulation of new meanings through the appropriation and dialectical juxtaposition of fragments in a new site and with regard to a wider context. The value that the eighteenth century gave to subjective experience helped develop a context in which montage could later flourish.

77 Benjamin, *The Origin of German Tragic Drama*, pp. 159–161.

Two distinct and contradictory models are evident in Benjamin's advocacy of montage. Offering a defined dialectic, the first is didactic and meant to shock. The directness and clarity of the message match the seamless combination of fragments into a coherent image. Turning the words and images of politicians against themselves, a John Heartfield photomontage is typical of didactic montage. In *Hurrah, the Butter is Finished*, 19 December 1935, a quotation from a speech by Hermann Goering, 'Iron always makes a country strong, butter and lard only fat', is juxtaposed to the image of a family chewing iron. A photograph of Hitler hangs on the wall behind. Benjamin's second model is less likely to shock and more likely to resist a single interpretation. Complex, incomplete, ambiguous and even confusing, it offers no clear dialectic and fully involves the reader, viewer or user in the formulation of meaning, which is seen to be cultural and transitory. Collectively, the six diverse sections of Benjamin's 1935, second draft for *Passagenwerk* (*The Arcades*

John Heartfield, *Hurrah, the Butter is Finished*, 19 December 1935. Courtesy of George Eastman House, International Museum of Photography and Film.

Project) – an investigation of the nineteenth-century Parisian arcades – are an example of ambiguous montage.[78] Unlike didactic montage, ambiguous montage shares authority between the producer and the user and is evident in the picturesque and modernism to some degree, as I discussed in Chapter 6 'The Weather of Our Houses'.

78 Benjamin, 'Paris, Capital of the Nineteenth Century', pp. 146–162; Benjamin, *The Arcades Project*.

Didactic montage consists of distinct material entities brought together in a new site: the montage of fragments. In addition to the fragments and the site, ambiguous montage juxtaposes a third element, creating the montage of gaps.[79] Indicating that something is unnoticed or hidden, absent or incomplete, a gap invites the user to imagine what is there and, thus, to make the montage anew. An opening between seemingly more substantial conditions, a gap may be spatial, sensual, semantic or temporal, for example. Rather than a literal absence, the spatial gap is a perceived emptiness, ready to be transformed by experience. The sensual gap occurs when either a number of senses contradict each other or one is depleted. The semantic gap occurs when certain characteristics expected of a building, such as solidity or utility, are absent or undermined. The temporal gap occurs when something is delayed or appears at the wrong time.

79 Hill, *Actions of Architecture*, pp. 109–128.

With the ruin as its emblem, the picturesque is a precedent for the montage of gaps, if not the non-organic work of art, as it conceals artifice more often than not. But declaring the manner of its construction, the Nordic Pavilion is a non-organic work of art as well as a montage of gaps. Spatial, sensual, semantic and temporal gaps arise because Venetian light is depleted into Nordic light. The absence of a physical threshold between building and garden and the presence of external elements inside as well as outside, such as trees and weather, add to the montage of gaps. The juxtaposition of Venetian and Nordic light is most apparent in summer when either the art or architecture Biennale is open. But whatever the season, the montage of gaps arises when dawn brings Nordic light to the Pavilion. I've experienced the Pavilion many times but it was actually most evocative when closed. One mild December day I entered the Biennale gardens to find the building boarded up for winter. Through gaps in the outer wall, I saw an interior empty except for three trees and a softly chilling light, mirroring a scene from a Norwegian winter. At the foot of each tree lay a scattering of leaves, having drifted down from the openings in the roof beams that extend around each trunk. Another cluster of leaves marked a roof opening where a tree had once grown and died, emphasising the emotive power of a ruin.

THREADS OF THOUGHT

In Salter's discourse on the poetics of construction – *TS: Intuition & Process*, 1989 – the first image is 'Chatsworth in the fog'. Architecture and nature are bleached and nearly unrecognisable, recalling Soane's lecture illustrations of Blenheim as well as Fehn's shadowless light.[80] Salter's first twentieth-century building is

80 Surrounded by a thousand-acre park, Chatsworth is the home of the Duke of Devonshire. Soane, quoted in Watkin, *Sir John Soane*, p. 373.

Peter Salter, *TS: Intuition & Process*, 1989. Cover. Courtesy of the Architectural Association, London.

Lewerentz's Flower Kiosk, which he praises as a 'sublime example of unequivocal building. The manipulation of the construction and the component details are generated and constrained by the design intention'.[81] Salter describes the Smithsons in comparable terms: 'One of the reasons why I like their work is that the strategy for making the design is evident in its construction.'[82] The well-used copy of *TS: Intuition & Process* in the Bartlett Library illustrates this argument well. Frayed threads extend outwards at the edges of its pale hessian cover, cataloguing the many times the book has been pulled from the shelves. The more it is used, the more its materiality and means of construction will become apparent.[83]

Fehn and Lewerentz shared the Smithsons' concern for history, nature, context and poetic and ethical construction, which opposed the wastefulness of consumer

81 Salter, 'An Essay in Eight Parts', p. 14.

82 Salter, in Boyarsky and Salter, p. 7.

83 Upper Lawn Pavilion subtly differs in that weathering has softened the various materials to gradations of soft grey.

society. But to understand and situate the present they emphasised a different past. Lewerentz indicated some debt to the picturesque, while it did not obviously concern Fehn although it is a precedent for the montage of gaps he created in the Nordic Pavilion. Instead, their obvious allegiance is to romanticism and national romanticism. The harsh Nordic climate does not encourage submission to the seasons and gentle weathering in the manner of Upper Lawn Pavilion. The dialogue with nature remains, but rather than the benign encounter of the picturesque or romantic classicism it is confrontational as well as celebratory and closer to the romanticism expressed in nineteenth-century landscape paintings. For an architect concerned with the subtleties of daily life in a harsh climate, actual immersion in nature is not an option. Instead, Fehn and Lewerentz recognised weather's metaphorical potential, making the evocation of a weather condition the purpose of a building. In a milder climate, Fehn combined architecture and nature to the extent that Nordic light became the Nordic Pavilion's principal material.

9

sweet garden of vanished pleasures

INTRODUCTION

Derek Jarman questioned the modernist eradication of history but as a film-maker had little concern for architectural modernism. His relevance to my theme depends on his attitude to the environment. Affirming the tradition that associates a people and a place with its landscape, Derek Jarman identified with the picturesque and romanticism in English art and poetry, as well as the pastoral films of the 1940s and 1950s, when a burgeoning neo-romanticism celebrated national identity. Jarman chose to live in a location that combined blissful childhood memories with the sublime threat of contemporary weather, which as an ever more complex hybrid recurred as a metaphor for time.

DUNGENESS

Two thousand years ago it did not exist.[1] Today Dungeness is one of the largest shingle expanses in the world. Covering more than seventy square kilometres and nearly twenty metres deep, the headland is gradually moving north-east along the coast as the tides collect and deposit shingle. Attempting to counter this daily drift, trucks carry shingle in the opposite direction.

Windswept and ignored, Dungeness developed without planning guidelines. Buildings, objects and artefacts litter the headland like detritus washed in on the morning tide. Dungeness is a laboratory layered with experiments past and present, each a memorial to a time and a technology:

100 wrecks, one a German submarine.
40 fishing boats.
Two lighthouses, three more destroyed.
A submarine oil pipeline to France built for Operation Pluto in 1944.
A National Nature Reserve (NNR) and Site of Special Scientific Interest (SSSI).
Railway carriages now used as houses.[2]
'Acoustic mirrors' to detect incoming aircraft.[3]
A one-third scale miniature railway.[4]
Pylons and power lines.
Fishermen's cottages, some still in use, others now second homes.
Two public houses.
A bird sanctuary and observatory.[5]
Gravel pits worked by rusting cranes.
A lifeboat station.

1 The name derives from the nearby Denge Marsh and the Old Norse term 'nes', meaning headland. The very earliest shingle deposits, to the west, began in 3000 BC but significant deposits only occurred in the last two thousand years. Plater, Stupples and Roberts, pp. 126, 210.

2 Left behind when the Southern Railway closed the station built to transport shingle excavated from the headland.

3 A few miles north-east of Dungeness, on a Ministry of Defence site at Denge, three concrete 'acoustic mirrors', each a parabolic reflector, face out to sea. Built between 1928 and 1930 as an experimental early warning system to detect incoming aircraft at sea they were ineffective and made obsolete by the invention of radar in 1932.

4 The best way to approach Dungeness is a 13-mile journey at 25mph. Following the coast, through woodland and marsh, past caravan parks and back gardens, the Romney, Hythe and Dymchurch Railway was founded in 1927.

5 Run by the Royal Society for the Protection of Birds (RSPB).

Dungeness, view of the giant timber 'T' left over from radar experiments, and towards the sea. Photograph, Jonathan Hill.

Second World War remains: anti-tank fencing, barbed wire, a concrete blockhouse, a giant timber 'T' left over from radar experiments.

The largest intervention is Dungeness nuclear power station. The UK government first made a commitment to nuclear energy in 1955. Dungeness A is a Magnox reactor that first became operational in 1966 and closed in 2006. Dungeness B is an Advanced Gas-cooled Reactor that opened in 1984 and became synonymous with inefficiency and expense.[6] Employing 550 full-time staff it is due to close in 2018. Both reactors will be subject to lengthy and costly site clearances. Financial and safety concerns – including operational failures, the decay of ageing reactors and long-term dangers of radioactive material – led successive British governments to reject further nuclear power stations. But as a means to limit carbon emissions and reduce reliance on foreign energy supplies, the Labour government promoted their revival in 2008 and confirmed eleven possible sites in January 2010. Later that year three sites, including Dungeness, were discarded from the

6 Hall, pp. 92–99.

Dungeness, view of a discarded and weathered fishing boat, and towards the sea. Photograph, Jonathan Hill.

initial list due to environment concerns.[7] The proposed nuclear programme is highly contentious, even more so after the Fukushima nuclear accident in 2011. Nuclear power stations need coastal locations because they require an abundant supply of cooling water. But due to global warming, the rising sea is a deterrent to their expansion. The marshes to the north and west of Dungeness, which lie between the shingle headland and higher ground, are increasingly susceptible to flooding. Projections suggest that a storm surge in a rising sea could breach the shingle ridge that protects the power station. But sites that remain on the list are also subject to coastal erosion. In 2007 the Middlesex University Flood Hazard Research Centre concluded: 'Given the uncertainties of climate prediction over a 200-year timescale, it is hard to escape the conclusion that the most sensible approach would be to reject all nuclear new-build on coastal sites.'[8]

Centuries of disregard and sporadic development have made Dungeness abundant in nature, with over 600 plant types and numerous coastal birds and

7 http://www.decc.gov.uk/en/content/cms/news/en_statement/en_statement.aspx (18 October 2010); http://news.bbc.co.uk/1/hi/uk_politics/7179579.stm (10 January 2008); http://www.bbc.co.uk/news/uk-politics-11564152 (18 October 2010).

insects, some very rare. But the situation is double-edged. Birds congregate around the outfall pipes from the nuclear power station, which discard warm water, radioactive waste and sewage that encourage sea-bound biological growth. While, on land:

> *Sea Kale,* Crambe maritima, *is the Ness's most distinguished plant. There are more of them here than anywhere else in England – they come up between the boats.* Crambe *are edible, but a radiologist told me that they accumulate radioactivity from the nuclear power station more than any other plant.*[9]

Natural sources account for more than half the radiation we receive. Everything is radioactive to a degree: the uranium in the ground, the cosmic rays in the atmosphere, the atoms in our bodies and the stones in our buildings. Man-made sources include nuclear power stations and X-ray machines. The long-term effects of low-level radiation are uncertain and difficult to measure. Although no amount is absolutely safe, the radiation generated by radio, television and sunlight is

8 Middlesex University Flood Hazard Research Centre, p. 3. (18 October 2010).

9 Jarman, *Derek Jarman's Garden*, p. 15.

Dungeness, view along the headland, and towards the nuclear power station. Photograph, Jan Kattein.

described as non-ionising because it is assumed to be too weak to cause serious damage.[10] But ionising radiation may damage biological tissue and cause cancer. In their day-to-day operations, nuclear installations release small doses of radioactive material, which emit ionising radiation into the surrounding environment and sea, while an accident may cause a larger 'uncontrolled release'. The annual average exposure to background radiation in the UK is around 2 mSv (millisieverts). Nuclear power station employees receive doses of radiation higher than the national average, as do people living close to a reactor. The maximum permissible dose for a power station employee is 50 mSv per annum, while for the public adjacent to a power station it is 5 mSv. In 1987 the Health and Safety Executive published *The Tolerability of Risk from Nuclear Power Stations*, an eerily pragmatic document that establishes the 'risk of death' for an employee at '1 in 1000 per annum' and at 1 in 10,000 for a member of the public.[11]

10 Kaku and Trainer, 'Radiation: Introduction', pp. 27–29.

11 Health and Safety Executive, pp. 13–23.

> *On this basis, we might define a major civil nuclear accident as one giving rise to an uncontrolled release of a size capable of giving doses of 100mSv at 3km. The actual harm caused by such an accident, which would of course activate the emergency procedures, would depend upon the weather conditions; but it is pessimistically estimated that an accident of this size might cause the eventual deaths from cancer of about 100 people. A bigger accident than this is possible, but the chance would be lower; and similarly there is a higher chance of smaller accidents.*[12]

12 Health and Safety Executive, p. 26.

The first major nuclear accident in the UK occurred at Windscale in 1957, when the fuel rods overheated and caught fire, releasing radioactive material into the atmosphere. Two vans were sent forth – one to the north, the other to the south – to measure the effects of the weather on the spread of radiation. Fearing that livestock would be contaminated, milk from nearby farms was destroyed. Subsequently, the ban was extended to an area of 500 square miles. Further uncontrolled releases at Windscale included an accident while processing spent oxide fuel in 1973, the contamination of the River Calder in 1975, and a radiation leak from a concrete storage solo in 1976. However, the subsequent Windscale Inquiry dismissed objections to the future of nuclear power on the site.[13] Commenting on the inspector who led the inquiry in 1977 and authored the report in the following year, Robin Cook MP caustically concluded: 'We are all practising politicians. We are all familiar with how telling the judicious choice of quotations can be. But I am bound to say that during the last week it has begun to appear as though Mr Justice Parker's skill in the selection of quotations puts us all to shame.'[14]

13 Hall, pp. 59–64, 149, 153, 159.

14 Cook, quoted in Hall, p. 162.

PROSPECT COTTAGE

On 26 April 1986 an explosion killed thirty-one people at the Chernobyl nuclear reactor in the Ukraine, which was then in the Soviet Union. Over a hundred thousand people were evacuated. The winds cast a radioactive cloud that spread across Asia and Europe and reached northern England in early May, contaminating the ground where rain fell and leading the UK to commission *The Tolerability of Risk from Nuclear Power Stations*.

Also in spring 1986, driving through Kent with Keith Collins and Tilda Swinton, searching unsuccessfully for a bluebell wood to film, Derek Jarman suggested a visit to Dungeness: 'There's a beautiful fisherman's cottage here, and if ever it was for sale, I think I'd buy it.'[15] Built in 1900 for the Richardsons, a local fishing family, Prospect Cottage had timber walls tarred black, bright yellow window frames, a black corrugated roof, black chimney and red clay chimney pots, colours that Jarman retained. Changing the windows to 'old-fashioned' ones with smaller glass panes, he stripped away carpets, wallpaper and plasterboard to reveal timber rooms: 'The house is a gem. It has four rooms off a central corridor and is lined with rich tongue and groove.'[16] In three rooms the timber boarding was waxed; the other room, at the front, was painted a 'clear translucent Naples yellow' with a white ceiling.[17] Jarman added simple furniture, 'much of it created from bits and pieces from scrapyards and from beachcombings'. Gradually he moved in many of his favourite possessions. Noting that 'The house is warm in the winter and cool in the heat', Jarman's diaries describe familiar pleasures: writing, reading, listening to the radio, watching planes pass overhead and the weather change.[18]

> *Prospect Cottage is the last of a long line of 'escape houses' I started building as a child at the end of the garden: grass houses of fragrant mowings that slowly turned brown and sour; sandcastles; a turf hut, hardly big enough to turn around in; another of scrap metal and twigs, marooned on ice-flooded fields – stomping across brittle ice.*[19]

15 Jarman, quoted in Collins, 'Preface', p. 5.

16 Jarman, *Derek Jarman's Garden*, p. 65.

17 Jarman, *Modern Nature*, p. 71.

18 Jarman, *Derek Jarman's Garden*, p. 66.

19 Jarman, *Modern Nature*, p. 276.

PROSPECT COTTAGE GARDEN

Jarman was 'always a passionate gardener – flowers sparkled in my childhood as they do in a medieval manuscript'.[20] When he was just four his parents gave him a copy of the four-hundred page *Beautiful Flowers and How to Grow Them*, 1926. '*Beautiful Flowers* was to be my bible for many years: I pored over its exotic pages,

20 Jarman, *Derek Jarman's Garden*, p. 11.

scribbled in coloured crayon across its illustrations and made my first drawings of flowers by copying it.'[21] His first 'garden' commissions were for an opera, John Gielgud's 1968 production of *Don Giovanni* for the English National Opera at the London Coliseum, and a film, *The Devils* directed by Ken Russell and released in 1970.[22] In 1973 he designed a garden at the Verzons near Ledbury, Herefordshire, for his sister and her husband, Gaye and David Temple. Each of these designs was for a formal garden with topiary, totems and obelisks.

21 Jarman, *Modern Nature*, p. 10.

22 Ken Russell, dir., *The Devils*, BFI, 1970.

Dungeness, view of Prospect Cottage and the front garden. Photograph, Jonathan Hill.

Dungeness is owned by the Paine Family Trust, the heirs to G.T. Paine, who bought the headland when the Southern Railway departed. Each property on the private estate is leased and no boundary delineation is permitted. At first, Jarman 'had no thought of building a garden. It looked impossible'.[23] But many of Jarman's materials – natural and man-made – are indigenous to the area. Combining two long-held fascinations – beachcombing and gardening – he concludes: 'There are no walls or fences. My garden's boundaries are the horizon.'[24] Lichens, plants, flowers, fruit; shells, stones, pebbles, flints, sea-ground bricks; driftwood, rusty metal, anchors, chains, fishing tackle.[25] All collected and combined into obelisks, totems and geometric shapes, the back garden loosely placed as though deposited by the tide, the front more obviously reminiscent of his earlier formal garden designs but on a smaller scale. The garden is arranged around the cottage – Prospect Cottage Garden – but, equally, the cottage is a feature of the garden – Prospect Garden Cottage. In its apparent informality, reaction to circumstance and combination of building and garden, Christopher Lloyd recognises a particularly English place:

Prospect Cottage is very much in the English garden tradition, showing a love of plants and growing them well as a personal satisfaction . . . The fact that he was not put off by being told that gardening at Dungeness was 'impossible', and of there being no protocol or guidance, is also in the English tradition.[26]

THE LAST OF ENGLAND

Jarman affirms the tradition that associates England with its landscape. English people and places rank high in his influences and affections: 'Blake and William Morris . . . all of them look backward over their shoulders – to a Paradise on earth. And all of them at odds with the world around them. I feel this strongly, chose a 'novelty' medium – film – in which to search.'[27] He also praises the English pastoral films of Humphrey Jennings and Michael Powell from the 1940s and 1950s, when a number of the arts used the picturesque and romantic to defend national identity and the genius of the place.[28] In 1960 Jarman enrolled at King's College, University of London, studying for a BA in English, History and History of Art. Jarman shared Pevsner's appreciation of the picturesque and its importance to England. Its relevance to modernist architecture did not concern him although he commented positively on some twentieth-century buildings and went on architectural walking tours with Pevsner, who later became a friend.[29]

23 Jarman, *Derek Jarman's Garden*, p. 12.

24 Jarman, *Modern Nature*, p. 3.

25 Jarman excavated shingle to create a planting hole, filled it with manure from a nearby farm and restored the shingle surface around the plant.

26 Lloyd created the nearby garden at Great Dixter, East Sussex, which Jarman admired. Lloyd, p. 152.

27 Jarman refers to William Blake. Jarman, *Modern Nature*, p. 25.

28 Jarman, *Kicking the Pricks*, p. 136.

29 Pevsner, 'Twentieth-Century Picturesque: An Answer to Basil Taylor's Broadcast', pp. 228–229. Jarman, *Modern Nature*, pp. 193–195.

If the English landscape is synonymous with a way of life, mourning one means mourning the other: 'In the short space of my lifetime I've seen the destruction of the landscape through commercialisation, a destruction so complete that fragments are preserved as if in a museum.'[30] Released in 1987 and set in the near future, Jarman's *The Last of England* depicts a derelict and decaying urban landscape ruled by the military.[31] The film's colours are Turner's and its title refers to the 1855 pre-Raphaelite painting by Ford Madox Brown, which depicts emigrants leaving England by sea.[32] Opposed to the modernist eradication of history Jarman identifies the continuity of the past with the present: 'It's a love story with England. It's not an attack. It's an attack on those things that I perceive personally as things without value. Things that have invaded the mainstream of British life. That's not an attack on England. It's the opposite.'[33]

Jarman's paternal grandfather emigrated from Devon to New Zealand in the late nineteenth century but his father returned in 1929, thirteen years before his birth. Many of Jarman's fondest childhood memories refer to the south-west of England. At Dungeness he was able to recall and recreate a number of the places in his fondest childhood memories. One is the Isle of Purbeck, Dorset, a headland rather than an island.[34] Used as a military range since the Second World War, it has avoided extensive farming and consequently contains some of the most varied wild plants and insects in southern England. Thomas Hardy is the author most associated with Purbeck. In his novels, many written at the end of the nineteenth century, the landscape and weather are the principal protagonists, often intervening to determine events.

Developed from Jarman's unrealised script on the Elizabethan alchemist, astrologer, geographer and mathematician John Dee, *The Angelic Conversation*, 1985, was filmed at Montacute House in Somerset, an Elizabethan mansion admired by Jarman.[35] Built between 1590 and 1601, Montacute has timber-panelled rooms ordered around a symmetrical plan and a formal garden abundant in topiary.[36] The most notable room is on the top floor. The 55m Long Gallery extends the full length of the house and has a bay window at each end, allowing the family to exercise and view the landscape when the weather was poor.

Visiting Kilve in Somerset, where the Quantock Hills meet the sea at an expansive shingle beach, was the 'happiest part' of Jarman's childhood.[37] There he went beachcombing and completed his first landscape paintings, a practice he continued however unfashionable. At the Slade School of Fine Art, University College London, in the early 1960s, he recalls that while others were absorbed by Pop art 'I was painting landscapes, close to the red earth of north Somerset, the flowers, the butterflies in the meadows.'[38] Kilve is close to Alfoxden and Nether Stowey, where William and Dorothy Wordsworth and Samuel Taylor Coleridge made

30 Jarman, *Kicking the Pricks*, pp. 136–138.

31 Derek Jarman, dir., *The Last of England*, Anglo International Films for British Screen, Channel 4 and ZDF, 1987.

32 Jarman, *Kicking the Pricks*, p. 245.

33 Derek Jarman, *Know What I Mean*, an interview preceding *A Night with Derek*, Channel 4 Television, 16 July 1994.

34 Peake, *Derek Jarman*, p. 25.

35 Derek Jarman, dir., *The Angelic Conversation*, BFI, 1985.

36 The architect was William Arnold, a local mason. Rogers, p. 11.

37 Jarman, quoted in Peake, p. 39.

38 Jarman started a Diploma in Fine Art at the Slade in 1963, with painting and drawing as his major subject and stage design as his subsidiary subject. Jarman, *Kicking the Pricks*, p. 41.

their homes at the end of the eighteenth century and produced some of their most influential work, notably *Lyrical Ballads*, 1798. Jarman enjoyed the area's association with the romantic poets and referred in particular to Dorothy Wordsworth's *Alfoxden Journal,* 1797–1798, a medium he enjoyed and practised: 'I too gathered worts on Danesborough, which she often climbed with Coleridge.'[39] Romanticism familiarly conceived industrialisation as a threat to the English landscape but Turner was a notable exception, as was William Wordsworth to a lesser extent. Jarman made films – a medium synonymous with industrialisation – and throughout his life maintained a concern for desolate and portentous landscapes with a brooding presence, whether natural or man-made. Typical of some romantics, the industrial landscape repelled and fascinated him but he only had distaste for the manicured gardens of the National Trust and the chocolate-box town of Rye, close to Dungeness.[40] Adjacent to Kilve there is a nuclear power station with the two same reactors as at Dungeness.[41] Begun when Jarman was fifteen, Hinkley Point nuclear power station was not a feature of his childhood but became important later. Jarman visited Kilve once again just before he bought Prospect Cottage:

> *The next week I drove to Somerset with Gerard to film on the beach at Kilve, where I spent afternoons as a child constructing driftwood sculptures for the incoming tide to sweep away. At Hinkley Point we took off the road to the nuclear power station which my Aunt Isobel and the village had fought from her cottage 'Great Beats'. Coming over the hill, it looked old and rusty: these power stations generate a strange atmosphere: the slight hum and the occasional whistle deepens the sense that those who ran them have left long ago.*[42]

39 Dorothy Wordsworth's journal was not intended for publication. Jarman, *Modern Nature*, p. 68.

40 Jarman, *Derek Jarman's Garden*, p. 41; Jarman, *Modern Nature*, p. 15.

41 Hinkley Point A is a Magnox reactor built between 1957 and 1965; Hinkley Point B is an Advanced Gas-cooled Reactor built between 1967 and 1975.

42 Jarman, *Kicking the Pricks*, pp. 239–240.

SUBLIME PROSPECT

Homeliness and other-worldliness drew Jarman to Dungeness: 'the bleakness of Prospect Cottage was what had made me fall in love with it'.[43] Dungeness evokes the sublime and the nuclear power station is one of its features. Burke attributed the sublime to buildings.[44] Especially since the industrial revolution, a terrifying and thrilling presence may be man-made as well as natural. Burke recognised natural weather as sublime, while Turner acknowledged the sublime potential of the hybridised weather of nature and industry. Today, Dungeness's sublime weather is also electromagnetic and radioactive.

In the centuries following Faraday's discovery of electromagnetic induction, the proliferation of electronic devices has produced an electromagnetic climate.

43 Jarman, *Derek Jarman's Garden*, p. 66.

44 Burke, *Philosophical Enquiry,* p. 76.

Unaffected by traditional building thresholds, electromagnetic weather is generated inside as well as outside, seeping into every corner. Electronic devices form volumetric electromagnetic fields that are an unseen presence in buildings, cities and beyond. Theorising this condition, Anthony Dunne and Fiona Raby even identify 'a new form of pollution, or electrosmog'.[45] In 1836, Faraday invented an electromagnetic shield to protect the interior of a room. The Faraday Cage is often used to isolate electronic equipment from unwanted discharges, such as a lightning strike. But as a respite from the electromagnetic spectrum, it also suggests that the challenge today may be to avoid electromagnetic fields as much as create them.[46]

45 Dunne and Raby, *Design Noir*, p. 21. Refer to Dunne, pp. 96, 105; Dunne and Raby, 'Notopia', p. 102.

46 Dunne and Raby, *Design Noir*, p. 26.

Dungeness, view of the back garden at Prospect Cottage and towards the nuclear power station. Photograph, Jonathan Hill.

However, denial was not Jarman's approach. Prospect Cottage cannot simply be understood as a rural retreat – a nostalgic primitive hut in the natural world – because the nuclear power station is ever present. In a nation such as Britain, with a nationally and globally interconnected infrastructure, a clear division between city and country is now untenable. Just as Turner allowed London's polluted air to enter his studio, Jarman chose a site next to a nuclear reactor, immersing himself in radioactive and electromagnetic weather to experience the sublime at home. 'The nuclear power station is a wonderment' but the glow and hum are so pressing that he imagines 'if I were to build a Howitzer I could hit Dungeness B'.[47] Tony Peake concludes that the nuclear power station provided 'the best visual metaphor' Jarman 'encountered for his own anger'.[48]

> *For the first twenty-five years of my life I lived as a criminal, and the next twenty-five were spent as a second-class citizen, deprived of equality and human rights. No right to adopt children – and if I had children, I could be declared an unfit parent; illegal in the military; an age of consent of twenty-one, no right of inheritance; no right of access to a loved one; no right to public affection; no right to an unbiased education; no legal sanction of my relationships and no right to marry.*[49]

On 22 December 1986 – the year he bought Prospect Cottage – Jarman was identified as a carrier of the AIDS virus, accentuating his anger and increasing his awareness of mortality.[50] The garden at Prospect Cottage marked his life from diagnosis to death. Describing his garden as 'a therapy and a pharmacopoeia',[51] Jarman proclaims: 'Like all true gardeners, I'm an optimist.'[52] But gardening is so absorbing that the gardener may forget any time except the present: 'The gardener digs in another time, without past or future, beginning or end. A time that does not cleave the day with rush hours, lunch breaks, the last bus home. As you walk into the garden you pass into this time – the moment of entering can never be remembered.'[53] So dependent on the weather and the seasons, the gardener also knows that life and death are necessary to one another.[54] On the south wall of Prospect Cottage are the words of John Donne's 'The Sunne Rising', 1633. As the two lovers will separate at daybreak, the poem boastfully teases the sun to delay or simply revolve around their bed:

> Busie old foole, unruly Sunne,
> Why dost thou thus,
> Through windowes, and through curtaines call on us?
> Must to thy motions lovers' seasons run?

47 Jarman, *Derek Jarman's Garden*, pp. 67, 64.

48 Peake, *Derek Jarman*, p. 366.

49 Jarman, Derek, *At Your Own Risk*, p. 4.

50 Peake, *Derek Jarman*, p. 378.

51 Jarman, *Derek Jarman's Garden*, p. 12.

52 Jarman, *Kicking the Pricks*, p. 151.

53 Jarman, *Modern Nature*, p. 30.

54 Unsettled weather accompanied Jarman's gardening. The years 1988, 1989 and 1990 were the warmest since records began in the seventeenth century and had some of the highest levels of drought while the winter of 1989–1990 was the wettest on record. O' Hare, Sweeney and Wilby, p. 265.

Sawey pedantique wretch, goe chide
Late schoole boyes and sowre prentices,
Goe tell Court-huntsmen, and that the King will ride,
Call countrey ants to harvest offices;
Love, all alike, no season knowes, nor clyme,
Nor houres, dayes, moneths, which are the rags of time . . .
Thou sunne art halfe as happy as wee,
In that the world's contracted thus.
Thine age askes ease, and since thy duties bee
To warme the world, that's done in warming us.
Shine here to us, and thou aret every where;
This bed this centre is, these walls thy spheare.[55]

55 Donne, as quoted in Jarman, *Derek Jarman's Garden*, p. 117.

Describing Prospect Cottage as 'more beautiful the older it becomes',[56] Jarman sees himself in his house and garden, vulnerable to the weather, subject to the seasons. In a section of his journals titled 'Borrowed Time' he is 'Like this old house in the gale . . . the clouds are blowing from the west, I'm drifting with them far away.'[57] Seeing another season means living a little longer: 'The day of our death is sealed up. I do not wish to die . . . yet. I would love to see my garden through several summers.'[58] Like General Dormer at Rousham, Jarman's garden preoccupied his last years, fulfilling the concern for life and death that pervades the picturesque. On 2 March 1994, just eight years after he moved to Prospect Cottage, 'The plain oak coffin was open. Jarman was dressed in a robe of glittering gold.'[59]

56 Jarman, *Derek Jarman's Garden*, p. 130.

57 Jarman, quoted in Peake, pp. 405, 407.

58 Jarman, *Modern Nature*, p. 310.

59 Jarman died on 19 February 1994, bequeathing Prospect Cottage to his partner, Keith Collins. Peake, p. 2.

My gilly flowers, roses, violets blue,
sweet garden of vanished pleasures,
Please come back next year.
Cold, cold, cold, I die so silently.[60]

60 Jarman, *Derek Jarman's Garden*, p. 81. Extract from an untitled poem.

HOME MOVIES

At Prospect Cottage there are numerous references to other gardens, including Elizabethan ones such as Montacute. But the two English traditions it most refers to are the picturesque garden and the cottage garden.[61] Redolent of Jarman's time there, his cottage's name relates to his prospecting and his prospect. It recalls the title of the first chapter – 'The Prospect' – in Hussey's influential *The Picturesque:*

61 Birksted, 'The Prospect at Dungeness', p. 256.

Studies in a Point of View, 1927.[62] In many picturesque gardens the focus is inward, as at Stourhead. While in others the views look out as well as in, as at Rousham. General Dormer's garden affirms the English Georgic tradition, which respects pleasure and production and implies benign management of land and labour. But it still enforces clear power relations between those who own the garden and those who work it. Jarman's obelisks, totems, tightly woven arrangement and meandering routes recall the picturesque, although the house is untypically at the centre. Confirming the legal requirement that no boundary delineation is permitted, the garden's edge is perceived rather than felt. The views look out as well as in but they are not framed and ordered as in the picturesque and the labour relations are those of the cottage garden. Growing fruit and vegetables to eat as well as flowers and shrubs to view, the cottage garden is decorative and practical. Pleasure and labour are combined; the owner is the designer and the gardener.

Whether beachcombing, gardening or film-making Jarman liked the ebb-and-flow of the creative process: 'I don't really feel that I've ever been a big controller-director. I just let everything "flow with the glue". There are no big plans which have to be fulfilled.'[63] Enjoying collaboration, he had no wish to be a figure of authority: 'I never saw myself as a film-director, I've never seen myself as one, I'm not one.' His longing for home-making and home-land combine in film-making: 'The home movie is a bedrock, it records the landscape of leisure: the beach, the garden, the swimming pool. In all home movies is a longing for paradise.'[64] Set around Prospect Cottage and released in 1990, *The Garden* is 'a home movie devoid of the innocent certainties of that form of film-making', writes Michael O'Pray.[65] Given that the film was 'inspired by Jarman's love of his own garden' and contains 'violence and sadism' that 'surpasses anything in his prior work', what sort of home is Prospect Cottage and its garden?[66] One that is typical.

Gardens appear in many of Jarman's films, 'where they are a metaphor for pain and pleasure, for Gethsemane and Eden'.[67] The subject of Prospect Cottage and *The Garden* is the pain and pleasure of home, made especially poignant by illness.[68] Jarman associates film-making with the sociability of home movies but home is synonymous with the private self. Much of his time at Prospect Cottage was spent alone. Jarman recalls the reaction of Swinton, a regular collaborator:

> *Tilda said she experienced* The Garden *quite differently from* The Last of England. *It was as if she was 'trapped' in my dream. She found the film intensely personal. The preoccupations of* The Last of England *were shared – here was something different. I feel the same way, can't really talk about the film. It's like talking about yourself!*[69]

62 Hussey, *The Picturesque*, pp. 1–17.

63 Jarman, quoted in Lippard, 'Interview', p. 167.

64 Jarman, *Kicking the Pricks*, p. 54.

65 Derek Jarman, dir., *The Garden*, Basilisk in association with Channel 4, British Screen, ZDF and Uplink, 1990. O' Pray, p. 179.

66 O' Pray, p. 178.

67 O' Pray, p. 38.

68 *The Garden* is 'an AIDS-related film but AIDS was too vast a subject to "film"'. Jarman, *Derek Jarman's Garden*, p. 91.

69 Jarman, *Modern Nature*, p. 296.

A recurring theme in architectural discourse states that the home is the origin and archetype of architecture, the manifestation of its most important attributes.[70] Defined by its separation from the world outside, the home is assumed to be the most secure and stable of environments. Banister Fletcher writes that 'Architecture . . . must have had a simple origin in the primitive efforts of mankind to provide protection against inclement weather, wild beasts and human enemies.'[71] The apparent stability of the home may provide gratification but it can also, simultaneously, create anxiety because the home can never be safe enough and is not always what it seems. In his 1919 essay on the uncanny Sigmund Freud considers what is 'Concealed, kept from sight, so that others do not get to know about it.'[72] The uncanny is a perception, not a property of a space; the most uncanny and threatening experience occurs within the home, when the hidden and repressed returns unexpectedly, rendering the homely unhomely.

70 Vitruvius, pp. 38–39.

71 Fletcher, p. 1.

72 Freud quotes from a dictionary, Daniel Sanders, *Wörtenbuch der Deutschen Sprache*, 1860. Freud, 'The "Uncanny"', p. 223.

HOME-MAKING

As the home-owner identifies with the home, mental unease and bodily disease – real or imagined – are easily projected onto building fabric. Jarman moved to Dungeness because a home there would be more vulnerable and thus more precious. Building and garden, natural and man-made, the last of his 'escape houses' is as flimsy as his first 'grass houses of fragrant mowings that slowly turned brown and sour'.[73] The fragility of his garden and cottage – so like one drawn by a child – makes his achievements in home-making more profound. A home is made, not found, and home-making lasts as long as a life. At Dungeness, due to the extreme weather it is obvious that a building must be tended like a garden:

> *Prospect has been re-tarred; it's shining and will remain so till the elements dull it. The west wall is the worst, sun and driving wet westerlies flake the paint in a year, so that it has to be painted continuously to keep the timbers in shape. Painting the house with tar varnish takes a day.*[74]

Prospect Cottage was built in response to its site and weather. Equally aware of local conditions, Jarman added a garden where it was least expected. Prospect Cottage is now associated with one author: *Derek Jarman's Garden*. Reflecting Jarman's heartfelt knowledge of the natural and cultural landscape of England, his design developed and evolved as he collected new plants, artefacts and ideas. But a design may be intensely personal while acknowledging other protagonists. Jarman

73 Jarman, *Modern Nature*, p. 276.

74 Jarman, *Derek Jarman's Garden*, pp. 68–69.

enjoyed the camaraderie of film-making. At Dungeness his collaborators were natural as well as human. The cottage and the garden are subject to the forces that make and transform Dungeness. The three natures and various weathers – natural, industrial, electromagnetic and radioactive – intermingle as one. Winds and tides, human interventions past and present, unforeseen events, all determine the character of the headland, cottage and garden. Dungeness is the model for the garden. And the garden is the model of Dungeness. At a different scale, the garden mirrors the arrangements, materials and conditions found across the headland.

Since the Italian Renaissance, it is often assumed that a significant building is the creation of a single architect – who conceives at a remove from construction – because artistic, intellectual labour is associated with the individual. Only occasionally is the contribution of a client, engineer or other architect acknowledged. Although Kent discarded plans, learnt from an existing topography and garden, accepted on-site advice, and encouraged alternative journeys and interpretations,

Dungeness, view along the headland. Photograph, Jonathan Hill.

Rousham is attributed to one author. So too is Jarman's garden. But Dungeness reveals a condition that is widespread: there are always a number of architectural authors at work. At Prospect Cottage and its garden, authorship is multiplied and juxtaposed, not dissolved. Multiplied because, rather than a sole author, a number of authors are identified, such as the designer, builder, gardener, visitor, site and weather. Juxtaposed because – sometimes competing, sometimes affirming – each author may inform or deny the other, as in a feisty dialogue of individual voices and unexpected conclusions. As natural and man-made forces affect each other on a global and a local scale, agents as well as authors are at work. An author is an initiating force while an agent responds, translates and transforms. As an author may also be an agent, the result is a complex interweaving of authorship and agency in which architecture and weather are connected rather than opposed and the production of architecture is shared and temporal.

conclusion

THINGS OF A NATURAL KIND

In the Renaissance, ideas were understood to be universal. But in *An Essay concerning Human Understanding*, 1690, Locke argued that ideas are provisional and dependent upon experience.[1] Countering the neo-Platonist and Cartesian traditions in which knowledge is acquired by the mind alone, empiricism emphasised that experience is key to understanding, which develops through an evolving dialogue between the environment, senses and mind. While Locke considered the natural world only so far as it affected human knowledge, Shaftesbury influenced a wider reverence.[2] Increasingly, the natural world was associated with subjective experience. One became a means to explore the other, drawing attention to the conditions that inform self-understanding. The changing weather became synonymous with changing perception and was considered to be as exceptional as the imagination. As material and metaphor, the weather was a means to appreciate the special and varied qualities of a time, a place and a person.

1 Locke, *An Essay concerning Human Understanding*, bk. 2, ch. 1, p. 105.

2 Shaftesbury, *Characteristicks*, vol. 2, p. 101.

The Renaissance raised the status of the visual artist to that of a sole author while restricting the imagination to absolute forms and proportions. Focusing attention on subjectivity, the eighteenth century transformed the visual arts, its objects, authors and viewers. No longer was architecture a cohesive body of knowledge. Rather than universal, ideas were provisional, changeable and dependent on experience at conception, production and reception. Empiricism established measured and modest behaviour as a model. But in drawing attention to the ambiguities of identity and limits of objectivity, its success could only be relative. Contradicting Locke's grounded reasonableness of a mechanistic mind, recognition that we make our own reality was increasingly exploited for its creative potential.

The new reverence given to subjectivity and nature in the eighteenth century, and the association of one with the other, encouraged a new type of design and a new way of designing, which valued the ideas and emotions evoked through experience. Marking a significant transformation in the role of the architect, the first convincing examples of such a design practice occurred in gardens, not buildings, because they appeared natural and were more clearly subject to change. Heightened concern for the fluctuating pleasures of perception and nature found expression in the picturesque, which is a deceptive term because it does not readily acknowledge the importance of the senses and the seasons to experience, understanding and the imagination in the eighteenth-century garden. Just as the daily weather was part of a larger weather pattern, the eighteenth-century picturesque garden was a means to engage the social as well as the subjective. History, politics, love and death were all represented and discussed among garden glades and monuments.

Although the pleasures and liberties of the picturesque were limited to the educated and prosperous, notable principles were established. Valuing the individuality of the designer and the visitor, the picturesque acknowledged that beauty is subjective. Loosening the ties of authorship, it encouraged varied allegories and diverse interpretations. Rather than being conceived according to the rules of geometry in a distant studio, the garden was designed the way it was experienced, by a figure moving across a landscape and imagining future movements, while special attention was given to drawings that explored the relations between site and experience. In a significant design innovation, the picturesque gave new emphasis to the environment, exploring human activity in dialogue with an evolving natural world. Rather than a complete and timeless object, a garden building was understood as an incident in an environment with which it conversed, establishing an architectural environmentalism that has had a profound influence on subsequent centuries.

In classical antiquity there were two distinct attitudes to atmospheric phenomena: one a theory of meteors, Aristotle's *Meteorologica*, the other a practical and poetic guide to the weather, Virgil's *Georgics*. Empiricism questioned both traditions because they did not depend on reasoned explanation. But scientific investigation was not immediately and extensively applied to the weather because it was assumed to lack reason and England's population was overwhelmingly rural. For a nation that was yet to feel the full effects of industrialisation, Virgil's farmer offered a model of benign management appropriate to Deism. Although a concern for the weather reflected a concern for the wider environment, the focus of a picturesque garden was often inward, recognising the pleasures within, not the labours without. But at Rousham the English Georgic tradition of labour and leisure was affirmed, acknowledging a poetic and practical appreciation of the weather. The early eighteenth-century garden also heralded an engagement with nature beyond the Georgic. Eulogising nature as the means of self-revelation, Rousham implied a burgeoning romanticism.

In eighteenth-century England the genius of the place was made as much as found, the fusion of new ideas, forms and spaces with those already in place, which were often the results of earlier migrations. Kent recalled the dream of rural life in classical antiquity and the gregarious interaction, mythological narrative and permeable organisation of the Italian Renaissance house and garden. Informed by the contemporary concern for experience, he heralded a newly picturesque landscape, which favoured nature and the weather as means to explore subjectivity. For the self-aware and questioning mind, the seasons drew attention to the past, present and future. Equating the seasons of a garden to the seasons of a life, Rousham's many references to impending winter, and death, are indicative of delights made sweeter because they are fleeting. Time is tangible in plants and trees and represented in monuments and buildings, which are also seen to age. The weather is Rousham's emblem.

THE GARDEN OF ARCHITECTURE

Drawing parallels between Rousseau's *Confessions*, Beckford's Fonthill Abbey and Sterne's *Tristram Shandy*, I regard Soane's house, museum and office at 12–14 Lincoln's Inn Fields as an intensely personal, highly self-conscious and purposively meandering autobiography in which the author edited, narrated and reinvented his life as he reflected upon it. Aware that no art form can fully describe a person and a life, Soane turned an impossible task to creative advantage. Number 12–14 Lincoln's Inn Fields is an appropriate monument to an era that lauded subjectivity but recognised it to be elusive and uncertain.

Visiting 12–14 Lincoln's Inn Fields today it is easy to ignore how different it was in Soane's lifetime. A building site for over forty years, Soane conceived 12–14 Lincoln's Inn Fields as a ruin and ruined as much as he built. In that era, the attention given to the ruin was due to the attention given to subjectivity and time, weather and decay. The ruin of a building was linked to the ruin of a life. But the ruin represented potential as well as loss, stimulating memory and the imagination. As Soane remained in Lincoln's Inn Fields while the three adjacent buildings were acquired, demolished, constructed, adjusted and rebuilt, living there was living in a living ruin unlike the preserved ruin we see today.

Soane often stated his fascination for the picturesque even though it was by then out of fashion. Equally inspired by Enlightenment architecture and the picturesque, he responded to Le Camus de Mézières' claim that a house and a garden can be designed according to similar principles by conceiving 12–14 Lincoln's Inn Fields as a garden of architecture, which engendered sensations and emotions, discourse as well as wonder. Avid for acquisition and adjustment, his inquisitive imagination guaranteed seasonal and yearly transformations. Drawings, paintings, windows and mirrors offer vistas and routes punctuated by ruins and monuments. Sculptures and antiquities cover every surface like architectural foliage, recalling the shaggy aesthetic of the late eighteenth-century picturesque as well as the intricately interconnecting spaces, alternative routes, deceptive dimensions and abundant allegories of Rousham's heavily wooded site.

In his lectures, Soane noted climate's creative influence on architectural development and emphasised the poetic effects of weather.[3] But in an increasingly secular society, the effect of humanity on nature was as much a concern as the effect of nature on humanity. With humanity conceived as an active agent of change at all scales and in all locations, greater demands were placed on building performance and the internal climate was subject to new scrutiny. Alongside a poetic appreciation of the weather, attempts to counter one climate with another were increasingly considered. Beyond the city Soane enjoyed the shifting modulations of mist and light. But in London his sensory appreciation extended no further than the boundaries of his home, concluding that retreat was the appropriate response. Creating a climate as much as a building, he designed a garden to exclude London. To create a meandering and habitable internal landscape he required central heating, employing an invention of the industrial era to counter one of its by-products, intense pollution. To bathe his garden in a golden light, he inserted coloured glass skylights and limited visits to sunnier days.

3 Soane, 'Lecture I', 'Lecture VIII', in Watkin, *Sir John Soane*, pp. 492, 595.

Soane fabricated a climate just as he fabricated a ruin. Only he determined his garden's growth and decay. Conceiving 12–14 Lincoln's Fields as a means of self-expression and morbidly concerned for his reputation, Soane displayed some of the characteristics of a romantic artist. But in attempting to deny the weather, Soane ignored a crucial aspect of the picturesque and isolated himself from the direct and unmediated engagement with nature that characterised romanticism.

PIGMENTS AND POLLUTION

Two attitudes to the weather developed alongside each other in the eighteenth and nineteenth centuries, each offering a contrasting relationship between humanity and nature. Responding to the rationalising demands of industry and agriculture as well as science, standard classificatory systems for the weather were devised in the early nineteenth century, more than sixty years after Linnaeus' classification of plants in *Critica Botanica*, 1737. The new science assumed Aristotle's title and his concern for a comprehensive account. But meteorology emphasised reasoned explanation not abstract theory or intuitive interpretation. Rather than the earlier coexistence with and within living nature, meteorology placed the detached specialist largely outside the natural world. Like any science, meteorology aimed for complete understanding of its subject. But weather's resistance to reason restricted meteorology's scientific status.[4]

4 Howard, *The Climate of London*, vol. 1, p. iii.

The two contrasting relationships between humanity and nature were complementary in that they were often applied to different landscapes; one terrain was transformed for productive purpose, the other was left fallow for spiritual purpose. In contrast to the direct control of nature, the unmediated exploration of uncultivated nature associated the weather with the imagination in a manner that united the self and the world. Nature was eulogised but the emphasis on the creative mind sometimes allowed the natural world to be wilfully misrepresented and, thus, subject to a more subtle manipulation. The close association of Coleridge and Davy, Faraday and Turner, indicated their mutual respect and overlapping concerns, undermining assumptions that the arts and sciences were necessarily opposed. The term 'romanticism' has been applied to science as well as art, and Wordsworth's *A Guide to the Lakes*, 1810, shows that poetry's appreciation of the weather accommodated intellect as well as emotion, and was not indifferent to reason.[5]

Turner's sketchbooks reveal how careful he was to record a landscape from different points of view, in different weathers, and at different times of the day. Many of his paintings focus on changes in the weather and human response to those changes. In the first volume of *Modern Painters*, 1843, Ruskin claims that Turner's genius depends on his ability to represent nature.[6] In the fourth volume in 1856, he refines his argument, recognising discrepancies between actual places and Turner's depictions. Rather than accurately represent physical topography, Ruskin states that 'Turnerian topography' truthfully depicts the impression of a place on an observer, taking into account the changing conditions and memories of associated journeys, places and paintings.[7] In the same volume, Ruskin describes the 'lower picturesque' as 'heartless' because it focuses on surface effects to the detriment of deeper social concerns. In contrast, he identifies the 'nobler', *'Turnerian Picturesque'*, concluding 'that the dignity of the picturesque increases from lower to higher, in exact proportion to the sympathy of the artist with his subject'.[8] Ruskin's analysis was beneficial in that it focused attention on human labour, which the picturesque had often ignored. But his assessment was a caricature, ignoring the range of social, cultural and environmental concerns that had been essential to the picturesque since the early eighteenth century. In characterising much of the picturesque as mere visual gratification, Ruskin affirmed a particularly English morality that denigrates aesthetics if it lacks an overt and glaringly obvious social purpose. If the picturesque continues to be unrecognised or misunderstood it is in some degree due to Ruskin's influence.

Ruskin's debt to the picturesque is seen in his fascination for ruination and weathering. But in 'that golden stain of time' he reserves praise for ageing due to the effects of use and weather and regrets the effects of industrialisation, which he believes to be dehumanising.[9] Extending the age-old affiliation of human misadventure with environmental retribution, he characterises industrial pollution as

5 Holmes, pp. xvi–xvii; Wordsworth, *A Description of the Scenery of the Lakes*, pp. 99–100.

6 Ruskin, *Modern Painters*, vol. 1, p. 180.

7 Ruskin, *Modern Painters*, vol. 4, pp. 27–47.

8 Ruskin, *Modern Painters*, vol. 4, pp.19, 23–26.

9 Ruskin, *The Seven Lamps of Architecture*, p. 177.

'the storm-cloud of the nineteenth century', which he associates with the spiritual abstinence of the modern world and his declining mental health.[10]

Soane avoided Ruskin's incessant moralising but the controlled climate he created at 12–14 Lincoln's Inn Fields denied the city's industries and weathers. In contrast, Turner allowed London's polluted air to infiltrate his studio through the broken roof. Rather than merely indicating his pessimism and old age, it is likely that Turner's treatment of his paintings was deliberate and necessary. Maybe he conceived the progressive decay and gradual ruination of a painting to be a means to convey the impression of a place in relation to time and weather. Subject to seasons and industries, the fusion of atmospheres and energies that defined early nineteenth-century London entered his work in pigments and pollution. Turner's subject, site and painting practice were perfectly aligned. Rather than a retreat to nature, Turner's romanticism fully acknowledged the complexity of his time, its climate and weather. Immersed in the hybridised atmospheres and energies that defined early nineteenth-century London, which nature and industry had together created, Turner offered an early indication of human-induced – anthropogenic – climate change.

Soane and Turner lived and worked barely a mile apart. But their attitudes to London's weather were distant. Soane created a clear division between a benign internal climate and a malign external one while Turner celebrated London's fog and smog in his dilapidated studio. Soane wished to control ruination while Turner accepted decay. Soane recognised the architectural potential of a climate while Turner acknowledged the weather as a significant authorial voice that complemented his own. To some extent, their differing professions determined their differing attitudes. Creating a comfortable environment, the architect has a responsibility to everyday use that need not concern the painter. But Soane and Turner also represent differing attitudes to architecture and authorship. There is a fundamental difference between an isolated interior in which the designer aims for complete control and a complex and inter-related environment in which the designer accepts other influences.

10 Ruskin, *The Brantwood Diary of John Ruskin*, p. 228; Ruskin, *The Storm-Cloud of the Nineteenth Century*, pp. 58–59.

NATURE AND INDUSTRY

The conceptual system that recognises three natures – mountains, fields and gardens – was begun in ancient Rome and established in the Renaissance. But the hybridised weather depicted by Turner paralleled a transformation in physical nature that we increasingly experience today. It is no longer possible to experience the first nature as an independent entity devoid of human intervention, while the second nature increasingly refers to infrastructure as well as agriculture, and the third is as likely to be concrete as much as clay. Their distinct characters are powerful conceptual tools but the three natures are interdependent and equally subject to human and natural influences.

THE WEATHER OF OUR HOUSES

Mies is regularly described as a leading modernist architect but his opinions frequently diverged from modernist orthodoxy. He dismissed functionalism and acknowledged the changeability of use, enjoyed the appearance of tectonic order more than its literal expression, promoted continuity as well as innovation, appreciated nature and prioritised spiritual needs. Modernist architecture is widely described as didactic. But citing Kent, Soane and Le Camus de Mézières, Tafuri offers an alternative modernism indebted to the 'relative value' and 'edifying play' of the picturesque.[11] The landscape that Tafuri identifies as the inspiration for modernism's 'ambiguous objects' was readily available to Mies due to the collaboration of Schinkel and Lenné on the Prussian royal estates at Potsdam in the early nineteenth century. The later development of the picturesque in German-speaking territories helps explain its conjunction with romanticism, which Soane shared to some extent. Rather than consistently advocating a particular philosophical position, Schinkel was informed by the evolving ideas of German nationalism, idealism and romanticism. Idealism's influence led German romanticism to emphasise the mind's ability to construct reality, placing less emphasis on the direct experience of wilder nature that fascinated English romanticism. Differentiating monuments, buildings and cities from plants, rivers and mountains, Schinkel describes architecture as 'complete in and of itself'.[12] But he remarks that architecture is like nature in that it develops according to a purpose: 'Architecture is the continuation of nature in her constructive activity. This activity is conducted through that natural product: Mankind.'[13] Influenced also by Alexander von Humboldt – a frequent visitor to the Court Gardener's House – Schinkel was concerned to promote the beneficial and poetic interdependence of the two worlds within the overriding natural order.

Baudelaire associated romanticism with the northern mist.[14] But the north and the south inspired Schinkel as much as his mentor in romantic classicism, Friedrich Gilly, and their successor, Mies. Indebted to the Court Gardener's House, the Barcelona Pavilion's allegiance to the picturesque, and also to romantic classicism, is evident in the dialogue it constructs between architecture, nature and perception.

11 Tafuri, *Theories and History of Architecture*, p. 82.

12 Schinkel, quoted in Bergdoll, 'The Nature of Mies's Space', p. 75.

13 Schinkel, quoted in Bergdoll, *Karl Friedrich Schinkel*, p. 208.

14 Baudelaire, 'What is Romanticism', p. 53.

The Pavilion is a creative stimulus to use precisely because it has no specific function and lacks many of the familiar environmental characteristics of a building, such as adequate heating and lighting. Rather than a conventional building, it can be occupied like a garden, in which uses are seasonal and the weather is always apparent.

The Farnsworth House does not subtly mediate between architecture and nature in the manner of the Court Gardener's House and Barcelona Pavilion; but neither does it keep them apart. The environmental conditions outside so temper and intrude on those inside that the relationship between architecture and nature is by no means visual alone. Within its vulnerable interior the full effects of weather and weathering are amplified and experienced, from the pleasant beauty of sunlight to the painful beauty of cold and condensation, from the majesty of thunder and lightning to the fearful flood when immediate danger overcomes the sublime. The Farnsworth House departed from romantic classicism, exemplifying instead the more fully romantic immersion in nature that is less familiar to German romanticism. Its vulnerability to anthropogenic climate change recalls the hybridised weather of nature and industry that Turner consciously engaged a century before. We do not know if such an immersion was Mies's intention. One response to this dilemma is to recognise the architect's debt to romantic classicism and speculate that his experience of the American landscape led him to a more extreme interaction between architecture and nature. Another is to focus less on the architect's intentions and more on the building's fate, recognising the weather's role in affirming the northern romantic tradition. Ambiguous because of the weather as much as the architect, the Farnsworth House is a hinge between the early modernist control of nature and the later modernist accommodation of nature, countering the technological bombast of the time.

SUBMITTING TO THE SEASONS

Many creative architects have looked to the past to imagine the future, studying an earlier architecture not to replicate it but to understand and transform it, revealing its relevance to the present. Kent admired Renaissance Italy, Soane looked to ancient Greece and Mies studied Schinkel. Countering the myth that modernism has no history, historians have resorted to different periods to give it a past. Associating a mild and misty climate with moderation and imagination, Pevsner identified the picturesque with a sensitivity to nature and place, 'liberalism and liberty', like others before him.[15] Aware of inter-war resistance to a new architecture,

15 Pevsner, 'The Genius of the Place', p. 232.

he saw the picturesque as a means to make modernism familiar to England. Critical of modernist disregard for cultural, social and geographic differences, Pevsner drew attention to the picturesque in order to question one modernism – international, mechanical and insensitive – in favour of another – local, emotive and environmentally aware. Identifying the picturesque with 'the modern revolution' as well as a later modernism, and associating the picturesque with England while affirming its wider relevance, he attempted a delicate balance of ideas.[16]

16 Pevsner, *The Englishness of English Art*, p. 183; Pevsner, 'The Genesis of the Picturesque', p. 139; Pevsner, 'Twentieth-Century Picturesque: An Answer to Basil Taylor's Broadcast', p. 229.

In 1955 Banham supported a new architectural movement, Brutalism, which he opposed to the picturesque and to Pevsner.[17] But the Smithsons also disappointed him. Like Pevsner, their fascination for the picturesque was a means to reassess and revise modernism. Rather than Banham's *tabula rasa* – a concern for technology and disposability that served a market-led economy – the Smithsons favoured the continuity of modernism with earlier centuries and opposed the banality and wastefulness of consumer society. In choosing a site and a name, retaining fragments, creating a 'half-building/half-ruin', allowing ivy to grow inside and out, and enjoying the weather, their approach was characteristic of the picturesque, in which design, construction and use are potentially interdependent and open-ended, as at Rousham and 12–14 Lincoln's Inn Fields.[18] Recalling the eighteenth century as a means to reconsider the twentieth century, and recognising no rupture between the past, present and future, Upper Lawn Pavilion is picturesque, modernist and Brutalist.

17 Banham, 'Revenge of the Picturesque', p. 267; Banham, 'The New Brutalism', p. 355.

18 Alison and Peter Smithson, 'Tisbury', p. 212.

Alison Smithson cites the Barcelona Pavilion and Farnsworth House as examples of environmentally sensitive '*light touch* inhabitation' in the tradition of Saint Jerome.[19] But Upper Lawn Pavilion was designed with weathering in mind, unlike Mies's designs. The Farnsworth House is immersed in nature – sometimes with delicacy, sometimes with violence – but we do not know if this was the architect's intention. At Upper Lawn Pavilion we can be certain that immersion was deliberate due to the architects' statements and gentle due to the mild climate, establishing a balance between architecture and weather. Submitting to the seasons to know them better, the Smithsons tested the assumption that some loss in environmental comfort is amply compensated by, and even necessary to, a more complete experience and understanding of nature.[20] Rather than celebrate the newly abundant consumer society, they accepted eighteenth-century levels of thermal comfort and energy consumption and continued the philosophy of 'make do and mend' that prevailed during war-time and post-war rationing. Affirming the urbanite's 'Virgilian dream' 'to build like a farmer', they created a simple and adaptable rustic machine.[21]Attuned to the environment and its limited resources, employing ad-hoc construction and arranged with objects of emotional more than financial value the

19 Alison Smithson, 'Saint Jerome', p. 225; Alison Smithson, 'Territory of the Pavilion', pp. 33–34.

20 Peter Smithson, in Alison and Peter Smithson, *Upper Lawn, Solar Pavilion Folly.*

21 Alison and Peter Smithson, *Without Rhetoric*, p. 14; Peter Smithson, *Conversations with Students,* p. 48.

Smithsons encouraged a poetic and pragmatic culture of repair and reuse that diminished consumption and waste.

FOG, GLARE AND GLOOM

Fehn and Lewerentz shared the Smithsons' concern for history, nature, context, and poetic and ethical construction, which opposed consumer society. But to understand the present they emphasised a different past. Lewerentz indicated some debt to the picturesque, which did not obviously concern Fehn although it is a precedent for the montage of gaps he created in the Nordic Pavilion. Their allegiance to romanticism was more obvious. In the early nineteenth century, nationalism and romanticism combined in German-speaking and Nordic countries, initially in opposition to French influence. Extending these traditions, national romanticism flourished across the arts in Germany and Scandinavia in the late nineteenth century and early twentieth century, which in each country was accompanied by nostalgia for an earlier era when it was most powerful. Rather than simply regressive, national romanticism was questioning and inventive. The romantic fascination for a dynamic interaction between a people and an environment was especially evident in Scandinavia due to the harsh climate, while the concern for primitive origins and the predominance of rural life affirmed the farmer as a poignant model rooted in nature and folklore.

Modernism spread throughout the Nordic countries between the two world wars but did not then take hold in Britain. Pevsner and the Smithsons drew attention to the picturesque in order to question one modernism in favour of another. From the start, Scandinavian modernism followed the second model, which Norberg-Schulz characterises as 'romantic modernism'.[22] Neither international nor revolutionary, Scandinavian modernism absorbed vernacular traditions and new developments alike, continuing national romanticism's concern for local building techniques and expressed construction.

22 Norberg-Schulz, *Nightlands*, p. 154.

The Nordic climate does not encourage submission to the seasons and gentle weathering in the manner of Upper Lawn Pavilion. The dialogue with nature remains, but rather than the benign encounter of the picturesque or romantic classicism it is confrontational as well as celebratory and closer to the romanticism expressed in nineteenth-century landscape paintings. As a painter as well as the architect of his studio, Turner exemplifies this tradition. So too does the Farnsworth House. But if we focus on stated intentions, its architectural equivalent is more often apparent in Scandinavia. According to Fehn, the Nordic light defines the region's architectural sensibility. While his inspiration was the fog, for Lewerentz it was the gloom. One has no shadow, the other is all shadow; but their effects are similar. Neither offers clarity. Rather, they result in ambiguity, which 'leads to romanticism', Fehn concludes.[23] For an architect concerned with the subtleties of daily life in a harsh climate, actual immersion in nature is not an option. Instead, Fehn and Lewerentz recognised weather's metaphorical potential, making the evocation of a weather condition the purpose of a building. Transferring the northern romantic mist to a milder climate, Fehn blurred architecture and nature to the extent that Nordic light is the Nordic Pavilion's principal material.

23 Fehn, in Lavalou, p. 85.

The weather also mattered to Fehn and Lewerentz because they identified the poetry of architecture in its construction. Reaffirming the romantic concern for in situ experience, they conceived construction as a means to define the genius of the place in the way that elements are made, brought together, and weather and decay during and after building. Evident in the picturesque and romanticism and continuing in picturesque and romantic modernism, the weather and weathering are means to acknowledge and calibrate time. In the fog, time stands largely still while the slow adjustment to the gloom is a journey back in time.[24] St Peter's is as archaic as its gloom. Rather than made *as new* the church was made *as old*. But the harsh light emanating from each window can be understood as modern as well as primitive, like the window's construction. Consequently, the breadth of time was apparent from the first, not only as the building aged.

24 Gregory, pp. 55–56.

SWEET GARDEN OF VANISHED PLEASURES

A recurring theme in architectural discourse states that the home is the origin and archetype of architecture, the manifestation of its most important attributes.[25] Defined by its separation from the external world, the home is assumed to be the most secure and stable of environments. This apparent stability may provide gratification but it can also, simultaneously, create anxiety because the home can never be safe enough and is not always what it seems. Unease generated within the home can be as disturbing as any external threat.

25 Vitruvius, pp. 38–39.

Jarman moved to Dungeness because a home there would be more vulnerable and thus more precious. He bought Prospect Cottage in spring 1986, when an explosion at the Chernobyl nuclear reactor cast a radioactive cloud across Europe, leading the UK government to publish *The Tolerability of Risk from Nuclear Power Stations* in the following year.[26] Prospect Cottage is not simply a primitive hut or rural retreat because the nuclear power station is ever present. Burke recognised

26 Health and Safety Executive, p. 26.

natural weather as sublime, while Turner acknowledged the sublime potential of the hybridised weather of nature and industry, which he allowed to enter his studio.[27] Dungeness's radioactive and electromagnetic weather is impervious to building thresholds. Reaffirming the romantic concern for immersive environments, Jarman chose to live next to a nuclear reactor, experiencing the sublime at home. At Dungeness, it is glaringly evident that the three natures and various weathers – natural, industrial, electromagnetic and radioactive among others – intermingle as one.

In December 1986 Jarman was identified as a carrier of the AIDS virus, accentuating his anger against society and increasing his sense of mortality.[28] The garden at Prospect Cottage marked his life from diagnosis to death. Like General Dormer at Rousham, Jarman's garden preoccupied his final years, fulfilling the temporal awareness that pervades the picturesque. So dependent on the weather and the seasons, the gardener knows that renewal and decay are necessary to one another. At Dungeness, due to the extreme weather, a building must be tended like a garden. As the home-owner identifies with the home, mental unease and bodily disease – real or imagined – are easily projected onto building fabric. Describing Prospect Cottage as 'more beautiful the older it becomes' Jarman saw himself in his house and garden, vulnerable to the weather, subject to the seasons.[29]

Keen to recognise his nation's history Jarman identified continuity between the past and the present. Affirming England's association with its landscape, the two garden traditions he most referred to are the picturesque garden and the cottage garden. Affirming the English Georgic tradition, Rousham enforces clear power relations between those who own the garden and those who work it. Jarman's obelisks, totems, tightly woven arrangement and meandering routes recall the picturesque, although the house is untypically at the centre. Confirming the legal requirement that no boundary delineation is permitted, the garden's edge is perceived rather than felt. The views look out as well as in but they are not framed and ordered as in the picturesque and the labour relations are those of the cottage garden. Growing fruit and vegetables to eat as well as flowers and shrubs to view, the cottage garden is decorative and practical. Pleasure and labour are combined; the owner is the designer and the gardener.

Since the Italian Renaissance, it is often assumed that a significant building is the creation of a single architect – who conceives at a remove from construction – because artistic, intellectual labour is associated with the individual. Although Kent discarded plans, learnt from an existing topography and garden, accepted on-site advice, and encouraged alternative journeys and interpretations, Rousham is

27 Burke, *Philosophical Enquiry*, pp. 39–40.

28 Peake, p. 378.

29 Jarman, *Derek Jarman's Garden*, p. 130.

attributed to one author. So too is Jarman's garden. But Dungeness reveals a condition that is widespread: there are always a number of architectural authors at work. At Prospect Cottage and its garden, authorship is multiplied and juxtaposed, not dissolved. Multiplied because, rather than a sole author, a number of authors are identified, such as the designer, builder, gardener, visitor, site and weather. Juxtaposed because – sometimes competing, sometimes affirming – each author may inform or deny the other, as in a feisty dialogue of individual voices and unexpected conclusions. As natural and man-made forces affect each other on a global and a local scale, agents as well as authors are at work. An author is an initiating force while an agent responds, translates and transforms. As an author may also be an agent, the result is a complex interweaving of authorship and agency in which architecture and weather are connected rather than opposed and the creation of architecture is shared and temporal.

THE METEOROLOGICAL PROJECT

The second nuclear reactor at Dungeness is projected to close in 2018. Financial and safety concerns led successive British governments to reject further nuclear power stations. But as a means to limit carbon emissions and reduce reliance on foreign energy supplies, new nuclear power stations are once again under consideration. The projected sites are highly susceptible to the rising seas of anthropogenic climate change, which has become the defining concern of meteorological science.

In principle, the roles of observer, theorist and forecaster have been fundamental to the meteorological profession since it was established in the early nineteenth century. In practice, the three roles were fully combined only in the twentieth century due to the initial research of the Bergen School and the later computational power of the Meteorological Project. However, the climate and weather have remained resistant to meteorology, in part because they are so complex and inconsistent, in part because they are culturally as well as scientifically defined.[30]

As an idea, 'nature' is a human construction that can be used to justify any modification or lead to reverence that hinders critical engagement.[31] But the places, species and phenomena that we include within 'nature' are real and not solely subject to our imagination and will. Just because we've named something does not mean that we have made it, or even understand it, whatever our influence on the natural world. Instead, the term 'coproduction' categorises nature–culture relations and the climates and weathers we inhabit.[32] As an idea, and the contemporary means to consider the relations between nature and culture, anthropogenic climate

30 Hulme, p. xxvii.

31 Refer to Morton, pp. 204–205

32 Rayner, p. 287.

change has allowed criticism to focus on the free-market economy and the isolationist policies of countries and corporations. Unlike the weather, which we can see and feel, we cannot directly experience climate because it is an idea aggregated over time. Climate always changes, whether by human agency or other means, but the term 'climate change' is sometimes used to imply that the current condition is an ideal that must be preserved. In arguing for the means to limit global warming, advocates of the current climate are not so far removed from other advocates of climate modification. Critics of global warming tend to affirm the tradition of the biblical flood, in which environmental catastrophe is the punishment for human failing, although few people propose a full-scale retreat from the benefits of modern society. The proposed scientific 'solutions' to anthropogenic climate change – large, monolithic and heavily funded – reaffirm a faith in technological progress that is consistent with the project of modernity, which began in the Renaissance, promoted scientific reason, led to industrialisation and has been the principal cause of anthropogenic climate change.[33] Such 'solutions' depend on General Circulation Models, which affirm the aspirations of meteorological science but cannot be guaranteed. If we assume that a GCM is true and respond with corrective measures that seem appropriate to our needs we may cause more harm than good, creating an ever more vicious circle. The dangers posed by anthropogenic climate change are real and need to be addressed. But in offering a subtle accommodation with the changing climate and weather, rather than resistance or rejection, the projects discussed in this book are compatible with a complex, creative and contextual engagement with climate change that is not solely driven by fear.[34] Cultural change is as inevitable as climate change. A causal link between climate and character is rare because numerous factors inform behaviour but we may consider with excitement as well as concern what will happen to northern romanticism once the mists subside.

33 Glover, pp. 22–23, 28–30, 86–88, 246–251.

34 Hulme, p. 363.

ON REFLECTION

Its supposed opposition to weather, which represents a physical and psychological threat, has often been used to define the limits of architecture. As David Sibley remarks: 'Nature has a long historical association with the other.'[35] In an early fifteenth-century demonstration of linear perspective, Brunelleschi depicted the square around the Baptistery in Florence. But rather than draw the sky he silvered part of a wooden panel so that it was seen in reflection, and a different sky was always present. Brunelleschi's demonstration seems to confirm the opinion that

35 Sibley, p. 26.

weather is outside architecture and outside architectural representation. But an alternative interpretation indicates the continuing importance of weather to architecture. First, because the dialogue between architecture and weather is a means to reconsider nature–culture relations. Second, because the weather locates architecture in a specific place, combating globalisation. Third, because attention to the changing climates and seasons encourages buildings that coexist with their immediate and wider environments. Fourth, because architecture is not just a mirror to the weather but can also be like the weather in all its subtle variation, both in the ways it is perceived and in its formal, spatial and material conditions. Fifth, because the weather makes architecture more ambiguous, unpredictable and open to varied interpretation, questioning established uses. Sixth, because the effects of weather on architecture are means to recognise, represent and reconsider time. Seventh, because a building is therefore understood not as a perfect, finite object but as provisional and open to change during its conception, construction, use and decay. Eighth, because the weather is a significant authorial voice over which architects have little control, tempering their claims to sole authorship.

In *Actions of Architecture,* 2003, I categorise users as passive, reactive or creative.[36] With a role as important in the formulation of architecture as that of the architect, the creative user either produces a new space or gives unexpected meanings and uses to an existing space. Architecture is usually experienced habitually, when it may not be the focus of attention. But even the familiar experience of architecture is not necessarily passive. Instead, as empiricism made evident, it can be a questioning intelligence acquired through continuing experience. Rather than necessarily a deviation from habit, creative use can instead establish, affirm or develop a habit that is itself creative. All buildings change, often slowly and subtly. But an architecture that is ever-changing like the weather will require constant re-evaluation, encouraging particularly questioning and creative relations between objects, spaces and users at varied scales and locations.

36 Hill, *Actions of Architecture*, pp. 88–89.

Informed by the weather signs tradition of Virgil's *Georgics*, architecture's relations with the weather were of interest to Renaissance architects and painters. Leonardo da Vinci wonderfully expressed his fascination for the weather in the title and subject matter of his painting *A Town Over-whelmed by a Deluge*, c.1515. He credited Sandro Botticelli for noticing that 'various inventions are to be seen' in a building stain and identified similar potential in weather: 'I have in the past seen in clouds and walls stains which have inspired me to beautiful inventions of many things.'[37] However, attention to the effects of weather and weathering is an architectural tradition principally developed from the picturesque, sublime and romanticism due to the combined fascination for subjectivity and the natural world

37 Da Vinci, pp. 201, 222.

in the eighteenth century, which reconfigured the relations between nature and culture and encouraged an expanded conception of architectural authorship that attributed creativity widely and to varied protagonists. Emphasising that a critical understanding of the past can be a catalyst to creativity, this tradition acquired renewed relevance in the mid-twentieth century as a means to reassess and revise modernism, while today it is increasingly relevant due to anthropogenic climate change.

Today's weather is especially complex and hybridised. As earlier buildings were porous, the weather was always inside as well as outside them. While means to exclude wind and rain have expanded, physical barriers – such as doors and walls – are especially permeable to new weather conditions such as electromagnetic pollution. Increasingly, architecture and weather are two inter-related elements of a complex system. Defining nature–culture relations, the term 'coproduction' applies to architecture as well as the weather. Just as the intermingling of natural and human forces creates the contemporary climate and weather, a building results from the relations between nature and culture that arise during its conception, construction and use. As architecture and the weather are each a product of nature–culture relations, they inform, affect and alter each other in a complex developmental process that is never one way. Critical awareness of the weather, its causes and effects, is a valuable basis for design because, in all stages of building, it recognises architecture's dependence on its immediate and wider environments.

As a metaphor, the weather is a means to understand time. But weathering is not necessarily equivalent to decay. It can be protective, as in the rust coating on Cor-ten steel, and stimulating, drawing attention to the transience of life and the possibility and potential of change.[38] In writing a history of architecture as a history of weather, my first purpose was to emphasise that environmental awareness is central to the architectural imagination while also recognising the weather as an architectural author in creative dialogue with the designer and user. In English, weather and time are two separate words. But in some languages their connection is explicit. For example, in French *temps* is both time and weather; while in Greek *kairos* is the weather and qualitative, momentary time in contrast to *chronos*, which is quantitative, sequential time. As my research progressed from Dormer, to Soane, to Jarman, focusing on subjective experience and the natural world, I increasingly realised that *Weather Architecture* is a story of time.

> Busie old foole, unruly Sunne,
> Why dost thou thus,
> Through windowes, and through curtaines call on us?[39]

38 Developed in the 1950s by the US Steel Corporation, Cor-ten is also known as 'weathering steel'. Refer to Leatherbarrow and Mostafavi, pp. 5, 104.

39 As quoted in Jarman, *Derek Jarman's Garden*, p. 117.

bibliography

Ackerman, James S. *Palladio*. Harmondsworth: Penguin, 1966.

Addison, Joseph. 'From *The Spectator* (21, 23 and 25 June 1712)'. In Mallgrave, pp. 234–239.

Addison, Joseph. 'From *The Spectator* (26 June 1712)'. In Mallgrave, pp. 253–256.

Addison, Joseph. *Selections from Addison's Papers contributed to The Spectator*. Ed. Thomas Arnold. Oxford: Clarendon Press, 1875.

Ahlin, Janne. 'Sigurd Lewerentz'. In Flora, Giardiello and Postiglione, *Sigurd Lewerentz*, pp. 378–381.

Ahlin, Janne. *Sigurd Lewerentz, Architect*. Cambridge, MA, and London: MIT Press, 1987. Originally published in Swedish in 1985.

Alberti, Leon Battista. *On the Art of Building in Ten Books*. Trans. Joseph Rykwert, Neil Leach and Robert Tavernor. Cambridge, MA, and London: MIT Press, 1988. Written around 1450 and published in 1485, its original title was *De re aedificatoria*. James, or Giacomo, Leoni first translated it into English as *Ten Books on Architecture* in 1726.

Albrecht, Donald. *The Work of Charles and Ray Eames: A Legacy of Invention*. New York: Harry N. Abrams, 1997.

Allison, Peter. 'Upper Lawn: The Invisible Restoration. A Conversation with Sergison Bates'. *2G*, no. 34, 2005, pp. 92–105.

Anderson, Stanford. 'The Fiction of Function'. *Assemblage*, no. 2, February 1987, pp. 19–31.

Andrews, Malcolm. *Landscape in Western Art*. Oxford: Oxford University Press, 1999.

Andrews, Malcolm. *The Search for the Picturesque: Landscape Aesthetics and Tourism in Britain, 1760–1800*. Aldershot: Scholar Press, 1989.

Andrews, Richard, ed. *James Turrell: Sensing Space*. Seattle: Henry Gallery, 1992.

Andrews, Richard and Chris Bruce. '1992 Interview with James Turrell'. In Andrews, *James Turrell: Sensing Space*, pp. 47–51.

Anstey, Tim, Katja Grillner and Rolf Hughes, eds. *Architecture and Authorship*. London: Black Dog Publishing, 2007.

Aristotle. *Meteorologica*. Trans. H.D.P. Lee. Cambridge, MA: Harvard University Press, 1952. First written *c.*350 BC.

Arrhenius, Svante. 'On the Influence of Carbonic Acid in the Air upon the Temperature of the Ground'. *The London, Edinburgh and Dublin Philosophical Magazine and Journal of Science*, April 1896, pp. 237–276.

Aspray, William. *John von Neumann and the Origins of Modern Computing*. Cambridge, Mass: MIT Press, 1990.

Ayres, Philip. 'Introduction'. In Shaftesbury, *Characteristicks*, pp. xiii–xxxviii.

Bacon, Francis. *Sylva Sylvarum: or A Natural History, in Ten Centuries*. London: Thomas Lee, 1676. First published in 1627.

Ballantyne, Andrew. *Architecture, Landscape and Liberty: Richard Payne Knight and the Picturesque*. Cambridge: Cambridge University Press, 1997.

Banham, Reyner. *The Architecture of the Well-tempered Environment*. Chicago: University of Chicago Press, 1984.

Banham, Reyner. *The New Brutalism: Ethic or Aesthetic*. London: Architectural Press, 1966.

Banham, Reyner. 'The New Brutalism'. *The Architectural Review*, vol. 118, no. 708, December 1955, pp. 355–361.

Banham, Reyner. 'Revenge of the Picturesque: English Architectural Polemics, 1945–1965'. In Summerson, *Concerning Architecture*, pp. 265–273.

Banham, Reyner. *Theory and Design in the First Machine Age*. London: The Architectural Press, 1960.

Banham, Reyner. 'This is Tomorrow'. *The Architectural Review*, vol. 120, no. 716, September 1956, pp. 186–188.

Baridon, Michel. 'Ruins as a Mental Construct'. *Journal of Garden History*, vol. 5, no. 1, January–March 1985, pp. 84–96.

Barrell, John. *The Dark Side of the Landscape: The Rural Poor in English Painting 1730–1840*. Cambridge: Cambridge University Press, 1980.

Barthes, Roland. *Mythologies*. Trans. Annette Lavers. London: Paladin, 1973.

Barthes, Roland. 'The New Citroën'. In Barthes, *Mythologies*, pp. 88–90.

Barthes, Roland. *The Pleasure of the Text*. Trans. Richard Miller. New York: Hill and Wang, 1979.

Bastide, Jean-François de. *The Little House: An Architectural Seduction*. Trans. Rodolphe el-Khoury. New York: Princeton Architectural Press, 1996.

Bate, Jonathan. 'Living with the Weather'. *Studies in Romanticism*, vol. 35, Fall 1996, pp. 431–447.

Bate, Jonathan. *Romantic Ecology: Wordsworth and the Environmental Tradition*. London and New York: Routledge, 1991.

Batey, Mavis. 'Introduction', in Müller, pp. 178–180.

Batey, Mavis. 'The Way to View Rousham by Kent's Gardener'. *Garden History*, vol. 11, no. 2, Autumn 1983, pp. 125–132.

Baudelaire, Charles. *Selected Writings on Art and Artists*. Trans. P.E. Charvet. Harmondsworth: Penguin, 1972.

Baudelaire, Charles. 'What is Romanticism'. In Baudelaire, *Selected Writings*, pp. 52–54.

Beckford, William. *An Arabian Tale, from an Unpublished Manuscript with Notes Critical and Explanatory. (Vathek).* Trans. Samuel Henley. London: J. Johnson, 1786. First published without Beckford being credited as the author.

Bending, Stephen. 'Horace Walpole and Eighteenth-Century Garden History'. *Journal of the Warburg and Courtauld Institutes*, vol. 57, 1994, pp. 209–226.

Bending, Stephen. 'Re-reading the Eighteenth-Century Landscape Garden', *Huntingdon Library Quarterly*, vol. 55, 1992, pp. 379–399.

Benjamin, Andrew, ed. *The Lyotard Reader*. Oxford: Basil Blackwell, 1989.

Benjamin, Walter. *The Arcades Project*. Ed. Rolf Tiedemann, trans. Howard Eiland and Kevin McLaughlin. Cambridge and London: Belknap Press of Harvard University Press, 1999.

Benjamin, Walter. 'The Author as Producer'. In Benjamin, *Reflections*, pp. 220–238.

Benjamin, Walter. *Illuminations: Essays and Reflections*. Ed. Hannah Arendt, trans. Harry Zohn. New York: Schocken Books, 1969.

Benjamin, Walter. *The Origin of German Tragic Drama*. Trans. John Osborne. London: New Left Books, 1977. Completed in 1928.

Benjamin, Walter. 'Paris, Capital of the Nineteenth Century'. In Benjamin, *Reflections*, pp. 146–162.

Benjamin, Walter. *Reflections: Essays, Aphorisms, Autobiographical Writings*. Ed. Peter Demetz, trans. Edmund Jephcott. New York: Schocken Books, 1978.

Benjamin, Walter. 'The Work of Art in the Age of Mechanical Production'. In Benjamin, *Illuminations*, pp. 217–252. First published in 1936.

Bergdoll, Barry. *Karl Friedrich Schinkel: An Architecture for Prussia*. New York: Rizzoli, 1994.

Bergdoll, Barry. 'Mies and Schinkel: Nature and Consciousness in the Modern House'. In Peik, pp. 125–135.

Bergdoll, Barry. 'The Nature of Mies's Space'. In Riley and Bergdoll, pp. 67–105.

Bergdoll, Barry, and Werner Oechslin, eds. *Fragments: Architecture and the Unfinished. Essays Presented to Robin Middleton*. London: Thames & Hudson, 2006.

Bermingham, Ann. *Landscape and Ideology: The English Rustic Tradition 1740–1860*. London: Thames & Hudson, 1987.

Bermingham, Ann. 'The Picturesque and Ready-to-wear Femininity'. In Copley and Garside, *The Politics of the Picturesque*, pp. 81–113.

Bhatia, Neeraj. 'The Post-Junkspace Globe'. In Mayer H. and Bhatia, pp. 236–251.

Bindman, David. 'Schinkel and Britain in 1826'. In Schinkel, *'The English Journey': Journal of a Visit to France and Britain in 1826*, pp. 12–20.

Birch, Dinah. *Ruskin on Turner*. London: Cassell, 1990.

Birksted, Jan. 'The Prospect at Dungeness: Derek Jarman's Garden'. In Birksted, *Relating Architecture to Landscape*, pp. 237–252.

Birksted, Jan, ed. *Relating Architecture to Landscape*. London: E & FN Spon, 1999.

Blake, Peter. 'A Conversation with Mies'. In Miller, *Four Great Makers of Modern Architecture*, pp. 93–104.

Blaser, Werner. *Mies van der Rohe: The Art of Structure.* New York: Whitney Library of Design, 1994. First published in 1965.

Blaser, Werner. *Mies van der Rohe, Farnsworth House: Weekend House/ Wochendenhaus*. Trans. Katja Steiner and Bruce Almberg. Basel, Boston and Berlin: Birkhäuser, 1999.

Blundell-Jones, Peter. *Modern Architecture Through Case Studies*. Oxford: Architectural Press, 2002.

Blundell-Jones, Peter. 'Sigurd Lewerentz, St Peter's Church, Klippan, Sweden, 1963–6'. In Blundell-Jones, *Modern Architecture Through Case Studies*, pp. 215–228.

Boas, Frank. *The Mind of Primitive Man*. New York: Free Press and London: Collier Macmillan, 1965. First published in 1911.

Bodansky, David. *Nuclear Energy: Principles, Practices and Prospects*. Woodbury, NY: American Institute of Physics, 1996.

Boia, Lucian. *The Weather in the Imagination*. London: Reaktion, 2005.

Bois, Yves-Alain. 'A Picturesque Stroll around Clara-Clara'. Trans. John Shepley. *October*, no. 29, Summer 1984, pp. 33–62.

Börsch-Supan, Helmut. 'Schinkel the Artist'. In Snodin, pp. 9–15.

Boullée, Étienne-Louis. 'From *Architecture, Essay on Art*'. In Mallgrave, pp. 210–215.

Bowen, Margarita. *Empiricism and Geographical Thought: From Francis Bacon to Alexander von Humboldt*. Cambridge: Cambridge University Press, 1981.

Boyarsky, Alvin, and Peter Salter. 'Fragments of a Conversation'. In Salter, *TS: Intuition & Process*, pp. 4–11.

Brassaï. *The Artists of My Life*. New York: Viking Press, 1982.

Breugmann, Robert. 'Central Heating and Forced Ventilation: Origins and Effects on Architectural Design'. *Journal of the Society of Architectural Historians*, vol. 37, no. 3, October 1978, pp. 143–160.

Brewer, John. *The Pleasures of the Imagination: English Culture in the Eighteenth Century*. New York: Farrar Straus Giroux, 1997.

Brimblecombe, Peter. *The Big Smoke: A History of Air Pollution in London Since Medieval Times*. London and New York: Routledge, 1988.

Brimblecombe, Peter. 'Interest in Air Pollution Among the Early Fellows of the Royal Society'. *Notes and Records of the Royal Society of London*, vol. 32, no. 2, March 1978, pp. 123–129.

Britton, John. *The Union of Architecture, Sculpture and Painting; Exemplified by a Series of Illustrations, with Descriptive Accounts of the House and Galleries of John Soane*. London, privately printed, 1827. Held in Sir John Soane's Museum, London.

Bronkman, H.A.N. 'Fonthill Abbey'. *The Architectural Review*, vol. 95, no. 570, June 1944, pp. 149–157.

Brown, David Blayney. *Romanticism*. London and New York: Phaidon, 2001.

Brown, John Croumbie, ed., trans. *French Forest Ordinance of 1669*. Edinburgh: Oliver and Boyd; London: Simpkin, Marshall and Co., 1883.

Bryson, Norman, ed. *Calligram: Essays in New Art History From France*. Cambridge: Cambridge University Press, 1988.

Bürger, Peter. *Theory of the Avant-Garde*. Trans. Michael Shaw. Manchester: Manchester University Press, 1985.

Burke, Edmund. *A Philosophical Enquiry into the Origin of our Ideas of the Sublime and Beautiful*. Ed. J.T. Boulton. London: Routledge and Kegan Paul, 1958. First published in 1757.

Butler, Marilyn. 'Romanticism in England'. In Porter and Teich, eds. *Romanticism in National Context*, pp. 37–67.

Callendar, Guy Stewart. 'The Artificial Production of Carbon Dioxide and its Influence on Temperature'. *Quarterly Journal of the Royal Meteorological Society*, no. 64, 1938, pp. 223–240.

Calvino, Italo. *Six Memos for the Next Millennium: The Charles Eliot Norton Lectures 1985–86*. Trans. Patrick Creagh. London: Penguin, 2009.

Campbell, Colen. *Vitruvius Britannicus, or the British Architect*. New York: Benjamin Blom, 1970. First published in three volumes between 1715 and 1725.

Cantor, Geoffrey, David Gooding and Frank A.J.L James. *Michael Faraday*. Atlantic Heights, NJ: Humanities Press, 1996.

Carpo, Mario. *Architecture in the Age of Printing: Orality, Typography and Printed Images in the History of Architectural Theory*. Trans. Sarah Benson. Cambridge, MA, and London: MIT Press, 2001.

Carson, Rachel. *Silent Spring*. Boston: Houghton Mifflin, 1987. First published in 1962.

Carter, Philip. *Men and the Emergence of Polite Society, Britain 1660–1800*. Harlow: Pearson, 2001.

Carter, Rand. 'Gartenreich Potsdam. Schinkel's, Persius's and Lenné's Summer Retreats for the Prussian Princes'. In Peik, pp. 71–81.

Casson, Hugh. 'Art by Accident: The Aesthetics of Camouflage'. *The Architectural Review*, vol. 96, no. 573, September 1944, pp. 63–68.

Casson, Hugh. 'Ruins for Remembrance'. In Casson, Colvin, and Groag, pp. 5–22.

Casson, Hugh, Brenda Colvin, and Jacques Groag. *Bombed Churches as War Memorials*. Cheam: Architectural Press, 1945.

Castell, Robert. *The Villas of the Ancients Illustrated*. London: Robert Castell, 1728.

Cereghini, Elisabetta. 'The Italian Origins of Rousham'. In Mosser and Teyssot, pp. 320–322.

Chambers, Douglas. *The Planters of the English Landscape Garden: Botany, Trees and the Georgics*. New Haven and London: Yale University Press, 1993.

Charney Report, The. *Carbon Dioxide and Climate: A Scientific Assessment*. Washington DC: National Academy of Sciences, 1979.

Christianson, Gale E. *Greenhouse: The 200-Year Story of Global Warming*. London: Constable, 1999.

Claridge, John. *The Shepherd of Banbury's Rules To Judge of the Changes of the Weather, Grounded on Forty Years Experience*. London: W. Bickerton, 1744.

Cofaigh, Eoin O., John A. Olley and J. Owen Lewis. *The Climatic Dwelling: An Introduction to Climate-Responsive Residential Architecture*. London: James and James, 1996.

Coffin, David. 'The Elysian Fields of Rousham'. *Proceedings of the American Philosophical Society*, no. 130, 1986, pp. 406–423.

Coleridge, Samuel Taylor. *Biographia Literaria*. Ed. Nigel Leask. London: J.M. Dent and Sons Ltd., 1997. First published in 1817.

Collins, Keith. 'Preface'. In Jarman, *Derek Jarman's Garden*, p. 5.

Collins, Peter. *Changing Ideals of Modern Architecture, 1750–1950*. London: Faber and Faber, 1965.

Colomina, Beatriz. ed., *Architectureproduction*. New York, Princeton Architectural Press, 1988.

Colomina, Beatriz. 'Reflections on the Eames House'. In Albrecht, pp. 127–149.

Colomina, Beatriz. 'Unbreathed Air 1956'. In Van den Heuvel and Risselada, pp. 31–49.

Colonna, Francesco. *Hypnerotomachia Poliphili: The Strife of Love in a Dream*. Trans. Joscelyn Godwin. London: Thames & Hudson, 1999. First published in 1499.

Colquohoun, Alan. 'Twentieth Century Picturesque: Letter to the Editors'. *The Architectural Review*, vol. 116, no. 691, July 1954, p. 2.

Constant, Caroline. 'The Barcelona Pavilion as Landscape Garden: Modernity and the Picturesque'. *AA Files*, no. 20, Autumn 1990, pp. 46–54.

Constant, Caroline. *The Woodland Cemetery: Toward a Spiritual Landscape, Erik Gunnar Asplund and Sigurd Lewerentz 1915-61*. Stockholm: Byggförlaget, 1994.

Cook, Peter. 'Regarding the Smithsons'. *The Architectural Review*, vol. 162, no. 1025, July 1982, pp. 36–43.

Copley, Stephen. 'William Gilpin and the Black-lead Mine'. In Copley and Garside, *The Politics of the Picturesque*, pp. 42–61.

Copley, Stephen, and Peter Garside. 'Introduction'. In Copley and Garside, *The Politics of the Picturesque*, pp. 1–12.

Copley, Stephen, and Peter Garside, eds. *The Politics of the Picturesque: Literature, Landscape and Aesthetics Since 1770*. Cambridge; Cambridge University Press, 1994.

Cornforth, John. 'The Genesis and Creation of a Great Interior'. In Moore, pp. 29–40.

Cotton, William R., and Roger A. Pielke Sr. *Human Impact on Weather and Climate*. Cambridge: Cambridge University Press, 2007, 2nd edition.

Cottrell, Alan. *How Safe is Nuclear Energy?* London: Heinemann Educational Books, 1981.

Cottrell Dormer, Frances Elizabeth. 'Account of Rousham Oxfordshire and of Some Persons and Places Connected With It'. Unpublished manuscript, 1902. Held in the Bodleian Library, Oxford.

Cowan, Brian. 'Reasonable Ecstasies: Shaftesbury and the Languages of Libertinism'. *Journal of British Studies*, vol. 37, no. 2, April 1998, pp. 111–138.

Craddock, Nigel. 'Sir John Soane and the Luminous Environment'. MPhil dissertation, Department of Architecture, University of Cambridge, unpublished, 1995.

Crary, Jonathan. *Techniques of the Observer: On Vision and Modernity in the Nineteenth Century*. Cambridge, MA, and London: MIT Press, 1990.

Crewe, Maurice. 'The Fathers of Scientific Meteorology – Boyle, Wren, Hooke and Halley: Part 2'. *Weather*, vol. 58, no. 4, April, 2003, pp. 135–139.

Curry, Patrick. *Prophecy and Power: Astrology in Early Modern England*. Cambridge: Polity Press, 1989.

Dal Co, Francesco. 'Between Earth and Sea: The Architecture of Sverre Fehn'. In Norberg-Schulz and Postiglione, pp. 7–18.

Damisch, Hubert. *A Theory of /Cloud/ Toward a Theory of Painting*. Stanford: Stanford University Press, 2002. First published in 1972.

Daniels, Stephen, and Charles Watkins. 'Picturesque Landscaping and Estate Management: Uvedale Price and Nathaniel Kent at Foxley'. In Copley and Garside, *The Politics of the Picturesque*, pp. 13–41.

Darley, Gillian. *John Soane: An Accidental Romantic*. New Haven and London: Yale University Press, 1999.

Darwin, Charles. *The Origin of Species*. Oxford: Oxford University Press, 1996. First published in 1859.

Davidson, Peter. *The Idea of North*. London: Reaktion, 2005.

Davies, Maurice. *Turner as Professor: The Artist and Linear Perspective*. London: Tate Gallery, 1992.

Davies, Norman. *A History of Europe*. Oxford: Oxford University Press, 1996.

Da Vinci, Leonardo. *Leonardo on Painting: An Anthology of Writings by Leonardo da Vinci*. Ed. Martin Kemp, trans. Martin Kemp and Margaret Walker. New Haven and London: Yale University Press, 1989.

Day, Aidan, *Romanticism*. London: Routledge, 1995.

Dean, Ptolemy. *Sir John Soane and London*. Aldershot: Lund Humphries, 2006.

De Bolla, Peter. *The Education of the Eye: Painting, Landscape, and Architecture in Eighteenth-Century Britain*. Stanford: Stanford University Press, 2003.

Defoe, Daniel. *An Historical Narrative of the Great and Tremendous Storm, Which Happened on Nov. 26th, 1703*. London: W. Nicoll, 1769. First published in 1704.

De Man, Paul. *The Rhetoric of Romanticism*. New York: Columbia University Press, 1984.

Derham, William. 'A Letter for the Reverend Mr William Derham, F.R.S. Containing his Observations Concerning the Late Storm'. *Philosophical Transactions*, 1704–1705, vol. 24, no. 289, pp. 1530–1534.

Descartes, René. *Discourse on Method, Optics, Geometry and Meteorology*. Trans. Paul Olscamp. Indianopolis: Hackett, 2001. *Discourse on Method* was first published in 1637 as an introduction to the three scientific treatises.

Descartes, René. *Meditations on First Philosophy*. Ed. Stanley Tweyman, trans. Elizabeth S. Haldane and G.R.T. Ross. London and New York: Routledge, 1993. First published as *Meditationes de Prima Philosophia* in 1641.

De Zurko, Edward. *Origins of Functionalist Theory*. New York: Columbia University Press, 1957.

Dickens, Charles. *Bleak House*. Ed. Stephen Gill. Oxford and New York: Oxford University Press, 1996. First published in nineteen instalments between 1852 and 1853.

Di Palma, Vittoria. 'Blurs, Blots and Clouds: Architecture and the Dissolution of the Surface'. *AA Files*, no. 54, Summer 2006, pp. 24–35.

Dobell, Clifford. *Antony van Leeuwenhoek and his 'Little Animals'*. London: John Bale, Sons and Danielsson, 1932.

Dodds, George. *Building Desire: On the Barcelona Pavilion*. London and New York: Routledge, 2005.

Dorey, Helen. 'Crude Hints'. In Woodward, *Visions of Ruin*, pp. 53–78.

Dorey, Helen. *John Soane & J.M.W. Turner: Illuminating a Friendship*. London: Sir John Soane's Museum, 2007.

Dorey, Helen. 'Sir John Soane's Courtyard Gardens at Lincoln's Inn Fields'. *The London Gardener or The Gardener's Intelligencer*, 1999–2000, vol. 5, pp. 14–21.

Drexler, Arthur. *The Architecture of Japan*. New York: Museum of Modern Art, 1966.

Drexler, Arthur. *Ludwig Mies van der Rohe*. New York: George Braziller, 1960.

Driscoll, Lawrence. '"The Rose Revived": Derek Jarman and the British Tradition'. In Lippard, *By Angels Driven*, pp. 65–83.

Du Prey, Pierre de la Ruffinière. *John Soane: The Making of an Architect.* Chicago: University of Chicago Press, 1982.

Dunne, Anthony. *Hertzian Tales: Electronic Products, Aesthetic Experience and Critical Design*. London: Royal College of Art, 1999.

Dunne, Anthony, and Fiona Raby. *Design Noir: The Secret Life of Electronic Objects*. London: August and Basel: Birkäuser, 2001.

Dunne, Anthony, and Fiona Raby. 'Notopia: Leaky Products / Urban Interfaces'. In Hill, *Architecture – the Subject is Matter*, pp. 91–106.

Dunster, David, ed. *John Soane*. London: Academy Editions and New York: St Martin's Press, 1983.

Edleston, R.S. '*Amphydasis betularia*', *Entomologist*, 1864–1865, no. 2, p. 150.

Edwards, Sebastian, Andrew Moore and Chloë Archer. 'The Catalogue' In Moore, pp. 82–150.

Eisenman, Peter. 'Introduction'. In Johnson, *Writings, Philip Johnson*, pp. 10–25.

Etlin, Richard A. 'Landscapes of Eternity: Funerary Architecture and the Cemetery, 1793–1881', *Oppositions*, vol. 8, 1977.

Evans, Robin. 'Figures, Doors and Passages'. In Evans, *Translations*, pp. 55–92.

Evans, Robin. 'Rookeries and Model Dwellings: English Housing Reform and the Moralities of Private Space'. In Evans, *Translations*, pp. 93–117.

Evans, Robin. 'Mies van der Rohe's Paradoxical Symmetries'. In Evans, *Translations*, pp. 233–277.

Evans, Robin. *The Projective Cast: Architecture and its Three Geometries*. Cambridge, MA: MIT Press, 1995.

Evans, Robin. *Translations from Drawing to Building and Other Essays*. London: Architectural Association, 1997.

Evelyn, John. *Fumifugium: Or, The Inconvenience of the Aer, and Smoake of London Dissipated*. Ed. Samuel Pegge. London: B. White, 1772. First published in 1661, with a slightly different title.

Evelyn, John. *Sylva, or A Discourse of Forest-Trees, and the Propagation of Timber in His Majesties Dominions*. London: Royal Society, 1664.

Fanning, Christopher. 'On Sterne's Page: Spatial Layout, Spatial Form, and Social Spaces in *Tristram Shandy*'. *Eighteenth-Century Fiction*, vol. 10, no. 4, July 1998, pp. 429–450.

Farnsworth, Edith. 'Memoirs'. Farnsworth Collection, Newberry Library, Chicago. Unpublished manuscript in three notebooks.

Fehn, Sverre. 'An Architectural Autobiography'. In Norberg-Schulz and Postiglione, pp. 244–247. First published in *The Poetry of the Straight Line: Five Masters of the North*, Helsinki: Museum of Finnish Architecture, 1992.

Fehn, Sverre. 'Has a Doll Life?'. In Norberg-Schulz and Postiglione, pp. 243–244. First published in *Perspecta*, 24, 1988.

Fehn, Sverre. 'How Our Dimensions Are Born'. In Norberg-Schulz and Postiglione, p. 247.

Fehn, Sverre. 'The Primitive Architecture of Morocco'. In Norberg-Schulz and Postiglione, pp. 242–243.

Fehn, Sverre. *The Pritzker Architecture Prize, 1997*. Los Angeles: The Hyatt Foundation, 1997.

Field, Ophelia. *The Kit-Cat Club*. London: Harper Perennial, 2009.

Filarete. *Treatise on Architecture: being the Treatise by Antonio di Piero Averlino, known as Filarete*. Trans John R. Spencer, 2 vols., New Haven and London: Yale University Press, 1965. Prepared between 1461 and 1465.

Finberg, A.J. *A Complete Inventory of the Drawings of the Turner Bequest: with which are included the twenty-three drawings bequeathed by Mr Henry Vaughan. Arranged chronologically,* 2 vols. London: Stationery Office, 1909.

Finberg, A.J. *The Life of J.M.W. Turner, R.A.* Oxford: Clarendon Press, 1961. First published in 1939.

Fisher, Nigel. *Harold Macmillan*. London: Weidenfeld and Nicolson, 1982.

Fitch, Raymond E. *The Poison Sky: Myth and Apocalypse in Ruskin*. Athens, Ohio, and London: Ohio University Press, 1982.

Fjeld, Per Olaf. *Sverre Fehn: The Thought of Construction*. New York: Rizzoli, 1983.

Fleming, James Rodger. *Historical Perspectives on Climate Change*. New York and Oxford: Oxford University Press, 1998.

Fletcher, Banister. *A History of Architecture on the Comparative Method*. London: B.T. Batsford, 1924, 7th edition.

Flora, Nicola, Paolo Giardiello and Gennaro Postiglione. 'Journey to Italy'. In Flora, Giardiello and Postiglione, *Sigurd Lewerentz 1885–1875*, pp. 35–43.

Flora, Nicola, Paolo Giardiello and Gennaro Postiglione, eds. *Sigurd Lewerentz 1885–1875*, Milan: Electa, 2002.

Flusser, Vilém. *The Shape of Things: A Philosophy of Design*. London: Reaktion, 1999.

Forty, Adrian. *Words and Buildings: A Vocabulary of Modern Architecture*. London: Thames & Hudson, 2000.

Foucault, Michel. *The Foucault Reader*. Ed. Paul Rabinow. London: Penguin, 1984.

Foucault, Michel. 'On the Genealogy of Ethics: An Overview of Work in Progress'. In Foucault, *The Foucault Reader*, pp. 340–372.

Fourier, Jean Baptiste Joseph. *The Analytical Theory of Heat*. Trans. Alexander Freeman. Cambridge, 1878. First published as *Théorie analytique de la chaleur* in 1822.

Fourier, Jean Baptiste Joseph. 'Remarques générales sur la températures du globe terrestre et des espaces planétaires'. *Annales de chimie et de la physique*, 1824, 2nd ser., no. 27, pp. 136–167.

Fourier, Jean Baptiste Joseph. 'Théorie de la chaleur' (Extrait). *Annales de chimie et de la physique*, 1816, 2nd ser., no. 3, pp. 350–376.

Fraser, Murray, with Joe Kerr. *Architecture and the 'Special Relationship': The American Influence on Post-War British Architecture*. London and New York: Routledge, 2007.

Freud, Sigmund. *The Standard Edition of the Complete Psychological Works of Sigmund Freud, Vol. 17*. Ed. James Strachey. Toronto: Clarke Irwin, 1955.

Freud, Sigmund. 'The "Uncanny"'. In Freud. *The Standard Edition*, pp. 217–252. Trans. Alix Strachey. First published in 1919.

Friedman, Alice T. *Women and the Making of the Modern House: A Social and Architectural History*. New York: Harry N. Abrams, 1998.

Furján, Helene. 'The Specular Spectacle of the House of the Collector'. *Assemblage*, no. 34, December 1997, pp. 56–91.

Gage, John, ed. *Collected Correspondence of J.M.W. Turner*. Oxford: Clarendon Press. 1980.

Gage, John. *Colour in Turner: Poetry and Truth*. London: Studio Vista, 1969.

Gage, John. *J.M.W. Turner: 'A Wonderful Range of Mind'*. New Haven and London: Yale University Press, 1987.

Gerard, W.B. *Laurence Sterne and the Visual Imagination*. Aldershot and Burlington: Ashgate, 2006.

Giardiello, Paolo. 'Building with Light: Between Shadows and Light in the Museums of Sverre Fehn'. In Norberg-Schulz and Postiglione, pp. 264–266.

Gibbon, Edward. *The Decline and Fall of the Roman Empire*. London: Everyman's Library, 1996, vols 1–6. First published between 1776 and 1788.

Giedion, Sigfried. *Space, Time and Architecture: The Growth of a New Tradition*. Cambridge, MA: Harvard University Press, 1956.

Gilpin, William. *Observations Relative Chiefly to Picturesque Beauty, Made in the Year 1772, On Several Parts of England; Particularly the Mountains, and Lakes of Cumberland, and Westmoreland*. London: R. Blamire, 1786, 2 vols.

Gilpin, William. *Remarks on Forest Scenery, and other Woodland Views (Relative Chiefly to Picturesque Beauty), illustrated by the Scenes of New-Forest in Hampshire*. London: R. Blamire, 1791, 2 vols.

Gilpin, William. *Three Essays: On Picturesque Beauty; On Picturesque Travel; and On Sketching Landscape*: to which is added a poem, on landscape painting. London: R. Blamire, 1792.

Gittings, Clare. 'Consolation and Condolence on the Death of Mrs. Soane'. In Waterfield, pp. 45–51.

Glacken, Clarence J. *Traces on the Rhodian Shore: Nature and Culture in Western Thought from Ancient Times to the End of the Eighteenth Century*. Berkeley, CA: University of California Press, 1967.

Glantz, Michael H. *Climate Affairs: A Primer*. Washington, Covelo and London: Island Press, 2003.

Glover, Leigh. *Postmodern Climate Change*. London and New York: Routledge, 2006.

Goethe, Johann Wolfgang von. 'On German Architecture (1772)'. In Goethe, *Goethe on Art*, pp. 103–112.

Goethe, Johann Wolfgang von. *Goethe on Art*. Trans. John Gage. London: Scholar Press, 1980.

Goethe, Johann Wolfgang von. *Goethe's Theory of Colours*. Trans Charles Eastlake. London: Frank Cass, 1967. First published in German in 1810 and in English in 1840.

Goethe, Johann Wolfgang von. 'Von deutscher Baukunst' (On German Architecture). In Goethe, *Goethe on Art*, pp. 103–112. First published in 1772.

Goldberger, Paul, and Lord Palumbo. 'Farnsworth House, April 2003'. In Sotheby's International Realty, pp. 22–24.

Golinski, Jan. *British Weather and the Climate of Enlightenment*. Chicago and London: University of Chicago Press, 2007.

Golinski, Jan. '"Exquisite Atmography": Theories of the World and Experiences of the Weather in a Diary of 1703'. *British Journal for the History of Science*, vol. 34, no. 2, June 2001, pp. 149–171.

Gordon, Susan. 'The Iconography and Mythology of the Eighteenth-Century English Landscape Garden'. PhD thesis, University of Bristol, 1999.

Gregory, Richard. *Eye and Brain: The Psychology of Seeing*. Oxford: Oxford University Press, 1998.

Grillner, Katja. 'Nature's Lovers: Design and Authorship in the Eighteenth Century Landscape Garden'. In Anstey, Grillner and Hughes, pp. 62–73.

Grillner, Katja. *Ramble, Linger and Gaze: Dialogues from the Landscape Garden*. Stockholm: KTH, 2000.

Gropius, Walter. *Apollo in the Democracy: The Cultural Obligation of the Architect*. New York: McGraw Hill, 1968.

Guardini, Romano. *Letters from Lake Como: Explorations in Technology and the Human Race*. Trans. Geoffrey W. Bromiley. Edinburgh: T and T Clark, 1994. First published as *Die Technik un der Mensch: Briefe von Comer See* in 1927.

Gunther, R.T. *Early Science in Oxford*, 4 vols. London: Dawson of Pall Mall, 1925.

Hackney, Stephen. 'The Condition of Turner's Oil Paintings'. In Townsend, *Turner's Painting Techniques in Context*, pp. 50–54.

Hall, Tony. *Nuclear Politics: The History of Nuclear Power in Britain*. Harmondsworth: Penguin, 1986.

Hamblyn, Richard. *The Invention of Clouds: How an Amateur Meteorologist Forged the Language of the Skies*. London: Picador, 2001.

Hamilton, James. *Faraday: The Life*. London: Harper Collins, 2002.

Hamilton, James. *Turner: A Life*. London: Hodder and Stoughton, 1997.
Hamilton, James. *Turner and the Scientists*. London: Tate Gallery Publishing, 1998.
Hammer-Tugendhat, Daniela. 'Is the Tugendhat House Inhabitable?'. In Hammer-Tugendhat and Wolf Tegethoff, pp. 29–34.
Hammer-Tugendhat, Daniela, and Wolf Tegethoff, eds. *Ludwig Mies van der Rohe: The Tugendhat House*. New York and Vienna: Springer Verlag, 2000.
Hardy, Thomas. *The Woodlanders*. Harmondsworth: Penguin, 1981. First published in 1887.
Harley, Trevor. '"Nice Weather for the Time of Year": The British Obsession with the Weather'. In Strauss and Orlove, pp. 103–118.
Harries, Karsten. *The Ethical Function of Architecture*. Cambridge, MA, and London: MIT Press, 1997.
Harris, Eileen. 'Sir John Soane's Library: "O, Books! Ye Monuments of Mind"'. *Apollo*, April 1990, pp. 242–247.
Harris, John. 'The Architecture of the House'. In Moore, *Houghton Hall: The Prime Minister, The Empress and the Heritage*, pp. 20–28.
Harris, John. *William Kent 1685–1748: A Poet on Paper*. London: Sir John Soane's Museum, 1998.
Harwood, Edward S. 'Personal Identity and the Eighteenth-Century Landscape Garden'. *Journal of Garden History*, vol. 13, nos. 1–2, Spring–Summer 1993, pp. 36–48.
Hawkes, Dean. *The Environmental Imagination: Technics and Poetics of the Architectural Environment*. London and New York: Routledge, 2008.
Health and Safety Executive. *The Tolerability of Risk from Nuclear Power Stations*. London: Her Majesty's Stationery Office, 1987.
Herder, Johann Gottfried. *Outlines of a Philosophy of the History of Man*. Trans. T. Churchill. London: J. Johnson, 1800. First published as *Ideen zur Philosophie der Geschichte der Menschheit* in 1784–1791.
Heynen, Hilde. *Architecture and Modernity: A Critique*. Cambridge, MA, and London: MIT Press, 1999.
Hill, Jonathan. *Actions of Architecture: Architects and Creative Users*. London and New York: Routledge, 2003.
Hill, Jonathan, ed. *Architecture – The Subject is Matter*. London and New York: Routledge, 2001.
Hill, Jonathan. *The Illegal Architect*. London: Black Dog Publishing, 1998.
Hill, Jonathan. *Immaterial Architecture*. London and New York: Routledge, 2006.
Hill, Jonathan. 'Weather Architecture (Berlin 1929–1930, Barcelona 1986–, Barcelona 1999–)'. In Hill, *Actions of Architecture*, pp. 159–175.
Hillier, Bill. *Space is the Machine*. Cambridge: Cambridge University Press, 1996.
Hipple, John Walter. *The Beautiful, the Sublime and the Picturesque in Eighteenth-Century British Aesthetic Theory*. Carbondale: Southern Illinois University Press, 1957.
Hitchcock, Henry-Russell. *Modern Architecture: Romanticism and Regeneration*. New York: Hacker Art Books, 1970. First published in 1929.
Hitchcock, Henry-Russell, and Philip Johnson. *The International Style*. New York: The Norton Library, 1966. First published in 1932 as *The International Style: Architecture Since 1922*.

Hofland, Barbara. *Popular Description of Sir John Soane's House, Museum and Library*. Ed. Arthur Bolton. London: Soane Museum, 1919.

Hofstadter, Albert, and Richard Kuhns, eds. *Philosophies of Art and Beauty*. Chicago: University of Chicago Press, 1964.

Holberton, Paul. *Palladio's Villas: Life in the Renaissance Countryside*. London: John Murray, 1990.

Holmes, Richard. *The Age of Wonder: How the Romantic Generation Discovered the Beauty and Terror of Science*. London: Harper Press: 2009.

Holtz, William V. *Image and Immortality: A Study of 'Tristram Shandy'*. Providence: Brown University Press, 1970.

House, Col. Tamzy J., Lt-Col. James B. Near Jr., Lt-Col. William B. Shields, Maj. Ronald J. Celentano, Maj. David M. Husband, Maj. Ann E. Mercer and Maj. James E. Pugh. *Weather as a Force Multiplier: Owning the Weather in 2025*. Unpublished research paper, August 1996.

Howard, Luke. *The Climate of London, Deduced from Meteorological Observations Made at Different Places in the Neighbourhood of the Metropolis*. London: W. Phillips, 1818 and 1820, 2 vols.

Hoyle, Fred, and Geoffrey Hoyle. *Commonsense in Nuclear Energy*. London: Heinemann Educational Books, 1980.

Hulme, Mike. *Why We Disagree About Climate Change*. Cambridge: Cambridge University Press, 2009.

Humboldt, Alexander von. *Cosmos: A Sketch of the Physical Description of the Universe*. Trans. E.C. Coté. Baltimore and London: John Hopkins University Press, 1997, 2 vols.

Hume, David. 'Of National Characters'. In Hume, *Selected Essays*, pp. 113–125. First published in 1748.

Hume, David. 'Of the Populousness of Nations'. In Hume, *Selected Essays*, pp. 223–274. First published in 1742.

Hume, David. 'Of the Standard of Taste'. In Hume, *Selected Essays*, pp. 133–154. First published in 1757.

Hume, David. *Selected Essays*. Ed. Stephen Copley and Andrew Edgar. Oxford: Oxford University Press, 1993.

Hunt, John Dixon. *The Afterlife of Gardens*. London: Reaktion, 2004.

Hunt, John Dixon. *Gardens and the Picturesque: Studies in the History of Landscape Architecture*. Cambridge, MA, and London: MIT Press, 1992.

Hunt, John Dixon. *Garden and Grove: The Italian Renaissance Garden in the English Imagination: 1600–1750*. Princeton: Princeton University Press, 1986.

Hunt, John Dixon. *Garden History: Issues, Approaches, Methods*. Washington DC: Dumbarton Oaks, 1989.

Hunt, John Dixon. *Greater Perfections: The Practice of Garden Theory*. London: Thames & Hudson, 2000.

Hunt, John Dixon. *The Picturesque Garden in Europe*. London: Thames and Hudson, 2002.

Hunt, John Dixon. '"The Question Opened by the Picturesque". Fragments and Fractures in Picturesque Criticism and Historiography'. In Bergdoll and Oechslin, pp. 267–274.

Hunt, John Dixon. 'Verbal Versus Visual Meanings in Garden History: The Case of Rousham'. In Hunt, *Garden History: Issues, Approaches, Methods*, pp. 151–181.

Hunt, John Dixon. *William Kent: Landscape Garden Designer*. London: Zwemmer, 1987.

Hunt, John Dixon, and Peter Willis, eds. *The Genius of the Place: The English Landscape Garden 1620–1820*. Cambridge, MA, and London: MIT Press, 1988.

Hunt, John Dixon, and Peter Willis. 'Introduction'. In Hunt and Willis, *The Genius of the Place*, pp. 1–46.

Hussey, Christopher. *English Gardens and Landscapes 1700–1750*. London: Country Life, 1967.

Hussey, Christopher. 'Introduction: The Aesthetic Background to the Art of William Kent'. In Jourdain, pp. 15–24.

Hussey, Christopher. *The Picturesque: Studies in a Point of View*. London: Frank Cass, 1983. First published in 1927.

Hutton, Louisa. 'Godparents' Gifts'. In Johnston, Ainley and Barrett, *Architecture is Not Made With the Brain: The Labour of Alison and Peter Smithson*, pp. 50–53.

Intergovernmental Panel on Climate Change. *IPCC Climate Change 2007: Synthesis Report*. http://www.ipcc.ch/pdf/assessment-report/ar4/syr/ar4_syr_spm.pdf.

Jackson, Hazelle. *Shell Houses and Grottoes*. Princes Risborough: Shire, 2001.

Jankovic, Vladimir. *Reading the Skies: A Cultural History of English Weather, 1650–1820*. Manchester; Manchester University Press, 2000.

Janowitz, Anne. *England's Ruins: Poetic Purpose and the National Landscape*. Oxford: Basil Blackwell, 1990.

Jarman, Derek, dir. *The Angelic Conversation*. BFI, 1985.

Jarman, Derek. *At Your Own Risk: A Saint's Testament*. London: Vintage, 1993.

Jarman, Derek. *Derek Jarman's Garden*. London: Thames & Hudson, 1995.

Jarman, Derek, dir. *The Garden*. Basilisk in association with Channel 4, British Screen, ZDF and Uplink, 1990.

Jarman, Derek. *Kicking the Pricks*. London: Vantage, 1996. First published in 1987 as *The Last of England*.

Jarman, Derek, dir. *The Last of England*. Anglo International Films for British Screen, Channel 4 and ZDF, 1987.

Jarman, Derek. *Modern Nature: The Journals of Derek Jarman*. London: Century, 1991.

Jarrett, Edward. 'Account of Thomas Coke's Grand Tour'. Held in the Bodleian Library, Oxford.

Jefferson, Thomas. *Notes on the State of Virginia*. Gloucester, MA: Peter Smith, 1976. First published in 1785.

Jefferson, Thomas. *The Writings of Thomas Jefferson*. Ed. Andrew A. Lipscomb and Albert Ellery Bergh. Washington DC: Thomas Jefferson Memorial Association of the United States, 1907.

Jellicoe, G.S.,and Neville Conder. 'Save Us Our Ruins'. *The Architectural Review*, vol. 95, no. 565, January 1944, pp. 139–146.

Jenner, Mark. 'The Politics of London Air: John Evelyn's *Fumifugium* and the Restoration'. *Historical Journal*, vol. 38, no. 3, 1995, pp, 535–551.

Johnson, Philip. *Mies van der Rohe*. New York: Museum of Modern Art, 1947.

Johnson, Philip. 'Schinkel and Mies'. In Johnson, *Writings, Philip Johnson*, pp. 164–181.

Johnson, Philip. *Writings, Philip Johnson*. Ed. Robert A.M. Stern. New York: Oxford University Press, 1979.

Johnson, Samuel. *The Idler and The Adventurer*. Ed. W.J. Bate, John M. Bullitt, L.F. Powell. New Haven and London: Yale University Press, 1963. *The Idler* was first published between 1758 and 1760.

Johnston, Pamela, Rosa Ainley and Clare Barrett, eds. *Architecture is Not Made With the Brain: The Labour of Alison and Peter Smithson*. London: Architectural Association, 2005.

Jones, Henry Bence. *Life and Letters of Michael Faraday*. London: Longmans, 1870.

Jones, Roger, and Nicholas Penny. *Raphael*. New Haven and London: Yale University Press, 1983.

Jormakka, Kari. 'The Eve of Destruction'. *Daidalos*, no. 63, March 1997, pp. 34–45.

Jourdain, Margaret. *The Work of William Kent*. London: Country Life, 1948.

Jury, Louise. 'British Museum's Long-hidden Treasures Find a New Home after Library's £8m Restoration'. *The Independent*, 11 December 2003, p. 23.

Kaku, Michio, and Jennifer Trainer, eds. *Nuclear Power: Both Sides. The Best Arguments For and Against the Most Controversial Technology*. New York and London: W.W Norton, 1982.

Kaku, Michio, and Jennifer Trainer. 'Radiation: Introduction'. In Kaku and Trainer, *Nuclear Power: Both Sides*, pp. 27–34.

Kames, Henry Home, Lord. *Elements of Criticism*. Dublin: Sarah Cotter, 1762. 2 vols.

Kant, Immanuel. *Kant's Critique of Judgement*. Trans. J.H. Bernard. London: Macmillan, 1931. First published in 1790.

Kant, Immanuel. *Immanuel Kant's Critique of Pure Reason*. Trans. Norman Kemp Smith. London: Macmillan, 1956. First published in 1781.

Keeling, Charles David. 'The Concentration and Isotopic Abundances of Carbon Dioxide in the Atmosphere'. *Tellus*, 1960, no. 12, pp. 200–203.

Kenda, Barbara, ed. *Aeolian Winds and the Spirit in Renaissance Architecture*. London and New York: Routledge, 2006.

Kenda, Barbara. 'Aeolian WInds and the Spirit of Renaissance Architecture'. In Kenda, *Aeolian Winds and the Spirit in Renaissance Architecture*, pp. 1–21.

Kent, Neil. *The Soul of the North: A Social, Architectural and Cultural History of the Nordic Countries, 1700–1940*. London: Reaktion, 2000.

Kent, Neil. *The Triumph of Light and Nature: Nordic Art 1749–1940*. London: Thames & Hudson, 1987.

Kent, William. 'Italian Diary of 1714–1715'. Held in the Bodleian Library, Oxford, MS. Rawl. D. 1162.

Kleinman, Kent, and Leslie Van Duzer. *Mies van der Rohe: The Krefeld Villas*. New York: Princeton Architectural Press, 2005.

Knight, Richard Payne. *An Analytical Inquiry into the Principles of Taste*. London: T. Payne, 1805.

Knight, Richard Payne. *The Landscape, A Didactic Poem, in Three Books, Addressed to Uvedale Price, Esq*. Farnborough: Gregg International Publishers, 1972. First published in 1794.

Knox, Tim. *Sir John Soane's Museum, London*. London and New York: Merrell, 2009.

Koerner, Joseph Leo. *Caspar David Friedrich and the Subject of Landscape*. London: Reaktion, 1990.

Kostof, Spiro, ed. *The Architect: Chapters in the History of the Profession*. New York and Oxford: Oxford University Press, 1977.

Kostof, Spiro. 'The Practice of Architecture in the Ancient World: Egypt and Greece'. In Kostof, *The Architect*, pp. 3–27.

Kostof, Spiro. 'The Architect in the Middle Ages, East and West'. In Kostof, *The Architect*, pp. 59–95.

Krauss, Rosalind 'The Grid, the /Cloud/, and the Detail'. In Mertins, pp. 133–147.

Krieg, Robert A. *Catholic Theologians in Nazi Germany*. New York and London: Continuum, 2004.

Kristeller, Paul Oskar. *Renaissance Thought and the Arts: Collected Essays*. Princeton: Princeton University Press, 1990.

Kristeller, Paul Oskar. 'The Modern System of the Arts'. In Kristeller, *Renaissance Thought and the Arts*, pp. 163–227.

Krucker, Bruno. *Complex Ordinariness: The Upper Lawn Pavilion by Alison and Peter Smithson*. Zurich: ETH Zurich, 2002.

Lamb, H.H. *Climate, History and the Modern World*. London and New York: Routledge, 1995.

Lambert, Phyllis. 'Mies Immersion'. In Lambert, *Mies in America*, pp. 192–589.

Lambert, Phyllis, ed. *Mies in America*. Montréal: Canadian Centre for Architecture / New York: Whitney Museum of American Art, 2001.

Lane, Barbara Miller. *National Romanticism and Modern Architecture in Germany and the Scandinavian Countries*. Cambridge: Cambridge University Press, 2000.

Lang, S, and Nikolaus Pevsner. 'Sir William Temple and Sharawaggi'. *The Architectural Review*, vol. 106, no. 636, December 1949, pp. 391–393.

Lansdown. *Recollections of the Late William Beckford*. Printed for private circulation, 1893.

Laugier, Marc-Antoine. *An Essay on Architecture*. Trans. Wolfgang and Anni Herrmann. Los Angeles: Hennessey and Ingalls, 1977. First published as *Essai sur l'Architecture* in 1753.

Lavalou, Armelle. 'Interview with Sverre Fehn', *L'Architecture d'Aujourd'hui*, no. 287, June 1993, p. 85.

Lavin, Sylvia. 'Sacrifice and the Garden: Watelet's *Essay sur les jardins* and the Space of the Picturesque'. *Assemblage*, no. 28, December 1995, pp. 16–33.

Leatherbarrow, David. 'Character, Geometry and Perspective: The Third Earl of Shaftesbury's Principles of Garden Design'. *Journal of Garden History*, vol. 4, no. 4, October–December 1984, pp. 332–358.

Leatherbarrow, David, and Mohsen Mostafavi. *On Weathering*. Cambridge, MA, and London: MIT Press, 1993.

Le Camus de Mézières, Nicolas. *The Genius of Architecture; or, the Analogy of That Art With Our Sensations*. Trans D. Britt. Santa Monica: The Getty Center, 1992. First published as *Le génie de l'architecture; ou, l'analogie de cet art avec nos sensations*, 1780.

Le Corbusier. 'A Coat of Whitewash: The Law of Ripolin'. In Le Corbusier, *The Decorative Art of Today*, pp. 185–192.

Le Corbusier. *The Decorative Art of Today*. Trans. James Dunnett. London: Architectural Press, 1987.

Le Corbusier. *Precisions on the Present State of Architecture and City Planning*. Cambridge, MA, and London: MIT Press, 1991. First published in 1930.

Le Corbusier. *Towards a New Architecture*. Trans. Frederick Etchells. London: Architectural Press, 1946. First published in French in 1923 as *Vers une architecture* and in English in 1927 as *Towards a New Architecture*.

Lefaivre, Liane. *Leon Battista Alberti's Hypnerotomachia Poliphili: Re-Cognizing the Architectural Body in the Early Italian Renaissance*. Cambridge, MA, and London: MIT Press, 1997.

Lévi-Strauss, Claude. *The Origin of Table Manners*. Trans John and Doreen Weightman. New York: Harper and Row, 1978. First published in French in 1968.

Lewerentz, Sigurd. 'Modern Cemeteries: Notes on the Landscape'. In Flora, Giardiello and Postiglione, *Sigurd Lewerentz 1885–1875*, pp. 44–45.

Li, Shiqiao. *Power and Virtue: Architecture and Intellectual Change in England 1660–1730*. London and New York: Routledge, 2007.

Ligo, Larry L. *The Concept of Function in Twentieth-Century Architectural Criticism*. Ann Arbor, MI: UMI Research Press, 1984.

Lippard, Chris, ed. *By Angels Driven: The Films of Derek Jarman*. Trowbridge: Flicks Books, 1996.

Lippard, Chris. 'Interview with Derek Jarman', in Lippard, *By Angels Driven*, pp. 161–169.

Lippard, Lucy. *Pop Art*. London: Thames & Hudson, 1966.

The Listener. 'Interview with Ludwig Mies van der Rohe'. *The Listener*, 15 October 1959, pp. 620–622.

Lloyd, Christopher. 'The Jarman Garden Experience'. In Wollen, pp. 147–152.

Locke, John. *An Essay concerning Human Understanding*. Ed. Peter H. Nidditch. Oxford: Clarendon Press, 1975. First published in 1690.

Locke, John. 'A Register of the Weather for the Year 1692, Kept at Oates in Essex'. *Philosophical Transactions*, vol. 24, no. 298, 1704–1705, pp. 1917–1937.

Locke, John. *Two Treatises of Government*. Ed. Peter Laslett. Cambridge: Cambridge University Press, 1988. First published in 1690.

Long, Antony J., Martyn P. Waller and Andrew J. Plater, eds. *Dungeness and Romney Marsh: Barrier Dynamics and Marshland Evolution*. Oxford: Oxbow Books, 2007.

Loos, Adolf. 'The Principle of Cladding'. In Loos, *Spoken into the Void*, pp. 66–69.

Loos, Adolf. *Spoken into the Void: Collected Essays 1897–1900*. Trans. Jane O. Newman and John. H. Smith. Cambridge, MA: MIT Press, 1982.

Lowie, Robert H. *Culture and Ethnology*. New York: Boni and Liveright, 1917.

Lukacher, Brian. *Joseph Gandy: An Architectural Visionary in Georgian England*. London: Thames & Hudson, 2006.

Lyotard, Jean-François. 'The Sublime and the Avant-Garde'. In Benjamin, *The Lyotard Reader*, pp. 196–211.

Macarthur, John. *The Picturesque: Architecture, Disgust and Other Irregularities*. London and New York: Routledge, 2007.

Macdonald, Chris, and Peter Salter, *Macdonald and Salter: Building Projects 1982–86, Mega III*, London: Architectural Association, 1987.

Macdonald, Chris, and Peter Salter. 'The Oriental Museum, Durham University'. *AA Files*, no. 7, September 1984, pp. 75–77.

MacDonald, William L. 'Roman Architects'. In Kostof, *The Architect*, pp. 28–58.

Maillet, Arnaud. *The Claude Glass: Use and Meaning of the Black Mirror in Western Art*. Trans. Jeff Fort. New York: Zone Books, 2004.

Mallgrave, Harry Francis, ed. *Architectural Theory, Volume I, An Anthology from Vitruvius to 1870*. Oxford: Blackwell, 2006.

Manley, Gordon. 'Weather and Diseases: Some Eighteenth-Century Contributions to Observational Meteorology'. *Notes and Records of the Royal Society of London*, vol. 9, no. 2, May 1952, pp. 300–307.

Manzelle, Mauro. *Carlo Scarpa at the Querini Stampalia*. Venice: Fondazione Querini Stampalia, undated.

Mayer H., Jürgen, and Nerraj Bhatia, eds. *Arium: Weather + Architecture*. Toronto: Daniels Faculty Publication, 2009.

McAtee, Cammie. 'Alien #5044325: Mies's First Trip to America'. In Lambert, *Mies in America*, pp. 132–191.

McGrath, Raymond. 'Looking into Glass'. *The Architectural Review*, vol. 71, January 1932, pp. 29–30.

McGrath, Raymond. *Twentieth Century Houses*. London: Faber & Faber, 1934.

McGrath, Raymond, and A.C. Frost. *Glass in Architecture and Decoration*. London: Architectural Press, 1937.

McLeod, Mary. '"Order in the Details", "Tumult in the Whole"? Composition and Fragmentation in Le Corbusier's Architecture'. In Bergdoll and Oechslin, *Fragments: Architecture and the Unfinished*, pp. 291–322.

Merchant, Carolyn. *The Death of Nature: Women, Ecology and the Scientific Revolution*. San Francisco: Harper, 1983.

Mertins, Detlef, ed. *The Presence of Mies*. New York: Princeton Architectural Press, 1994.

Middlesex University Flood Hazard Research Centre. 'The Impacts of Climate Change on Nuclear Power Station Sites: A Review of Four Proposed New-build Sites on the UK Coastline'. Greenpeace: http://www.greenpeace.org.uk/files/pdfs/nuclear/8176.pdf, 2007. (18 October 2010).

Middleton, Robin. 'Introduction'. In Le Camus de Mézières, *The Genius of Architecture*, pp. 17–64.

Middleton, Robin. 'Soane's Spaces and the Matter of Fragmentation'. In Richardson and Stevens, pp. 26–37.

Middleton, Robin, and David Watkin. *Neoclassical and 19th Century Architecture/1: The Enlightenment in France and in England*. London: Faber and Faber, 1987.

Mies van der Rohe, Ludwig. 'Build Beautifully and Practically! Stop this Cold Functionality'. In Neumeyer, *The Artless Word*, p. 307. First published in 1930.

Mies van der Rohe, Ludwig. *Drawings from the Collection of the Museum of Modern Art, New York*. New York: Museum of Modern Art, 1969.

Mies van der Rohe, Ludwig. 'Notebook (1927–1928)'. In Neumeyer, *The Artless Word*, pp. 265–296.

Mies van der Rohe, Ludwig. 'Skyscrapers'. In Neumeyer, *The Artless Word*, p. 240. First published in 1922.

Millenson, Susan Feinberg. *Sir John Soane's Museum*. Ann Arbor, MI: UMI Research Press, 1987.

Miller, Charles A. *Jefferson and Nature: An Interpretation*. Baltimore and London: John Hopkins University Press, 1993.

Miller, Richard et al. *Four Great Makers of Modern Architecture: Gropius, Le Corbusier, Mies van der Rohe, Wright*. New York: De Capo Press, 1963.

Moggridge, Hal. 'Notes on Kent's Garden at Rousham'. *Journal of Garden History*, no. 6, 1986, pp. 187–226.

Moholy-Nagy, László. *The New Vision 1928 fourth revised edition 1947 and Abstract of an Artist*. Trans. Daphne M. Hoffmann. New York: George Wittenborn, 1947.

Molina, Mario J, and F.Sherwood Rowland. 'Stratospheric Sink for Chlorofluoromethanes: Chlorine Atom-Catalysed Destruction of Ozone'. *Nature*, no. 249, 28 June 1974, pp. 810–812.

Monbiot, George. *Heat: How to Stop the Planet Burning*. London: Penguin, 2007.

Montesquieu, Charles Louis de Secondat, Baron de. *The Spirit of Laws*. London: J. Nourse and P. Vaillant, 1750, 2 vols. First published in 1748.

Moore, Andrew, ed. *Houghton Hall: The Prime Minister, the Empress and the Heritage*. London: Philip Wilson, 1996.

Morel, Jean-Marie. *Théorie des jardins*. Paris: Pissot, 1776.

Morton, Timothy. *Ecology Without Nature: Rethinking Environmental Aesthetics*. Cambridge, MA, and London: Harvard University Press, 2007.

Mosser, Monique, and Georges Teyssot, eds. *The History of Garden Design: The Western Tradition from the Renaissance to the Present Day*. London: Thames & Hudson, 1991.

Mowl, Timothy. *Gentlemen & Players: Gardeners of the English Landscape*. Stroud: Sutton, 2000.

Mowl, Timothy. 'William Beckford: A Biographical Perspective'. In Ostergard, pp. 17–32.

Mowl, Timothy. *William Kent: Architect, Designer, Opportunist*. London: Jonathan Cape, 2006.

Müller, Ulrich. 'Rousham: A Transcription of the Steward's Letters, 1738–42'. *Garden History*, vol. 25, no. 2, Winter 1997, pp. 178–188.

Nebeker, Frederick. *Calculating the Weather: Meteorology in the 20th Century*. San Diego: Academic Press, 1995.

Neumeyer, Fritz. *The Artless Word: Mies van der Rohe on the Building Art*. Trans. Mark Jarzombek. Cambridge, MA, and London: MIT Press, 1991.

Neumeyer, Fritz. 'Search for Reflection: Block Versus Pavilion'. In Schulze, *Mies van der Rohe; Critical Essays*, pp. 148–171.

Newman, Oscar, ed. *CIAM '59 in Otterlo*. London: Tiranti, 1959.

Newton, Isaac. *Mathematical Principles of Natural Philosophy*. Trans. Florian Cajori. Berkeley: University of California Press, 1962. First published in 1687 as *Philosophiae Naturalis Principia Mathematica*.

Newton, Isaac. *Opticks*. New York: Dover, 1979. First published in 1704, this, the third edition was published in English in 1723.

Nicolson, Marjorie Hope. *Mountain Gloom and Mountain Glory: The Development of the Aesthetics of the Infinite*. New York: Norton, 1963.

Norberg-Schulz, Christian. *Genius Loci: Towards a Phenomenology of Architecture*. London: Academy, 1980.

Norberg-Schulz, Christian. *Modern Norwegian Architecture*. Oslo, Bergen, Stavanger, Tromso: Norwegian University Press, 1986.

Norberg-Schulz, Christian. *Nightlands: Nordic Building*. Cambridge, MA, and London: MIT Press, 1996.

Norberg-Schulz, Christian. 'The Poetic Vision of Sverre Fehn'. In Norberg-Schulz and Postiglione, pp. 19–51.

Norberg-Schulz, Christian. 'A Talk with Mies van der Rohe'. In Neumeyer, *The Artless Word*, pp. 338–339. First published in *Baukunst und Werkform*, 11, no. 11, 1958, pp. 615–618.

Norberg-Schulz, Christian and Gennaro Postiglione, eds. *Sverre Fehn: Works, Projects, Writings, 1949–1996*. New York: Monacelli, 1997.

Norri, Riitta. 'Interview with Sverre Fehn: About Rationalism and the Spiritual Content'. In Norberg-Schulz and Postiglione, pp. 248–250. First published in April 1986.

O'Hare, Greg, John Sweeney and Robin Wilby. *Weather, Climate and Climate Change: Human Perspectives*. Harlow: Pearson Education, 2005.

O'Pray, Michael. *Derek Jarman: Dreams of England*. London: British Film Institute, 1996.

Ostergard, Derek E., ed. *William Beckford 1760–1844: An Eye for the Magnificent*. New York: Bard Graduate Center / New Haven and London: Yale University Press, 2001.

Oxford University Press. *The Compact Edition of the Oxford English Dictionary*, Oxford: Oxford University Press, 1971.

Padovan, Richard. 'Seven Small Thoughts on the Architects' Writings'. In Webster, pp. 194–205.

Palladio, Andrea. *The Four Books on Architecture*. Trans. Robert Tavernor and Richard Schofield. Cambridge, MA: MIT Press, 1997. First published as *Quattro Libri dell' Archittetura* in 1570.

Palmer, Susan. 'From Fields to Gardens: The Management of Lincoln's Inn Fields in the Eighteenth and Nineteenth Centuries'. *The London Gardener or the Gardener's Intelligencer*, 2004–2005, vol. 10, pp. 11–28.

Palmer, Susan. 'Sir John Soane's Garden at the Royal Hospital Chelsea'. *The London Gardener or The Gardener's Intelligencer*, 2003–2004, vol. 9, pp. 11–20.

Palmer, Susan. *The Soanes at Home: Domestic Life at Lincoln's Inn Fields*. London: Sir John Soane's Museum, 1997.

Palumbo, Peter. 'Foreword'. In Vandenburg, *Farnsworth House: Ludwig Mies van der Rohe*, p. 8.

Panofsky, Erwin. *Idea: A Concept in Art Theory*. Trans. Joseph J.S. Peake. Columbia: University of Southern Carolina Press, 1968. First published in 1924.

Peake, Tony. *Derek Jarman*. London: Little, Brown, 1999.

Peik, Susan M. *Karl Friedrich Schinkel: Aspects of his Work*. Stuttgart/London: Axel Menges, 2001.

Pelletier, Louise. *Architecture in Words: Theatre, Language and the Sensuous Space of Architecture*. London and New York: Routledge, 2006.

Pérez-Gómez, Alberto. *Architecture and the Crisis of Modern Science*. Cambridge, MA: MIT Press, 1983.

Petri, Mathilde. 'Interview with Sverre Fehn'. In Norberg-Schulz and Postiglione, pp. 250–252. First published in 1990.

Pevsner, Nikolaus. 'The Anti-Pioneers'. In Pevnser, *Pevsner on Art and Architecture*, pp. 293–307.

Pevsner, Nikolaus. 'Conclusions'. In Pevsner, *The Picturesque Garden and its Influence Outside the British Isles*, pp. 117–121.

Pevsner, Nikolaus (using the pseudonym Peter F.R. Donner). 'Criticism'. *The Architectural Review*, October 1941, pp.124–126.

Pevsner, Nikolaus. *The Englishness of English Art: An Expanded and Annotated Version of the Reith Lectures Broadcast in October and November 1955*. London: Architectural Press, 1956.

Pevsner, Nikolaus. 'The Genesis of the Picturesque'. *The Architectural Review*, vol. 96, no. 575, November 1944, pp. 139–146.

Pevsner, Nikolaus. 'The Genius of the Place'. In Pevsner, *Pevsner on Art and Architecture*, pp. 230–240.

Pevsner, Nikolaus (Peter F.R. Donner). 'The Lure of Rusticity'. *The Architectural Review*, vol. 93, no. 553, January 1943, p. 27.

Pevsner, Nikolaus. *Pevsner on Art and Architecture: The Radio Talks*. Ed. Stephen Games. London: Methuen, 2002.

Pevsner, Nikolaus. *Pioneers of the Modern Movement from William Morris to Walter Gropius*. London: Faber and Faber, 1936.

Pevsner, Nikolaus, ed. *The Picturesque Garden and its Influence Outside the British Isles*. Washington DC: Dumbarton Oaks, Harvard University, 1974.

Pevsner, Nikolaus. 'Twentieth-Century Picturesque: An Answer to Basil Taylor's Broadcast'. *The Architectural Review*, vol. 115, no. 688, April 1954, pp. 227–229.

Pevsner, Nikoalus. 'Twentieth Century Picturesque: Reply to Alan Colquohoun'. *The Architectural Review*, vol. 116, no. 691, July 1954, p. 2.

Phibbs, John. 'Pleasure Grounds in Sweden and Their English Models'. *Garden History*, vol. 21, no. 1, Summer 1993, pp. 60–90.

Plater, Andrew J., Paul Stupples and Helen M. Roberts. 'The Depositional History of Dungeness Foreland'. In Long, Waller and Plater, *Dungeness and Romney Marsh: Barrier Dynamics and Marshland Evolution*, pp. 108–154.

Plato. *Philebus*. Trans. J.C.B. Gosling. Oxford: Clarendon Press, 1975.

Plato. *Timaeus, Critias, Cleitophon, Menexenus, Epistles*. Trans. R.G. Bury. Cambridge, MA: Harvard University Press, 1929.

Plato. *The Republic*. Ed. Terence Irwin. Trans. A.D. Lindsay. London: Everyman, 1992.

Plot, Robert. In *The Natural History of Oxfordshire, Being an Essay toward the Natural History of England*. Oxford and London: S. Millers, 1677.

Pococke, Richard. *The Travels through England of Dr. Richard Pococke*. Ed. J.J. Cartwright. London: Camden Society,1888.

Pope, Alexander. *The Correspondence of Alexander Pope*, vols. 1–5. Ed. George Sherburn. Oxford: Oxford University Press, 1956.

Porter, Roy. *English Society in the Eighteenth Century*. London: Penguin, 1991.

Porter, Roy. *Enlightenment: Britain and the Creation of the Modern World*. London: Penguin, 2001.

Porter, Roy. *Flesh in the Age of Reason: How the Enlightenment Transformed the Way We See Our Bodies and Souls*. London: Penguin, 2004.

Porter, Roy, and Mikulás Teich, eds. *Romanticism in National Context*. Cambridge: Cambridge University Press, 1988.

Posner, Donald. 'Concerning the "Mechanical" Parts of Painting and the Artistic Culture of Seventeenth-century France'. *Art Bulletin*, vol. 75, no. 4, December 1993, pp. 583–598.

Powell, Cecilia. 'Turner's Sketches: Purpose and Practice'. In Townsend, *Turner's Painting Techniques in Context*, pp. 55–60.

Prawer, S.S. ed. *The Romantic Period in Germany*. London: Schocken, 1970.

Pretor-Pinney, Gavin. *The Cloudspotter's Guide*. London: Hodder & Stoughton/Sceptre, 2006.

Price, Cedric. 'The Folly'. *Osaka Follies*. London: Architectural Association, 1991, p. 7.

Price, Uvedale. *Essays on the Picturesque, as Compared with the Sublime and the Beautiful; and, on the Use of Studying Pictures for the Purpose of Improving Real Landscapes*. London: J. Mawman, 1810, 3 vols.

Price, Uvedale. *An Essay on the Picturesque, as Compared with the Sublime and the Beautiful; and, on the Use of Studying Pictures for the Purpose of Improving Real Landscapes*. London: J. Robson, 1794. First published in Hereford in 1794.

Psarra, Sophia. *Architecture and Narrative: The Formation of Space and Cultural Meaning*. London and New York: Routledge, 2009.

Pugh, Simon. *Garden – Nature – Language*. Manchester: Manchester University Press, 1988.

Puttfarken, Thomas. *The Discovery of Pictorial Composition: Theories of Visual Order in Painting 1400–1800*. New Haven and London: Yale University Press, 2000.

Quetglas, Jose. 'Fear of Glass: The Barcelona Pavilion'. Trans. Stan Allen, Beatriz Colomina and Mari Marratt. In Colomina, *Architectureproduction*, pp. 121–151.

Ramanathan, V. (Ram). 'Greenhouse Effect Due to Chlorofluorocarbons: Climate Implications'. *Science*, vol. 190, issue 4209, 3 October 1975, pp. 50–52.

Ramanathan, V. (Ram), et al. 'Trace Gas Trends and Their Potential Role in Climate Change'. *Journal of Geophysical Research*, vol. 90, no. D3, 20 June 1985, pp. 5547–5566.

Rawnsley, H.D. *Past and Present at the English Lakes*. Glasgow: MacLehose and Sons, 1916.

Rayner, Steve. 'Domesticating Nature: Commentary on the Anthropological Study of Weather and Climate Discourse'. In Strauss and Orlove, *Weather, Climate, Culture*, pp. 277–290.

Redford, Bruce. *Dilettanti: The Antique and the Antic in Eighteenth-Century London*. Los Angeles: J. Paul Getty Museum, 2008.

Reed, Arden. *Romantic Weather: The Climates of Coleridge and Baudelaire*. Hanover and London: University Press of New England, 1983.

Repton, Humphry. *The Landscape Gardening and the Landscape Architecture of the Late Humphry Repton, Esq*. Ed. J.C. Loudon. Farnborough: Gregg International Publishers, 1969. First published in 1840.

Reynolds, Joshua. *Letters of Sir Joshua Reynolds*. Ed. Frederick W. Hilles. Cambridge: Cambridge University Press, 1929.

Richards, J.M., Nikolaus Pevsner, Osbert Lancaster and H. de C. Hastings. 'The New Empiricism: Sweden's Latest Style'. *The Architectural Review*, vol. C1, no. 606, June 1947, pp. 199–204.

Richardson, Charles James. *A Popular Treatise on the Warming and Ventilating of Buildings: Showing the Advantage of the Improved System of Hot Water Circulation*, 2nd edition, London: John Weale Architectural Library, 1839. First published in 1837.

Richardson, Lewis Fry. *Weather Prediction by Numerical Process*. New York: Dover, 1965. First published in 1922.

Richardson, Margaret. *Building in Progress: Soane's View of Construction*. London: Sir John Soane's Museum, 1995.

Richardson, Margaret, and MaryAnne Stevens, eds. *John Soane Architect: Master of Space and Light*. London: Royal Academy of Arts, 1999.

Ricks, Christopher. 'Introductory Essay'. In Sterne, *The Life and Opinions of Tristram Shandy*, pp. xi–xxxii.

Riemann, Gottfried. *Karl Friedrich Schinkel: Reisen nach Italien. Tagebücher, Briefe, Zeichnungen, Aquarelle*. Berlin: Rütten & Loening, 1979.

Riemann, Gottfried. 'The 1826 Journey and Its Place in Schinkel's Career'. In Schinkel, pp. 1–11.

Riley, Terence. 'Making History: Mies van der Rohe and the Museum of Modern Art'. In Riley and Bergdoll, pp. 10–23.

Riley, Terence, and Barry Bergdoll, eds. *Mies in Berlin*. New York: Museum of Modern Art, 2001.

Risselada, Max. 'Another Shift'. In Van den Heuvel and Risselada, pp. 50–59.

Rittel, Horst, and Melvin Webber. 'Dilemmas in a General Theory of Planning', *Policy and Sciences*, vol. 4, no. 2, 1973, pp. 155–169.

Robson-Scott, W.D. 'German Romanticism and the Visual Arts'. In S.S. Prawer, pp. 259–281.

Rodner, William S. *J.M.W. Turner: Romantic Painter of the Industrial Revolution*. Berkeley, Los Angeles and London: University of California Press, 1997.

Rogers, Malcolm. *Montacute House*. London: National Trust, 1991.

Rosenblum, Robert. *Modern Painting and the Northern Romantic Tradition: Friedrich to Rothko*. London: Thames & Hudson, 1975.

Rousseau, Jean-Jacques. *The Confessions of Jean-Jacques Rousseau*. Trans. J.M. Cohen. London: Penguin, 1953. First published in 1781.

Rousseau, Jean-Jacques. *Émile*. Trans. Barbara Foxley. London: Dent and Sons, 1972. First published in 1762.

Rousseau, Jean-Jacques. *Lettre à Monsieur D'Alembert sur les spectacles*. Paris: Flammarion, 1967. First published in 1758.

Rousseau, Jean-Jacques. *Reveries of the Solitary Walker*. Trans. Charles E. Butterworth. Indianapolis and Cambridge: Hackett, 1992. First published in 1782.

Rowe, Colin. 'The Mathematics of the Ideal Villa'. In Rowe, *The Mathematics of the Ideal Villa and Other Essays*, pp. 1–27.

Rowe, Colin. *The Mathematics of the Ideal Villa and Other Essays*. Cambridge, MA: MIT, 1976.

Rowe, Colin. 'Neo-"Classicism" and Modern Architecture I'. In Rowe, *The Mathematics of the Ideal Villa and Other Essays*, pp. 119–138.

Rowe, Colin. 'Neo-"Classicism" and Modern Architecture II'. In Rowe, *The Mathematics of the Ideal Villa and Other Essays*, pp. 139–158.

Rowe, Colin, and Leon Satkowski. *Italian Architecture of the Sixteenth Century*. New York: Princeton Architectural Press, 2002.

Ruskin, John. *The Brantwood Diary of John Ruskin: Together With Selected Related Letters and Sketches of Persons Mentioned*. Ed. Helen Gill Viljoen. New Haven and London: Yale University Press, 1971.

Ruskin, John. *The Elements of Drawing*. New York: Dover, 1971. First published in 1857.

Ruskin, John. *Modern Painters*, vol. 1. London: George Allen, 1888. First published in 1843.

Ruskin, John. *Modern Painters*, vol. 3. London: Smith Elder & Co, 1873. First published in 1856.

Ruskin, John. *Modern Painters*, vol. 4. London: George Allen, 1904. First published in 1856.

Ruskin, John. *Modern Painters*, vol. 5. London: George Allen, 1905. First published in 1860.

Ruskin, John. *The Seven Lamps of Architecture*. New York: Farrar, Straus and Giroux, 1984. First published in 1849.

Ruskin, John. *The Stones of Venice*, 3 vols. London: Smith, Elder & Co., 1851–1853.

Ruskin, John. *The Storm-Cloud of the Nineteenth Century*. Orpington: George Allen, 1884.

Ruskin, John. *The Works of John Ruskin*. Eds. Edward T. Cook and Alexander Wedderburn. London: George Allen, 1903–1912.

Rutter, John. *Delineations of Fonthill and its Abbey*. Shaftesbury: J. Rutter / London: Charles Knight and Co. et al., 1823.

Rybczynski, Witold. *Home: A Short History of an Idea*. London: Penguin, 1986.

Rykwert, Joseph. *On Adam's House in Paradise: The Idea of the Primitive Hut in Architectural History*. New York: Museum of Modern Art, 1972.

Rykwert, Joseph. *The First Moderns: The Architects of the Eighteenth Century*. Cambridge, MA, and London: MIT Press, 1980.

Saisselin, Rémy. 'Architecture and Language: The Sensationalism of Le Camus de Mézières'. *British Journal of Aesthetics*, vol. 15, no. 3, Summer 1975, pp. 239–253.

Salter, Peter. 'Building in Nature'. In Birksted, *Relating Architecture to Landscape*, pp. 261–268.

Salter, Peter. *4+1 Peter Salter: Building Projects*. London: Black Dog Publishing, 2000.

Salter, Peter. 'An Essay in Eight Parts by Peter Salter'. In Salter, *TS: Intuition & Process*, pp. 13–107.

Salter, Peter. 'Peter Smithson Obituary'. *The Architectural Review*, vol. 213, no. 1276, June 2003, pp. 25–28.

Salter, Peter. *TS: Intuition & Process – Projects by Students Under the Tutelage of Peter Salter*, Themes VI, London: Architectural Association, 1989.

Salter, Peter, and Lorenzo Wong, eds. *Climate Register: Four Works by Alison and Peter Smithson*. London: Architectural Association, 1994.

Sarti, Raffaella. *Europe at Home: Family and Material Culture: 1500–1800*. Trans. Allan Cameron. New Haven and London: Yale University Press, 2002.

Savi, Vittorio E., and Josep M. Montaner. *Less is More: Minimalism in Architecture and the Other Arts*. Barcelona: Colegio de Arquitectos de Cataluña y Actar, 1996.

Schama, Simon. *The Embarrassment of Riches: An Interpretation of Dutch Culture in the Golden Age*. London: Fontana, 1991.

Schinkel, Karl Friedrich. *'The English Journey': Journal of a Visit to France and Britain in 1826*. Ed. David Bindman and Gottfried Riemann. Trans. F. Gayna Walls. New Haven and London: Yale University Press, 1993.

Schmidt, Leo, Christian Keller and Polly Feversham, eds. *Holkham*. Munich: Prestel, 2005.

Schnaidt, Claude. *Hannes Meyer: Buildings, Projects and Writings*. Teufen: Arthur Niggli, 1965.

Schulze, Franz. *The Farnsworth House*. Plano, IL: Palumbo, 1997.

Schulze, Franz. *Philip Johnson: Life and Work*. New York: Alfred A. Knopf, 1994.

Schulze, Franz. *Mies van der Rohe: A Critical Biography*. Chicago and London: University of Chicago Press, 1985.

Schulze, Franz. *Mies van der Rohe; Critical Essays*. New York: Museum of Modern Art, 1989.

Scully, Vincent. *Architecture: The Natural and the Manmade*. New York: St Martin's Press, 1991.

Serlio, Sebastiano. *The Five Books on Architecture: An Unabridged Reprint of the English Edition of 1611*. Trans. Simon Stafford and Robert Peake. New York: Dover, 1982. First published as *Tutte l'opere d'architettura e prospective* in 1584.

Serres, Michel. *Genesis*. Trans. Geneviève James and James Nielson. Ann Arbor: University of Michigan Press, 1995.

Serres, Michel. *The Natural Contract*. Trans. Elizabeth MacArthur and William Paulson. Ann Arbor: University of Michigan Press, 1995.

Serres, Michel. 'Turner translates Carnot'. Trans. Stephen Bann. In Bryson, *Calligram*, pp. 154–165.

Shaftesbury, Anthony Ashley Cooper, third Earl of. *Characteristicks of Men, Manners, Opinions, Times*. Ed. Philip Ayres. Oxford: Clarendon Press, 1999, 2 vols. First published as a three-volume collection in 1711.

Shaftesbury, Anthony Ashley Cooper, third Earl of. *The Life, Unpublished Letters, and Philosophical Regimen of Anthony, Earl of Shaftesbury*. Ed. Benjamin Rand. London: Swan Sonnenschein, 1900.

Shaftesbury, Anthony Ashley Cooper, third Earl of. *Second Characters; or, the Language of Forms.* Ed. Benjamin Rand. Cambridge: Cambridge University Press, 1914.

Shaw, Philip. *The Sublime*. London and New York: Routledge, 2006.

Sibley, David. *Geographies of Exclusion: Society and Difference in the West*. London: Routledge, 1995.

Sicca, Cinzia Maria. 'On William Kent's Roman Sources'. *Architectural History*, vol. 29, 1986, pp. 134–157.

Simons, Paul. *Since Records Began: The Highs and Lows of Britain's Weather*. London: Collins, 2008.

Skirbekk, Gunnar, and Nils Gilje. *A History of Western Thought: From Ancient Greece to the Twentieth Century*. London and New York: Routledge, 2001.

Smith, Robert Angus. *Air and Rain: the Beginnings of a Chemical Climatology.* London: Longmans Green, 1872.

Smith, Steven R. 'John Evelyn and London Air'. *History Today*, vol. 23, no. 3, March 1975, pp. 185–189.

Smithson, Alison. *AS in DS: An Eye on the Road*. Baden: Lars Müller, 2001. First published by Delft University Press, 1983.

Smithson, Alison. *Imprint of India*. London: Architectural Association, 1994.

Smithson, Alison. 'The Landscape that Can Survive and the Lewerentz Connection'. In Flora, Giardiello and Postiglione, *Sigurd Lewerentz*, pp. 373–374.

Smithson, Alison. 'Mies' Barcelona Pavilion, Myth and Reality, extracts from a lecture, Barcelona, 1986'. In Alison and Peter Smithson, *Changing the Art of Inhabitation*, pp. 35–37.

Smithson, Alison. 'And Now Dhamas are Dying Out in Japan'. *Architectural Design*, vol. 36, no. 9, September 1966, pp. 447–449.

Smithson, Alison. 'Patio and Pavilion, 1956, Reconstructed U.S.A. 1990'. *Places: A Quarterly Journal of Environmental Design*, vol. 7, no. 3, 1991, pp. 10–14.

Smithson, Alison. 'Saint Jerome The Desert . . . The Study'. In Van den Heuvel and Risselada, pp. 224–231.

Smithson, Alison. '"Territory of the Pavilion", extracts from a lecture. Unpublished'. In Alison and Peter Smithson, *Changing the Art of Inhabitation*, pp. 33–34.

Smithson, Alison. '"Three Pavilions of the Twentieth Century: the Farnsworth, the Eames, Upper Lawn", a lecture given in connection with the seminar "A Fragment of an Enclave", held in Barcelona, November 1985'. In Alison and Peter Smithson, *Changing the Art of Inhabitation*, pp. 141–143.

Smithson, Alison and Peter. *Alison and Peter Smithson: The Shift (Architectural Monographs 7)*. London: Academy Editions, 1982.

Smithson, Alison and Peter. 'Banham's Bumper Book on Brutalism, Discussed by Alison and Peter Smithson'. *The Architects' Journal*. vol. 144, no. 24, 14 December 1966, pp. 1590–1591.

Smithson, Alison and Peter. *Changing the Art of Inhabitation: Mies' Pieces, Eames' Dreams, The Smithsons*. London, Zürich, Munich: Artemis, 1994.

Smithson, Alison and Peter. *The Charged Void: Architecture.* New York: Monacelli Press, 2001.

Smithson, Alison and Peter. 'Cluster City: A New Shape for the Community'. *The Architectural Review*, vol. 122, July–December 1957, pp. 332–336.

Smithson, Alison and Peter. 'Folly at Fonthill, Wilts.'. *Architectural Design*, vol. 33, no. 10, October 1963, pp. 482–483.

Smithson, Alison and Peter. *The Heroic Period of Modern Architecture*. London: Thames & Hudson, 1981.

Smithson, Alison and Peter. 'House of the Future', *Daily Mail Ideal Home Exhibition, Olympia, 1956*, catalogue to the exhibition.

Smithson, Alison and Peter. 'Mies van der Rohe', *Architectural Design*, vol. 39, no. 7, July 1969, pp. 363–366.

Smithson, Alison and Peter. 'The New Brutalism'. *Architectural Design*, vol. 27, no. 4, January 1955, p. 1.

Smithson, Alison and Peter. 'The New Brutalism; Alison and Peter Smithson Answer the Criticisms on the Opposite Page'. *Architectural Design*, vol. 27, April 1957, p. 113.

Smithson, Alison and Peter. *Ordinariness and Light: Urban Theories 1952–1960 and their Application in a Building Project 1963–1970*. London: Faber and Faber, 1970.

Smithson, Alison and Peter. 'The Pavilion and the Route'. *Architectural Design*, vol. 35, no. 3, March 1965, pp. 143–146.

Smithson, Alison and Peter. 'The Silent Architects'. *Sigurd Lewerentz 1885–1975: The Dilemma of Classicism*. London: Architectural Association, 1989, p. 5.

Smithson, Alison and Peter. 'Tisbury'. Ed. Jeremy Baker. *Architectural Association Journal*, vol. 81, no. 899, February 1966, pp. 212–213.

Smithson, Alison and Peter. *Upper Lawn, Solar Pavilion*. Barcelona: Edicions UPC, 1986.

Smithson, Alison and Peter. *Without Rhetoric: An Architectural Aesthetic 1955–1972*. London: Latimer New Dimensions, 1973.

Smithson, Peter. 'Conglomerate Ordering'. In Webster, pp. 182–193.

Smithson, Peter. *Conversations with Students: A Space for our Generation*. Eds. Catherine Spellman and Karl Unglaub. New York: Princeton Architectural Press, 2005.

Smithson, Peter. 'Going Back, Workpoints'. In Alison and Peter Smithson, *Changing the Art of Inhabitation*, pp. 31–32.

Smithson, Peter. 'Just a Few Chairs and a House: An Essay on the Eames-aesthetic'. *Architectural Design*, vol. 36, no. 9, September 1966, pp. 443–446.

Smithson, Peter. 'Letter to America'. *Architectural Design*, vol. 28, no. 3, March 1958, pp. 93–102. Reprinted and credited to Alison and Peter Smithson in *Ordinariness and Light*, pp. 135–143.

Smithson, Peter. 'A Sensibility Primer'. In Alison Smithson, *AS in DS*, p. 1.

Snodin, Michael, ed. *Karl Friedrich Schinkel: A Universal Man*. New Haven and London: Yale University Press, 1991.

Soane, Eliza. 'Mrs Soane's Note Books, 1804–1813'. Held in Sir John Soane's Museum, London.

Soane, John. 'Crude Hints towards an History of my House in L(incoln's) I(nn) Fields'. In Woodward, *Visions of Ruin*, pp. 61–75.

Soane, John. *Description of the House and Museum on the North Side of Lincoln's-Inn-Fields, the Residence of John Soane*. London, privately printed, 1830. Held in Sir John Soane's Museum.

Soane, John. *Description of the House and Museum on the North Side of Lincoln's-Inn-Fields, the Residence of Sir John Soane*. London, privately printed, 1832. Held in Sir John Soane's Museum.

Soane, John. *Description of the House and Museum on the North Side of Lincoln's Inn Fields, the Residence of Sir John Soane*. London, privately printed, 1835. Held in Sir John Soane's Museum.

Soane, John. *Memoirs of the Professional Life of an Architect, between the Years 1768 and 1835. Written by Himself.* London, privately printed, 1835. Held in Sir John Soane's Museum, London.

Soane, John. 'Soane's Note Books'. 14 vols. Held in Sir John Soane's Museum.

Solà Morales, Ignasi de, Christian Cirici and Fernando Ramos. *Mies van der Rohe: Barcelona Pavilion*. Trans. Graham Thomson. Barcelona: Editorial Gustavo Gili, 1993.

Sotheby's International Realty. *Ludwig Mies van der Rohe, The Farnsworth House, 1945–1951*. Auction Catalogue, Sale 7957, Lot 800, 12 December 2003, New York.

Stanhill, Gerald. 'Climate Change Science is Now Big Science'. *Eos, Transactions of the American Geophysical Union*, vol. 80, no. 35, 1999, pp. 396–397.

Steel, Carolyn. 'The Geography Man', *Blueprint*, no. 113, December 1994–January 1995, pp. 26–31.

Steenbergen, Clemens M., and Wouter Reh. *Architecture and Landscape: The Design Experiment of the Great European Gardens and Landscapes*. Munich: Prestel, 1996.

Sterne, Laurence. *The Life and Opinions of Tristram Shandy, Gentleman*. Ed. Melvyn New and Joan New. London: Penguin, 2003. First published in nine volumes between 1759 and 1767.

Stevens, William K. *The Change in the Weather: People, Weather and the Science of Climate*. New York: Delta, 2001.

Strauss, Susan, and Ben Orlove, eds. *Weather, Climate, Culture*. Oxford and New York: Berg, 2003.

Sullivan, Louis. *The Autobiography of an Idea*. New York: Dover, 1956. First published in 1924.

Summerson, John, ed. *Concerning Architecture: Essays of Architectural Writers and Writings Presented to Nikolaus Pevsner*. London: Allen Lane, 1968.

Summerson, John. 'Soane: the Man and the Style'. In Dunster, pp. 9–23.

Summerson, John. 'Sir John Soane and the Furniture of Death'. *The Architectural Review*, vol. 163, no. 973, March 1978, pp. 147–155.

Summerson, John, and Helen Dorey. *A New Description of Sir John Soane's Museum*. London: Trustees of Sir John Soane's Museum, 2001, 10th edition.

Swenarton, Mark. *Artisans and Architects: The Ruskinian Tradition in Architectural Thought*. Basingstoke: Macmillan, 1989.

Tafuri, Manfredo. *Architecture and Utopia: Design and Capitalist Development*. Trans. Barbara Luigia La Penta. Cambridge, MA: MIT Press, 1976.

Tafuri, Manfredo. *The Sphere and the Labyrinth: Avant-Gardes and Architecture from Piranesi to the 1970s*. Trans. Pellegrino d'Acierno and Robert Connolly. Cambridge, MA, and London: MIT Press, 1987.

Tafuri, Manfredo. *Theories and History of Architecture*. Trans. Giorgio Verrecchia. London: Granada, 1980.

Tafuri, Manfredo and Francesco Dal Co. *Modern Architecture: Vol. 1*. Trans. Robert Erich Wolf. London: Faber and Faber, 1986.

Tanizaki, Jun'ichiro, *In Praise of Shadows*. Trans. Edward J. Harper and Edward G. Seidensticker. Stony Creek, CT: Leete's Island Books, 1977.

Tarnas, Richard. *The Passion of the Western Mind: Understanding the Ideas That Have Shaped Our World View*. London: Pimlico, 1996.

Tatarkiewicz, W. 'Classification of the Arts'. In Wiener, vol, 4, pp. 456–462.

Taylor, Charles. *Sources of the Self: The Making of Modern Identity*. Cambridge: Cambridge University Press, 1989.

Taylor, Frederick W. *The Principles of Scientific Management*. New York: Norton, 1967. First published in 1911.

Tegethoff, Wolf. 'Catching the Spirit: Mies's Early Work and the Impact of the "Prussian Style"'. In Riley and Bergdoll, pp. 135–151.

Thacker, Christopher. *The Wildness Pleases: The Origins of Romanticism*. London and New York: Croom Helm and New York: St Martin's Press, 1983.

Thomas, Keith. *Man and the Natural World: Changing Attitudes in England 1500–1800*. London: Allen Lane, 1983.

Thomson, James. 'A Poem Sacred to the Memory of Sir Isaac Newton'. In Thomson, *The Seasons*, pp. 241–252.

Thomson, James. *The Seasons*. London: John Millan, 1730.

Thornbury, Walter. *The Life of J.M.W. Turner RA*. London: Ward Lock Reprints, 1970. First published in 1861.

Thornton, Peter, and Helen Dorey. *A Miscellany of Objects from Sir John Soane's Museum*. London: Laurence King, 1992.

Townsend, Joyce. *Turner's Painting Techniques*. London: Tate Publishing, 1993.

Townsend, Joyce, ed. *Turner's Painting Techniques in Context*. London: UKIC, 1995.

Townsend, Joyce. 'Turner's Use of Materials, and Implications for Conservation'. In Townsend, *Turner's Painting Techniques in Context*, pp. 5–11.

Treib, Marc, ed. *Modern Landscape Architecture: A Critical Review*. Cambridge, MA: MIT Press, 1993.

Tugendhat, Grete. 'On the Construction of the Tugendaht House'. In Hammer-Tugendhat and Wolf Tegethoff, pp. 5–10.

Turner, J.M.W. 'Diary of a Tour in Part of Wales, 1792'. In Gage, *Collected Correspondence of J.M.W. Turner*, pp. 11–19.

Tuveson, Ernest Lee. *The Imagination as a Means of Grace: Locke and the Aesthetics of Romanticism*. Berkeley and Los Angeles: University of California Press, 1960.

Tyndall, John. 'Note on the Transmission of Heat through Gaseous Bodies'. *Proceedings of the Royal Society of Great Britain*, 1859, no. 10, p. 37.

Vanbrugh, John. 'From Letter to the Duchess of Marlborough (1709)'. In Mallgrave, pp. 230–232.

Vandenburg, Maritz. *Farnsworth House: Ludwig Mies van der Rohe*. London: Phaidon, 2003.

Van den Heuvel, Dirk, and Max Risselada, eds. *Alison and Peter Smithson – from the House of the Future to a House of Today*. Rotterdam: 010, 2004.

Vasari, Giorgio. *Vasari on Technique*. Trans. Louisa S. Maclehose. New York: Dover, 1960. First published as *Le vite de' più eccelenti pittori, scultori e architettori* (The Lives of the Most Eminent Painters, Sculptors and Architects) 2nd edition, 1568.

Vaughan, William. *Romanticism and Art*. London: Thames & Hudson, 1994.

Venning, Barry. *Turner*. London and New York: Phaidon, 2003.

Vidler, Anthony. 'Preface'. In Bastide, pp. 9–18.

Vigarello, Georges. *Concepts of Cleanliness: Changing Attitudes in France since the Middle Ages*. Trans. Jean Birrell. Cambridge: Cambridge University Press, 1988.

Vismann, Bettina, and Jürgen Mayer H. 'The Perspiration Affair, or the New National Gallery Between Cold Fronts'. Trans. Sara Ogger. *Grey Room*, Fall 2002, pp. 80–89.

Vitruvius. *The Ten Books on Architecture*. Trans. Morris Hicky Morgan. New York: Dover, 1960. First published as *De Architectura Libri Decem* in the first century BC.

Vogtherr, Christoph Martin. 'Views and Approaches: Schinkel and Landscape Gardening'. In Zukowsky, pp. 68–83.

Voitle, Robert. *The Third Earl of Shaftesbury, 1617–1713*. Baton Rouge: Louisiana State University Press, 1984.

Voogd, Peter Jan de. 'Tristram Shandy as Aesthetic Object'. *Word & Image*, vol. 4, no. 1, January–March 1988, pp. 383–392.

Waagen, Gustav Friedrich. *Karl Friedrich Schinkel als Mensch und Künstler: die erste Biografie Schinkels im Berliner Kalendar von 1844*. Ed. Werner Gabler. Düsseldorf: Werner, 1980. First published in 1844.

Walpole, Horace. *The Castle of Otranto*. London: Grey Walls Press, 1950. First published in 1764.

Walpole, Horace. *The History of the Modern Taste in Gardening*. New York: Ursus Press, 1995. Written in the late 1760s and printed in 1771 but not published until 1780 as part of Walpole's *Anecdotes of Painting in England*. In 1785 it was published on its own.

Warner, Deborah Jane. 'The Landscape Mirror and Glass'. *Antiques*, vol. 105, no. 1, January 1974, pp. 158–159.

Watelet, Claude-Henri. *Essay on gardens: a chapter in the French picturesque translated into English for the first time*. Ed., trans. Samuel Danon. Philadelphia: University of Pennsylvania Press, 2003. First published in 1774 as *Essai sur les jardins*.

Waterfield, Giles, ed. *Soane and Death: The Tombs and Monuments of Sir John Soane*. London: Dulwich Picture Gallery, 1996.

Watkin, David. 'Beckford, Soane, and Hope: The Psychology of the Collector'. In Ostergard, *William Beckford*, pp. 33–48.

Watkin, David. 'Built Ruins: The Hermitage as a Retreat'. In Woodward, *Vision of Ruins*, pp. 5–14.

Watkin, David. *The English Vision: The Picturesque in Architecture, Landscape and Garden Design*. London: John Murray, 1982.

Watkin, David. 'John Soane: Architecture and Enlightenment'. *Casabella*, vol. 62, no. 660, 1998, pp. 72–83.

Watkin, David. 'Karl Friedrich Schinkel: Royal Patronage and the Picturesque'. *Architectural Design*, vol. 49, no. 8–9, 1979, pp. 56–72.

Watkin, David. 'Monuments and Mausolea in the Age of Enlightenment'. In Waterfield, *Soane and Death: The Tombs and Monuments of Sir John Soane*, pp. 9–25.

Watkin, David. *Sir John Soane: Enlightenment Thought and the Royal Academy Lectures*. Cambridge: Cambridge University Press, 1996.

Watkin, David. 'Soane and his Contemporaries'. In Dunster, pp. 40–59.

Watkin, David, and Tilmann Mellinghoff. *German Architecture and the Classical Ideal*. Cambridge, MA: MIT Press and London: Thames & Hudson, 1987.

Weart, Spencer R. *The Discovery of Global Warming*. Cambridge, MA, and London: Harvard University Press, 2003.

Weber, Nicholas Fox. *Le Corbusier: A Life*. New York: Alfred A. Knopf, 2008.

Webster, Helena, ed. *Modernism Without Rhetoric: Essays on the Work of Alison and Peter Smithson*. London: Academy, 1997.

Webster, Tom. 'Writing to Redundancy: Approaches to Spiritual Journals and Early-Modern Spirituality'. *Historical Journal*, 1996, vol. 39, no. 1, pp. 33–56.

Westheim, Paul. 'Mies van der Rohe: Entwicklung eines Architekten'. *Das Kunstblatt*, vol. 11, no. 2, February 1927, pp. 55–62.

Weston, Richard. *Materials, Form and Architecture*. London: Laurence King, 2003.

Whale, John. 'Romantics, Explorers and Picturesque Travellers'. In Copley and Garside, *The Politics of the Picturesque*, pp. 175–195.

Whately, Thomas. *Observations on Modern Gardening, Illustrated by Descriptions*. London: T. Payne, 1771. First published in 1770.

Wheeler, Dennis. 'The Great Storm of November 1703: A New Look at the Seamen's Records'. *Weather*, vol. 58, no. 11, pp. 419–427.

Whiteley, Nigel. *Reyner Banham: Historian of the Immediate Future*. Cambridge, MA, and London: MIT Press, 2002.

Whyte, Iain Boyd. 'Charlottenhof: the Prince, the Gardener, the Architect and the Writer', *Architectural History*, vol. 43, 2000, pp. 1–23.

Wiedman, August. *Romantic Art Theories*. Henley-on-Thames: Gresham Books, 1986.

Wiedman, August. *Romantic Roots in Modern Art: Romanticism and Expressionism: A Study in Comparative Analysis.* Old Woking: Gresham Books, 1979.

Wiener, Philip P., ed. *Dictionary of the History of Ideas.* New York: Charles Scribner's Sons, 1973.

Wigley, Mark. *White Walls, Designer Dresses: The Fashioning of Modern Architecture*. Cambridge, MA, and London: MIT Press, 1993.

Williams, Raymond. *The Country and the City*. St Albans: Paladin, 1975.

Willis, Peter. 'William Kent's Letters in the Huntington Library, California'. *Architectural History*, vol. 29, 1986, pp. 158–167.

Willmert, Todd. 'Heating Methods and Their Impact on Soane's Work: Lincoln's Inn Fields and Dulwich Picture Gallery'. *Journal of the Society of Architectural Historians*, vol. 52, no. 1, March 1993, pp. 26–58.

Wilson, Colin St John. 'Sigurd Lewerentz: The Sacred Buildings and the Sacred Sites'. In Flora, Giardiello and Postiglione, *Sigurd Lewerentz 1885–1875*, pp. 11–34.

Wilson, Michael. *William Kent; Architect, Designer, Painter, Gardener, 1685–1748*. London: Routledge & Kegan Paul, 1984.

Wilton, Andrew. *The Life and Work of J.M.W Turner*. London: Academy, 1979.

Wilton, Andrew. *Turner and the Sublime*. London: British Museum, 1980.

Wilton, Andrew. *Turner as Draughtsman*. Aldershot: Ashgate, 2006.

Wilton, Andrew. *Turner in his Time*. London: Thames & Hudson, 1987.

Wilton, Andrew. *Turner in the British Museum: Drawings and Watercolours*. London: British Museum, 1975.

Wittkower, Rudolf. *Architectural Principles in the Age of Humanism*. London: Academy and New York: St. Martin's Press, 1988. First published in 1949.

Wollen, Roger, ed. *Derek Jarman: A Portrait. Artist, Film-maker, Designer*. London: Thames & Hudson, 1996.

Woodbridge, Kenneth. 'Kent's Gardening: The Rousham Letters'. *Apollo*, vol. C, no. 152, October 1974, pp. 282–291.

Woodbridge, Kenneth. 'William Kent as Landscape-Gardener: A Reappraisal'. Apollo, vol. C, no. 150, August 1974, pp. 126–137.

Woodward, Christopher. *In Ruins*. London: Vintage, 2001.

Woodward, Christopher, ed. *Vision of Ruin: Architectural Fantasies and Designs for Garden Follies*. London: Sir John Soane's Museum, 1999.

Wordsworth, William. *A Description of the Scenery of the Lakes in The North of England*. London: Longman, Hurst, Rees, Orme, and Brown, 1822. First published as *Guide to the Lakes* as an introduction to Joseph Wilkinson's *Select Views in Cumberland, Westmoreland and Lancashire*, 1810.

Wordsworth, William. *Lyrical Ballads*, 2 vols. London: Longman, 1802. First published in 1798.

Wordsworth, William. *William Wordsworth: The Major Works*. Oxford: Oxford University Press, 1984.

Worn, Alan. 'Communicative Construction: Sigurd Lewerentz's Flower Kiosk'. MA dissertation, Department of Architecture, University of Cambridge, unpublished, 2004.

Wrede, Stuart. *The Architecture of Erik Gunnar Asplund*. Cambridge, MA, and London: MIT Press, 1980.

Yoshida, Nobuyuki, ed. *A + U* (Sverre Fehn – Above and Below the Horizon), January 1999, no. 340.

Yoshida, Nobuyuki. 'Editor's Preface'. In Yoshida, *A + U* (Sverre Fehn – Above and Below the Horizon), pp. 4–5.

Yoshida, Nobuyuki, ed. 'Interview with Sverre Fehn'. In Yoshida, *A + U* (Sverre Fehn – Above and Below the Horizon), pp. 15–19.

Zanten, David van. 'The Harmony of Landscape, Architecture, and Community: Schinkel's Encounter with Huyot, 1826'. In Zukowsky, *Karl Friedrich Schinkel*, pp. 84–96.

Zukowsky, John, ed. *Karl Friedrich Schinkel 1781–1841: The Drama of Architecture*. Tübingen and Berlin: Ernst Wasmuth, 1994.

Zweinger-Bargielowska, Ina. *Austerity in Britain: Rationing Controls and Consumption*, 1939–1955. Oxford: Oxford University Press, 2000.

INDEX

Page numbers in *italics* denotes an illustration